Reuben Adeolu Alabi, Joy Alemazung, Hans H. Bass,
Achim Gutowski, Robert Kappel, Tobias Knedlik,
Osmund Osinachi Uzor, Karl Wohlmuth (Eds.)

Africa and the Global Financial Crisis – Impact on Economic Reform Processes

African Development Perspectives Yearbook

Edited by the

Research Group on African Development Perspectives:
Reuben Adeolu Alabi, Joy Alemazung, Hans H. Bass,
Achim Gutowski, Robert Kappel, Tobias Knedlik,
Osmund Osinachi Uzor, Karl Wohlmuth

Vol. XV

LIT

Reuben Adeolu Alabi, Joy Alemazung,
Hans H. Bass, Achim Gutowski, Robert Kappel,
Tobias Knedlik, Osmund Osinachi Uzor,
Karl Wohlmuth (Eds.)

Africa and the Global Financial Crisis – Impact on Economic Reform Processes

LIT

Bibliographic information published by the Deutsche Nationalbibliothek
The Deutsche Nationalbibliothek lists this publication in the Deutsche Nationalbibliografie; detailed bibliographic data are available in the Internet at http://dnb.d-nb.de.

ISBN 978-3-643-10648-3

A catalogue record for this book is available from the British Library

Fresnostr. 2 D-48159 Münster
Tel. +49 (0) 2 51-620 320 Fax +49 (0) 2 51-922 60 99
e-Mail: lit@lit-verlag.de http://www.lit-verlag.de

Distribution:
In Germany: LIT Verlag Fresnostr. 2, D-48159 Münster
Tel. +49 (0) 2 51-620 32 22, Fax +49 (0) 2 51-922 60 99, e-mail: vertrieb@lit-verlag.de
In Austria: Medienlogistik Pichler-ÖBZ, e-mail: mlo@medien-logistik.at

In the UK: Global Book Marketing, e-mail: mo@centralbooks.com

In North America by:

Transaction Publishers
New Brunswick (U.S.A.) and London (U.K.)

Transaction Publishers
Rutgers University
35 Berrue Circle
Piscataway, NJ 08854

Phone: +1 (732) 445 - 2280
Fax: + 1 (732) 445 - 3138
for orders (U. S. only):
toll free (888) 999 - 6778
e-mail: orders@transactionpub.com

Contents Volume 15
African Development Perspectives Yearbook, 2010/2011
AFRICA AND THE GLOBAL FINANCIAL CRISIS – IMPACT ON ECONOMIC REFORM PROCESSES

Foreword

At the onset of the Global Financial Crisis (GFC) in the middle of 2008, the likely impact of the crisis on Africa was largely underestimated. However, the continent which has recorded rapid economic growth between 2000 and 2008 relative to the 1990s was hit by a severe external shock. The growth rate of the gross domestic product declined from 5.6 percent in 2008 to 2.5 percent in 2009. Taking an annual population growth rate of about 2.5 percent into account, GDP per capita did not grow at all in 2009. Prior to the GFC, the region was confronted with a food crisis due to various factors related to low productivity in agricultural sector, drastic price increases of imported food, negative effects induced by climate change (draught and flood), and drastic increases in oil prices and prices of other primary commodities including agricultural products in international markets. Consequently, food security became a worrying problem such that 21 countries in the region are currently under conditions of an acute food security crisis. The proportion of income in poor households spent on food is well over 50 per cent in many countries in the region (UNCTAD, 2009). The food security crisis was then followed in Africa by the effects of the global financial crisis.

The GFC has affected Africa mainly via two channels (Kato, 2009, UNU-WIDER, 2009). The first is a negative demand shock for African export products due to the decline in global demand for almost all kinds of commodities, including primary commodities such as crude oil, minerals, and agricultural products, resulting in declining export prices. The effects of the trade channel have been aggravated by a second channel, the transfer and capital flow channel. Potential dangers of the GFC included the decline of external transfers such as foreign aid and remittances. Whilst remittances declined significantly in many countries and by an estimated 6.6 per cent for the whole continent between 2008 and 2009, foreign aid is, however, expected to flow relatively constant in 2009 and 2010 (AfDB, OECD 2010, IOM, 2009). The path on ever-increasing foreign direct investment (FDI) inflows, which Africa enjoyed during the 2000s, came to an abrupt end in 2009. In 2009, FDI inflows were expected to decline by 36 percent (as compared with 2008). Africa's decline in FDI goes hand-in-hand with similarly declining rates in other developing countries (AfDB, OECD 2010). Also access to credit was affected by the GFC. The slowdown in world trade reduced government revenues considerably, while government expenditures were on the increase also because of stimulation packages in some African countries. Additionally, this put pressure on fiscal positions in many African countries, thereby subjecting the progress made in poverty reduction and public investment.

One would then ask whether Africa is at another economic and political crossroad. Over two and a half decades many countries in the region have been engaged in economic policy reforms. The policy reforms were aimed at restructuring the economies to a more market-based development path. Multiple crises (food crisis and financial crisis) of such a magnitude imply that gains recorded from the policy reforms in countries like Botswana, Mauritius, Ruanda, Ghana, South Africa, etc. are in danger. Countries like Nigeria, that has made progress in banking and capital market reforms, face difficulties in managing the external shock. The SANE countries (South Africa, Algeria, Nigeria and Egypt), seen as the emerging economies that can drive the economic direction of the continent, were hit by second round effects of the crisis, especially on stock markets. For some observers, the influence of China in Africa became another source of concern since the Chinese development cooperation strategy failed to recognise the fundamental principle of economic and political reform in the region. The danger is that policymakers in the region may seek alternative ways out by reversing policies in order to respond to the crisis. New global powers may emerge as stumbling blocks to reform as countries in the region look for different development paradigms and seek alternative trade partners in the global market. Although the global financial crisis seems to be an event of the past in the developed world, the impacts on Africa are still present and severe.

In volume XV of the African Development Perspectives Yearbook, the Research Group on African Development Perspectives investigates the impact of the GFC on economic reform processes in Africa. The analysis is structured in such a way so as to reflect the opportunities and dangers of policy reversals in the face of the GFC. The impact of the crisis on different types and forms of governance in the region is considered. The central question is therefore which macro-economic policy instruments have to be applied in order to overcome the crisis and to continue with sustainable development. The further question is raised how the GFC has affected Africa's external economic relations and if the path of opening up to the world markets is continued. Another question raised is how the crisis has affected social cohesion, impacted on poverty alleviation strategies and the achievement of Millennium Development Goals (MDGs). All these questions are discussed in the various contributions which comprise general studies and country case studies. The authors also looked into the role of international financial institutions during and after the crisis.

The volume XV of the African Development Perspectives Yearbook is structured into three Units. Unit 1 addresses general issues regarding the impact of the GFC on economic reform processes in Africa. The main issues for Africa are how to assess the impact of the GFC on economic reform processes, and how to continue in the aftermath of the GFC with deeper economic reforms. Three contributions present the agenda for more fundamental reforms after the GFC so as to reduce the vulnerability of African economies; three other contributions highlight concrete reform steps deriving lessons from the impact of the GFC and the reactions to it for Africa: use of fiscal and countercyclical policies, use of policies for stabilising trade and pushing for export diversification, and use of policies for financial market regulation. Unit 2 presents case studies from countries and sub-regions. Three African sub-regions (West Africa, Central Africa, and Southern Africa) are covered in the contributions, but also the impacts of the GFC on ECOWAS and its member countries are discussed. The steps towards a West African Monetary Union (WAMU) highlight future options to strengthen the regional economies. Various contributions on Nigeria highlight important macroeconomic, human development and sector issues. Because of the important role of Nigeria (as a SANE country) for the further development of its neighbouring countries, the concentration on Nigeria in Unit 2 gives the possibility to reflect on the importance of necessary macroeconomic, human development, and sector reforms. The impact of the GFC on the economic reform processes is considered in all contributions, reflecting on the chances to continue with deeper economic reforms. Unit 3 presents reviews and book notes of current literature focussing on issues of African development perspectives. There is a concentration on books, reports and documents discussing GFC and developing countries, GFC and African countries, GFC and Global and African Economic Reports, GFC and development finance, but there are also reviews and notes on publications about post-conflict stabilization in African countries as these countries suffered most from the GFC and need special assistance in their economic reform processes.

Previous versions of the articles in this volume of the African Development Perspectives Yearbook have been presented at a conference on the theme hosted by the Bremen University of Applied Sciences in 2010. Financial support has been provided by the European Centre for Development Policy Management (Brussels), the Faculty of Economics and Business Administration, Bremen University of Applied Sciences, the Deutsche Bundesbank (HV Hannover), the International Office of the University of Bremen, and the Wolfgang Ritter Foundation (Bremen). The support is greatly appreciated.

References

AfDB, OECD (2010). African Economic Outlook, African Development Bank & OECD.

Kato (2009). What The Global Financial Crisis Means for Sub-Saharan Africa Speech by Mr. Takatoshi Kato, Deputy Managing Director, IMF At the Twelfth African Union (AU) Summit Addis Ababa, Ethiopia February 3, 2009.

IOM (2009). The Impact of the Global Economic Crisis on Migrants and Migration. www.globalmigrationgroup.org/pdf/Economic Crisis.March09.Eng.pdf.

UNCTAD, (2009). Food security in Africa: learning lessons from the food crisis United Nations Conference on Trade and Development TD/B/EX(47)/3 www.unctad.org/en/docs/tdbex47d3_en.pdf.

UNU-WIDER, (2009) The Global Economic Crisis after One Year: Is a New Paradigm for Recovery in Developing Countries Emerging? Policy brief No. 2.

The Research Group on African Development Perspectives

The aggravating social, political and economic crisis of the African continent forces institutions, organisations, researchers, development practitioners, ad hoc working groups and networks on Africa, and all others involved in African development affairs to intensify the analytical and conceptional work on alternative development visions and designs for Africa. There exist a growing number of plans and programmes, conceptions, researches, and ideas being published worldwide and focussing on the peculiarity of the African crisis, the chances for structural adjustment, the issue of planning development beyond mere adjustment, and on the necessary responses to the globalisation trend. The discussion referring to Africa's development problems and perspectives is widening. However, it is difficult to get an overall view of the different approaches and proposals and, subsequently, to make the discussion useful for the programming and co-ordinating of development policies. So there is a need for a comprehensive publication that compiles, evaluates, and analyses the scattered material and the often not easily available sources.

To fill this gap, the Research Group on African Development Perspectives established at the University of Bremen is presenting the African Development Perspectives Yearbook, being published since Volume 1 in 1989. Research activities of the group members comprised over the years country studies and comparative country analyses, macroeconomic policies and strategies, aspects of labour market policies and informal sector activities, human development policies and strategies, agriculture and food security policy, resources development and environmental policy, promotion of small-scale industries, private sector development policies, entrepreneurship development, assessments of sector and structural adjustment policies, trade and regional integration policies, as well as economic diversification options.

The African Development Perspectives Yearbook is the first English-speaking periodical published in Germany relating to development problems and perspectives in Africa. African, European and North-American experts from universities, international and regional organisations, and from non-governmental and donor organisations are reporting on problems and on possible solutions, on new political and economic approaches, on specific economic programmes, and on visions for alternative African development paths.

Africa's future will depend on both, on its economic and political connections with the international community at the Pan-African, regional, national, sub-regional and sectoral levels, and on local projects and development efforts at the micro level. Most important are own African development visions, programmes, strategies and policies. The African Development Perspectives Yearbook contains information and analyses with regard to these various dimensions. Global analyses, regional and country studies, sectoral studies and individual project evaluations are published in the African Development Perspectives Yearbook, as well as statements and declarations submitted as the result of international conferences, important documents of African regional organisations and individual African states, and important programmes of African civil society organisations and self-help groups.

Beside the analytical, comparative and documentary character of the African Development Perspectives Yearbook, the editors successfully established an extensive network for the exchange of news and information and are so relating and connecting development organisations and research institutions that are working in and for Africa. The members of the Research Group on African Development Perspectives are interested to deepen the contacts with partners that are sharing similar objectives.

The African Development Perspectives Yearbook is targeted to decision-makers and research personnel in development policy and to experts and staff in project consultancies, media, research and development, donor and aid institutions, and to all others that are interested in Africa's development. It offers comprehensive analyses and information about recent developments with regard to the African continent. Main focus is on development perspectives. Thus, the African Development Perspectives Yearbook is reporting on

- visions and conceptions with regard to long-term development strategies for Africa;
- strategies that emphasise a longer-run planning process that goes beyond conventional structural adjustment policies;
- successful projects and programmes concerning countries, regions, institutions, or specific sectors of African economies, by analysing the conditions of their success;
- resourceful and creative activities of socio-economic interest groups, local development initiatives and NGOs, which could serve as models for other regions;
- innovative strategies for and prospects of regional integration in Africa; and on
- economic, social, and political trends in Africa's sub-regions, nation-states, provinces, towns and local communities.

The African Development Perspectives Yearbook takes into account sources and information from all relevant levels of action, planning, discussion, and research, i.e. from international, regional, and national organisations and institutions, committees, working groups, and NGOs, but with particular emphasis given to those ideas and approaches originating from Africa.

Address:
Research Group on African Development Perspectives
c/o Tobias Knedlik, Coordinating Editor
Steigerstrasse 21
D-99096 Erfurt
Germany

Telephone: +49-345-7753740
Fax: +49-345-775369740
E-mail: Tobias.Knedlik@iwh-halle.de
Internet: http://www.iwim.uni-bremen.de/africa/africanyearbook.htm

Abbreviations and Acronyms

AAF-SAPs	The African Alternative Framework to Structural Adjustment Programmes
ACP	African, Caribbean, Pacific states
ADF	Augmented Dickey Fuller unit root test
ADL	Autoregressive Distributed Lag
AEG	Augmented Engle Granger Cointegration Test
AfDB	African Development Bank
AFEM	Autonomous Foreign Exchange Market
AfT	Aid for Trade
AGOA	African Growth and Opportunity Act
ANCs	Antenatal clinics
APRM	African Peer Review Mechanism
ASEAN	Association of South East Asian Nations
AU	African Union
AUC	African Union Commission
BCBS	Basel Committee on Banking Supervision
BBC	British Broadcasting Corporation
BCEAO	Banque Centrale des Etats de I'Afrique de I'Ouest
BEAC	Banque des Etats de L'Afrique Centrale
BMF	Bundesministerium für Finanzen
BRICS	Brazil, Russia, India, China and South Africa
BRVM	Bourse Regionale des Valeurs Mobilieres
BTI	Bertelsmann Transformation Index
CAP	Common Agricultural Policy of the EU
CASE	Cairo and Alexandria Stock Exchange
CBN	Central Bank of Nigeria
CBWAS	Central Bank of West African States
CBCAS	Central Bank of Central African States
CDC	Cameroon Development Cooperative
CEMAC	Communauté Économique des États d'Afrique Centrale
CENEEMA	National Centre for Studies and Experimentation in Agricultural Mechanisation
CERA	Cambridge Energy Research Associates
CFA Franc	Communite Financiere Africain Franc
CIA	Central Intelligence Agency
CIMI	Common Investment Market Initiative

CMH	Commission for Macroeconomics and Health (Nigeria)
COM	Commission of the European Communities
CRR	Cash reserve requirement
CRTV	Cameroon Radio and Television
C-10	Committee of Ten (The Committee of Ten African Ministers of Finance and Central Bank Governors)
DAC	Development Assistance Committee (of OECD)
DAS	Dutch Auction System
DCI	Department of Commerce and Industry
DFI	Development Finance International
DFQF	Duty free and quota free
DOW or DJIA	Dow Jones Industrial Average
DW	Durbin Watson Statistic
EBID	ECOWAS Bank for Investment and Development
ECA	Economic Commission for Africa
ECCAS	Economic Community of Central African States
ECIC	ECOWAS Common Investment Code
ECOWAS	Economic Community of West African States
EDIS	Explicit Deposit Insurance Scheme
EIPF	ECOWAS Investment Policy Framework
EMCP	ECOWAS Monetary Cooperation Program
ERM	Exchange Rate Mechanism
ESEC	ECOWAS Securities and Exchange Commission
ESIPC	ECOWAS Securities Insurance Protection Commission
ESUT	Enugu State University of Science and Technology
ETLS	ECOWAS Trade Liberalization Scheme
EU	European Union
FCT	Federal Capital Territory
FCFA	Franc de la Communite Financière en Afrique Centrale
FDI	Foreign Direct Investment
FFR	Finance Facility for Remittances
FGN	Federal Government of Nigeria
FSB	Financial Stability Board
FSF	Financial Stability Forum
ETF	Education Tax Fund
FTSE	Financial Times Stock Exchange
G 20	Group of Twenty major countries

GDP	Gross Domestic Product
GFC	Global Financial Crisis
GM	Genetically Modified
GNI	Gross National Income
HCS	Health Care System
HDI	Human Development Index
HIPC	Highly-Indebted Poor Countries initiative
HIV/AIDS	Human Immunodeficiency Virus/Acquired Immune Deficiency Syndrome
HWWI	Hamburgisches WeltWirtschafts-Institut
IBRD	International Bank of Reconstruction and Development
ICPs	Industrial Core Projects
ICT	Information and Communication Technology
IDAs	Industrial Development Acts
IDPS	Implicit Deposit Protection Schemes
IFAA	Institute for African Alternatives (in London)
IFAD	International Fund for Agricultural Development
IFCI	International Finance Corporation Investibles
IFI	International Financial Institutions
IFS	International Financial Statistics
ILO	International Labour Organisation
IMF	International Monetary Fund
IRA	Institute of Agronomic Research
IRIN	Integrated Regional Information Networks
IRZ	Institute of Zoo-technical Research
ISMED	Investment Small and Medium Scale Enterprises Development
JSE	Johannesburg Stock Exchange (South Africa
LDC	Least Developed Countries or Listed Domestic Stocks
LE	Egyptian Pound
LEEDS	Local Economic Empowerment Strategy
LPA	Lagos Plan of Action
MC	Market Capitalisation
MDGs	Millennium Development Goals
MFIs	Micro Finance Institutions
MFN	Most-Favoured Nation
MIDEN	North West Development Authority

MIDEVIV	Mission de Developpement des Cultures Vivrières, Marachaires et Fruitières
Mn	Million
MOU	Memorandum of Understanding
MPR	Monetary policy rate
MSCI	Morgan Stanley Capital International index
MSMEs	Micro, Small and Medium Scale Enterprises
N	Naira
NAB	New Arrangements to Borrow
NAFDAC	National Agency for Food and Drug Administration and Control
NBER	National Bureau of Economic Research,
NBS	National Bureau of Statistics
NDI	National Democratic Institute
NDIC	Nigeria Deposit Insurance Corporation
NDLEA	National Drug Law Enforcement Agency
NDP	National Development Plan
NEEDS	National Economic Empowerment and Development Strategy
NEP	Nigerian Enterprises Promotion
NEPAD	New Partnership for Africa's Development
NEPC	Nigeria Export Promotion Council
NGOs	Non- Government Organizations
NHIS	National Health Insurance Scheme
NIDs	National Immunization Days
NIKKEI	Nihon Keizai Shimbun of Japan
NIPC	Nigerian Investment Promotion Commission
NLDB	Nigeria Local Development Board
NPC	National Planning Commission
NPCA	NEPAD Planning and Coordinating Agency
NPI	National Programme on Immunization
NPTEA	Nigerian Primary Teacher Education Association
NSE	Nigerian Stock Exchange
OAU	Organization of African Unity
ODA	Official Development Assistance
ODI	Overseas Development Institute
OECD	Organization for Economic Co-Operation and Development
PEs	Public Enterprises

PHC	Primary Health Care
PIIGS	Portugal, Italy, Ireland, Greece and Spain
PRSP	Poverty Reduction Strategy Paper
R&D	Research and Development
RHS	Right Hand Side
SAP	Structural Adjustment Program
SDR	Special Drawing Rights
SEEDS	State Economic Empowerment Development Strategy
SITC	Standard International Trade Classification
SMEs	Small and Medium Enterprises
SMEDAN	Small and Medium Enterprises Development Agency of Nigeria
SMEEIS	Small and Medium Enterprises Equity Investment Scheme
SSA	Sub-Saharan Africa
TCPC	Technical Committee on Privatization and Commercialization
TI	Transparency International
TNC	Transnational Corporations
ToT	Terms of Trade
TR	Turnover Ratio
TUNINDEX	Tunisia Stock Index
UBE	Universal basic education
UEMOA	Union Economique Monetaire de l'Ouest Africain (West African Monetary Union)
UK	United Kingdom
UN	United Nations
UNCR	United Nations Committee Report
UNCTAD	United Nations Conference on Trade and Development
UNDP	United Nations Development Program
UNECA	United Nations Economic Commission for Africa
UNESCO	United Nations Educational, Scientific and Cultural Organization
UNU-WIDER	United Nations University – World Institute for Development Economics Research
US or USA	United States of America
USD	US Dollar

VAR	Vector Auto Regressive Model
VAD	Vitamin A Deficiency
VASP	Vitamin A Supplement Programme
WACU	West African Currency Unit
WADA	Wum Area Development Authority
WAMA	West African Monetary Agency
WAMI	West African Monetary Institute
WAMU	West African Monetary Union
WAMZ	West African Monetary Zone
WASC	West African School Certificate
WB	World Bank
WDI	World Development Indicators, World Bank
WHO	World Health Organization
WTO	World Trade Organization
XAF	ISO currency code for the Central African CFA franc

Unit 1: General Issues

Setting the Agenda for Africa's Long-term Growth and Structural Transformation in the Aftermath of the Global Economic Crisis

Afeikhena Jerome[1], Oluyele Akinkugbe[2], Francis Chigunta[3]

Abstract

While, initially, it was thought that Africa was relatively sheltered from the global financial crisis, perhaps ironically, due to its generally weak integration with the rest of the global economy, the continent has been hit severely by the crisis; its growth rate dipped to 1.6 percent in 2009 for the first time since 2002. This paper examines the nature, causes and implications of the global financial crisis for Africa, on-going initiatives to mitigate the crisis, and proffers an agenda for long term growth and structural transformation. It notes that, although the immediate impact of the crisis may have been mitigated, African economies are faced with severe threats of growth deceleration, which is undermining recent progress in reducing poverty. Substantial negative effects have been already observed in terms of losses of values on stock markets, currency depreciation, and worsening of macroeconomic balances (current account deficits, budget deficits). A new development paradigm is therefore needed if Africa is to reclaim its development course. In the search for this paradigm, the paper recommends that Africa should revisit its key documents that were never implemented, such as the Lagos Plan of

[1] African Peer Review Mechanism Secretariat, Midrand, South Africa, Email: afeikhenaj@nepad.org

[2] Division of Economic Affairs, Government of Barbados, Warrens office Complex, Warrens, St. Michael, Barbados, West Indies, Email: oluyelea@yahoo.co

[3] Department of Development Studies, University of Zambia, Lusaka, Zambia, Email: fchigunta@yahoo.co.uk

Action (LPA), the African Alternative Framework to SAPs (AAF-SAPs), the Arusha Declaration on Popular Participation, the Abuja Treaty, and the NEPAD Framework document among others. This does not necessarily imply delinking itself from the rest of the world.

1 Introduction[4]

A crisis of historic proportions struck financial institutions, in the United States (US) and globally in September, 2008. The global credit markets came to a halt as a result of a series of bank and insurance company failures triggered by the continuous decline in the United States mortgage market, the over-exposure of US and European banks in the US market for sub-prime mortgages that led to the accrual and accumulation of serious and mostly hidden losses. This, in turn, created a crisis of confidence in the global financial system as banks refused to lend money to each other regardless of the credit standing. At the same time, the flow of capital to the global market for structured products dissipated. In the process, the liquidity problems encountered by US and European banks escalated to such a degree as to develop into a full blown financial crisis which has been described by leading economists as the worst financial crisis since the Great Depression of the 1930s.[5] Financial markets froze, output plummeted, especially in the advanced economies, world trade shriveled in the final months of 2008, and the world economy teetered on the edge of calamity, fuelling unprecedented government intervention. Like a hurricane, the crisis quickly spread across the entire world. However, the crisis and its speed of propagation across the global economy differ from previous crises; inter-linkages among financial institutions are much stronger now than before, and world economies—developed and developing—are much closely interconnected.

At present, the storm has been broken and the sense of panic has subsided. Although the worst may have been avoided, much pain remains. The global recovery is still fragile and new challenges are surfacing for many

---

[4] We would like to thank Prof. Karl Wohlmuth for the very constructive comments on an earlier draft. The views expressed in the paper are solely those of the authors and they should not be ascribed to the respective institutions in which they work.

[5] For example, Nouriel Roubini, Kenneth Rogoff, and Nariman Behravesh, three top American Economists all agreed in a wide-ranging conversation with Cambridge Energy Research Associates (CERA) Chairman Daniel Yergin and an audience of nearly 1,000 people at CERAWeek 2009 in Houston that the 2009 Financial Crisis has been the worst since the Great Depression, http://www.allbusiness.com/economy-economic-indicators/economic-conditions-depression/11782365-1.html.

countries. The fear of the second wave of the crisis came to the surface on November 25, 2009 when Dubai's flagship company – the Dubai World – announced its intention to postpone debt service payments for six months, until the company is restructured. While the scale of Dubai's debts is comparatively modest at $80 billion, the surrounding uncertainty led financial markets across the world to react very negatively. Greece is currently in the headlines. Its runaway debt and deficit due to unrestrained spending, cheap lending and failure to enforce financial reforms, accentuated by the financial crisis, has precipitated a crisis that may soon spiral into a "PIIGS" – Portugal, Italy, Ireland, Greece and Spain – disaster, threatening to destabilize the Euro zone[6].

The impact of the world financial crisis on African economies has been the subject of much debate in academic, business and popular circles. While Africa was largely shielded from the worst of the global downturn because of its limited exposure, it was not immune. Africa was hit hard by the crisis and it suffered more than any other region. The crisis is threatening to reverse the continent's recent hard-won economic growth and progress in attaining the Millennium Development Goals after twenty-five years of widespread economic reforms, significant debt relief related to reforms, and notable improvements in governance. Estimates provided by the World Bank indicate that there was a sharp drop in growth (from 5 percent in 2008 to 1.7 percent in 2009), throwing 7-10 million more Africans into poverty, and leading to the deaths of 30,000 - 50,000 additional infants before their first birthday (World Bank, 2010a). Moreover, it is also taking place at a time when the region is slowly recovering from the negative effects of the fuel and food price shocks of 2007 and 2008 that put inordinate strains on the growth prospects of African countries.

On the global scene, the economic crisis has also exposed the shortcomings of the current development paradigm and a number of deficiencies in financial regulation and financial architecture, particularly in the treatment of financial institutions with system-wide importance, in the assessment of systemic risks and vulnerabilities, and in the resolution of financial institutions. Moreover, the global nature of the financial crisis has made it clear that financially integrated markets, while offering many benefits, can also pose significant risks, with large real economic consequences.

Amid signs that the global economy is emerging from the worldwide recession of late 2008 and 2009, African economies appear to be recovering from the crisis with a growth rate of 4.5 per cent as projected for 2010 by the

---

[6] The Euro zone, led by Germany, with support of the IMF have since waged into this, to ensure that stability returns, to Greece and such stability is important to shield the zone from much larger negative effects.

International Monetary Fund (IMF)[7]. Attention is again shifting towards longer-term policies, reviving the debate on Africa's broad socio-economic development trajectory and priorities.

This paper examines the nature, causes, and implications of the global financial crisis for Africa, on-going initiatives to mitigate the crisis, and proffers an agenda for long term growth and structural transformation. The chapter is structured in six sections. Section 2 appraises the nature of the crisis in relation to Africa, while Section 3 focuses on the impact of the crisis on Africa, and Section 4 provides Africa's responses. The thrust of Section 5 is an agenda for Africa's long-term growth, and Section 6 concludes.

2 The Nature of the current Global Financial Crisis and Africa

A majority of the economic and financial crises over the past few decades originated in developing and emerging countries, often resulting from abrupt reversals in capital flows, and from loose domestic monetary and fiscal policies. In contrast, the global financial crisis of 2008 to 2009 had its roots in the USA. The proximate cause of the financial turbulence is attributed to the subprime mortgage sector in the USA. The sustained rise in asset prices, particularly house prices, on the back of excessively accommodative monetary policy and lax lending standards during 2002-2006 coupled with financial innovations, resulted in a large rise in mortgage credit to households, particularly low credit quality households. At a fundamental level, however, the crisis could be ascribed to the persistence of large global imbalances, which, in turn, were the outcome of long periods of excessively loose monetary policy in the major advanced economies during the early part of this decade (Mohan, 2007; Taylor, 2008).

The crisis has already consumed some high profile institutions in the financial sector. By mid 2008, it was glaring that the crisis in the subprime market in the US and the associated liquidity crunch was having a major impact on banks and financial institutions in several countries. The first sign of the severity of the crisis appeared in the United Kingdom (UK), where there was a run on the deposits of Northern Rock in September 2007, a medium size UK commercial bank with a focus on the residential mortgages market, and it had to be effectively nationalized – the first such move in 150

[7] In a speech in Nairobi, Kenya, in March 2010, Mr. Dominique Strauss-Kahn, Managing Director of the International Monetary Fund, stated that African economies were recovering faster than expected from the global downturn. He noted further that an urgent imperative is for Africa to rebuild policy foundations shaken by the Global Economic Crisis (IMF, 2010).

years – in order to save it from imminent collapse.[8] This was followed by the posting of massive losses by big US-based commercial and investment banks such as Citigroup, Merrill Lynch, and some of the biggest European Banks, such as UBS. In March 2008, JP Morgan took over Bear Stearns, one of America's largest Wall Street Investment Banks, in a deal facilitated by the Federal Reserve to prevent a wider systemic crisis. The crisis intensified in the third quarter of 2008, with a number of collapses, notably Lehman Brothers, and a generalized loss of confidence that hit all financial institutions. As a result, several banks failed in Europe and the USA, while others received government recapitalization towards the end of 2008 (Kirkpatrick, 2009). The intensification of bank bailouts in itself, no doubt, represents an abrupt change in policy towards banks.

The financial crisis soon spiraled into the real economy and to the rest of the world, thereby threatening jobs, savings, pensions and public services everywhere, and resulting in a worldwide recession, while the public bears the cost. The cost for developing countries was high. A recent study by the World Bank (2010c), monitoring progress in MDGs in the post crisis period, indicates that prior to the global economic crisis in 2008–09, overall progress on the MDG targets was particularly strong on poverty reduction, even in Africa. Progress was also made on gender parity in primary and secondary education, on maternal mortality, and on reliable access to improved water. The crisis has, nonetheless, generated predictions of rising mortality rates and closed schools, as governments reduce services in response to falling output and public revenues. It reached the following conclusion:

> "Despite policy improvements and efforts to sustain social spending and ramp up safety nets, preliminary indications of the impact of the crisis on human development point to serious problems. An important reason is the size of the shock - it is the largest global downturn since the Great Depression. Thus while developing countries' efforts have been important in mitigating the impact of the crisis, the crisis nevertheless has been a severe setback to poverty reduction". (World Bank 2010c, p. 51)

---

[8] For more details, see House of Commons Public Accounts Committee, The Nationalisation of Northern Rock, Thirty-first Report of Session 2008–09, Report, together with formal minutes, oral and written evidence. Published on 25 June 2009 by authority of the House of Commons London: The Stationery Office Limited, http://www.voltairenet.org/IMG/pdf/Nationalisation_of_Northern_Rock.pdf.

The current financial crisis is undoubtedly more global than any other period of financial turmoil since the Great Depression of the 1930s. While some of these factors are reminiscent of past bouts of financial crises, four new factors played important roles with regard of the severity and the global scale of the crisis - particularly, with respect to its transmission and amplification - that intensified the disruptions of several markets in the fall of 2008. These were: 1) the widespread use of complex and opaque financial instruments; 2) increased interconnectedness among financial markets, nationally and internationally, with the U.S. at the core; 3) high degree of leverage of financial institutions; and 4) the central role of the household sector (Claessens, et. al. 2010).

In many respects, Africa was not responsible for the global financial crisis but an innocent victim. Financial markets in Africa remain largely underdeveloped, and this, until recently is perceived as a major weakness as it implies weak financial integration with the rest of the world. Virtually no banks or other financial institutions in Africa outside of South Africa held U.S. or European subprime mortgage-backed securities or other risky derivative securities. Even South Africa, which is by far Africa's largest economy and the most integrated into the global financial system, had an exposure that was quite limited, given the continuing existence of rather pervasive capital and foreign exchange controls. In addition, tight regulation by national and (in the case of West Africa) regional supervisory authorities and restrictions in some countries on foreign ownership of banks have served to limit the impact of the financial crisis on Africa.

Prior to the crisis, several African countries did many things right, adopting prudent macroeconomic policies and building up foreign exchange reserves. At the same time, the external environment was quite favorable - commodity prices were high, trade boomed, and the international community put a high priority on aid and debt relief.

3 The Impact of the Global Financial Crisis on Africa

The impact of the Global Financial Crisis on Africa has enjoyed intense scrutiny in recent years and was the focus of several engagements on Africa (see, for example, ODI, 2008; UNU-WIDER, 2009; and African Development Bank, 2009 and 2010). At the onset of the crisis, the widely held view was that the impact on African countries would be minimal because of the limited integration of African economies into the global economy. But this turned out to be untrue as the continent was hard hit by the crisis. However, the biggest threat to the African economy was not the credit crisis itself given the continent's limited exposure to structured financial products and low levels of financial integration, but its secondary effects through loss of export earnings (both manufactured exports and commodities), net outward flow of capital, loss of services earnings (e.g. tourism and migrants' remittances), and reduced aid and other development assistance flows.

Consequently, the global financial crisis prompted an economic slowdown in Africa, a continent where most countries were already hit by the rise in the prices of food and energy.

After what has been tagged as the "lost decade" for Africa in the 1980s, the continent's political and economic landscape has recorded notable progress in recent years. Economic growth across a broad swath of African countries improved significantly in the last decade. While performance varied across countries, the region as a whole saw average annual real gross domestic product (GDP) growth rates of around 5.0 percent between 1995 and 2007 as shown in Figure 1, or annual increases in per capita GDP of over 2.0 percent as a result of improved macroeconomic policies, favorable commodity prices, and significant increases in aid, capital flows and remittances. These growth rates brought Africa in line with the trends for other developing countries (World Bank, 2010a).

Figure 1: Economic Growth in Africa (1997 to 2009)

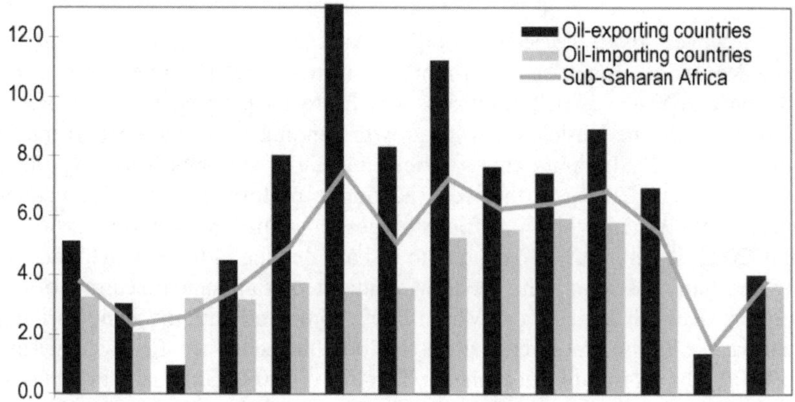

Note: Oil exporting countries are Angola, Cameroon, Chad, Republic of Congo, Equatorial Guinea, Gabon, and Nigeria. All other African countries are net oil importers.

Source: Arieff, A./ M. Weiss/V. Jones (2010), using the IMF Sub-Saharan Africa Regional Economic Outlook Database.

However, the decade-long, sustained and accelerating growth came to a grinding halt as a result of the global crisis of 2008-2009. Per capita income fell by nearly 1.0 percent in 2009 – the first such contraction in a decade (World Bank, 2010). However, improved policies in the face of the crisis helped the continent get through the storm better than expected. GDP is projected to expand by around 4.2 percent in 2010 and by 4.9 in 2011, what is a faster turnaround than in previous crises. African countries were able to take appropriate measures to mitigate the turbulence because policies before the crisis were good, allowing them to build reserves, cut debt, and open up fiscal space to combat the recession.

The crisis is also threatening to reverse the continent's progress in attaining the Millennium Development Goals (MDGs). Even though prior to the crisis sub-Saharan Africa (SSA) lagged behind other regions on all the MDGs, including poverty reduction, because of what has been acknowledged as lower initial starting conditions, practically all the MDG curves for sub-Saharan Africa have been headed in the right direction for more than 10 years. Although the effects will not be apparent for many more years, the crisis has interrupted this progress (World Bank, 2010c). More unpleasing, the crisis of 2008-2009 seems to have occurred at a time when the region was slowly recovering from the negative effects of the fuel and food shocks of 2007 and 2008 that put inordinate strains on the growth prospects of African countries.

However, given the heterogeneity of African countries, the crisis has impacted on some countries much more than on others. The region's middle-income and resource-rich countries, which are more integrated into global markets, were the hardest hit, with growth slipping by about 4.5 percentage points in 2009. Slumping energy prices depressed earnings of oil-exporting countries, contributing to the weak economic performance of these economies. South Africa, which is Africa's biggest economy, went into recession in May 2009, its first in 17 years, due to a sharp decline in the key manufacturing and mining sectors. The economy contracted at an annualized rate of 6.4 per cent between January and March 2009, compared with the same period a year earlier. In the first three quarters of 2009, the economy shed a staggering 959,000 jobs (Assubuji/Luckscheiter/Ben-Zeev, 2009). Similarly, in a period of nine months, between May 2008 and February 2009, Zambia experienced a sharp contraction of 40.0 percent in copper export earnings as a result of the collapse of copper prices which slid from US$ 8,500 per ton in July 2008 to slightly below US$ 3,000 per ton at the beginning of 2009 (Kryticous, 2009). Copper exports account for almost 80.0 percent of total exports of Zambia, playing a major role in sustaining growth, which has averaged 6.1 percent between 2006 and 2008. In Botswana, GDP dropped by 10.3 per cent, the strongest decline in economic activity in Africa in 2009, owing to lower production and prices of diamonds. Between January and August 2009, Kenyan horticultural products exports fell by 35.0 percent in volume terms compared with the same period in 2008. Tourist revenues in Tanzania fell to $302.1 million between January and April 2009 compared with $388.2 million for the same period in 2008 (UNECA, 2010).

a) Stock markets, financial Sector and exchange rates

Stock markets across the world – developed and developing – are so closely linked that share prices followed mirror patterns throughout the world. The onset of the crisis also put in motion serious stock market volatility, and substantial losses were soon to manifest the major stock exchanges. For example, share prices tumbled between 12 and 19 per cent in the USA, UK and Japan in just one week, while the MSCI[9] emerging market index fell by 23 per cent. This includes stock markets in Brazil, India and China (Malik/Ullah/Azam/Khan, 2009). Volatility was not limited to the developed and emerging economies only. Through their financial links with other regions in the world, South Africa, Nigeria, Ghana, and Kenya were hit first, suffering falling equity markets, capital flow reversals, and pressures on exchange rates. In Nigeria, the stock market indices declined by about 67 per cent between March 2008 and March 2009, the steepest quarterly decline in more than a decade. The Johannesburg Stock Exchange - the largest in the region - ended 2008 with a 25.7 percent loss. Significant losses have also been reported in Egypt, Kenya, Mauritius, Zambia and Botswana (UNECA, 2009).

Financial sectors in sub-Saharan Africa are also vulnerable to several risks. The downturn in African stock markets is beginning to have significant negative effects on the financial sector and on aggregate demand. Both the IMF (2009) and UNECA (2009) provide growing evidence that it has had a negative effect on bank balance sheets and warns that, if present trends continue, non-performing loans in the banking sector would likely increase, with dire consequences for financial stability in the region. In Ghana, the ratio of non-performing loans to gross loans was found to have increased from 7.9 per cent to 8.7 per cent between 2006 and the third quarter of 2008, and in Lesotho it increased from 2 per cent to 3.5 per cent over the same period (IMF 2009).

---

[9] The MSCI Emerging Market index was created by Morgan Stanley Capital International (MSCI) and it is designed to measure equity market performance in global emerging markets. It consisted of indices in 26 emerging economies: Argentina, Brazil, Chile, China, Colombia, Czech Republic, Egypt, Hungary, India, Indonesia, Israel, Jordan, Korea, Malaysia, Mexico, Morocco, Pakistan, Peru, Philippines, Poland, Russia, South Africa, Taiwan, Thailand, Turkey and Venezuela.

Record of bank failures has been minimal in Africa, largely because most banks do not have any significant exposure to the sub-prime mortgage market and asset-backed securities. However, as recovery continues to happen at a slower than expected pace, risks could grow from a protracted economic slowdown that elevates credit risks especially in countries where foreign shareholding is substantial, such as Botswana, Cape Verde, Central African Republic, Chad, Côte d'Ivoire, Equatorial Guinea, Lesotho and Zambia. In these countries foreign ownership of banks is quite high. The financial sector, especially banks, must be monitored closely in order to minimize vulnerabilities and mitigate risks.

The foreign exchange markets in several African countries have also been under enormous stress as a result of the crisis. In the first quarter of 2009, the Ghanaian currency, cedi, depreciated against the United States dollar by 14 per cent, and the Nigerian naira declined by 10 per cent. The Zambian kwacha also lost 13 per cent of its value relative to the United States dollar over the same period (UNECA, 2009a).

b) Exports, imports, and terms of trade

Primary commodity exports have been the main drivers of growth in many African countries. Strong growth in the emerging economies of China and India has propelled the increase in the prices and demand for commodities, thus enabling several African countries, especially oil exporters, to accumulate substantial reserves and to increase the fiscal space to undertake major public investment programs and to repay foreign debt. It is estimated that by 2007, Africa had accumulated foreign exchange reserves totaling around USD 369 billion, with Algeria leading the pack at USD 110 billion, Libya with USD 79 billion, and Nigeria with USD 51 billion (African Development Bank, 2009).

The financial crisis has had a negative impact on world growth prospects and seriously has dampened expectations on commodity futures markets. This induced falling prices and demand for most commodities. Not surprisingly, several African countries were affected as a result of the significant decline in the prices of key commodities exported by African countries since the second half of 2008. The steepest decline was recorded in the crude oil sector where prices declined by more than 50 per cent between February 2008 and February 2009. The prices of copper, coffee, cotton, and sugar also declined by more than 20 per cent on average over the same period as shown in Figure 2.

The slowdown in economic growth in three key export markets - Europe, the United States, and China - affected the demand for exports from Africa. The growth of Africa's exports in real terms fell from 4.5 per cent in 2007 to

3 per cent in 2008. Import growth fell from 14 per cent in 2007 to 13 per cent in 2008 (UNECA, 2009). The decline in commodity prices and export volumes led to a decrease in export revenues in African countries. For example, in Burundi, coffee earnings were estimated to have declined by 36 per cent between October and November 2008; in Angola, export earnings were also estimated to have dipped from USD 67 billion in 2008 to USD 23 billion in 2009; while in Cape Verde, they are expected to fall from USD 90 million in 2008 to USD 84 million in 2009. In Côte d'Ivoire, earnings are expected to decline from USD 10.4 billion in 2008 to USD 7.7 billion in 2009 (UNECA, 2009:4-5).

Many African governments rely disproportionately on revenue from commodity exports. For example, oil generates more than half of all revenues for Congo, Equatorial Guinea, Gabon, and Nigeria. As a result of the fall in global demand, export revenues are declining sharply, leading to a deterioration of the current account balances, to an erosion of foreign exchange reserves, and to losses in trade tax revenue.

Figure 2: Trends in Price Indices of Major Commodity Groups

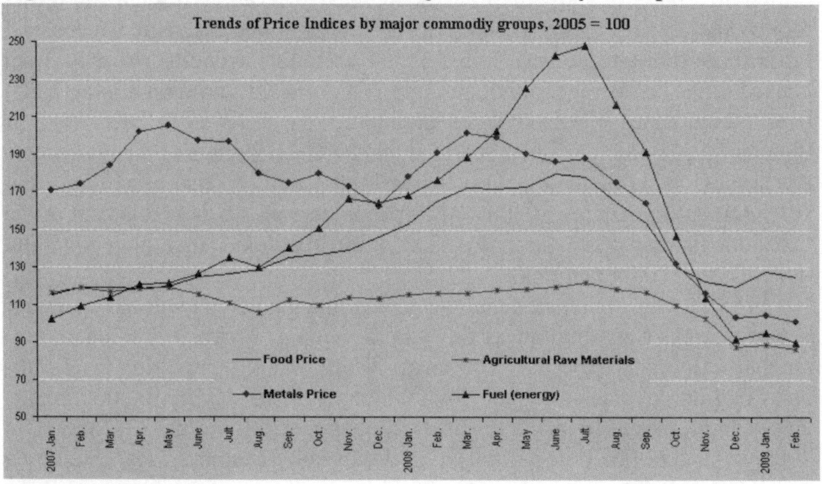

Source: UNECA 2009

In 2009, current account balances deteriorated remarkably in Sub-Saharan Africa as a whole; balances were estimated to have moved from a deficit of 0.4 percent of GDP in 2008 to 6.75 percent of GDP in 2009 (IMF 2009: 4-6). The deterioration was more remarkable in countries with stronger trade ties with Europe, the United States and China. In oil-exporting countries, the current account balances deteriorated by as much as 8.0 percentage points of GDP. In the case of oil importers, their current account deficits registered an improvement of 2.0 percent of GDP between 2008 and 2009, while low-income countries also saw mild improvements in their current account of 1.2 percentage points to a deficit of 9.2 percent of GDP (World Bank, 2010c, 2010d).

There was a marked contraction in the fiscal space in many economies in Africa, with the fiscal balance turning from a surplus of about 1.0 percent of GDP in 2008 to a deficit of more than 5.5 percent of GDP (World Bank, 2010c, 2010d). The bulk of the deterioration occurred in oil-exporting and middle income countries, notably South Africa. Noteworthy, the prices of several commodities rebounded sharply in 2009 and are continuing their upward trend in 2010 as the global recovery gains momentum.

c) Remittances

Since the beginning of the millennium, remittances have become an important source of external capital for Africa. It is estimated that remittance inflows to Sub Saharan Africa increased from $4.6 billion in 2000 to $18.59 billion in 2007 to $20 billion in 2008, nearly rivaling foreign aid flows though the actual amount is likely to be higher, since the region receives a large share through informal transfers. In 2008, this accounts for only 2 per cent of GDP on average, although there is significant variation among countries. Remittances in Lesotho, for example, were reported to be as high as high as 27 per cent of GDP (World Bank 2009). Nigeria and Kenya receive the highest value of remittances. Increasingly, they are also assuming a poverty-mitigating role as millions of Africans depend on their relatives in the Diaspora to send them funds for their daily livelihood, including food and other essential commodities.

While it was anticipated that the global financial crisis will have a major negative impact on remittances flows to the region, Africa is holding up better than originally expected. The recent World Bank's migration brief indicates that unlike private capital flows which declined sharply in 2009, remittances have remained more resilient. Globally, it fell from $336 billion in 2008 to $316 billion (6.0 percent) in 2009. In Sub Saharan Africa, it fell by a modest 3 percent with only a weak recovery expected in 2010 and 2011 (World Bank, 2010b).

Though evidence is only just emerging, the impact has been uneven in different countries. In Ghana, a rapid appraisal of the impact of the Global Financial Crisis commissioned by the World Bank reported that remittances experienced a sharp drop in the first half of 2009, leading to children missing classes or deferring their studies and families resorting to in-country family networks for support (Dogbe and Marshall, 2009).

Remittances to Kenya (which depend on the US economy) have been hit hard, with the Central Bank estimating a 38 percent year-to-year drop in August 2008 according to the report prepared by Cali, Massa, and te Velde (2008).

d) Foreign direct investment and equity investment

After six years of uninterrupted growth, FDI inflows in Africa declined by 36.2 percent between 2008 and 2009. In absolute terms, it declined from $87.6 billion in 2008 to $55.9 in 2009 as the impact of the global financial and economic crisis continued to unfold (UNCTAD, 2010). In fact, the decline was widespread as it affected 33 countries due to the crisis-induced lull in the global demand for commodities, which is a major driver for FDI in Africa. The cancellation of some cross-border M&A (merger and acquisition) deals combined with the absence of any exceptionally large one-off acquisitions, depressed the value of cross-border M&A operations in Africa during 2009 compared to the previous year (UNCTAD 2010).

Portfolio investment has also been affected negatively. Prior to the crisis, countries such as Ghana and Gabon successfully issued bonds in international capital markets. As a result of the crisis, this source of external finance has dried up and several African countries (for example, Nigeria and Kenya) are facing difficulties issuing bonds in international capital markets. Firms in Burkina Faso have delayed mining ventures because of difficulties in obtaining finance. In the Democratic Republic of the Congo, BHP Billiton, a major foreign investor, has suspended nickel prospecting because of low mineral prices. The drying up of these sources of external finance has constrained growth and development in the region (African Development Bank, 2009).

e) Aid Flows

Several African countries depend on official development assistance (ODA) for the financing of government programs. However, while the promises of increased aid at the Gleneagles summit in 2005 were already off track just three years later, it was feared that development aid to Africa could be dramatically reduced in 2009 as a consequence of the global crisis.

New figures presented by the OECD show continuing growth in development aid in 2009, despite the financial crisis. Total official development assistance from OECD member states "rose slightly" by 0.7 percent in 2009 to US$ 119.6 billion, representing 0.31 percent of donor countries' gross national income (GNI) (OECD, 2010). This means that earlier aims for rapid aid growth in 2009 were not met, but the results were nevertheless encouraging.

In 2009, net bilateral aid to Africa was US$ 28 billion, representing an increase of 3.0 percent over 2008. US$ 25 billion of this aid went to sub-Saharan Africa, an increase of 5.1 percent over 2008 (OECD, 2010). A cursory analysis of the figures revealed that several donor countries substantially reduced aid in 2009. Austria and Italy cut aid by over 30.0 percent, German aid fell by 12.0 percent, and Japan's aid by 11.0 percent. Interestingly, these countries were not the most affected by the crisis. These reductions were outweighed by many other donors, significantly increasing their aid in 2009. USA aid grew overall by over 5.0 percent in 2009 and to sub-Saharan Africa by 10.5 percent, fulfilling its promise to double its aid to sub-Saharan Africa between 2004 and 2010. However, USA still spends only 0.20 percent of its GDP on development aid, less than half of the share of the European countries.

The Gleneagles pledges to strongly beef up aid to Africa have so far ended up as empty words as less than half of the extra aid that was promised had been actually received. Aid flows also remain volatile and uncoordinated, adding to the difficulty of macroeconomic management.

f) Social Impact of the Global Financial Crisis

The financial crisis has discernable impacts on the social sectors. It has indirect effects on poverty through its impact on unemployment. The International Labour Organization (ILO) in its annual Global Employment Trends (2010) reported that the number of unemployed worldwide reached nearly 212 million in 2009, following an unprecedented increase of 34 million compared to 2007. In 2009, the unemployment rate is estimated to have risen to 8.2 per cent in sub-Saharan Africa and to 10.6 percent in North Africa, and this rising trend is unlikely to change in 2010.

Five years from the target date for attainment of the Millennium Development Goals (MDGs), available statistics and projections from international development partners seem to suggest that Africa is not on track to meet many of these goals; more so as the continent continues to grapple with the previously discussed negative impacts and the resource cut-backs of the global financial crisis. Before the global economic crisis in 2008–09, overall progress on the MDGs targets was particularly strong on poverty reduction, even in Africa. The proportion of Africans living on less than $1.25 a day fell from 58.0 percent in 1990 to 51.0 percent in 2005, but the absolute number of poor people rose from 296 million to 388 million (World Bank, 2010c).

The crisis attacked two critical drivers of progress toward the MDGs: faster growth and better service delivery. The World Bank (Global Monitoring Report 2010) estimates that, with slower growth rates, drastic cut back in aid and other development assistance flows consequent upon the crisis, the delivery of aid-financed social services in many African countries continues to suffer (World Bank, 2010c). Projected numbers reveal that the poverty rate for Sub-Saharan Africa will be 38.0 percent by 2015, rather than the 36.0 percent it would have been without the crisis. The continent will therefore fall short of MDG Goal 1 of halving 2000 poverty rate by 2015. The crisis will thus leave an additional 20 million people in extreme poverty by 2015 (World Bank 2010c: 6).

The crisis is also affecting progress on other human development indicators. Prior to the crisis, the World Bank estimated that Africa was the region with the fastest progress in primary school completion: the average primary completion rate increased from 53 percent to 65 percent between 2000 and 2008. This was a noticeable progress in several low income countries, including Mozambique, Rwanda, Ethiopia, and Burundi, that had a 50 percent or higher improvement in completion rates, admittedly starting from a low base. African countries also made substantial progress in closing the gender gap in primary school enrollment ratios. More and more girls have been enrolling in primary schools. Improvement varied between a 5 to 40 percent increase for low income countries in Africa: Benin, Burkina Faso, Ethiopia, Guinea, and Liberia saw a 20 percent increase in their gender parity index between 2000-2008; changes were less for Zambia and Rwanda, which had much higher initial values in 2000 (World Bank, 2010c). The crisis may have halted this progress as many African countries reverted to cutting spending rather than risk a new debt crisis. For example, Zambia slashed its health spending by a third in 2010, while Mali, Benin, and Niger reduced their budget for schools (Kyrili and Martin, 2010).

The crisis has also negatively affected infant mortality. Friedman and Schady (2009) estimate that additional 30,000-50,000 infants may have died in 2009 as a result of the global financial crisis. Most of these additional deaths are likely to be poorer children (born to women in rural areas and with lower education levels) and are overwhelmingly female.

Research undertaken by the Institute of Development Studies (IDS) which present evidence from five countries, including Kenya and Zambia in Africa, shows that households have been coping with the crises by spending a greater share of income on food, buying lower cost items, reducing the quality and diversity of food, gathering wild foods, eating less, or going hungry. Food intake in communities in Kenya was reported to have declined in quantity and in quality with women eating last and least. Children are particularly vulnerable to hunger and malnutrition, and this is affecting their ability to learn and/or hindering them from attending school altogether (Hossain and Eyben, 2009).

4 Response to the Crisis: Africa and Beyond

The response to the financial crisis was as dramatic as its causes. In a bid to relieve the global financial system of the ripples, Central Banks across the world announced sweeping rescue plans. From the Americas and Europe to Asia and Africa, the crisis prompted nations to inject huge funds into the banking sector in an effort to keep economic activities on track. The United States Federal Reserve, the European Central Bank, the Swiss National Bank, the Bank of England, the Bank of Canada and the Bank of Japan injected cash totaling $247 billion.[10] In the same light, African countries took several steps to mitigate the impact of the financial crisis on their economies: interest rate reductions, recapitalization of financial institutions, increasing liquidity to banks and firms, fiscal stimulus packages, trade policy changes, and financial sector regulatory reforms were some of the measures instituted. Strategies and policies adopted differ from country to country, depending on the available fiscal space as well as the degree of vulnerability to the crisis. For example, oil-exporting countries in the region with relatively more fiscal space were able to undertake counter-cyclical policies because they had accumulated huge foreign exchange reserves during pre-crisis oil price hikes. On the other hand, in the non-oil exporting economies, a counter-cyclical policy was not much of an option. In addition to the above measures, some countries set up task forces or committees to monitor the financial crisis and to advise government on how to respond. Rwanda, Kenya, Nigeria, and the Democratic Republic of the Congo are examples of countries that adopted this approach (African Development Bank, 2009b).

a) Fiscal stimulus

Governments in both OECD and non-OECD countries launched economic stimulus packages to address the economic downturn. Table 1 gives an indication of the size of the recovery packages of OECD countries which were directed towards diverse areas such as investment in modern infrastructure, research and development (R&D), support to innovation and to small and medium-sized enterprises (SMEs), education, and the greening of the economy.

---

[10] The European Central Bank injected up to $110 billion, the Swiss National Bank $27 billion, the Bank of Japan $60 billion, the Bank of England $40 billion and the Bank of Canada $10 billion. In addition, the Federal Reserve has pushed $55 billion into the US banking system.

Table 1: Fiscal packages (Public Revenue and Spending Measures 2008-2010, in USD Millions)

United States	804, 070
Germany	107,789
Japan	99,992
Canada	61,551
Spain	56,754
Australia	45, 673
Korea	42,667
United Kingdom	38,003
France	18,565
Netherlands	13,367
Sweden	13,109
Denmark	8,668
Finland	8,575
Belgium	8,016
Czech Republic	6,500
New Zealand	5,404
Poland	5,145
Austria	4,600
Switzerland	2,486
Luxembourg	1,968
Portugal	1,963
Slovak Republic	35

Source: OECD (2009)

African countries have responded better to this crisis than in the past. The fiscal policy measures adopted in several countries also constituted a clear break from the pro-cyclical policies during the past crises and the pre-crisis boom. Unlike in previous crises, some African countries responded decisively to the current economic turmoil through counter-cyclical monetary, fiscal and financial policies.

Taking a cue from the responses to the crisis in developed and emerging economies, a number of African governments implemented fiscal stimulus packages that include increases in public investment expenditure as well as tax reductions (see table 2).

Table 2: Stimulus packages adopted by African Countries

Egypt	The government introduced its "first" fiscal stimulus package of LE 15.5 billion ($2.81 billion) in 2008/09, mostly to finance accelerated investments in public utilities. Though the additional outlays were formally ratified by Parliament in March of 2009, several projects under the package were already off the ground in September 2008, financed through budgeted contingencies.
Mauritius	The Government announced in January 2009 a stimulus package of 10.4 billion of Mauritian Rupees (USD 330 Million), or approximately 3 percent of Mauritius GDP, to boost domestic demand and increase job creation.
Nigeria	Launch of a Presidential Steering Committee on the Global Economic Crisis in January 2009. The Committee is responsible for developing a framework to respond to the global crisis. The government was mulling whether to use its USD 52 billion foreign exchange reserves to shore up the economy through a stimulus package. It however decided to inject N70 billion (USD 0.477) billion into the textile industry through guarantees in February 2009.
South Africa	In the State of the Nation address, the President on 6th February, 2009 announced a stimulus package that entails increased funding for public investment projects with allocation of R 690 billion (about USD 80 billion) over the next three years.
Tanzania	$1.3 Billion

Sources: Compiled from various sources including Report of the Committee of African Finance Ministers and Central Bank Governors to the G20 of March 2009 (AfDB, 2009b and Ministry of Finance, 2009).

As the Report from the Committee of African Finance Ministers and Central Bank Governors that was established to monitor the crisis reveals (African Development Bank, 2010b), the Government of Mauritius put in place in January 2009 a stimulus package worth 10.4 billion Mauritian Rupees (USD 0.3 billion), or approximately 3.0 percent of its GDP to boost domestic demand and to increase job creation[11]. In South Africa, the government has increased funding for public investment projects with an allocation of R 690 billion (about USD 80 billion) over the three-year period 2009 to 2011. Similar actions were taken in Cape Verde, Sudan and Uganda. In Tunisia, the 2009 budget included a significant increase in public investments in line with its plan to increase external competitiveness and employment, and to strengthen social protection programmers.

As indicated in Table 2, the scope for counter-cyclical measures has varied with the level of income as it was Africa's relative rich countries that instituted stimulus packages with the exception of Tanzania. In absolute terms, South Africa's stimulus package is the largest in the region and would even rank forth in the world juxtaposed against Table 1. In relation to the size of countries' economies, Tanzania's stimulus package is one of the largest in the region, worth 6.4 per cent of GDP ($1.3 billion in total). The Tanzanian stimulus package took the form of limited and time-bound support to banks that have extended non-performing loans to sectors that have been affected by the crisis. It also instigated measures to ease constraints on production, processing and manufacturing, and trading, including maintaining infrastructure investments, stabilizing farmers' incomes, guaranteeing loans, maintaining fertilizer subsidies, and recapitalizing the Tanzanian Investment Bank (Oxfam 2010: 64).

b) Collective Measures

In addition to individual country actions in Africa, there were also a number of collective measures to mitigate the aftermath of the crisis. The African Development Bank, in collaboration with the Economic Commission for Africa (ECA), the African Union Commission (AUC), and NEPAD, convened a conference of African Ministers of Finance in Tunis in November 2008 to fashion out appropriate policy responses and to mobilize the calls for international support to the continent.[12] Its role is to monitor the impact of the

---

[11] See the Report of the Committee of African Finance Ministers and Central Bank Governors to the G20 of March 2009 (AfDB 2009b).

[12] The Committee of Ten African Ministers of Finance and Central Bank Governors (The C-10) was created during the November 2008 meeting in Tunis. Members of the C-10 are: Algeria, Botswana, Cameroon, Egypt, Kenya, Nigeria, South Africa, Tanzania, the Central Bank of West African States (CBWAS), and the Central Bank of Central African States (CBCAS). The Tunis meeting was convened to assess the potential impacts of the then looming global financial and economic crisis on Africa, and to deliberate on effective responses. It was sponsored and organized by the African Development Bank (AfDB), the United Nations Economic Commission for Africa (UNECA), and the African Union Commission (AUC).

financial crisis on African economies and related developments, and to develop proposals on how best to contribute to the international deliberations in the context of the G20. It also acts as a platform for sharing domestic and regional responses to the crisis.

The Committee has since met several times. Its first meeting was in Cape Town in January 2009 where it stressed the importance of mobilizing G20 members to support strong African participation in the London Summit. It subsequently met in Dar Es Salaam, Tanzania in March 2009 on the margins of the IMF Conference to prepare a submission to the G 20 Meeting, documented in a report titled ‘Impact of the Crisis on African Economies – Sustaining Growth and Poverty Reduction: African Perspectives and Recommendations to the G20’. This report was presented to the then British Prime Minister, Mr. Gordon Brown, host of the G20 Summit in London in April 2009 (AfDB 2009b).

The Committee met again in Abuja on 14 July 2009 for its third session. It reviewed information pertaining to the impact of the crisis on Africa, took stock of internal and international developments. The Committee then prepared an African perspectives report to feed into global discussions, in particular those leading up to the G20 Leaders Summit in Pittsburgh on 26 September 2009.

Regional institutions, such as the African Development Bank (AfDB) Group and the UNECA, have also been at the forefront of efforts at analyzing the crises’ impact on Africa and providing financial and technical support to regional member countries. For instance, the African Development Bank Board of Directors in 2009 inaugurated four products to counter the crises. These include: (1) an Emergency Liquidity Facility, with a US$ 1.5 billion budget; (2) a US$ 1 billion Trade Finance Initiative launched in two phases to support trade finance by African banks; (3) a Framework for Accelerated Resource Transfer of African Development Fund Resources to eligible countries; and, (4) Enhanced Policy Advisory Support (African Development Bank, 2009c).

This response is largely based on the recommendations of the African Finance Ministers and Governors of Central Banks’ Conference held on November 12, 2008 in Tunis.

5 Setting the Agenda for Africa’s Long-term Growth

As the depth and relative durability of the crisis have become apparent, the dominant economic paradigm (the neo-liberal "Washington Consensus”) has fallen into increasing disrepute. What was being hailed yesterday as the only road to ‘growth and prosperity’ is now under fierce attack by the same countries and institutions that promoted it for years. In leading developed countries, states have drawn up massive rescue plans to bail out industries or to nationalize banks and financial institutions. As previously highlighted, countries such as the USA, UK, Germany, France, and Japan, provided trillions of dollars between 2008 and 2009 in this wise. The aftermath of the crisis is also a pointer to the ever present concerns that Africa needs to reclaim the debate on its development; it has to take responsibility for its actions, and has to harness all available resources—human and natural—as well as the pile of previously crafted documents and strategies in this regard.

In the 1950s and early 1960s, Africa was largely seen as a very promising and prosperous continent. On the contrary, Asia was mired in seemingly irredeemable poverty and ravaged by wars. It was thus caught in a low-level equilibrium trap, with large and growing populations, unstable governments, and in many cases a weak natural resource base. In 1960, the per capita GDP[13] of several African countries including South Africa (USD 2,207.37), Gabon (USD 1,659.43), Algeria (USD 1,280), Liberia (USD 683.69), and Democratic Republic of Congo (USD 617.28) were far higher than those of China (USD 105.46) and Thailand (USD 329.25). In fact, in 1968, Gunnar Myrdal, the 1974 Nobel Laureate in Economics, published a three volume opus entitled *Asian Drama: An Inquiry into the Poverty of Nations*, depicting the Asian continent as the global economic 'soft-case'—unable to enforce the discipline that was needed to implement development plans.[14]

Moreover, after a spurt of post-independence economic growth, external shocks, poor policy responses and ineffective development strategies brought economic stagnation to many African countries, causing even front-runners such as Kenya and Cote d'Ivoire to lose momentum (Roemer, 2007). As the African dream was being shattered, the East Asia economic miracle was being rekindled. Since the 1970s, the world has witnessed a reversal of fortune. The spectacular growth of many economies in East Asia, especially Hong Kong, South Korea, Singapore, and Taiwan, collectively known as the "Four Tigers" over the past three decades, has amazed the economics profession and has evoked a torrent of books and articles attempting to explain the phenomenon. From 1973 to 1993, in all the rapidly growing economies of East and Southeast Asia—China, Hong Kong, Indonesia, Malaysia, Singapore, South Korea, Taiwan and Thailand—income per capita grew by 4 to 9 percent a year, doubling or even, as in Korea, quintupling over those 20 years

---

[13] The per capita GDP in 2000 prices for 1960 are available in the link: http://www.nationmaster.com/graph/eco_gdp_per_cap_con_2000_us-per-capita-constant-2000-us&date=1960

[14] See Tim Lankester (2004:1).

(Roemer, 1996). In addition to the four tigers, spectacular growth performances were also recorded by Indonesia, Malaysia and Thailand over the same period and by China since 1978. Together, these eight countries grew at a rate about twice of what was witnessed in the rest of East Asia and the industrial economies; they grew about three times as fast as those in Latin America and South Asia, and about five times as fast as those in sub-Saharan Africa.

Growth rates in the transition economies of China and Vietnam in the last three decades further reinforce the argument as to how important it could be for Africa to take a cue from the East Asian experiences in terms of understanding the underlying factors in sustainable growth and development. None of the countries in East Asia followed the orthodox policies of the 'Washington Consensus' to the letter, and most of them were predominantly state-dominated—so termed "benevolent dictators" held reign. The underlying characteristics of their growth trajectories could be pinned down to the following closely integrated and mutually reinforcing factors

- Dynamic agricultural sector;
- Rapid growth of exports;
- Rapid demographic transition;
- High investment and saving rates; and,
- High investments in human capital.

For example, export orientation and export growth created a demand for skilled workers and this justifies the value of investments in education and human development. The dynamic agricultural sector allowed labor to shift into export industries. Rapid demographic transition also heightened the need for more investment in education as sustainable avenues were being created for the growing pool of savings; resources were being invested in the development of needed physical and social capital. All of these are indications of the benefits of fostering interactions between growth drivers in an economy for the accelerated development of key sectors.

Bad governance and poor policy choices certainly played a key role in the African growth tragedy. Park Chung-Hee's 18-year reign in Korea, the Kuomintang's hold on Taiwan, Britain's colonial regime in Hong Kong, Lee Kuan Lee's long dominance of Singapore, Suharto's 29- year rule in Indonesia, and Mahathir's long-tenured rule in Malaysia all coincided with rapid developments in those countries. Thailand is a special case: although prime ministers changed frequently until the recent political reforms, the popularly revered monarchy has been able to protect and entrench high-ranking officials who make economic policy. On the other hand, governance in Africa has been catastrophic, combining to a large extent limited capacity for forward-looking and growth-promoting policy choices, with continuing reliance on externally imposed programs that served only the strategic interests of the development partners. This contrasted rather sharply with experiences of the East Asian economies whose 'benevolent dictators' displayed a very high degree of economic pragmatism. African leaders, even in the rare instances where they were not plunderers, tended to be ideologically driven and deficient in the ability to harness growth potentials that are abound domestically.[15]

Despite positive trends achieved in Africa for close to a decade before the onset of the global crisis, economic growth did not raise incomes high enough to sufficiently trigger any notable progress in meeting the Millennium Development Goals (MDGs) and other antipoverty benchmarks. A number of structural factors - high ratio of foreign debt to national income; lack of far-reaching investment in agriculture and upstream agribusiness; poor communication and transportation infrastructure; high population growth; and the burden of disease, continue to constrain growth and development prospects. Many countries still rely on external aid to balance their budgets and to provide basic social services. Political instability - continues in many areas, and few states constitute a transparent and representative democratic governance system.

The foregoing can only point in one direction: it is time for the continent to review its development strategies and to make them more resilient against future external shocks, and focus on the delivery of social and economic services more broadly and inclusively. African countries need to lead the debate on the continent's development and take bold and decisive actions when the need arises. Genuine development needs are to be viewed more as endogenous processes rather than as initiatives that can be 'imported' from abroad. It is imperative that Africans restore their self-confidence, trust African expertise, and promote the use of African endogenous knowledge and technology.

In the search for an alternative paradigm, Africa should revisit key documents, such as the Lagos Plan of Action for the Economic Development of Africa (LPA) (OAU 1980/republished UNECA 1980); the African Alternative Framework to SAPs (AAF-SAP) (UNECA, 1989); the African Charter on Popular Participation and Transformation (African Union, 1990), and the NEPAD Framework Document (NEPAD, 2000), among others.

The *Lagos Plan of Action (LPA)* covered a wide spectrum of issues of topical concern to Africa: (a) the development of priority sectors; (b) skills and training for participation; and (c) institutional development at the nation-

[15] The 'benevolent dictators' in Africa, unfortunately, did and do no more than sit-in-office-till-death-do-us-part.

al, sub-regional and regional levels. With regard to industry, the Plan accords high priority to the establishment of a sound industrial base in Africa, and was explicitly critical of previous approaches to industrial development in most African countries which have tended to be carbon-copies of foreign patterns of industrialization (Sekgoma 2006: 68-72). According to the LPA, those earlier approaches only resulted in industries which had a very high import content and low value added. The products from most of the industries tended to be luxury goods which did not satisfy the basic needs of the majority of African population. The Plan therefore denounced such approaches to industrial development and advocates an industrial sector which would aim at - (a) satisfaction of the basic needs of the population; (b} fostering local linkages by exploiting local natural resources; (c) creating jobs; (d) establishment of a base for the development of other sectors; and (e) achievement of regional self-reliance.

To address the development tragedy of the 1980s on the African continent, the *African Alternative Framework to SAPs (AAF-SAP)* put to fore policy instruments that include reduction in defense spending; expenditure-switching to ensure that an average of 30 percent of total government expenditure goes to the social sector; selective use of subsidies to ensure availability of essential commodities; selective use of trade and fiscal policies, including high taxes on conspicuous consumption; and a guaranteed minimum price for food crops managed through strategic food reserve (Bade Onimode 1992: 34-35). For the productive sectors, policies advocated in the AAF-SAP include:

- Land reforms for better access and entitlement to land for productive use; enhancement of the role of women as agents of change and the modernisation of the food production sector;
- Allocation of an increasing share of foreign exchange for imports of vital inputs;
- Sectoral allocation of credit using credit guidelines that would favour the food subsector and the manufacture of essential goods;
- Use of selective nominal interest rates in such a way that interest on loans for speculative activities would be greater than the rates on loans for productive activities;
- Rehabilitation and rationalisation of installed productive and infrastructural capacities;
- Removal of subventions to parastatals other than those in the social sector and nationally important strategic basic industries; and
- Use of limited, realistic and decreasing deficit financing for productive and infrastructural investments that have little import content.

On the other hand, *the African Charter for Popular Participation* called for the emergence of a new era in Africa—an Africa in which democracy, accountability, economic justice and development for transformation become internalized and an Africa in which the empowerment of people, initiative and enterprise, and the democratization of the development process are the order of the day in every country (UNECA, 1990: 1-2).

The latest of the incantations, the *New Partnership for Africa's Development (NEPAD),* is a programme of the African Union (AU), adopted in 2001 by African leaders in Lusaka, Zambia, with the primary objectives of poverty eradication, promotion of sustainable growth and development, and the empowerment of women through building genuine partnerships at country, regional and global levels. It is a pledge by African leaders, based on a common vision and a firm and shared conviction, that they have a pressing duty to eradicate poverty and to place their countries, both individually and collectively, on a path of sustainable growth and development, and, at the same time, to prepare them to participate actively in the world economy and in global politics. It is anchored on African ownership and management of the development process. NEPAD identifies seven priority areas of intervention:

- Strengthening mechanisms for conflict prevention, management and resolution;
- Promoting and protecting democracy and human rights;
- Restoring and maintaining macroeconomic stability;
- Revitalizing and extending the provision of education, technical training and health services, with high priority accorded to HIV/AIDS, malaria, and other communicable diseases;
- Promoting the role of women in social and economic development;
- Building the capacity of the states in Africa; and
- Promoting the development of infrastructure, agriculture and its diversification.

NEPAD[16] calls for adapted policy reforms and increased investments in the priority areas of agriculture and food security, science and technology,

[16] As part of the process to integrate NEPAD into the African Union structures and processes, the 14th African Union (AU) Summit, held in Addis Ababa, Ethiopia from 25 January – 2 February 2010, decided to strengthen the NEPAD programme by transforming the NEPAD Secretariat into an implementation Agency – the NEPAD Planning and Coordinating Agency (NPCA).

environment, trade and market access, governance, infrastructure (energy, transport and water sanitation, and information and communication technologies), gender, and capacity development.

An elaborate review of these documents is needed to take into account more recent developments in the global environment. The integration of contributions by academics, the private sector, and of civil society organizations in the areas of gender equality, trade, finance, food sovereignty, and human and social rights should all be harnessed for the development of a framework for Africa's new growth and development paradigm. Within this framework, the role of the state in promoting economic growth and development needs to be redefined.

Of note from the documents cited and developments debates of more recent times from concerned stakeholders on the continent is that the *laissez-faire* prescriptions assigned in the past three to four decades to the role of governments - less activist and more enabling - are to be replaced by active interventions of governments in economic activities (especially in the social service sectors), and through mitigating measures as the economic stimulus packages. There is need for a review and rebalancing of the roles of the state and that of the market within development, growth and poverty-reduction strategies. Needless to say, too, records of achievements in the South East Asian countries have shown that the state just cannot be the only player. It has to work with the private sector and the civil society, in this drive for inclusive development.

It is also important to revisit export-oriented strategies. Without necessarily advocating a swing towards inward-looking strategies, it is important that domestic demand be significantly strengthened. At the same time, measures for active and competitive participation in the global value chains need to be accelerated. Further redirection efforts lie in the treatment of environmental issues (including measures to address climate change and biodiversity loss) as part of the solution to the crisis, by fostering a more sustainable development policy.

Africa is particularly vulnerable to climate change although it is the continent least responsible for climate change, because of its overdependence on rain-fed agriculture, compounded by factors such as widespread poverty and overall weak intervention and implementation capacity. The main longer-term impacts include: changing rainfall patterns affecting agriculture and reducing food security; worsening water security; decreasing fish resources in large lakes due to rising temperature; shifting vector-borne diseases; and rising sea level affecting low-lying coastal areas with large populations (Africa Partnership Forum, 2007). Africa, thus, needs to plan for 'Green Growth' that emphasizes environmentally sustainable economic progress to foster a low-carbon, and socially inclusive development.

There is need for reform of the global financial architecture, including the exchange rate system, in order to underpin macroeconomic stability and to avoid debt traps and speculation. This would involve going "back to the basics" – to the rules invented at the 1944 Bretton Woods Conference – in particular, fixed but adjustable exchange rates reflecting fundamentals such as inflation rates. Keeping real exchange rates stable would prevent major distortions in international trade and currencies. Africa and other developing countries have been unjustifiably left out of mitigation measures[17]. It is imperative that they are included in the quest for solutions and the governance architecture of international financial institutions.

The downturn has also heightened the imperative of strengthening intra-African integration; African countries need to strengthen efforts aimed at promoting economic integration as a central component for the continent's development in an increasingly globalizing world economy. Regional integration in Africa is currently among the lowest worldwide. As UNCTAD (2009) indicated in its African Report, intraregional trade represents only 9 per cent of exports, compared to 71 per cent in Europe and 46 per cent in developing Asia - both regions in which it has clearly served as a stepping stone for economic development. Similarly, intra-African investment accounts for only 13 per cent of all inward FDI, less than half the figure for ASEAN countries. For Africa, strengthening regional integration, especially through trade, investment and movement of labour, could mitigate the adverse effects of the current crisis and make the continent more resilient to future external shocks.

Regional integration could support the development of infrastructure in such key sectors as transportation, communications, and energy by allowing for economies of scale in their production.

Finally, one of the many big lessons of the global crisis is that African countries need to deepen their policy and regulatory frameworks as well as their structural reform measures in order to attract sufficient private capital flows, diversify their export basket, and insulate the financial system from complex but unmanageable financial instruments. They will also need to rationalize and strengthen the various institutions that they have created to enhance such efforts. Evidently, the launching of NEPAD and the African Peer Review Mechanism (APRM), and the aid-trade-investments complementarities inherent in BRICS's African agenda within the redefined G20, have been acclaimed as important initiatives that have a high potential to give a new boost and direction to the development efforts of African countries[18]. It is hoped that the smooth and efficient functioning of these institutions and

---

[17] Only South Africa is a member of the reconfigured G20.

[18] BRICS is the acronym for Brazil, Russia, India, China and South Africa.

alliances move Africa in the desired direction of enhanced South-South and triangular cooperation.

6 Conclusion and Policy Recommendations

This paper has examined the nature, the causes and the implications of the global financial crisis for Africa, on-going initiatives to mitigate the crisis, and proffers an agenda for long term growth and structural transformation. The paper shows that, although the immediate impact of the crisis may have been mitigated, African economies are faced with severe threats of growth deceleration, which have undermined recent progress in reducing poverty. Substantial negative effects have been already observed in terms of losses on stock markets, currency depreciation, and a worsening of macroeconomic balances (current account deficits, budget deficits). The continent is also vulnerable to extreme weather events such as faster desertification, rising sea levels, and more frequent droughts.

Regional solutions to the problems facing Africa have so far remained elusive. A new development paradigm, that draws largely from a number of past documents and pronouncements—the Lagos Plan of Action for the Economic Development of Africa (LPA), the African Alternative Framework to SAPs (AAF-SAP), the African Charter on Popular Participation and Transformation, and the NEPAD Framework Document—is needed. Such a demand is reinforced by more recent developments in the global environment, and the realization of the new paradigm is ensured by the integration of contributions by academics, the private sector, and of civil society organizations in the areas of gender equality, trade, finance, food sovereignty, and human and social rights; they should all be harnessed if Africa is to reclaim its development options.

It is clear that African countries and their leaders should seek proactive economic policy measures and reforms to mitigate the effects of the crisis on African economies. In charting the way forward, in addition to the recommendations given in section 5 towards a new development paradigm, the key priorities are succinctly examined below:

- Until the onset of the financial and economic crisis, macroeconomic policies in Africa tended to be pro-cyclical, rather than counter-cyclical, with sometimes dire consequences for growth and poverty reduction. The dependence on primary commodities, limits on government borrowing spending[19], or debt accumulation over many years all combined to give governments less room to conduct discretionary fiscal policy. Not surprisingly, fiscal policy tends to be expansionary during booms and tight during downturns, thereby amplifying and exacerbating the adverse effects of shocks on output. In the monetary policy arena, the conventional wisdom was that the primary objective of monetary policy should be the maintenance of low and stable inflation. Given this mindset, Central Banks in the region were thus more concerned about the impact of their policy actions on inflation rather than on the implications for output. Consequently, they are often hesitant to follow expansionary monetary policy during downturns for fear that it would create inflation and undermine macroeconomic stability. Also, in the 1980s and 1990s, several African countries that adopted SAPs were required to follow both restrictive monetary and fiscal policies in response to economic turmoil with severe economic and social costs.

- The current crisis has exposed the limitations of this approach to the conduct of macroeconomic policy. It has demonstrated that monetary policy is not an end in itself. It is useful to the extent that it supports the overall development efforts of countries. In this regard, the focus of monetary policy should not be on inflation alone. It should also explicitly take into account growth and financial stability issues in order to minimize the impact of shocks to the economy. There is thus the need to alter existing mandates of central banks to include growth and financial stability objectives especially in countries pursuing inflation targeting. The crisis has also demonstrated that an active fiscal policy is necessary to cushion the effects of shocks on output. African countries thus need to create fiscal space for counter-cyclical policy responses in the future by managing revenue from commodity booms more effectively and building resilience to external shocks through the development of productive capacity. This could be accomplished by infrastructure development, promoting technology, and improving manufacturing export competitiveness.

---

[19] Thorton (2008) and UNCTAD (2010) appraised exhaustively why African countries and developing countries in general adopt pro-cyclical macroeconomic policies rather than counter-cyclical policies that would support their development efforts.

- The crisis has underscored the importance of diversification of the economic bases[20]. In order to overcome the one-sided dependence from exporting commodities in unprocessed form, agro-industrial development is an option for many African countries which is not yet exploited. The crisis has also created opportunities for accelerating progress with implementing structural reforms in the areas of private sector development, financial sectors, labor markets, and social safety nets as well as with deepening regional integration.

- The crisis has—paradoxically—provided a unique opportunity to accelerate growth and poverty reduction in Africa. The awareness of global interdependence and of the huge impact of the Global Financial Crisis on Africa's development path has increased. Aid to Africa must increase by more than the shortfall in the Gleneagles Commitments in order to help low-income countries in the region resume and accelerate progress on the MDGs. Current financing constraints make it even more important for donors to ensure, in keeping with the Paris Declaration, that aid is predictable, transparent, and aligned with the policy priorities of the recipients. Aid would be particularly useful now as fiscal pressures are building up, to prevent undue compression of investment budgets, and to make it possible to maintain the scope and size of social safety nets. Although many donor countries face problems of their own, aid flows are still a relatively small share of their budgets and can be accommodated even with the new competing demands; and,

- Trade talks need to resume with a view to stimulating global growth and welfare. The Doha round, which was started in 2001, has in effect been stalled for nearly two years. Successful conclusion of the Doha Round would help to better integrate developing countries, including those in sub-Saharan Africa, into the global trading system, which would spur global and regional growth and facilitate Africa's attainment of the MDGs. Temptations to respond to weakening balance of payments positions with protectionist measures need to be avoided. Less global trade would likely harm all countries.

---

[20] This was the focus of Vol. 11 (2005/2006) and Vol. 12 (2007) of the African Development Perspectives Yearbook entitled: "Africa - Escaping the Primary Commodities Dilemma" and "Africa - Commodity Dependence, Resource Curse and Export Diversification" respectively (Wohlmuth et al. 2006, 2007).

References

AfDB/African Development Bank (2009a), 'Impact of the Financial Crisis on African Economies: An Interim Assessment', Paper presented at the Meeting of the Committee of Finance Ministers and Central Bank Governors, Cape Town, South Africa, 16 January, African Development Bank, Tunis

AfDB/African Development Bank (2009b), 'Impact of the Crisis on African Economies: Sustaining Growth and Poverty Reduction, African Perspectives and Recommendations to the G20', A Report from the Committee of African Finance Ministers and Central Bank Governors (C-10) to the British Prime Minister to the British Prime Minister as Part of the Agenda for the April 2009 G20 Summit in London, African Development Bank, Tunis

AfDB/African Development Bank (2009c), The African Development Bank Group Response to the Economic Impact of the Financial Crisis, March, The African Development Group, Tunis

Africa Partnership Forum (2007), Africa and Climate Change, 8th Meeting of the Africa Partnership Forum Berlin, Germany, 22-23 May 2007, see: http://www.africapartnershipforum.org/dataoecd/57/7/38897900.pdf

AU/African Union (1990), African Charter for Popular Participation in Development and Transformation, African Union, Tanzania, February 16, 1990, see: http://www.africanreview.org/docs/civsoc/arusha.pdf

Arieff, A./ M. Weiss/ V. Jones (2010), The Global Economic Crisis: Impact on Sub-Saharan Africa and Global Policy Responses, Congressional Research Service Report, for Congress, 7-5700, see: www.crs.gov R40778

Assubuji P./J. Luckscheiter/ K. Ben-Zeev, Editors (2009), The Global Economic Crisis and South Africa Perspectives, No 3, 09, Heinrich Böll Stiftung, Southern Africa, Cape Town, see: http://www.boell.org.za/downloads/Perspectives_3-09.pdf

Cali, M/ I. Massa/ D. Willem te Velde, (2008), "The Global Financial Crisis: Financial Flows Into Developing Countries Set to Fall by One Quarter," Overseas Development Institute. http://www.odi.org.uk/resources/download/2523.pdf

Claessens S. /G. Ariccia/D. Igan/L.Laeven (2010), Lessons and Policy Implications from the Global Financial Crisis, IMF Working Papers, WP/10/44, February

Dogbe, T. and C. Marshall (2009), 'A Rapid Assessment of the Impact of the Global Economic Crisis in Ghana', Kumasi: Participatory Development Associates Ltd.

Friedman, J./ N. Schady (2010), How Many More Infants Are Likely to Die in Africa as a Result of the Global Financial Crisis?, World Bank Policy Research Working Paper, #5023, August

Holmqvist, G., 2009, 'Africa and the Global Recession', Nordic Africa Institute, Uppsala, Sweden

Hossain, N./ R. Eyben, (2009), "Accounts of Crisis: Poor People's Experiences of the Food, Fuel and Financial Crises in Five Countries, Institute of Development Studies: Brighton

IMF (2009), Impact of the Global Financial Crisis on Sub-Saharan Africa, African Department, International Monetary Fund, Washington DC

IMF (2010), IMF Managing Director Strauss-Kahn Calls on Africa to Rebuild Policy Foundations Shaken by Global Economic Crisis, Press Release No. 10/73, March 8, 2010, in: http://www.imf.org/external/np/sec/pr/2010/pr1073.htm, accessed 10 June 2010

ILO/International Labour Organization (2010), Global Employment Trends, International Labour Organization, Geneva: ILO

Kyrili, K. / M. Martin (2010), The Impact of the Global Economic Crisis on the Budgets of Low-Income Countries, Research report, DFI for Oxfam, July

Kryticous, N. P. (2009), The Impact of the Global Financial Crisis on the Zambian Economy, Economic Injustice, Volume 2, Number 4 (May), Open Society Initiative for Southern Africa

Lankester, Tim (2004), 'Asian Drama': The Pursuit Of Modernization In India And Indonesia, in: *Asian Affairs,* Vol. XXXV, No. III, November, Pp. 291-304

Massa, I. and D. Willem Te Velde (2008), 'The Global Financial Crisis: Will Successful African Countries Be Affected?', Overseas Development Institute, London, in: http://www.odi.org.uk/resources/projects/background-papers/2008/12/financial-crisis-african-countries-poverty-development.pdf

Malik, N. I./S. Ullah/K. Azam/A. Khan (2009), The Impact of the Recent Global Financial Crisis on the Financial Institutions in the Developing Countries: Global Perspectives, *International Review of Business Research Papers, Vol. 5, No. 5, pp. 85-89*

Ministry of Finance (2009), Egypt Response to the Global Crises, Macro Fiscal Policy Unit, Cairo, Egypt, http://www.mof.gov.eg/MOFGallerySource/English/Egypt%20Response%20to%20the%20Global%20Crisis.pdf, Accessed 22 August 2010

Mohan, R. (2008), Global Financial Crisis – Causes, Impact, Policy Responses and Lessons, Speech by Dr Rakesh Mohan, Deputy Governor of the Reserve Bank of India, at the 7th Annual India Business Forum Conference, London Business School, London, 23 April

OECD (2009), Policy Responses to the Economic Crisis: *Investing in Innovation for Long-Term Growth,* Organization for Economic Co-Operation and Development, Paris, June

OECD (2010), Development aid rose in 2009 and most donors will meet 2010 aid targets, see: http://www.oecd.org/document/11/0,3343,en_21571361_44315115_44981579_1_1_1_1,00.html, Accessed 10 June 2010

Onimode, B. (1992), *A future for Africa: beyond the politics of adjustment,* Earthscan/IFAA: London, pp.34-35

OAU/Organization of African Unity (1980), "Lagos Plan of Action for the Economic Development of Africa, 1980-2000", republished by the United Nations Economic Commission for Africa, April 1980, see: http://www.uneca.org/itca/ariportal/docs/lagos_plan.pdf

Kirkpatrick, G. (2009), The Corporate Governance Lessons from the Financial Crisis, OECD,in: www.oecd.org/dataoecd/32/1/42229620.pdf, Accessed 28 July 2010

Sekgoma , G.A. (2002), Pula: The Botswana Journal of African Studies, Vol. 8. No. 2, pp. 68-94

South Centre (2009), Key Issues in the Policy Response to the Economic Crisis: South Centre's View, South Bulletin, June, Issue 37, Geneva

Roemer, M. (1996), Could Asian Policies Propel African Growth?, Harvard Institute for International Development, July 1996, Boston, USA: Harvard University

Taylor, J. (2009), "The Financial Crisis and the Policy Responses: An Empirical Analysis ofWhat Went Wrong", Working Paper 14631, January, NBER/National Bureau of Economic Research, New York, USA

UNCTAD (2009), Economic Development in Africa, Strengthening Regional Economic Integration for Africa's Development, New York and Geneva: United Nations

UNCTAD (2010), Global Investment Trends Monitor No. 2 - Newsletter 1, Global and Regional Trends in FDI in 2009, Geneva, January

UNECA/United Nations Economic Commission for Africa (1989), African Alternative Framework to Structural Adjustment Programmes for Socio-Economic Recovery and Transformation (AAF-SAP), see: www.uneca.org/publications/ESPD/old/aaf_sap.pdf

UNECA/United Nations Economic Commission for Africa and Africa Union (1990), "*African Charter for Popular Participation in Development*", Adopted at the International Conference on Popular Participation in the Recovery and Development in Africa, Arusha, United Republic of Tanzania, 12 – 16 February, 1990, UNECA: Addis Ababa

UNECA/United Nations Economic Commission for Africa and African Union (2009), Meeting of the Committee of Experts of the 2nd Joint Annual Meetings of the AU Conference of Ministers of Economy and Finance and ECA Conference of Ministers of Finance, Planning and Economic Development, *Cairo, Egypt 2-5 June 2009*

UNECA/United Nations Economic Commission for Africa and AU/Africa Union (2010), Overview of Economic and Social Conditions in Africa in 2009, Meeting of the Committee of Experts of the 3rd Joint Annual Meetings of the AU Conference of Ministers of Economy and Finance and ECA Conference of African Ministers of Finance, Planning and Economic Development, Lilongwe, Malawi 25 – 28 March 2010

Te Velde, Dirk Willem (2008), The Global Financial Crisis And Developing Countries, Which Countries Are At Risk and What Can Be Done?, Background Note, Overseas Development Institute, October

Thornton J (2008), Explaining Pro-Cyclical Fiscal Policy in African countries, in: *Journal of African Economies,* Vol. 17, No. 3

UNCTAD (2010), The Financial Crisis, Macroeconomic Policy and the Challenge of Development in Africa, Trade and Development Board, Fiftieth executive session, Geneva, 8 July 2010.

Wohlmuth, Karl/Philippe Burger/Achim Gutowski/Mohammed N. Hussain/Tobias Knedlik/Mareike Meyn, Eds., (2006), African Development Perspectives Yearbook 2005/2006, Africa - Escaping the Primary Commodities Dilemma, Vol. 11, LIT Verlag Münster – Hamburg – London

Wohlmuth, Karl/Chicot Eboue/Achim Gutowski/Afeikhena Jerome/Tobias Knedlik/Mareike Meyn/Touna Mama, Eds., (2007), African Development Perspectives Yearbook 2007, Africa - Commodity Dependence, Resource Curse and Export Diversification, Vol. 12, LIT Verlag Munster – Hamburg – London

World Bank (2009), Migration and Development Brief 11, Migration and Remittances Team Development Prospects Group, World Bank, published 3 November 2009, Washington D. C.

World Bank (2010a), Africa's Pulse, An Analysis of Trends Shaping Africa's Economic Future, World Bank, Washington, D. C.

World Bank (2010b), Migration and Development Brief Number 12, Outlook for Remittance Flows 2010-11, Migration and Remittances Team, Development Prospects Group, World Bank, published 23 April 2010, Washington D. C.

World Bank (2010c), Global Monitoring Report 2010, The MDGs after the Crisis, The International Bank for Reconstruction and Development/The World Bank, Washington D. C.

World Bank (2010d), Global Economic Prospects, sub-Saharan Africa, The International Bank for Reconstruction and Development/The World Bank, Washington D. C., http://siteresources.worldbank.org/INTGEP2010/Resources/Appendix-SSA.pdf

African Economic Integration, the Millennium Development Goals and African Reform Challenges in View of the Global Financial Crisis

Arno J. van Niekerk[1]

Abstract

The impact of the global financial crisis (GFC) on Africa's economies has left considerable doubt about the way forward for Africa in terms of its economic integration. Not only, for instance, are policy reforms even more under scrutiny as a result of the crisis, but policy coordination among African countries has now become more problematic. The continent's strong aims regarding economic integration and the Millennium Development Goals (MDGs) are being seriously challenged by the 'new economic normal' situation that is taking shape as the worst of the GFC is dissipating. By investigating the changed, crisis-induced context of these key African priorities, the paper will assist in policy decision-making, taking current conditions into consideration and providing perspective on reform requirements for progress in regional economic integration and the MDGs. In the wake of the GFC, Africa is certainly at a crossroads regarding its progression, especially in deciding on the strategy it will follow to promote both intra-integration among its economies and inter-integration with external partners, with both presumably leading to an improvement in Africans' quality of life. The decisions Africa will make now will have a momentous impact on closing the divide between itself and most of the rest of the world – i.e. arguably its last window of opportunity.

---

[1] PhD, Senior lecturer, University of the Free State, South Africa. With thanks to the National Research Foundation (NRF) for providing funding.

1 Introduction

Since the start of the global financial crisis (GFC) with the subprime crisis in August 2007, economic conditions in Africa have deteriorated alarmingly. Its six leading economies (out of 53) – accounting for 65% of the continent's gross domestic product (GDP) – are primarily the ones that have felt the brunt of this impact, mainly due to them being the most integrated into global financial markets. South Africa (SA), Nigeria, Algeria, Egypt, Morocco and Angola have all experienced a significant weakening in their GDP growth rates – even up to 99% in the case of Angola (from 2007 to 2009) as global trade collapsed (IMF, 2009: 90). For Africa as a whole its real GDP growth rate has declined by over 70%, from 6.3% in 2007 to 1.7% in October 2009. In global terms, the GFC has caused world output to fall from 5.2% real GDP growth in 2007 to -1.1% in 2009. World trade, in terms of volume, has fallen by 11.9% from 2008 to 2009 (IMF, 2009: 184, 169). The GFC's impact has particularly been felt by almost all countries' current accounts and fiscal balances, resulting in 'twin-deficits'. Regions with current account surpluses experienced a reduction in these surpluses since 2008, namely Japan and developing Asia, including China (ECA, 2009: 2). Latin America has moved from a small surplus to a small deficit, while the Middle Eastern countries are experiencing the highest current account surpluses due to high oil revenues. These are, however, expected to decline in line with the falling oil price. The fiscal balance deteriorated in industrialised countries as a whole and in all major countries and regions. This is mainly driven by lower revenues due to the growth slowdown and higher expenditure as countries dealt with the effects of the GFC – both developed and developing economies.

In view of increasing globalisation, or perhaps rather triadisation among the three centers of global economic power (the United States (US), Europe and Japan (and now also China and India)), of particular concern for Africa is how the GFC will affect two key focus-areas which are regarded as essential for Africa's efforts to catch up with the rest of the world: achieving the Millennium Development Goals (MDGs) and deeper regional and economic integration on the continent. Africa's progress towards the MDGs, and especially the reduction of poverty (Goal 1), are in serious jeopardy due to the GFC. So also are the plans of the African Union (AU) to intensify African economic integration and to implement, by 2021 (or eventually), a single African currency (Jefferis, 2007: 83). The paper investigates the impact of the GFC on Africa's economic progress, with specific emphasis on the implications it could have for Africa's aspirations to achieve the dual aims of (1) reaching the MDGs by 2015 and (2) deepening African economic integration *en route* to 2021 (for instance). It firstly aims to explore what challenges Africa's crisis-affected economic conditions are now posing as regards attaining these dual aims, and secondly, to examine what economic reform requirements are among those most essential for achieving the dual aims. Comprising of sections three to four, this will be preceded by section two, which provides vital background through succinctly considering Africa's historical experience with factors like globalisation, dictating actions and ideological influences, and especially African regionalisation – all factors that are now particularly in the spotlight due to the GFC and its impact on the two focus-areas (dual aims) mentioned.

2 History: Africa, globalisation, reform and regional integration

After what is known as 'European scramble for Africa' at the Berlin Conference in 1884, colonialism forced Africa's primary role in the global economy, of acting as a reservoir of human and natural resources to continue to enrich the economy of the colonial center at its own expense, upon itself (Shrestha *et al.*, 2008: 4). This set Africa on the path of underdevelopment as the capitalist class in Europe used their control of international trade to ensure that Africa specialised in exporting captives (Rodney, 1974: 91). Only after World War II, when it became enormously difficult and costly for the European colonisers to maintain their colonialism, and when rising tides of anti-colonialism across Africa were taking its toll on the imperium, did the bell of independence began to rang during the 1950s. Being the last continent to be colonised, Africa was also the last to be politically free from the clutches of colonialism. Ever since this period, when the slave trade had a most devastating effect on the continent, Africa has struggled with the issue of colonisation: its origins, its earlier justification and its after-effects, resulting in an innate resistance to swaying Western influences – often to their own detriment as in the case of globalisation. For many Africans globalisation is a modern-day version of colonisation that must be desisted (Makinda & Okumu, 2008: 81). With this inertia-approach, plus a general lack of competitive ability, many African countries have robbed themselves of the opportunity to react quicker and reap more of the benefits of globalisation.

Later, during the 1980s, when reforms through the structural adjustment programmes (SAPs) were less than successful in many African countries, mainly due to their lack of taking country-specific conditions sufficiently into consideration, it became evident that its economies had gained little in terms of becoming more globalised (Clapham, 2006: 7). It was from this experience, primarily, that the duality between African marginalisation and globalisation developed. Leys (1994: 46) conclude that the failure of World Bank and International Monetary Fund (IMF) austerity policies in Africa has moved the continent from "crisis" to "tragedy". In response to the failure of the SAPs, even in 1989, the Economic Commission for Africa (ECA) initiated the African Alternative Framework to Structural Adjustment Programme for Socio-Economic Recovery and Transformation (AAF-SAP). Being on the whole concerned with 'adjustment with transformation', AAF-SAP stressed the need for capital investment for economic growth in Africa (Loots, 2006: 4). After the Washington Consensus[2], during the 1990s, when neo-liberal policy approaches got deeper ingrained in prescriptions, African economies became even more vulnerable as the winds of increased globalisation became icier and Africa's global competitiveness waned (Collier, 2007: 14). There is no doubt that the continent presents a challenge to globalisation's advocates. Today, in light of the GFC, the hegemony of neo-liberal policy approaches and American-style capitalism – for many the true roots of the crisis – are under serious scrutiny. Ironically, Africa had arguably paid the highest price for these partly-flawed neo-liberal policy approaches, into which its economies (even those who initially resisted it like Nigeria and Tanzania) were forced via conditionality.

In combination with these developments, over the past century, Africa has consistently attempted to promote regional integration. Perhaps the word most frequently used in African political discourse is 'unity', signifying a deep-seated desire by Africans to join forces in order to compete better in an increasingly globalised economy. Regional economic cooperation in Africa dates as far back as the beginning of the last century. By 1919 an East African Currency Board (EACB) was created by Kenya, Uganda and Tanzania (then Tanganyika) to help facilitate monetary integration. The cooperation primarily focused on the facilitation of international trade and payments, as well as infrastructure. In the process of deepening cooperation, African countries have formed (and evolved) a number of regional economic communities (RECs) with overlapping memberships, which ended up in the 'galaxy' as shown in Figure 1 below. However, the presence of these groupings is yet to translate into a substantial increase in trade within the continent (ECA, 2008: 183). Although the share of African countries' exports to other African countries grew from about 4% in the 1980s to 12% in the first half of the 2000s, this growth is very low compared to other regional groupings outside the continent: 66% in Western Europe, 50% in Asia-Pacific and 40% in North America (Siddiqi, 2006: 25). More efforts are needed to promote trade within the various RECs. Furthermore, there has been very little manufacturing or intra-industry trade, with petroleum, cotton, livestock, maize and cocoa accounting for most of the trade within Africa.

---

[2] Later the Santiago (1998) and Monterrey (2002) Consensuses followed with second-generation reforms.

Figure 1: The African galaxy – overlapping regional groupings

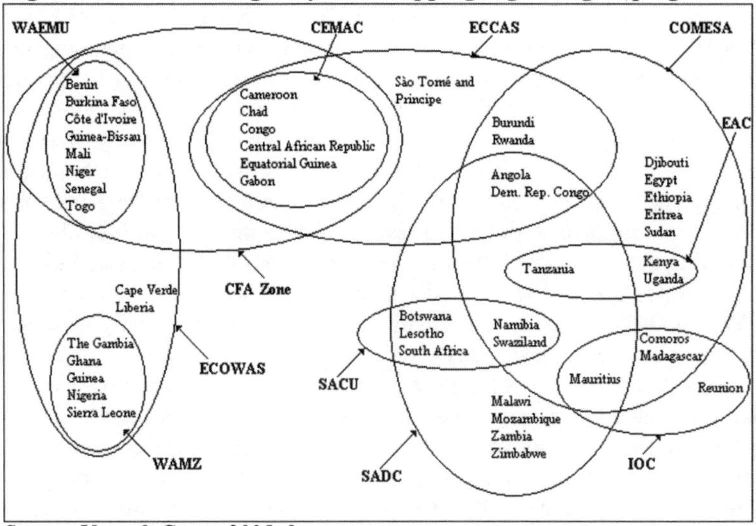

Source: Yang & Gupta, 2005: 9
Note: See full list of these regional groupings' abbreviations and dates in Appendix A.

Makinda and Okumu (2008: 13) make an interesting observation that a large part of the reason why there is an inherent desire by Africans to unite is because of their colonial heritage, and more specifically, the collective humiliation that they endured. It, in fact, "helped to give them an identity" in which the interests of liberation and integration were closely tied. Colonialism thus helped the pan-African cause that culminated, under the inspiration of Kwame Nkrumah, in the establishment of the Organisation for African Unity (OAU) in Addis Ababa, Ethiopia, on May 25, 1963 by the political leaders of 31 African countries. However, the OAU had mainly three weaknesses that seriously limited its success in terms of improving the living standards of the African people and creating intra-African cooperation: it often behaved like a mutual preservation club (discounting good governance and coddling some of the world's worst dictators); its failure to make clear the OAU's relationship with the RECs (a symptom, perhaps, of not dealing with underlying subregional power struggles, e.g. between Nigeria and Ghana, culminating in increased competition between their respective sub-regional blocs); and its failure to pursue vigorously the economic goals and principles stipulated in its Charter (which Nkrumah emphasised as essential – for economic cooperation to complement regional integration). The OAU co-existed with a number of RECs, including SADC and ECOWAS, while the EAC existed before its emergence. So also did the United Nations (UN) ECA, whose lead was later followed by the OAU (with its headquarters also in Addis Ababa) as it began to cede the power for economic decision-making to the ECA. Hence, the OAU took part in negotiations on major economic initiatives, including the discussion on the New International Economic Order and the Lomé Conventions. Other key economic initiatives that the OAU took, but could not deliver on, was the Lagos Plan of Action in 1980 and the Abuja Treaty of 1991, both of which called for the strengthening of existing RECs as a basis for integrating Africa. Even though the OAU tried to harmonise policies between regional organisations, it did not prevent an uncontrolled proliferation of RECs during the 1970s and 1980s that created serious inefficiencies, duplication, unintended overlap, and even dissipating efforts and scares resources.

With the belief in getting strength out of unity and regional integration not having died – even to this day – the process of deepening OAU relations with RECs was pursued with vigor from the 1990s, especially after African leaders concluded, in the aftermath of the Cold War, that the challenges of persistent conflict, underdevelopment, poverty and globalisation could best be addressed through integration (Onimode, 2004: 193). Hence, in recognising the structural weakness that had prevented the OAU from responding effectively to fratricidal intrastate conflicts, the African Union was formed in Durban, SA, on July 8, 2002. Africa needed a new organisation that could take risks and responsibility in promoting development, peace and security. With Mbeki becoming the first Chair of the AU, he pursued the ideals that Nkrumah had enunciated, especially that of establishing African unity through economic cooperation. For this he proposed the African Renaissance and New Partnership for Africa's Development (NEPAD) initiatives. NEPAD, with its support for a peer review mechanism, was regarded as an appropriate governance tool for debt-ridden Africa, and with its integrated agenda and specific policy options, it was seen as a strong instrument to help harmonise policies and engender socio-economic transformation. Although, unlike the AU, NEPAD does not enjoy universal support in Africa, the G8 responded at its Kananaskis Summit in 2002, strongly confirmed it through its *G8 Africa Action Plan*. Notably, the principles of the AU (e.g. socio-economic development, good governance and social justice, gender equality) and the ideals of NEPAD (e.g. attracting foreign investment for African wealth creation) significantly correspond with the MDGs, which the UN proposed in 2000. This shows how interrelated, even in their progression, the development path sketched out by both African economic integration through the AU and the RECs, and the MDGs are.

Throughout the progression of African economic integration there were always efforts towards monetary integration. Apart from the well-known CFA Franc (now euro) zone and the EACB, which was terminated in 1967, a monetary system similar to that of East Africa, was established as the Southern Rhodesia Currency Board in 1938 by a colonial Act, but was replaced by a currency board in 1954 and later dissolved in 1963. Another initiative was the Rand Monetary Agreement in 1974, with the rand as the only legal tender in Botswana, Lesotho, Swaziland and SA. The rand zone, which was amended in 1986, was similar to the euro zone in terms of the sharing of seigniorage and the flexibility of the peg *vis-à-vis* the outside world (ECA, 2008: 187). Eventually, it came to be that most of the RECs in Figure 1 have initiated some form of monetary cooperation arrangement that is focusing on establishing macroeconomic convergence criteria.

Following the success of the European Monetary Union (and since the AU has largely been modeled on the European Union (EU)) and the desire to strengthen the continental integration agenda, the AU has adopted, as a formal objective, the creation of a single currency and central bank by 2021 to establish continent-wide monetary integration. This is in the hope that a common currency would protect African countries from contagious or correlated capital movements and financial crises. Hence, plans are clearly set in motion to complete African integration – a 'United States of Africa', as envisioned by Nkrumah. Whether this will help Africa to become more globalised, only time will tell. Ultimately, in view of the continent's historical pathway, it is entirely plausible to postulate that Africa will prove to be the final frontier of globalisation in the global economy.

3 Impact of the global financial crisis on Africa's economy

Notwithstanding the current global recession, the economic situation in Africa has improved in recent years. Impressive growth rates and increasing levels of foreign direct investment (FDI) supported an economic resurgence over the past decade: between 2001 and 2008, Africa experienced an average annual growth rate of 5.9% in GDP. This was helped by an improved macroeconomic environment as well as better governance and a reduction in levels of armed conflict. High economic growth helped to reduce poverty, and agricultural growth, in particular, contributed to enhancing food security as well as reducing hunger and malnutrition (Kirk & Puetz, 2009: 10). However, it is also true that, even before the GFC had affected Africa, the continent has – in view of globalisation – increasingly been fighting an uphill battle to gain recognition as a competitor in the global economy. Africa has more states than any other continent. Its small, fragmented, and shallow markets do not offer economies of scale. 40% of Africans live in landlocked countries, many of which are amongst the world's poorest performing economies (World Bank, 2009a: 56). Contributing to this, though, the GFC did make matters worse for Africa as global demand – of especially African merchandise (and their prices) – fell to exceptionally low levels, reducing export-earnings dramatically as the balance on Africa's current account fell from US$32,4 billion in 2008 to US$-37,1 billion in October 2009 (IMF, 2009: 186). Despite a lack of demand, the current GFC has also affected other growth drivers of Africa such as capital inflows that are falling and promises of increased aid that have not materialised yet. Africa therefore faces serious uncertainties over its growth and development prospects as questions are increasingly raised about whether its pre-crisis growth performance can be sustained.

Figure 2: Vulnerabilities in SSA compared to other developing regions

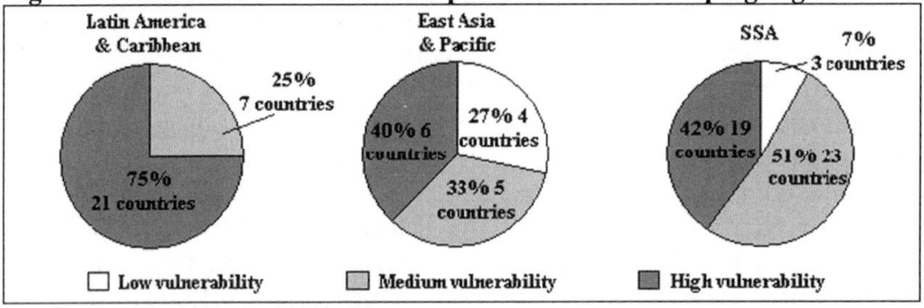

Source: World Bank, 2009b: 32

Early indications are that the global economic downturn is much deeper than expected, and the recovery will be gradual and uncertain (World Bank, 2009b: 23). Having originated in the developed world, the GFC – for which there has been no equal in over 70 years – grew into an economic crisis and is now becoming an unemployment crisis, i.e. a human and social crisis. Sparing no country or region, it has spread quickly and inexorably to the developing world. The poor countries are especially vulnerable as they lack the resources to respond with ameliorative actions. This poses serious threats to the hard-won gains in boosting the economic growth of many developing countries, particularly Africa, as well as achieving progress toward the MDGs. The confluence of weak economic activity, drastic swings in commodity prices, steep declines in foreign exchange reserves, and financial market instability, coupled with an intensified adverse feedback loop between the slowdown in the real economy and financial markets, is causing increasing vulnerabilities in developing countries, most notably in Africa. As Figure 2 illustrates, in Sub-Saharan Africa (SSA) 93% of countries are currently in either the high or medium vulnerability[3] categories. Although the situation in

[3] Vulnerability is measured on the basis of developments in exports, FDI, remittances flows, external debt ratios (emerging markets), and aid flows (low-income countries).

Latin America and the Caribbean might be worse, less countries are affected, which is also the case in East Asia and the Pacific. This poses a threat to global recovery, because developing countries can provide a growth platform to help the global economy pull out of the crisis. Some of the key factors that contribute to Africa's high vulnerability are considered below.

3.1 Impact on trade and capital flows – two key engines of economic growth

Although the effect of the global recession was initially felt most strongly in those African economies more highly integrated into global financial markets (e.g. SA, an oil importer), the impact of the fall in financial flows spread to oil exporters (including Algeria, Angola, Libya, Nigeria), manufacturing exporters (Morocco and Tunisia), and commodity exporters (Botswana) as global trade collapsed. This is illustrated in Figures 3 and 4 below. In the case of the latter, Africa's current account fell to -3% of GDP, of which SSA's has fallen from -8% of GDP in 2008 to over -10% in 2009 (IMF, 2009: 34).

Figure 3: Industrial production

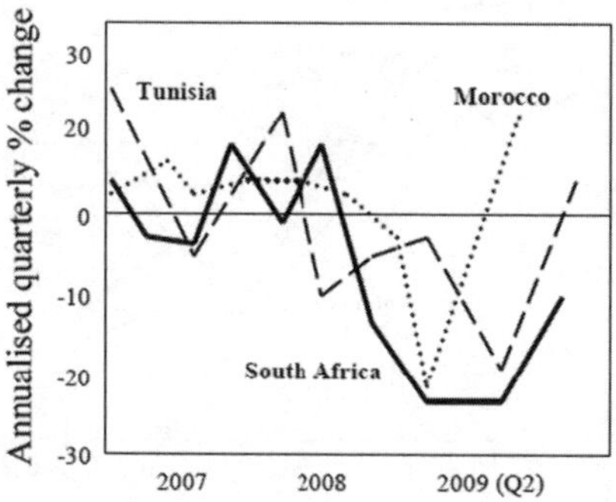

Figure 4: Current account balance

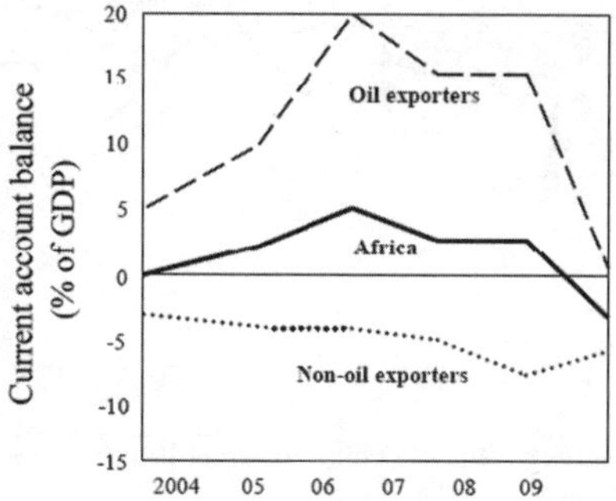

Source: IMF, 2009: 89

International trade continued to decline in 2009, from 2008 (see Figure 5 below), for the first time in 27 years (World Bank, 2009b: 139). Declining demand has been compounded by a contraction in the available finance for trade flows. As Figure 5 shows, the second half of 2008 saw a sharp slowdown in merchandise trade – most notably for SSA. For the year as a whole, growth in the volume of world trade moderated to 3.4% in 2008, from an average of 7.9% during 2003-07. The world trade volume in goods and services contracted over 6% in 2009, with a noticeably sharper decline in trade volumes of manufactured goods. Total trade in services – not one of Africa's strengths – appeared to be more resilient than in manufactures. For Africa, oil and mineral exports have suffered the largest losses. Nigeria and Angola alone experienced a combined shortfall of about $76 billion in export receipts, while for mineral exporters, Zambia and the Democratic Republic of the Congo (DRC), together it amounts to approximately $6 billion (ADB, 2009a: 2). By the first quarter of 2009, a number of African countries recorded major declines in key commodity exports. In Uganda, coffee exports were 34% lower than the year before. Having benefited from the earlier primary commodity boom, Africa experienced a loss of almost 50% of its exports value in 2009 (ADB, 2009b: 20). Making the situation worse, losses in export growth rates have not been compensated for by decreasing import growth rates in value terms, resulting in a deterioration of trade balance for most African countries. However, the decline in food prices should mitigate the impact of the GFC on African countries, especially on the balance of payments and government budget.

Figure 5: Export growth by region during 2008

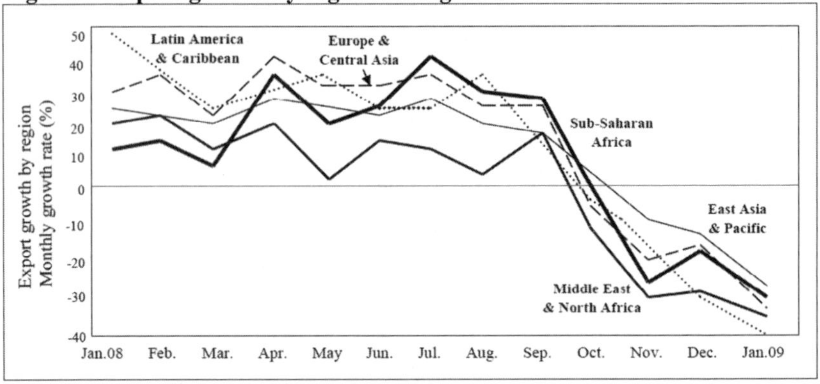

Source: World Bank, 2009b: 139

According to the IMF (2009: 90), many low-income countries in Africa that have more diversified commodity exports seem to be weathering the global recession fairly well and may quickly return to higher growth paths. However, as the African Development Bank (ADB) (2009b: 8) points out, for the majority of Africa's economies, the adverse impact of the GFC on export commodity prices (although price increases are already taking place) and resource inflows threatens to reverse the gains from the recent economic performance. Key consequences include: declining foreign reserves, non-profitability of some oil fields that have high extraction costs, reduction in government funding capacity and cancellation or postponement of a number of investments in extractive industries that are highly dependent on FDI. Furthermore, a significant implication of declining trade flows is trade taxes that fall dramatically. In 2009, Africa suffered a shortfall in trade tax of roughly $15 billion, representing 1% of GDP and 4.6% of government revenue (ADB, 2009a: 2). These trade tax shortfalls may grow even larger as the crisis deepens.

As far as capital flows are concerned, the GFC threatens to reverse Africa's recent progress in attracting public and private capital inflows. The shortage of liquidity and increased risk (and deteriorating risk perception of African markets) are causing a decline in badly needed capital inflows and curtailing the availability of trade finance (ADB, 2009c: 2). With the seizing up of the global financial markets in 2008, emerging market countries were the first among developing countries to feel the impact of the GFC, given their heavier reliance on private capital flows. Private capital flows to the developing world are seeing their sharpest decline ever, with net flows turning negative in 2009 – a more than $700 billion fall from the peak in 2007 (World Bank, 2009b: 1). Many low-income countries are also affected by the private credit crunch; private flows to these countries, including several in Africa that had increased in several years, are now falling. Even remittances, which have become a major source of external financing for African countries, have, according to the ADB (2009b: 11), been negatively affected by the slowdown in developed countries. In some African countries, remittances exceed official development assistance (ODA) as a source of external financing. For countries such as Lesotho and Comoros where remittances account for over 20% of GDP, the effect of the crisis could be more devastating if the trends continue. Remittances between African countries have fallen following job cuts and the decline in activity in the mining sector.

Somewhat surprisingly, as Table 1 confirms, whereas global FDI declined sharply by about 21% in 2008 (to $1.4 trillion, and is expected to be worse in 2009), FDI inflows to Africa increased by 16.8% from 2007 to 2008 (ADB, 2009b: 20). However, there are large discrepancies across countries: while Morocco and Egypt respectively reported a decline -7% and -5.6%, FDI in SA more than doubled in 2008. The recent rise in capital flows to SA is expected to contribute to a recovery, particularly given the recent upgrade in its sovereign credit rating (IMF, 2009: 90). Although capital inflows to SA[4] increased further in 2009, it is the exception to the rule as far as the Afri-

[4] This by no means suggests that the SA economy was not severely scarred by the GFC. While inflation fell to 5.8% in 2009, real GDP growth was negative (-1.8% in 2009, compared to 3.7% in 2008), manufacturing production was down about 40% from mid-2008 and trade volume was down over 40% (SARB, 2009: 29).

can economy as a whole is concerned as the ADB (2009c: 2) already indicated that FDI is projected to decline by about 18% in 2009, from $62 billion to $50.8 billion, with severe implications on private sector activity. This could well increase the region's financial marginalisation as growth in foreign capital dependent sectors such as natural resources are undermined. Portfolio flows have already decreased by 62%, from $15.7 billion in 2007 to $5.9 billion in 2008. Notably, these declines in capital flows point to a financing gap that will further slow down Africa's recovery prospects, given the strong reliance on FDI and portfolio flows to cover current account deficits. The ability of governments to mobilise capital on global markets has been severely affected by the GFC. Since October 2008, sovereign debt spreads have been on the increase. Thus, several African countries, including Tanzania, Tunisia, Uganda and Kenya, decided to postpone bond issue in global financial markets to mobilise resources for financing growth, turning instead to weakened local markets.

Table 1: Africa: Capital flows (2005-08) (billions of US$)

Type of capital flow	2005	2006	2007	2008
FDI: net inflows				
Africa [% world total]	26.8[2.4%]	38 [2.6%]	51 [2.3%]	62 [4.4%]
Developing economies	272.3	348.2	501.7	n/a
Developed economies	836.4	1097.4	1617.6	n/a
World	1116.3	1457	2139.3	1408
Net foreign direct investment	21.6	21.4	n/a	n/a
Portfolio investment	10.8	15.5	15.7	5.9
ODA	35.2	43.1	38.2	44.4

Source: WDI, 2009: 1; IMF, 2009: 89; ADB, 2009c: 3

3.2 Implications for reaching the MDGs

There are just five years to go to the deadline set by the international community for achieving the MDGs. The trouble is, as the Organisation for Economic Cooperation and Development (OECD) (2009: 31) pointed out, it appears that no SSA-country will achieve all the goals by 2015. Undermining gains in poverty reduction, the triple jeopardy of the food, fuel and the financial crises brought new challenges to the continent. The pre-GFC rise in food prices between 2005 and 2008 pushed an estimated 160 million to 200 million more people worldwide into extreme poverty, of which most are African. The GFC has amplified the impact of the food crisis, especially on the urban poor and the rural population. For food-importing countries (e.g. Lesotho (67% reliance on food imports), Gambia (82%), Mauritania (32%) and Malawi (31%)), the GFC has further weakened current account and fiscal balances, and accelerated the depreciation of currencies. This has worsened food insecurity and together with the growth slowdown added to the poverty impact of high food prices. In Rwanda, it is estimated that poverty would have decreased from its 2005 level of 53% to 33% in 2015 if food prices had changed at the same pace as the Cost Price Index (ADB, 2009a: 8). The reduced growth in SSA will cost the 390 million people living in extreme poverty about 20% of their per capita income (or $46 per person), according to the UN Educational, Scientific and Cultural Organisation (UNESCO) (2009: 3). The percentage of workers earning less than $2 per day will increase from 82.2% in 2007 to 86.6% in 2009 in Africa, representing 27 million new poor people in 2009. The unemployment rate in SSA could also increase by 8.5% in 2009, that is an additional 3 million unemployed. The extractive industry has been hit the hardest. In the DRC, the closure of 40 mines led to the loss of 300 000 jobs, while in Zambia, 3000 jobs have been lost since December 2008 as copper mines and smelters ceased operation (ADB, 2009a: 9). Given that three out of five SSA-workers are considered 'extreme working poor[5]', such rises in unemployment (not to mention manufacturing, construction and service), have profound implications for poverty conditions. Having to create 2.4 million more new jobs per year to make any impact on poverty rates, Africa's current situation detracts severely from any MDG-achievement.

The UN (2009: 6) indicated that SSA lags on all MDGs and is unlikely to fully achieve much of the goals, based on current trends. With decreasing incomes and soaring food prices, the poor are forced to allocate more income to food and reduce expenditures on health and education. Poor children will be particularly affected. Child malnutrition and infant mortality is expected to increase dramatically in 2009, by between 200 000 and 400 000 additional deaths (UNESCO, 2009: 7). Low-income African countries which have made efforts to improve universal primary education will suffer setbacks as governments are unable to finance subsidised educational programs, while poor households are not in a position to pay fees. Moreover, food insecurity is amplified by the decline in food aid. Out of the $12.3 billion that was pledged in June 2008, only $1 billion was disbursed by donors by February 2009 (ADB, 2009a: 8). It is thus essential that donors deliver on their commitments to increase foreign aid to Africa to help slow, or even avert, people sliding

---

[5] Extreme working poor reflects vulnerable employments; those employed but still being in a poverty-trap.

back into poverty. A new push is now required to counter the threat the crisis poses to some of the progress Africa has already made. As can be seen in Figure 6, almost half of Africa's countries find themselves 'below average' as far as Goal 1 is concerned, while a third are in this category for four more goals (Goals 2, 4, 5 and 7).

Figure 6: Missed goals: Distribution of African countries' status by MDG (2008)

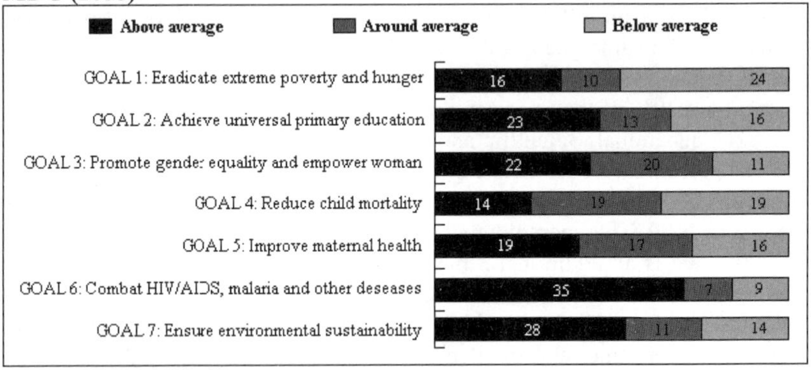

Source: OECD, 2009: 87

3.3 Implications for African economic integration

It is now certain that reaching the MDGs by 2015 and intensifying African economic integration to the extent that it is ready to establish a continent-wide monetary union by 2021 is now under real threat. Even prior to the GFC, African regional integration was slow, with a persistence of under-funded regional and sub-regional organisations, lack of political will and slow progress in creating infrastructure linking land-locked countries and remote regions of coastal countries to the centers of demand and to ports (Kirk & Puetz, 2009: 4). The GFC has slowed the drive towards African regional integration as the focus shifted to global concerns (e.g. the credit crunch) and country-specific economic challenges. At the regional level, according to the ADB (2009d: 3), the crisis has dampen-ed prospects for intra-regional trade by worsening financing constraints for the RECs[6]. African governments have not been able to fully provide for the financial requirements of RECs during the growth periods. The GFC have compounded the

[6] Not all RECs, however, have been completely adversely affected by the GFC – for example the EAC.

inability of these countries to meet their financial obligations to RECs, undermining their ability to effectively carry out their mandates. The poor condition of infrastructure and trade facilitation in Africa are among the main factors contributing to lower intra-African trade. The drying up of external financing is having an adverse impact on the implementation of large projects, including large infrastructure projects that are critical for regional integration. In SSA, infrastructure projects that have been delayed or cancelled amount to $1.35 billion.

Over the past decades, financial integration programs in various African RECs have been underpinned by progress in macroeconomic and financial sector reforms, leading to stable exchange rates, reductions in inflation rates, the strengthening of the banking systems as well as sustainable fiscal balances (Jefferis, 2007: 89). With the GFC, macro-economic convergence, which many RECs have made a core aspect of their financial integration programs, is threatened by weakening national economies (ADB, 2009c: 3). The risk arises that, because African countries may respond differently to the crisis, economic structures may begin to diversify, thus negating previous efforts towards convergence and heightening countries' vulnerability to asymmetric shocks. The crisis has complicated policy choices in the sense that regional and country interests are now at times in conflict. Increased impediments is thus a grave concern as regional integration is vitally important for Africa's ability to withstand the shocks and integrate into the global economy, notably through market expansion, improved competition and gains for economies of scale.

4 Africa's dual-aim challenge: Key economic reforms required at a critical time

The GFC has brought Africa at a crossroads in terms of identifying what areas of economic reform are, given the 'new crisis-induced reality', most critical for successfully addressing the (now increased) challenge of enhancing both its economic development (to reach the MDGs) and to facilitate deeper economic integration through improved policy coordination and coherence. Complicating matters, these two important focus-areas are certainly reinforcing towards each other in terms of their outcomes, but not necessarily/always so in terms of their respective requirements for achievement. This is a serious challenge on the continent's road of progress that, if not managed well, from a regional perspective, has the potential to actually intensify the friction among African states in stead of deepening cooperation – especially now that countries will be scampering to try and make up as much as possible of the economic loss caused by the GFC. In view of the limited time available for Africa to catch up with the rest of the world, economic-wise – while the global drive towards a recovery speeds up – and given the priority that Africa gives to the MDGs and regional economic integration as primary vehicles for aligning itself with the rhythm of progress of leading economies, it is proposed that at least three areas of economic reform and management actions be urgently attended to by all African countries. However, before examining this, important context is necessary to stress Africa's delicate task/response at hand. As Clapham (2006: 8) aptly observes, the escalation of globalisation, primarily due to more and more countries adopting neo-liberal policy approaches, has undoubtedly contributed to increased global systemic risk and contagion, which, after a series of crises[7], culminated in the current GFC – the worst since the Great Depression. Given the policy-uncertainty (and -confusion) that this is now creating for an appropriate response, the challenge (and pressure) is so much greater for Africa to now address the right areas to progress economically and help safeguard itself against crises:

1. Macroeconomic stabilisation. Although there has been a marked improvement in Africa's macroeconomic policy environment the past decade, the GFC has severely strained policy instruments. It is now crucial that African countries maintain supportive macroeconomic policies, at least until the recovery is on a firm footing. Arguably the most important of these is preserving and strengthening endogenous growth drivers. The gains through structural reforms should be consolidated and not slide back on economic reforms and avoid the build-up of unsustainable debt. The challenge is that African countries must do so while simultaneously avoiding drastic cuts in public expenditures (in cooperation with development partners). Growth driven by domestic investment and consumption should be promoted. In the face of declining and volatile external flows, domestic resource mobilisation must be improved, notably by enhancing the development of domestic and regional bond markets. This will help reduce aid-dependence. Supply-side bottlenecks must be alleviated, especially by increasing investment in infrastructure (new infrastructure and maintenance of existing stocks) and increasing access to credit for the local private sector. Regional economic integration should also be fostered through a greater role for regional actors, including pan-African institutions and regional financial institutions. They can provide budget support and balance of payments support as short-term measures to address resource constraints for African countries (ADB, 2009c: 4). It is critical that African countries harness these growth drivers to move back to closer to 7% growth rates, which is required for achieving the MDGs. It is

---

[7] The 1994 Mexican crisis, the 1997 Asian and Japanese financial crises and 1998 Russian financial crisis.

vital that economic growth is supported in a way that keeps inflation under control, as most African countries have already taken steps to stimulate economic activity through expansionary monetary and fiscal policies, and further stimulus may be needed in 2010. This is also key for harmonising countries in African RECs' agreed-upon macroeconomic convergence targets, so as to keep progression as regards monetary integration in tact. This not only serves the purpose of supporting the process of monetary integration, it also reflects a broader aim of achieving macroeconomic stabilisation in the region as a whole.

2. Strengthening financial sector regulations and improving the investment climate. African financial systems are significantly more stable than before and have largely been insulated from the worst of the GFC due to their limited international exposure. However, Africa's financial systems are still characterised by shallowness, their high costs (as exemplified by high interest rate spreads), and by limited access to finance. Although the GFC has not fully exposed these weaknesses, it has heightened the need to strengthen Africa's financial sector regulations, especially in relation to incentive-compatible banking surveillance and supervision. Better risk assessment and monitoring as well as adequate capital adequacy requirements are fundamental. This will facilitate savings mobilisation and encourage private sector lending while minimising credit risk (ADB, 2009a: 12). African countries also need to pursue prudent capital control strategies to promote private capital flows while minimising the risk of abrupt capital reversals that are detrimental to currency stability. Moreover, African countries should design measures that encourage foreign capital allocation diversification across sectors. This would particularly promote those activities with the highest potential for employment creation and export diversification. To make Africa a more attractive investment destination, apart from lessening restrictions in the business environment and consolidating political stability through increased regional cooperation, it needs to deepen its financial sector. It cannot reach the MDGs without sufficient capital. Sophisticated capital markets are inseparable from economic progress. One suggestion for capital market deepening is for African governments to adopt a sub-regional approach to the support and development of capital markets, so as to strengthen their catalytic role in mobilising savings. Regional integration – together with further macroeconomic and structural reforms – could help African capital markets develop and overcome the impediments related to size and liquidity (Anyanwu, 2006: 65). African governments should support developing African regional and continental stock exchanges because this will facilitate the development of more efficient and competitive markets throughout Africa. Multiple listings and cross-border trade in securities, for example, could be an option in setting up sub-regional stock markets. In addition, it is critical that African stock markets be made more effective. In this regard, four essential requirements that are geared towards attracting more investment include: (1) a set of substantive legal rules that meets a set of clear, well-functioning, and reliable securities laws; (2) improved trading infrastructure; (3) increased participation by local institutions, and (4) increased market liquidity combined with promising future listings.

3. Trade diversification, human capital development and fostering regional integration. It is critical that African countries reduce their vulnerability to international shocks (e.g. a deceleration of global demand) through economic diversification and improved management of income from natural resources. With over 75% of Africa's exports still primary commodities dominated by crude oil, natural gas, precious and base metals and agricultural produce (specifically cocoa, coffee and tea), the concern remains the relatively low levels of manufactures and total merchandise trade (Siddiqi, 2006: 24). Africa's trade diversification should primarily focus on these areas to ensure not only an increase in export earnings and competitiveness, but also the enhancement of the continent's production capacity (also through the utilisation of more skilled workers) to ensure sustainable growth regarding exports' contribution to economic growth and development. A high premium is thus placed on human capital development (for knowledge-intensive production and diversification) through education and training to be able to make better (and at a broader scale) use of available modern technologies. To move beyond the constraints for agro-industrial development, the development of regional value chains for agriculture should be pursued more. With over 60% of African workers employed by the agricultural sector, and with three-fifths of African farmers being subsistence farmers, advancement in agriculture can make an instant impact on living standards. According to the ECA (2009: 151), intra-African trade data show that a growth strategy for higher-valued products destined for domestic and regional markets as well as non-African markets could revitalise agriculture in all regions of Africa. Instead of raw agricultural commodities and related jobs and processing industries being exported, the expansion of forward-linked agribusiness and agro-processing could substantially increase employment and non-farm incomes for rural populations in many African countries. Hence, the development of such intra-regional African markets would contribute to rapid job creation, food security and poverty reduction – all essential for attaining the MDGs.

NEPAD has identified an 'infrastructure gap' and regards it as one of the main factors that constrain economic growth and job creation in Africa. Given its importance for facilitating trade and it being a main determinant of competitive advantage of African goods in local and international markets (e.g. by affecting product prices), bridging the infra-structure gap has become a critical element of promoting regional integration. Trade within Africa would significantly benefit from more investment in transport and telecommunications infrastructure. Intra-African trade would also benefit from improving the regulatory environment (customs reform) so that – unlike as is currently the case – it is not more affordable and less time-consuming to ship cargo to Japan than transiting through a neighboring African country. Furthermore, to improve Africa's connectivity to global markets by bridging the infrastructure gap, Aid-for-Trade is becoming increasingly valuable as a long-term strategy. It is essential, though, that it involves predictable aid flows which can be fed into African countries' budgeting processes. As regards external trade relations, China and India have shown particular interest in emerging African countries in the 21st century. Investment in Africa by China and African trade with China have increased dramatically in recent years, even regardless of the GFC. Opportunities to gain bargaining power has now arisen for Africa in that increased investment in Africa by China has attracted the attention of the EU and US and has provoked talks of competitive investment. This is an ideal opportunity for the AU to provide leadership as far as enhancing African trade relations through strategic decision-making are concerned.

5 Conclusion

Although African economies are less linked to global financial markets than other parts of the world, the region has not been spared from the fall-out of the GFC. The balance of risks has firmly shifted from inflation to financial instability and deteriorating growth. In fact, the easing of inflationary pressures is probably the only positive that has come out of the GFC. However, it is particularly in attempting to achieve the dual aims of the MDGs by 2015 and continent-wide monetary integration by 2021 (or simply just deeper regional integration), that the impact of the GFC on Africa has been most wounding. With a historical background of colonialism, despotism, SAPs as well as the tendency to always return to integration-efforts despite conflicts, the region has increasingly been marginalised to the periphery of global economic activity. To date, the challenge posed by globalisation has simply been too demanding for Africa. In recent years, however, Africa has shown remarkable economic growth (6.1% from 2002-07), albeit from a low base. The GFC have had a severe impact on Africa as key drivers of economic growth such as export-earnings and capital inflows fell drastically, donor support faded and its economies became more vulnerable. It has also affected countries differently. African countries with accumulated reserves from the recent commodity boom now had to use these reserves to boost domestic demand and mitigate the impact of the GFC on their economic and social development (ECA, 2009: 38). Countries with limited reserves and high dependence on donor support have suffered the most, making it much harder for these low-income countries to make any MDG-progress.

Currently, it appears that the GFC has started to retard the whole of Africa's progress towards the MDGs (UN, 2009: 48). This impact is felt on all MDGs, but especially the goals for poverty reduction and human development. Most of Africa's economies are seriously at risk of falling behind as they are highly vulnerable to shocks and have very little capacity to respond with ameliorative actions. The growth slowdown is a particular concern for poverty, which has already started to increase as African unemployment levels rose sharply in a number of sectors – most notably extractive and manufacturing. As a result of the GFC, African regional integration now has more challenges as countries' reserves have been depleted and donor support has started to decrease. It has also become more difficult for countries in African RECs that pursue monetary integration, to harmonise macroeconomic convergence targets. Yet, the dream of a United Africa, which is over 100 years old, still lives strong. It is an opportune time, in the wake of the GFC, for the AU, the most ambitious stage of Pan-Africanism, to take the lead in terms of stimulating regional cooperation and assisting in policy coordination. To become the central-figure-organisation that it envisions, it must now step up to the fore-front and provide much-needed direction to African countries. Since regional integration is seen, by not only Africa but also the international community, as a priority instrument for promoting economic growth and poverty reduction, it has to be pursued fastidiously. To avoid being trapped in a cycle of inertia and procrastination, policy-makers have to react swiftly to the challenges exacerbated by the GFC and its implications for reaching the dual aims. Central among the reforms African policy-makers should consider is:

- *Ensuring macroeconomic stabilisation* by limiting the widening of the twin deficits of current account and budget deficits without building up unsustainable debt. Growth drivers must be strengthened by regional cooperation to fight poverty.
- *Strengthening financial sector regulations* through better risk assessment and monitoring to mobilise savings and create a more attractive investment environment.
- *Diversifying trade and production* to reduce African countries' vulnerability to external shocks and increase export earnings and competitiveness as well as skills.

Finally, it should be underlined that, to ensure economic success, Africa requires strong leadership (the AU, RECs and governments) and political will to make the right policy-decisions now and ensure their sustainable impact through intensive management. The slogan of an African disability group *'nothing about us without us'* is very apt and should be adopted by all African leaders, policy-makers and managers as it suggests that Africans must play a decisive part in any initiative that determines Africa's progress.

References

African Development Bank (ADB) (2009a): Africa and the Global Economic Crisis: Strategies for Preserving the Foundations of Long-term Growth. *ADB Working Paper Series*, 98, pp. 1-20.

African Development Bank (ADB) (2009b): Impact of the Global Financial and Economic Crisis on Africa. *ADB Working Paper Series*, 96, pp. 1-25.

African Development Bank (ADB) (2009c): Africa and Financial and Economic Crisis: An Agenda for Action. *Policy Briefs on the Financial Crisis*, 13, pp. 1-11.

African Development Bank (ADB) (2009d): The Financial Crisis, Trade and Regional Integration in Africa. *Policy Briefs on the Financial Crisis*, 10, pp. 1-13.

Anyanwu, J. (2006): Promoting of Investment in Africa. *African Development Review,* pp. 42-71.

Clapham, C. (2006): The Evolution of Africa's International Relations. In U. Engel and G. Olsen (eds.). *Africa and the North: Between Globalisation and Marginalisation.* Cambridge: Routledge.

Collier, P. (2007): The Bottom Billion. New York: Oxford University Press.

Economic Commission for Africa (ECA) (2008): Assessing Regional Integration in Africa: Towards Monetary and Financial Integration in Africa. Addis Ababa: ECA.

Economic Commission for Africa (ECA) (2009): Economic Report on Africa 2009: Developing African Agriculture Through Regional Value Chains. Addis Ababa: ECA.

International Monetary Fund (IMF) (2009): World Economic Outlook – October 2009: Sustaining the Recovery. Washington, D.C.: IMF.

Jefferis, K. (2007): The Process of Monetary Integration in the SADC Region. *Journal of Southern African Studies,* 33(1), pp. 83-106.

Kirk, C. and D. Puetz (2009): Facing the Financial Crisis: The Imperative for Regional Action for Agriculture in Africa. *Paper presented at the 4th Annual African Economic Conference in Addis Ababa*. 11-13 November 2009.

Leys, C. (1994): Confronting the African Tragedy. *New Left Review,* March, pp. 33-47.

Loots, E. (1996): Road Map for Africa's Recovery: Challenges and Recommendations for Structural Reform. *Africa Insight*, 36(3-4), pp. 11-25.

Makinda, S. and F. Okumu (2008): The African Union: Challenges of Globalisation, Security, and Governance. New York: Routledge.

Onimode, B. (2004): African Development and Governance Strategies in the 21st Century. London: Zed Books.

Organisation for Economic Cooperation and Development (OECD) (2009): African Economic Outlook 2009. Paris: OECD.

Rodney, K. (1974): How Europe Underdeveloped Africa. Washington, D.C.: Howard University Press.

Shrestha, N.R., L. McKinley-Floyd, B. Mtwige (2008): Introduction to the Special Issue: Management in Africa in the Global Context. *Journal of African Business*, 9(1), pp. 1-26.

Siddiqi, M. (2006): Is Africa a Poor Trader? *African Business,* 318, pp. 24-25.

South African Reserve Bank (SARB) (2009): Quarterly Bulletin: December. Pretoria: SARB.

United Nations (2009): Millennium Development Goals Report 2009. New York: UN.

United Nations Educational, Scientific and Cultural Organisation (UNESCO) (2009): Global Crisis Hits the Most Vulnerable. Paris: UNESCOPRESS.

World Bank (2009a): World Development Report 2009: Reshaping Economic Geography. Washington, D.C.: World Bank.

World Bank (2009b): Global Monitoring Report 2009: A Development Emergency. Washington, D.C.: World Bank.

Appendix A: Abbreviations and establishment dates for African regional groupings

CEMAC	Economic and Monetary Community of Central Africa	1999
CFA zone	African Financial Community	1945
EAC	East African Community	1967
ECCAS	Economic Community of Central African States	1966
ECOWAS	Economic Community of Western African States	1975
COMESA	Common Market for Eastern and Southern Africa	1994
IOC	Indian Ocean Commission	1984
SACU	Southern African Customs Union	1910
SADC	Southern African Development Community	1980
WAEMU	West African Economic and Monetary Union	1994
WAMZ	West African Monetary Zone	2000

External and internal factors of the crisis in Africa

Hartmut Elsenhans*

Abstract

Because of its special shape, globalization has today become an issue. It is based on the devaluation below purchasing power parity and its limits are food surpluses and high levels of employment in the catching-up economies. In the meanwhile, wage restraint in the leading economies is counter-productive as it slows down employment creation in the catching-up economies and intensifies tendencies of under-consumption and the unregulated expansion of financial markets. Because of its food dependence, Africa is not well placed to follow the Asian economies, of which success provides African countries with new rents from raw material exports. Under the influence of liberal economics, there is no perspective of creating the social and economic conditions necessary for the productive use of rents, so that politically disguised forms of rent appropriation will most likely rise. Africa suffers much more than the Asian countries from rents and, for the wastefulness of the African state classes, this appears to be more important than specific cultural traits. Therefore, Africa should base alternative strategies of development on a non-neoliberal evaluation of the possibilities of using rent for economic diversification, including the necessary changes in the internal political power relations.

Globalisation is a long term process. It began with European expansion during the 16th century. Simultaneously, it hit sub-Saharan Africa: the slave trade with its loss of human lives and productive labour, the militarisation of many African societies, and also the specialisation in cash crops had their influence on sub-Saharan Africa's economic social and political structures (even if there were also internal causes). This debate on the external versus internal causes of sub-Saharan African underdevelopment is not really the focus of my contribution. My topic will be narrower: What are the new challenges sub-Saharan Africa faces in the actual crisis; not only with respect to

* Prof. em. Dr. Hartmut Elsenhans, University of Leipzig, Germany.

the crisis on financial markets, but also to the foundations of the crisis on the financial markets which also may hit Africa?

The financial crisis has not led to a breakdown of the world economy comparable to the 1930s, but has rather been successfully managed by global co-operation between the leading industrial economies; at least with respect to the protection of their own interests and the maintenance of the global architecture of the world economy. The pattern of crisis solution leads to new conditions in the global economy. What new challenges will sub-Saharan African economies and societies face? What are the internal factors that keep sub-Saharan Africa from exploiting the opportunities which emerge from the mode of crisis solution?

I will therefore examine the various causal factors of the actual crisis, that explain these new tendencies and which are of particular relevance for sub Saharan Africa

1 Capitalism and mass empowerment: Some Keynesian remarks

The financial crisis of 2007 to date is but an epiphenomenon of a deeper imbalance in the global economic system. Capitalism was imposed on pre-capitalist ruling classes of a tributary type only in some regions of the world on the basis of a largely accidental empowerment of labour, North-western Europe. Because of this empowerment, labour became capable of reducing rent, the politically based appropriation of surplus by powerful lords. Because of labour resistance, the only possible escape for the lords consisted in using labour ever more productively by improving the techniques they applied. This escape was facilitated by two aspects of the results of an increasing orientation of economic resources to the production of goods for the consumption of an increasingly scarce workforce; which because of its scarcity could improve the conditions for its productive effort, its wages or the payment for its products.

On the one hand the structure of demand was increasingly characterised by a higher share of mass consumption goods, which at least apart from agriculture could be produced in higher quantities. In addition to lower quality requirements for products which went into consumption of lower income strata, higher quantities meant greater homogeneity of demand and production.

Since the invention of the pottery disc, greater homogeneity and larger production runs have invariably allowed the use of mechanical devices, which are useful to execute repetitive operations. Add non-human energy in power delivery systems to mechanical devices and you have the machine as the centre piece of the physical aspects of production during the industrial revolution.

On the other hand, a significant expansion of mass consumption was not possible by just redirecting rent from the wasteful luxury consumption to mass consumption. The dreams of agrarian communism in the utopias of the early "bourgeois" movement were unrealistic. Rising mass incomes required better technologies and those among the rentiers together with flexible climbers from the lower strata who were able to design, produce and operate such new technologies could be sure to have paid for them by sales on markets. Because their new technologies and their cost efficient use in the Bortkiewicz/Okishio sense (Bortkiewicz 1907: 456-459, Okishio 1961), their cost price was lower than the cost price of those who used older technologies. Under perfect competition, the accumulation of physical capital is always covered from returns and can be financed by banks. Such financial institutions existed long before the transition to capitalism in many of the more differentiated pre-capitalist societies. Without these improvements in technology, the existing productive apparatus could not respond to rising mass demand. Rising mass purchasing power would evaporate in inflation if additional capacities of production did not emerge. Inflation would have enriched the owners of existing production facilities by supplying them with the financial means for accumulation. Labour can not "redistribute" that part of national income which goes into the construction of new productive capacities. Investors who create purchasing power by constructing machinery cannot be deprived of their profit as their outlays constitute socially necessary costs of production. Profit to the difference of rent does not depend on power but on "socially necessary" net spending on investment goods, because these investment goods are necessary to produce the products required to satisfy the rising final demand. Profit can do without the power structures of the tributary modes of production which therefore slowly fall in decay. Profit is compatible with the existence of a market economy where day to day power no longer counts. Rentiers who feel forced to defend their privileges shift their assets from luxuries like palaces into machinery. They can maintain their privileged position by becoming capitalists who use the larger part of their resources for accumulation, displace other rentiers and certainly change their outlook to have it compatible with the new social and economic practices they have to follow in order to survive. The old Weberian argument and its critics are equally in line and confirm the Marxist view: culture follows challenges, but the more smoothly the adaptation is achieved, the more efficiently the new behavioural patterns contribute to accelerating the process which they are related to, i.e. accumulation.

As cost efficient investment in mass consumption oriented production serves only the rising mass demand, there is no increase in mass consumption oriented investment without an increase in mass demand. If mass demand increases, investment contributes via more employment to demand. Neoliberal thinking formalises this aspect through the theory of the wage drift. Keynesians disagree because liquidity preference in an economy with paper money allows withholding investment so that there might be no full employment and no basis for the wage drift, at least in the downturn of the cycle.

Capitalism is not the utopia of labour. It is however the result of the admittedly limited implementation of the utopias of labour because labour becomes scarce under specific conditions. On the economic side, the absence of marginality has to be mentioned: increases in agricultural productivity lead to higher average productivity and higher marginal productivity and these higher productivities are no longer used for increasing rates of population growth, which once more would have driven marginal productivity below the level of subsistence. If working people had aspired to consume more material goods instead of producing more children, labour would have become scarce and hence capable of negotiating better terms for its services. Mass incomes grew and created outlets for machine-produced products so that the accumulation of capital became profitable. Rent decreased to the benefit of profit and mass incomes. Increasing mass incomes stabilised profit, destabilised rent and kept increasing part of the productive apparatus on an orientation to mass consumption (Elsenhans 1983a; 1983b; 1992). Increasing the political clout of labour supported this process by keeping labour powerful even in periods of recession during the business cycle but depended ultimately on the scarcity of labour.

This mechanism is threatened by the patterns of the expansion of capitalism to societies where these foundations of capitalism (i.e. a high marginal product of labour) have not yet emerged, especially because of a still low marginal product of labour in agriculture.

2 The actual crisis as a result of the erosion of the economic and social bases of capitalism at the global level

The standard view on globalisation focuses on newly approaching locations of production into the international division of labour. These new locations become competitive in the exportation of manufactured goods. As overall levels of development of productive forces are low, the average incomes of average skilled labour are low. Exporters can produce with cheap labour. With their access to cheap labour they can undersell producers who still produce in the high wage economies of the old industrial countries. These producers either have to succeed in raising productivity in the old industrial countries, reduce wages of their labour, or shift their production to the cheap labour countries.

A global race to the bottom is said to become inevitable. All industries compete for cheap labour by trying to employ the labour with the lowest real wages. Workers who do not accept low real wages lose their jobs.

This scenario is misleading: the successful exporters of the South do not produce in the low wage areas of sub-Saharan Africa, but in East and South East Asia where poverty is less pronounced. The reason for this geographical contradiction to the model of the race to the bottom lies in the causes for internationally cheap labour. Labour is cheap in international currency not because real physical consumption is low, but because its international price is low. Low international costs may coincide with relatively high levels of real wages, provided that the goods consumed by this labour are locally produced and difficult to be traded in the world market. This paradox can be explained by the interaction of comparative advantage and the exchange rate.

Specialisation follows comparative advantage and not "absolute" advantage. An economy has comparative advantage in the production of a good if in its production its productivity is relatively better than in the production of another good, even if its productivity here is lower than in another technically more advanced economy. In the Ricardian example, England produces more cloth and more wine than Portugal, with the same amount of labour. England has, however, an interest in specialising in cloth, because it can buy more wine from Portugal by selling additional cloth than its hitherto wine producing labour produced before specialisation. In order that the English housewives buy Portuguese wine, this wine has to be cheaper. It becomes cheaper through changes between the levels of cost between the two countries. In the initial situation of equal gold wages in both countries, Portugal sells nothing to England and buys cloth and wine from this country. Its gold stock decreases and with it its average price level. Gold flows to England so that the English price level increases. The first product where Portugal becomes competitive is wine. At an appropriate decline of the Portuguese price level, Portugal becomes competitive in the product where it has a comparative advantage. In the contemporary world, this adjustment is achieved by changes in the exchange rate between the currencies of the trading partners. I add that this mechanism was partially operating in the 19th century in favour of the competitiveness of the not yet developed world. Latin America, China, and many other countries of the South had silver currencies and kept from following the industrial world in the adoption of the gold standard.

Comparative advantage is transformed into cost competitiveness through the exchange rate. Hence it should be expected that there is no purchasing power parity between the underdeveloped world and the highly industrialised countries. Our youngsters are quite aware of it. They consider India as a cheap country: They can buy in India for the money they bring with them more then they could buy at home. Our Indian colleagues make the opposite experience: For them everything is expensive here. The World Bank therefore documents the per capita income of countries by two indicators: at the exchange rate the per capita incomes of most Asian countries are about one fourth of the per capita income at purchasing power parity. It has been calculated that a Chinese household can buy in Beijing up to ten times as much than if this household converted its income into Canadian dollars and went shopping in Canada (Chen, Gordon, Zhiming 1994). It surprises me that European labour unions never burst with curiosity when research institutes tell them that labour in Asia earns less than 1/50 of labour here, because anybody can see that no worker in Germany can live with 1/50 of average income here. The relief rates for a standard family are nearly 80% of average wages for average skilled labour here.

What has to be addressed in order to maintain the competitiveness of industrial countries' labour is not the low wage in the emerging countries or even excessively high wages in highly industrialised countries, but the capacity to devalue the currency by emerging countries.

The ever consistent national organisation in many aspects of the global economy leads however to national approaches to this issue in the highly industrialised countries: This renders even more difficult the problems of the world economy. The highly industrialised countries can not prevent emerging economies from having exchange rates which correspond to equilibria on the world markets for foreign exchange. They are trying to limit their real wages in national currency. According to my analysis this cannot have a lasting positive effect on competitiveness. For long periods before the introduction of the Euro, it led in the German case only to an appreciation of the German currency, especially in relation to its partners in the Common Market. In addition, real wage cuts in leading industrial countries concern less the highly skilled workers in export industries who compete with imports but unskilled workers in the internal market oriented industries and services, where tradable goods are not produced.

Limiting the expansion of real wages implies limiting the expansion of the demand: early on the supporters of globalisation argued that jobs in leading industrial countries were not "delocalized" due to being exported into catching-up economies, but were lost because the growth of productivity in the leading industrial countries was too fast in relation to production growth (Rowthorn/Ramaswamy 1999: 31, Appelbaum/Schettkat 1995: 611, Hsieh 1973: 16, Begg/Fagerberg/Guerrieri 1999: 228). Jobs are lost because of productivity outpacing production. This loss can not be attributed to excessively high real wages in relation to productivity growth, the usual neoclassical explanation for unemployment. Productivity outrunning production should cause high profit rates and allow business to accelerate capital accumulation. But the potentially high profit rates in this situation seem not to be "realised" because of lack of demand. The loss of jobs through productivity growth instead of delocalisation into emerging catching-up economies can only be based on a Keynesian explanation of capitalism: in the case of too high productivity growth capitalism does not produce the demand necessary for full employment. Production growth does not follow theoretically available growth potential.

The configuration of productivity outrunning production growth demonstrates that the maintenance of sufficient demand is decisive and no longer guaranteed at the global level, because of the pattern of adjustment of the leading industrial countries. In order to maintain demand in relation with the possibilities of consumption, the increase in consumption in leading economies has to go beyond the rise in their productivity. In a world economy based on devaluation driven export growth of catching up economies, the leading economies would have to increase real consumption not only in line with their own productivity growth, but beyond this level according to the improvement in the terms of trade between the newly delocalized branches and the rest of their economy.

For sub-Saharan Africa, two major conclusions cannot be avoided:

– local competition for manufactured exports will intensify because more and more countries become capable of devaluation driven manufactured exports,

– sub-Saharan Africa is poorly positioned in this race for world markets in manufactured exports because it is poor and characterised by food dependence. Because of food dependence sub-Saharan Africa cannot apply the successful strategies of the East and South East Asians, i.e. devaluation below purchasing power parity

3 The limits to devaluation-driven growth

Devaluation below purchasing power parity has limits: full employment and the size of the surplus of locally produced mass consumption goods (Elsenhans 2006a: 237 f.).

Increasing exports of manufactured goods at exchange rates below purchasing power parity implies exploitation (in Marxist terms) or subsidy (in WTO terms). Workers are employed in manufacturing firms that produce export goods which they sell against foreign currency. They pay salaries in national currency to their workers. If the exchange rate is lower than purchasing power parity these salaries can buy more products locally than can be imported on the basis of their share in the export earnings of the enterprise from the world market. The firm transfers to its workers more purchasing power than the corresponding export earnings. There is therefore a difference in the quantity of products the workers can buy locally and the quantity of products which can be additionally imported. These products have to be supplied by somebody. As they cannot be supplied from imports, this somebody has to be a local producer.

Devaluation driven exports of manufacturers are based on a locally produced surplus of wage goods. At lower levels of real wages, consumption spending of additional export workers is comprised mostly of food (about 50%). The other items are cloth, shelter, household equipment, and miscellaneous items. Most of these items are produced by local small and medium scale enterprises, often the so-called informal sector. The workers of these enterprises also receive relatively low real wages which are spent on the same items, hence mostly on food. Devaluation for increasing manufactured exports depends therefore on the availability of a surplus of local agriculture and a dynamic local informal sector which is capable of producing simple industrial wage goods. The "modern" items which enter into household consumption such as refrigerators and TV sets, but perhaps not more sophisticated electronic products (like cell phones) are also produced locally at least in most of the countries which were successful in export-led growth.

Export-orientation hence is based on nearly the same requirements as so-called self-centred development; i.e. the dynamisation of local wage goods production, especially food production. Export-led growth creates the additional demand for local wage goods production by making relatively unskilled labour prices competitive on the world market with export products. It avoids the danger of rent-seeking in state-led self-centred development where "empowerment" in the form of purchasing power of this labour depends on policies of distribution, hence on political measures which imply power struggles.

The alternative is not between the export orientation or mass-oriented self-centred development, but between accepting exploitation in the exchange of getting access to a mechanism of administratively simple empowerment of labour through additional demand for that labour versus state-based rent-seeking aiming at such empowerment of labour by politics and planning.

All larger economies, which have been successful in export-oriented manufacturing, have also done well with the Green Revolution. This fact shows the importance of an agricultural surplus. The city-states like Hong Kong and Singapore are special cases which do not contradict the argument since they are surrounded by rich agricultural regions such as Vietnam and Thailand (although similar metropolises have also grown elsewhere on major trade routes like Mumbai). No larger country has successfully engaged in export-manufacturing without having achieved at least initially self-sufficiency in food production. Rice economies are prominent among them, because high yielding varieties allowed triple cropping and increased de facto the agriculturally useful cropping area. In two regions, the Green Revolution has not been successful: the semi-arid Arab world and sub-Saharan Africa.

As nobody can risk a new Holocaust by blocking agricultural progress in the South, devaluation driven export-oriented manufacturing will continue as long as its other limit is not reached. This other limit consists in the achievement of full employment. In an economy characterised by full employment, export surpluses will lead to competition for scarce labour and wage increases in local currency beyond productivity increases. At this level, wages increase not only in the export branches but in the whole economy. Korean authors nicely described this threshold as a turning point (Bai 1982, Osborne 2000: 128, Manning 1995: 77, Blumenthal 1968: 24). At this threshold persisting undervaluation of the economy leads to inflationary pressures which counteracts devaluation. The best case for this achievement is West Germany in the late 1950s. When high levels of employment were reached by devaluation driven exports, Germany either had to accept inflation or appreciation of its currency, which was imposed by the then Minister of economics, Ludwig Erhardt. Mainland China seems to be approaching this turning point.

The adoption of wage repression by the leading industrial countries is therefore diametrically opposed to the requirements for the smooth absorption of the actual globalisation drive. As long as there is structural unemployment in the South, the West should increase its consumption beyond the increase of its own productivity in order to push the South to full employment. The leading industrial countries should accept balance of trade deficits, as did Britain in the late 19th century in favour of the continental European economies and the USA after 1945 in favour of the reconstruction of Western Europe and Japan.

4 The reluctance of the West due to the dangers of being overtaken

The global system is largely conditioned by the refusal of major Western economies to let their internal markets expand. Two aspects at the basis of this behaviour are relevant for the management of the actual crisis.

The processes through which the South has acquired comparative advantage in some manufacturing industries and become capable of transforming them into cost competitiveness have started long before the last decades of the 20th century. Indian textiles were already competitive at the end of the 19th century and were blocked from exports by the policies of the (colonial) British raj of keeping the rupiah high in relation to the English pound, especially during the interwar period. The policies of the postcolonial newly independent states of defending the international purchasing power of their (traditional) raw material exports implied high exchange rates. Only those economies which had no raw materials at all, like Korea and Taiwan, had to follow Japan. Japan was the first economy to exploit the possibility of devaluation-driven exports with an exchange rate in 1919 at about 50% of purchasing parity.

As long as leading industrial economies could adjust by shifting to more demanding goods and branches for which their own expanding internal markets were important, they experienced minor employment problems. This configuration went with the idea of path dependence of technical progress as popularised by the theory of the product cycle (Vernon 1966). The introduction of human capital into foreign trade theory has greatly strengthened this view of path dependence. Human capital is difficult to define. It is only a theoretical construct to indicate something that is not of full comprehension. When it was introduced as a capital good produced in the form of periods of training, India and Pakistan presented their bills of training for their medical and engineering staff, who entered as immigrants into the United States and Canada. They asked for compensation for their "reverse technical assistance". The concept was redefined. Just as the phlogiston of early chemistry, it was defined by its effects. The pay difference between skilled and unskilled labour was interpreted as caused by human capital. Assuming a certain interest rate, the value of the capital could be calculated. When income differences based on skill decrease because the labour force becomes more skilled, (and hence human capital more abundant) the measured amount of human capital decreases. In a three factor HOS-model, the richer economy always has more human capital than the poorer one if the wages between these two economies are compared because there are inter-country wage differences. If both countries are compared on the basis of their own intra-country wage differences, the richer and more egalitarian one has less human capital than the other. Only in simplistic models it therefore should have always comparative advantage in branches where the highest amount of human capital is required, hence the most technically progressive branches.

This result is not ratified if we turn back to Ricardo and have comparative advantage depending on differences in productivity differences instead of on differences in factor endowments. Let us assume that productivity growth depends on learning, which is created in the overall process of economic change, following endogenous growth theory. We imagine that this is a process of learning by doing, not only directly in the production processes, but also in related areas, such as the adaptation of infrastructures, institutions, etc. Let us call this the technical innovation system. A leading economy may be more productive in all branches than a less advanced economy, but it may have comparative advantage in old industries although it is certainly more productive than a less advanced economy in the most modern branches. It is unlikely that the effects of learning by doing are equally beneficial in an older established and a newly emerging branch. Certainly, learning in an established already demanding branch has positive effects on the adaptation of the labour force to the requirements of a new branch. But the emphasis is on "equally". If somebody has learned French, he will pick up Italian more easily than somebody who has learned neither language. If two people, both being now in Italy and learning both Italian, have to co-operate and earn their money with tasks, half of each requiring either French or Italian, the one having already learned French will specialise on the tasks involving French, despite being superior also in Italian.

According to this argument, France, technically at least equal to England in the 18th century, was kept from competing with England in the production of low quality mass consumption goods, because of her superiority in luxuries. The "paradox" of the high industrial productivity of French industry in the early 19th century in relation to Britain is caused by this specialisation on well-earning luxuries (O'Brien/Keyder 1978: 91). The inventions of the second Industrial Revolution (electrical machinery, chemistry) were made in Britain and Germany at roughly the same time but exploited by Germany: Britain earned so well from its old (textile) industries that it left these industries to Germany. In the 1970s Germany was not present in the microelectronics revolution, despite the facts that Germany built the first computer and invented the first fax machine.

The leading economy can maintain its position of leadership only if its productivity advances in new industries are at least as great as the old industries. Such an outcome would imply that there is no branch-specific effect of the learning by doing in a particular branch. This is unrealistic. There is therefore a real danger of the leading industrial countries being overtaken by catching-up economies. To this they react inappropriately by cutting their wage costs.

It is by accident that this danger has been realized in the phase of the demise and collapse of real socialism in Eastern Europe. Especially in Germany during the Cold War, business felt necessary a new approach to deal with labour in a cooperative manner in order to prevail in the Cold War political competition between the two social systems for legitimacy. This led to neo-corporatism and Rhenish capitalism (Albert 1991: 122 ff.). The gradual (already decades before the Berlin Wall fell) and then cataclysmic removal of this constraint facilitated the offensive of "monetarism". It weakened the previous ideological hegemony of welfare capitalism in the West. The inflexibility of labour and the welfare state as interpreted as a rigid labour market were accused of causing the economic problems; although labour had never been more flexible than in the period of full employment during the 1950s and 1960s. Wage increases parallel to productivity increases were rejected on the argument that not only apparent productivity had to be taken into account but also the productivity of the rising number of the unemployed, whose productivity was considered to be very low or zero, although unknown and not measurable (Sinn 2007: 57). Unemployment was no longer the result of insufficient demand (Keynes), but instead was the result of excessively low productivity of labour (at least according to some models).

In the real world these developments were greatly supported by the rise of two economies which were shaped culturally by the fear of balance of trade deficits: Germany and Japan. In both countries, the majority of public opinion saw the balance of trade deficits as an unmistakable sign of decay.

5 The financial crisis is as an expansion of an underconsumptionist crisis of the real economy

In a rentier world, where potentially available surplus is produced because those who appropriate it can use it even if there are no possibilities for investment, the amount of surplus produced is dependent on the non-rentiers' reduction of consumption; especially the consumption of labour. In a capitalist world with Keynesian active money, surplus as the result of investment spending depends on expectations about future sales of the goods made available with the newly created capacities of production at prices that yield a profit. As profit depends on the net investment spending, profitable sales ultimately depend on the rate of accumulation.

If the expansion of mass consumption does not follow the increasing productivity there is no incentive to spend on additional manufacturing plant and equipment. When productivity outruns production, the rate of net accumulation decreases. In Germany, investment in physical capital in the real economy is financed increasingly from amortisation, so that net investment tends to decline.

Profits for companies no longer depend on net investment spending if there are barriers to entry and possibilities of oligopolistic price formation. This is the situation in the large scale industry, especially with transnational companies. Imperfect competition implies the reduction of quantities produced to the absorptive capacity of markets at acceptable margins. This leads to further underconsumptionist tendencies, but corresponds with high profit rates in the oligopolistic sector of industry as shown by profit rates in transnational companies of more than 10% far in excess of the average profit rate in the real world economy and unrealistic with respect to the rate of capital accumulation. Higher profit rates in the oligopolistic sector should lead to further concentration of the economy. Globalisation has therefore been associated with mergers and acquisitions instead of new "greenfield" investment: accumulation and by dispossession (Nitzan 2001). As available financial resources cannot be fully invested in new plant and equipment, alternative uses have to be found. This is the basic argument about a lack of investment spending because of liquidity preference.

In financial markets the rate of profit is not only the result of real surplus earned by companies in their production and handed over to shareholders as dividends, but of expectations about the future stock trends. The more these stocks are expected to increase, the more the stocks will be in demand and rise independently on dividend payments (even in the future). Profit rates on unregulated financial markets are fed with increasing credit money and lead to increases of the mass of credit money, which national central banks will not curtail. The rise in stock prices is not interpreted as inflation since it does not lead to increasing prices for goods and services of the real economy. Instead, a rise in stock prices is interpreted as a sign of increasing wealth.

As long as speculators get credit from banks, they can continue to acquire additional stocks. This possibility of making money on the basis of the difference between actual prices of financial titles and their predicted future prices is greatly enhanced if only part of the financial titles (for example the difference between the actual and the future expected prices) have to be financed by the speculators. This reduction in the cost of speculation is achieved by the development of derivatives. Increasing assets expected from such derivatives yields further increases in credit lines for speculators by the banking system.

In principle, credit expansion in a Keynesian world is no different from money printing by the state. Reducing the cost of credit expansion means lowering costs for money creation and hence (at least in financial market booms) more money creation.

High costs of trust in financial places (London or New York) creates earning capacities on those places. In the competition for income generating possibilities cheapening the cost of speculation is an instrument of creating new activities which cannot be outcompeted by newly competitive manufacturing sites.

Britain and the U.S. first participated in the expanding financial industry, followed by the attempts if many other industrial and newly-industrializing countries. In the realm of culture this was accompanied by changes in language: speculation was called investment, speculators investment bankers, and high risk financial titles were called products.

Deregulation was universally followed. Public opinion that did not revolt as the inflation on the financial markets did not lead to price rises for the consumers. A mass of financial resources emerged for which there was no corresponding value in the real economy and which however was considered as valuable on the basis of a money illusion of the financial community. This money illusion was shared in most parts of society and the political class due to the offensive of neoliberalism against the necessarily labourist character of actual existing capitalism. This labourist conception of capitalism had been imposed by system competition after 1945. Business was forced to acknowledge it for political reasons. The money illusion vanished because more and more doubtful titles of the real economy had to be included into the assets on which financial titles where based.

The process of expansion of the financial markets resembles the "construction" of reality in the fairytale of *The Emperor's New Clothes*. Critics were silenced for being traditional and uninformed, just as in this fairytale.

6 The solution to the crisis will enhance the underconsumptionist tendencies

In contrast to the 1930s, Keynesian thinking is actually strong enough to be easily adopted. Nobody objects to the injection of huge amounts of money by governments and central banks into the financial markets by pretending that this increases the distortions which have led to the actual crisis. The theoretical basis on which this is done is constituted by the integration of Keynesian thinking into mainstream economics in the form of so-called monetary Keynesianism. The political basis which supports this adoption of monetary Keynesianism is constituted by the hope of resolving the crisis by saving the banks and their share in artificially created wealth. The banks have accepted monetary Keynesianism with an enhanced role of the state because they expect to minimise their losses, i.e. to transform their artificial wealth into real wealth. The economic basis consists in the hope of saving the share of the banks in the process of adapting the artificial wealth to the actually existing assets by shifting the burden of the losses to be imposed on holders of artificial wealth on the non-banks, which are considered as not structurally essential for the global financial architecture.

In a Keynesian logic of sufficient demand for keeping real investment at the full employment level, there is ambiguity. Is demand primarily insufficient because final demand is too low, or is the production of investment goods temporarily insufficient? When Keynes argued that even the building of pyramids could bring the economy back to high levels of demand (and hence also investment induced by the additional final demand), there was no hope of the pyramids contributing in any way to increased productivity. Additional spending is not intended to contribute to earning capacities of the owners of the newly created assets. Pyramids are equally valueless as armaments or subsidies to poor households. Hence the absence of a theory of the microeconomic efficiency of state spending in Keynes' work should not be surprising. Unused financial resources and even money in the hands of capitalists who will not invest them can be taken out of their hands and given to those who will use them unproductively. These financial resources can even contribute to more profit in the real economy provided that they are spent on goods and create through additional demand incentives to invest for business which then uses other financial resources productively.

When Keynes suggests using instruments of monetary policy, especially the lowering of the interest rate, he expects that investment is supported; which later contributes to productive capacity. But no private entrepreneur can invest in plant and equipment, which ultimately does not yield a surplus by producing goods for a market. Monetary Keynesianism expects this market from supporting private investment. It does not require an explicit increase in mass incomes by redistribution. Real Keynesianism insists on the possibility that the expansion of final demand is insufficient for creating the demand for investment goods, which keeps the economy on a full employment path. On the one hand the solution of the classical authors of the destruction of artificial financial resources is necessary, not by crisis but by redistribution to unproductive consumers. This has to be combined on the other hand with a "wasteful" increase in final demand in order to raise labour incomes to the level of marginal productivity of labour.

This picture becomes more complicated if households lose trust and start to save, so that household incomes no longer are used as demand for goods and services of the real economy. This would imply that business has to engage in debt-financed investment in risky plant and equipment (Elsenhans 1999: 116-123)

With the massive injection of public money into the banking system, governments of the leading industrial countries protect financial capital from painful liquidation of financial assets which have no counterpart in the real economy. The increase of public money occurs mainly in the rescue of banks that are considered vital for the global financial architecture. Losses of other investors in financial markets are not cared for. The limited adjustment of the nominal value of financial assets is born by non-banks without supporting governments from the industrial countries. For political reasons, the losses of one category of actors on financial markets are kept secret: the governments of raw material, especially oil exporting countries who thought to preserve their rent incomes by placing them on financial markets instead of accelerating their national development by industrial diversification.

Two categories of speculators emerge: those who benefit from the support of industrial countries governments and the others. Financial assets are increasingly concentrated in the hands of those who enjoy the support of governments, which because of the productive capacity of the industry in their country, can credibly create money in the currency in which their real economy is paid. The second category has no such productive capacity behind it. To this category belong the rent-collecting governments of the South.

From this it follows that the mirage, created by increasing raw material exports from sub-Saharan Africa to the newly industrialising economies of Asia with competition between India and China for African mineral deposits, should be considered with caution.

I expect that the capacity of monetary Keynesianism, to ease the problems the world economy, will prevent a reorientation of national and globally co-ordinated economic policies with the goal of promoting rising mass incomes and investment in the real economy for stabilising the growth of the world economy. Real Keynesianism will not replace financialisation. We will not return to the welfare oriented predominance of the real economy which characterised the three golden post-World War II decades. High profit rates in financial markets will continue to attract "investors", especially from the oligopolistic sector. Job creation will depend on the non-oligopolistic sector and newcomers, the growth of which is rather hampered by the dominance of the oligopolistic sector. Growth of production and employment will be lower than possible because of the limits to the expansion of mass demand.

Monetary Keynesianism prevents the destruction of financial assets to a necessary degree as well as a reorientation in the growth of the real economy via rising mass incomes. The positive effect of defending mass incomes in the emerging economies which has already achieved satisfactory levels of economic diversification will not trickle down to the sub-Saharan African countries. This is the case of China, Brazil, Peru and Mexico where programs defending the purchasing power of the poor have been implemented.

Therefore, I assume that devaluation-driven competition will continue. In this context globalisation will continue to be used as an instrument to discipline labour in the leading industrialised countries. Labour leadership will not oppose this instrumentalisation because it justifies the failures of the labour movement to mobilise, which however may be due not to globalisation but to other causes of the decline of social democratic labour in the West.

7 Sub-Saharan Africa has difficulties in participating in the globalisation of manufacturing production and will remain hindered in its development through better raw material prices

In the intensifying competition for manufactured exports sub-Saharan Africa suffers from a disadvantage which renders more attractive the alternative of opting out from industrial diversification in favour of more raw material exports.

Sub-Saharan Africa is not self-sufficient in food production. This is surprising given the relatively low population density in comparison to India and China and the high potential for agricultural exports. The competition of densely populated Asian countries for land concessions in sub-Saharan Africa indicates that there are resources which can be exploited provided that there is demand. The colonial powers and the postcolonial states have been able to have African peasants adopt cash crop production by mixtures of economic incentives and coercion. It is therefore fair to assume that the fact that foreign countries are searching for land in Africa to grow food, indicates that African peasants could use their own land themselves (provided that there was demand for the food they grow). The lack of adequate food production in order to achieve food self-sufficiency might therefore be explained by a preference of the urban population for foreign food at least at the prevailing price relations. Foreign food seems to be relatively cheap in relation to local food because incomes for cash crops are high, because there are rents from raw mineral materials or because foreign assistance trickles down to the urban population directly or indirectly from employment by the rent receiving privileged strata.

Without a change in the orientation of the local agriculture, sub-Saharan Africa's capacity to cheapen the export of manufactured products by devaluation below purchasing power parity cannot be expected.

A larger number of studies have shown that the richness of sub-Saharan Africa in natural resources (including agriculture) leads to a pattern of behaviour in the economies quite different than the reaction of Asian economies to devaluation. If Africa devalues, over a wide range of rates of devaluation sub-Saharan African economies increase their competitiveness in traditional and new cash crops. Instead of manufacturing industries becoming competitive on the local factor markets, more raw material branches become competitive (Fontaine 1993: 409, Kappel 1999: 52, Godfrey 1985: 37, Rittenberg 1986: 177). Devaluation with continued specialisation on raw materials (with low price elasticity of demand) is wasteful, as devaluation is only justified as an instrument of economic diversification and rising employment, with hopefully large multiplier effects.

Sub-Saharan Africa is still too rich to prosper on the basis of the mobilisation of its own labour for food self-sufficiency and manufactured exports.

Devaluation-driven exports of manufactured products are unattractive: export earnings will initially decline; a new deal would have to be struck with the peasantry where the urban population would lose; the success of devaluation-driven industrialisation in Asia provides sub-Saharan Africa with new raw material rents.

New opportunities will maintain existing power relations in sub-Saharan African societies. Despite the crisis of the development state, the decline of terms of trade and economic liberalisation imposed by the donors, the self-proclaimed modern sector of the African population is economically weak with respect to its quality as a producer. The sector of small and medium enterprises is either limited or strongly linked to the "foreign" sector, which is based on the donors and non-market organisations. These new private entities (the "civil scene") replace the faltering state by a façade of private business forms of organisation. However, these entities are viable primarily on the basis of market imperfections. A formally private sector has emerged on the ruins of the state. Its dominant social class has been capable of erecting barriers against new entrants and of maintaining informal webs of coordination especially through its privileged access to the resources of donors from abroad.

In such a configuration, it can be expected that increased raw material earnings will be largely absorbed by these networks and benefit a middle class based on clientelistic vertical and horizontal relations. There will be no incentive to engage resources in the less remunerative industries for diversification or to engage oneself in the local production of food.

When the appropriation of rents became an issue for development strategies, oil rents were especially popular in the focus of discussion. Oil rents can be appropriated by centrally organised institutions. Many of the cash crop rents are more difficult to appropriate, especially as previous institutions are discredited (marketing boards). Centralised government organisations for rent collection will be considered as a return to previous state dominance, which everybody knows to have been pernicious. A continued specialisation in raw materials will therefore coincide with an opaque form of appropriation of the rent. The simplest form of such a mode of appropriation will be a high exchange rate.

This new mode of appropriation will be justified on terms of neoliberal thinking. This is because in an economy with differences in backwardness in productivity and low degrees of backwardness in price-inelastic products, there are multiple equilibria in foreign trade. As levels of employment are low at high exchange rates (with low bargaining power of labour) and purchasing power for imports is high through better terms of trade, those better off will be able to increase their share of national income with a high share of imported goods. With a skewed income distribution in favour of the rich, the consumption of industrial products will be diversified and oriented to high quality products in relatively limited quantities. The growth-impeding structures of consumption will persist.

The rise in raw material exports will not lead to the mobilisation of labour and the emergence of mass demand for simple products that a local small and medium scale industry could manufacture. Sub-Saharan Africa is not becoming a case of the staple theory of growth via raw material exports where raw material production creates mass markets which trigger broad industrialisation. Such had been the case in the regions of 19th century European settlement and 19th century Scandinavia.

8 Rent and alternatives of development

Sub-Saharan Africa has the problem of comparative advantage in the wrong branches. It receives from the rest of the world development assistance and (in the case of increasing raw material exports) incomes which are sufficient to maintain balance of payments equilibria at low levels of employment and structures of income distribution which maintain growth-impeding social structures. Economic liberalisation does not destroy this structure, but replaces the state-controlled mechanism of rent appropriation and rent allocation by a decentralised network-based structure which is still less accountable than the old state-based system. Here rent appears as a natural income at the prevailing price structure to which a social class has access which is able to erect barriers to entry that the excluded population cannot pull down, as it is kept from employment by the level of the exchange rate and the structure of internal demand. The rent is hidden in a more than favourable exchange rate and hence too high incomes for limited and privileged groups of the population. How can the rent be brought to use for an alternative development strategy which favours mass employment and mass consumption?

I do not want to develop in extense the approach of capitalist development on the basis of rising mass demand, which pushes the growth of a small and medium industrial sector (Elsenhans/Kleiner/Dreves 2000: 42-74, Elsenhans 1975; 1982; 1995). I admit, however, that this mechanism becomes more and more difficult to rely on, when modern communication products like cell phones become important items of mass consumption. The international demonstration effect makes transnational cooperation for such products indispensable. A strategy of mass-consumption-based industrial diversification can no longer be implemented in the form of dissociation from the world market, even if it strives to be self-centred. By increasing the local linkages through appropriately low exchange rates and a concentration in the production of goods for mass demand in large series an early local production of products can be achieved where technical dependence on transnational enterprises cannot be avoided.

Equality of distribution, state intervention in the economy, and the promotion of foreign direct investment can go together. There is no opposition between an opening to the world market and state intervention with the goal of sector-specific industrial policies. Tiger nations of East Asia also had to deal with the problem that competitiveness in new industries and diversification of industrial exports required exchange rates which implied undesirable reductions of foreign exchange earnings. They adopted, together with export orientation, strategies of rent appropriation and rent-based finance of industrial diversification which resembled in basic characteristics, but not in the pattern of implementation, to import-substituting industrialisation based on rents from raw material exports. South Korea in the 1970s faced declining terms of trade for its simple textile products in the world market. Prices fell more rapidly than quantities rose. Export earnings tended to decline just in a similar way as the export earnings of countries with tropical agricultural products in the Singer-Prebisch theory. South Korea blocked the import of textile machinery. Textile exporters had to address their local suppliers of spare parts. The prices of new locally produced machinery were higher than the prices of imported ones in local currency. The export prices of textiles in local currency rose (due to the low price elasticity of demand) with low losses in export earnings. The result was the same as would have been if textile exports had been taxed and the additional tax income had been used for a government-sponsored program of subsidising a local textile machinery industry. Administrative costs were low, bureaucratic inflexibility and corruption were avoided, and textile exporters were probably much better technical advisers for new machinery producers than bureaucrats in charge of a governmental investment programme for textile machinery production.

All successful new industrial economies have followed industrial policies. Foreign investors were forced to increase the local content of their production. Brazil succeeded by this mechanism to attract most of the world's automobile part subcontractors.

Raw material rich sub-Saharan African economies initially will not have large industrial sectors they can use to climb up the production chain. They cannot use rents appropriated in the export-oriented production chains of which major technical characteristics are already known to them and major channels of commercialisation are accessible to them just by increasing the local share of production in existing export units. In raw materials, climbing the chain of production is notoriously difficult, especially because of the high complexity of mineral production equipment. Sub-Saharan Africa may enjoy increasing raw material exports earnings but cannot avoid state responsibility in managing supplies (arrangements for export taxes, fees for mineral concessions, production sharing in contracts with foreign companies) and in channelling the additional financial resources into industrial projects the short term profitability is not assured.

Such decisions depend on planning investment on the basis of a projected industrial structure, as first did the late colonial industrialisation plan for

Algeria (Plan de Constantine 1958) (Elsenhans 2000: 644 ff.). Orienting such a process to mass consumption requires information on the structure of consumption of poor and slightly less poor households, especially with respect to those technically more demanding products which poor households buy early on if their incomes increase, as well as with respect to basic inputs required for an expanding industrial production.

As far as I can see, all the information on household consumption in sub-Saharan Africa is deficient. I have not found documentation comparable to India on technology available for small-scale industrial production. I assume therefore that information for industrial policies, which aim at diversification on the basis of mass consumption is, perhaps no longer, available. I suspect that the interests of western donors in economic liberalisation have led to disinterest in this type of information. Sub-Saharan Africa seems to be kept from the informational resources which a strategy of the East Asian type would require.

As the pattern of indirect channelling of rent through climbing up the chain of production cannot be used initially in a sub-Saharan African strategy of diversification because of the rather low level of industrial development and still high comparative advantage in raw materials, a sub-Saharan strategy of alternative development requires the making visible of the rent. Instead of accepting high exchange rates (which make middle strata happy), devaluation should be used to lower the international price of local factors of production. At the same time the international prices of the already competitive price-inelastic products should be defended by export taxes. It is this procedure which I call rendering rents visible, in order to make those with access to these rents accountable (Elsenhans 1993: 19-24). As rent does not simply disappear in the case of economic liberalisation, I defend this policy against indiscriminate liberalisation where the rent seeps away in the form of the consumption of imported items by the better off.

The allocation of rent to investment projects against criteria of short-term profitability and in view of probable profitability under the conditions of a future but not yet existing structure of demand and inter-industrial linkages (whether through a central planning authority or decentralised bodies including larger participation of private business or civil society organisations) is always threatened by particularistic interests in rent seeking. The market sanction of decisions through losses because of absence of profitability is necessarily weakened and this creates a selection problem, an information problem, and a control problem (Elsenhans 1987: 83-87). There are many actors, public and private ones, who see their power enhanced if projects in their area of influence are implemented. They will present those projects in an overoptimistic manner and eventually lie. In order to do so, information is carefully "presented", unfavourable information withheld. Lack of achievement is "explained" by adverse conditions for which in underdeveloped economies "proofs" are abundant (lack of skills, deficient infrastructures, etc.). Success in this manipulation of information depends on alliances. Information becomes sticky and is negotiated. The planning, implementation and monitoring process is politicised. Western donors have not escaped this danger of losing contact to reality in the monitoring of their own projects. Allocation of rent is the result of power struggles.

In the attempt to "rationalise" these power struggles, developmental thinking has joined the "cultural turn". Inefficiency in the use of inevitably emerging rents is explained by cultural norms of the elites who control rents. I have described these elites as state classes which are pulled between their aspiration to (wasteful) privilege and some obligation to remain in their privileged position by producing (some) legitimacy.

In the cultural turn approach, the sub-Saharan African problem in using rents less efficiently than the East and South East Asians is explained by differences in culture between Asia and sub-Saharan Africa, but Nepal is certainly not more efficient, and Saddam Hussein's Iraq was certainly not less despotic than the highly criticised African tyrants.

I am inclined to consider that in countries which had previously experienced bureaucratic empires and so-called tributary mode of production, there may exist traditions of the bureaucratic rationality. I admit that long-lasting struggles for independence with high ratios of participation of non-propertied middle strata may constitute an asset. But in sub-Saharan Africa, where demand conditions are favourable for the emergence of a small and medium scale informal industrial sector, it emerged like in many of the larger cities, although the skills and diversity of the sector seem to be lower in sub-Saharan Africa than in countries like India, Pakistan or Bangladesh.

I assume therefore that cultural differences are less important than the objective possibilities for launching small and medium scale industries and the influence such industries can exercise on the definition of legitimacy of the rent-appropriating class. Instead of lamenting on specific cultural characteristics in sub-Saharan Africa, the micro-institutions which impose growth-enhancing uses of rents and the macro-social conditions which favour such behaviour should be investigated together with the possibilities of influencing culture.

9 On influencing culture

Having a fair exposure to cultural distance through field work, teaching and even a close family experience, I find the cultural turn in its form of post-colonial studies surprising by its lack of empirical roots. Elite behavioural patterns, which are rational on the basis of rent, are condemned despite their microeconomic, micro-social and micro-political rationalities. Elite production in cultural items is privileged, whereas day to day culture which creates values and norms is not investigated.

When political economy rose in political science, some reception of the results of the neighbouring discipline, economics, was realised. Admittedly, this started with a rather uncritical reception of Marxian economics and shifted (due to the crisis of real socialism), to a crude neoclassical model. Both have converged in the globalisation discourse with the idea of a race to the bottom, which has already been criticised above. When the hope of revolution vanished, Marxist theory with its isomorphy in neoclassical economics could but end theoretically and politically in a neoclassical rejection of the possibility of politically shaping markets and hence influencing incentives on markets. I have not seen even a slight opening of the cultural turn discourse to the respective neighbouring discipline: psychoanalysis.

As far as I can see, psychiatry is an undeveloped science in poor countries because most of the potential clients are so poor that they cannot consume it, whereas the available consumers are mostly Western oriented. Where contributions are found, (for example the "fahlawi" personality in the Arab world; Dessouki 1973: 190) the link between the absence of socialisation via labour and the illusion of access to resources by prestige and impressing on others are highlighted. "Hanging around" as an instrument of social status promotes obviously conspicuous consumption, power playing, and the acceptance of "big man behaviour".

This brings me to the hypothesis that the specific cultural traits in rent-based societies are less received from learning a cultural tradition but that this cultural tradition is picked up as if it were readily available (one will not learn things totally inaccessible) and then "learned" because it fits into the existing economic structures. Such cultural traditions are hence continuously created and recreated as long as rents are not "tamed".

In rent-dominated economies the culture of rent may be dominant but it is never universal. Rents never trickle down to everyone, and those without access to rent have to live on the income they get from the sale of their products and their efficiency in producing these products. Invariably they have to be rational in the Weberian sense: the literature is full of X-efficient market women as well as innovative and thrifty peasants and craftsmen in Africa, too. De Soto's (de Soto 1989, esp. 171 ff.) conclusions may be exaggerated as he reduces the obstacles for this behaviour to problems of secure property rights, but the evidence on which he bases himself is universally shared in the literature about agriculture and the benefits of the predominance of owner-operated farms or about the dynamism of the informal sector provided that there are expanding markets.

In agriculture, owner operated farms tend to maintain a competitive market due to the fact that land and resources are generally equally distributed. In order to reinforce the market orientation against rent orientation in culture, a dynamic and relatively egalitarian agriculture has to be preserved or, in the case of concentration in property in land, brought into existence.

In sub-Saharan Africa such peasantries exist. The process of economic and political liberalisation has rarely touched them. They are not visible in these processes and do not play an important role. I should mention that the differences in outcomes of liberalisation in the People's Republic of China and the Soviet Union seem to have been caused by the differences in importance of owner-operated farms.

According to my arguments about the origin of profit in net investment goods production, investment goods production triggered by increases in consumption, and local investment goods production being favoured by a high share of simpler products in demand, the growth of market-oriented behaviour can be expected from a rather egalitarian distribution of incomes and assets. Social justice would hence be a precondition of market-oriented behaviour, even if social justice is in turn reinforced by market-orientation. Market orientation and equality could then constitute two elements of a virtuous circle.

As rent is considered inevitable in the process of transition to development, the question of cultural norms becomes important. I see two opposite positions in the actual debate, which in the real world appear in mixed forms. Following neoclassical thinking about the natural tendency to equilibrium, any economic transaction which takes the form of an exchange contributes to the stabilisation of market relations. Such a conception favours disguised rents with underemployment equilibria. In a Keynesian view, macroeconomic stability can only be expected if final demand triggers off a sufficient level of investment spending. If this condition is not fulfilled, all players will try to save themselves by engaging in rent seeking. Only rising mass incomes prevent wasteful spending and maintain the mechanism of competition between those in control of the surplus. Hence rising mass incomes are constitutive for the successful and persisting transition to capitalism and the support of the struggle against rent.

Here ideological struggles matter: social groups as well as political and economic decision-makers behave much less on the basis of their wishes and their values but much more on the basis of their expectations. Nobody will spend money on investment if they do not believe that it will work. Under the usual assumptions of neoclassical theory, rent seeking does not work because capitalists are more efficient than rent seekers, achieve a higher return on their capital invested than rentiers on their assets. If they invest their surplus by employing labour becomes scarce, and as a result of this also the labour the rentiers wants to employ. At a level of demand, where capitalists can invest all their resources, capitalists have to destroy rent and are able to do so. By destroying the economic basis of the rentiers, scarcity-constrained capitalists also destroy their culture. Capitalists survive only by staying attached to their own culture, which they therefore produce "uno actu" with their efforts to remain competitive. However, as long as capitalists cannot destroy rents because they cannot empower labour via full employment, capitalists themselves will try to become rentiers themselves. Being a rentier is much more comfortable than being a capitalist who has to compete on markets. By showing the link between empowerment of labour and profit, in economies with still important rents, a labourist discourse can strengthen those forces which ease an orientation of economic policies to the aim of empowering labour.

Western discourse therefore matters: the discourse linked to the mainstream neoclassical insistence on markets may reduce some of the more wasteful and politically dangerous form of rent seeking, but not rent itself. A discourse which establishes the link between mass incomes and profit reduces the basis of rent in the long-run, even if it is associated with politically controlled rent appropriation in the pursuit of higher levels of employment. Which discourse prevails in the West has an important implication on the South, especially in cases of societies which are highly dependent on the transfer of Western resources, money and ideas. This influences their internal power structures, as is the case for the sub-Saharan African countries

The actual ideological debate in sub-Saharan Africa is largely determined by the interaction of two economic worldviews. First, the popular "vulgar" Marxian worldview of a zero sum game between exploitation and mass consumption is politically no more acceptable but constitutes the background of the debate because of the training of many intellectuals. It is completely compatible with the neoclassical interpretation of capitalism the international agencies work with. The second being the Keynesian view, is absent because it is universally accepted that the deformation of underdeveloped economies does not allow the operation of the mechanism of rising mass incomes leading to a smooth adjustment of the economy through accumulation and market-driven investment. Planning would be necessary for restructuring the productive apparatus but is excluded for political reasons.

The only theoretical approach open now for underprivileged groups consists in the rejection of any worldview which focuses on economics. The defence of the interests of the underprivileged groups is based on an a-economic worldview, which is based on the rejection of any consistent overall economic theory, which is replaced by a concentration on moral arguments and values.

This shift to moral economy takes place also elsewhere in the South but under overall conditions quite dissimilar from those prevailing in sub-Saharan Africa.

The rise of the moral economy is associated in many areas of the South with the rise of new cultural identitarian movements (Elsenhans (1989). Their social bases are new and old middle classes who have lost their hope in the modernising state of the import-substituting industrialisation as well as the marginalised poor. The secular state classes did not succeed in eradicating marginality and in achieving self-sustained growth. The old middle classes (in India: the traders) see in the state only a rapacious government eager to collect taxes and bribes. The new middle class has emerged as a result of the undoubtedly successful efforts for education in the modernising state and face an overcrowded public sector which is staffed by strata having close links to Western culture, especially in the realm of linguistic skills.

In the post-communist countries of East Asia and in the successful early export-oriented economies of East and South East Asia the combination of state intervention, radical social (agrarian) reforms have created high levels of employment through export orientation and a universal hope that economic progress may trickle down to most of the population. Even with limited democratisation, political stability is maintained.

In Latin America the rise of discontent takes the form of populism. This is because there is no cultural identity which would be fundamentally opposed to the "Occident".

Only in South and some parts of South East Asia and the Arab world does the failure of the secular nationalists who had won independence and the dissatisfaction about the limits of the state-led modernisation project take the form of new cultural identitarian movements because this project has been successful enough to create new social strata outside the traditional established groups.

The moral economy principles of populism and of the new cultural identitarian movements pursue pragmatic and eclectic economic policies. These economic policies combine social measures for the marginals, the protection of small and medium-sized businesses and some more are less efficient industrial policies for employment creation within a framework of limited opening up to the world market (Elsenhans 2004; 2006b). Within such admittedly incoherent approaches the creation of mass demand and employment may dynamise the small and medium-scale industrial sector and lead to the removal of the bottlenecks which Keynesian strategies face in underdeveloped economic structures. The already mentioned programs for the defence of the incomes of the poor in some of the major countries of Asia and Latin America are examples.

There are no new cultural identitarian movements in sub-Saharan Africa, even if religion as a political factor is on the rise. Elites in sub-Saharan Africa cannot adopt religious identity in order to organise large multi-class coalitions with the two major elements, the middle classes and the marginals, with the goal of creating solidarity on the basis of more rights for the poor, more market orientation and reforms in the name of religion in order to reduce privileges, the "hogra" denounced by the Islamists, and corruption.

Elites in sub Sahara Africa can not base their power on increasing the small and medium state industries which want to be protected from a modern sector; which the secular state and the West have spoon-fed and provided with monopolistic privileges. Instead of cultural nationalism they adopt a discourse which mainly refers to the Western ideals of 1776 and 1789. Tiny bridgeheads try to impress the donors whose perception of the South is largely determined by Western non-governmental organisations. These non-governmental organisations reproduce themselves economically by producing political and social realities which they can use in relation to their Western audiences as "certificates of good conscience". The critique of the established elites in the South as corrupt, the denunciation of cultural nationalists as anti-modern and even fascist, and the praising of their local rarely politically representative clientele are the ideological vehicles for presenting this "de facto" neo-colonial set-up as progressive.

This configuration is not dissimilar from the ideologies and roles of the 19th century missionary societies of the West with their claim to fulfilling a humanitarian mission.

The local bridgehead of this worldwide civil society is extremely dependent and cooperates in enabling this neo-colonial setup determining what is politically correct. It has been maintained that despite its humanitarian approach, this set-up in reality precludes the empowerment of the poor (Petras 1997).

When discussing similar observations I made during a recent trip to West Africa with some of my Africanist friends in Germany, I was not only confirmed but also told that empirical research in order to determine the extent of the isolation of the Western bridgeheads in their own societies in Africa would be difficult to realise. It was argued that the opposition of the NGO community would be too strong.

I would therefore suggest as a hypothesis that the cultural turn in Western development thinking has become instrumental for keeping out from the area of legitimate consideration the actually existing non-Western forces of civil society, established traditional power holders and new cultural identitarian movements to which most of the cultural turn scientific community seems to have no real contact.

The cultural turn approach can be therefore be considered as wonderfully fitting into the attempts of maintaining the hegemony of the neoliberal economic discourse against the admittedly incoherent uttering of the moral economy discourse and this would serve the disguising of rent seeking as compatible with market orientation and political democracy. Maybe my contribution can be seen as a small effort for asserting an alternative view of capitalism in order to break some ground for an alternative mass-oriented praxis.

References

Albert, M. (1991): Capitalisme contre capitalisme, Paris: Editions du Seuil.

Appelbaum, E.; Schettkat, R. (1995): Employment and Productivity in Industrialized Economies, in: *International Labour Review*, 134, 4/5; pp. 605-623.

Bai, M.-K. (1982): The Turning Point in the Korean Economy, in: *Developing Economies*, 20, 1 (March); pp. 117-140.

Begg, I.; Fagerberg, J.; Guerrieri, P. (1999): Conclusions and Policy Implications, in: Fagerberg, J.; Guerrieri, P.; Verspagen, B. (eds.): *The Economic Challenge for Europe: Adapting to Innovation-Based Growth*, Cheltenham, Northampton: Edward Elgar; pp. 229-237.

Blumenthal, T. (1968): Scarcity of Labour and Wage Differentials in the Japanese Economy, 1958-1964, in: *Economic Development and Cultural Change*, 17, 1 (October); pp. 15-32.

Bortkiewicz, L. v. (1907): Wertrechnung und Preisrechnung im Marxschen System 83), in: *Archiv für Sozialwissenschaft und Sozialpolitik*, 25, 2; pp. 445-489.

Chen, H.; Gordon, M.J.; Zhiming, Y. (1994): The Real Income and Consumption of an Urban Chinese Family, in: *Journal of Development Studies*, 31, 1 (October); pp. 201-213.

Dessouki, A.E.H.: Arab Intellectuals and Al-Nakba: The Search for Fundamentalism, in: *Middle Eastern Studies*, 9, 2 (April); pp. 187-195.

Elsenhans, H. (1975): Overcoming Underdevelopment. A Research Paradigm, in: *Journal of Peace Research*, 12, 4 (December); pp. 293-313.

Elsenhans, H. (1982): Die Überwindung von Unterentwicklung durch Massenproduktion für den Massenbedarf – Weiterentwicklung eines Ansatzes, in: Nohlen, D.; Nuscheler, F. (eds.): *Handbuch der Dritten Welt (1): Unterentwicklung und Entwicklung – Theorien, Strategien, Indikatoren*, Hamburg: Hoffmann & Campe; pp. 152-182.

Elsenhans, H. (1983a): Égalité et développement. L'expérience européenne et le monde sous-développé d'aujourd'hui, in: *Cultures et développement*, 15, 2; pp. 187-216.

Elsenhans, H. (1983b): Rising Mass Incomes as a Condition of Capitalist Growth: Implications for the World Economy, in: *International Organization*, 37, 1 (Winter); pp. 1-38.

Elsenhans, H. (1987): Dependencia, Underdevelopment and the Third World State, in: *Law and State*, 36; pp. 65-94.

Elsenhans, H. (1992): English Poor Law and Egalitarian Agrarian Reform in the Third World, in: Elsenhans, H.: *Equality and Development*, Dhaka: Center for Social Studies; pp. 130-162.

Elsenhans, H. (1993): Integrating Political Economy in the Comparative Study of Administration, in: Asmeron, H.K.; Jain, R.B. (eds.): *Politics, Administration and Public Policy in Developing Countries*, Amsterdam: Vrije Universiteit Press; pp. 16-35.

Elsenhans, H. (1995): Überwindung von Marginalität als Gegenstand der Armutsbekämpfung, in: Schäfer, H.B. (ed.): *Bevölkerungsdynamik und Grundbedürfnisse in Entwicklungsländern. Schriften des Vereins für Socialpolitik 246*, Berlin: Duncker und Humblot; pp. 193-221.

Elsenhans, H. (1999): Individualistische Strategien der Haushalte zur Zukunftssicherung: Grundlage für den Niedergang des wohlfahrtstaatlichen Kapitalismus, in: *Comparativ. Leipziger Beiträge zur Universalgeschichte und vergleichenden Gesellschaftsforschung*, 9, 3; pp. 114-142.

Elsenhans, H. (2000): La guerre d'Algérie 1954–1962. La transition d'une France à une autre. Le passage de la IV à la Ve République, Paris: Publisud.

Elsenhans, H. (2004): L'OMC, la mondialisation et les nouveaux mouvements politiques du sud: le cas de l'Inde, in: *NAQD - Revue d'Études et de Critique Sociale*, 19/20; pp. 227-264.

Elsenhans, H. (2006a): Globalization between a Convoy Model and an Underconsumptionist Threat, Münster: LIT Verlag.

Elsenhans, H. (2006b): The WTO, Globalisation and New Political Movements of the South, in: Elsenhans, H.; Jain, R.K. (eds.): *India, the European Union and the WTO*, New Delhi: Radiant Publishers; pp. 51-98.

Elsenhans, H. (2009): Rising New Cultural Identitarian Movements in Africa and Asia, Paper read at the Leipzig Converence 1989 in a Global Perspective. International Conference 14-16 October Leipzig, Germany. In reviewing process

Elsenhans, H.; Kleiner, E.; Dreves, R.J. (2000): Développement, équité et extension du marché des masses. Une autre alternative. Le cas algérien. L'enjeu des PME industrielles, Paris: Publisud.

Fontaine, J. (1993): Demande et investissement dans le processus d'ajustement, in: *Tiers Monde*, 34, 135 (July-September); pp. 491-512.

Godfrey, M. (1985): Trade and Exchange Rate Policy in Subsaharan Africa, in: *IDS Bulletin*, 16, 3 (July); pp. 31-38.

Hsieh, C.-T. (1973): Measuring the Effects of Trade Expansion on Employment. A Review of Some Research, in: *International Labour Review*, 107, 1 (January); pp. 1-29.

Kappel, R. (1999): Die anhaltende Unterentwicklung Afrikas, in: *Internationale Politik und Gesellschaft*, 1; pp. 38-54.

Manning, C. (1995): Approaching the Turning Point? Labor Market Change under Indonesia's New Order, in: *Developing Economies*, 33, 1 (March); pp. 52-81.

Nitzan, J. (2001): Regimes of Differential Accumulation: Mergers, Stagflation and the Logic of Globalization, in: *Review of International Political Economy*, 8, 2 (Summer); pp. 226-274.

O'Brien, P.K.; Keyder, Ç. (1978): Economic Growth in Britain and France 1780–1914. Two Paths to the Twentieth Century, London: Allen & Unwin.

Okishio, N. (1961): Technical Change and the Rate of Profit, in: *Kobe University Economic Review*, 7; pp. 85-99.

Osborne, E. (2000): Labor Surplus in Korea: A Reassessment, in: *International Economic Journal*, 14, 4 (Winter); pp. 125-141.

Petras, J. (1997): Imperialism and the NGOs in Latin America, in: *Monthly Review*, 49, 7 (December); pp. 10-27.

Rittenberg, L. (1986): Export Growth Performance of Less Developed Countries, in: *Journal of Development Economics*, 24, 1 (November); pp. 167-177.

Rowthorn, R.; Ramaswamy, R. (1999): Growth, Trade and Deindustrialization, in: *IMF Staff Papers*, 46, 1 (March); pp. 18-41.

Sinn, H.-W. (2007): Internationaler Vergleich der Arbeitskosten. Warum Deutschland keine starken Lohnerhöhungen veträgt, in: *IFO-Schnelldienst*, 60, 4 (February); pp. 54-58.

Soto, H. de: El otro sendero: La revolución informal, Lima: Editorial Ausonia.

Vernon, R. (1966): International Investment and International Trade in the Product Cycle, in: *Quarterly Journal of Economics*, 80, 2 (May); pp. 190-207.

The Freetown Declaration of Economic Policy Independence: Countercyclical Policy for Africa south of the Sahara and the Global Financial Crisis

John Weeks[*]

Abstract

In August 2009 the African finance ministers issued the Freetown Declaration in which they committed their governments to "implement fiscal stimulus measures" to counter the effects of the international financial crisis on their economies. This paper analyzes the feasibility of realizing this commitment. It considers the availability of policy instruments in the sub-Saharan countries for countercyclical intervention. On the basis of this, the paper proposes a fiscal stimulus tailored to the conditions and constraints of the countries of the region. In a majority of the countries the fiscal expansion could be financed domestically, in other countries governments would require additional external funding, and for a few countries would a stimulus not be appropriate.

1 Introduction[1]

In August 2009 the Caucus of African Governors of the IMF, World Bank and African Development Bank (also known as the Caucus of African

---

[*] John Weeks is Professor Emeritus of the School of Oriental and African Studies of the University of London, London, UK. Email Address for communication: John Weeks [jw10@soas.ac.uk]

[1] This paper is based on the author's keynote address to the Caucus of African Governors of the IMF, World Bank, African Development Bank, Sierra Leone, 12-13 August 2009

Finance Ministers) met in Freetown, Sierra Leone.[2] Responding to the crisis in the international economy, the meeting unanimously issued the Freetown Declaration, in which they collectively committed themselves to implement a fiscal stimulus and called for the international agencies to support it.[3]

This paper considers the feasibility of a fiscal stimulus for the sub-Saharan countries, most of which are low-income and exporters of primary products. Section 2 reviews the policy recommendations in the Freetown Declaration which are relevant to a fiscal stimulus. Section 3 treats counter-cyclical interventions analytically to identify instruments and outcomes. Section 4 considers in detail the policy instruments available to sub-Saharan governments to implement effectively a stimulus program. The final and concluding section 5 indicates how donors and lenders could support countercyclical fiscal policy by the governments of the region.

2 The Recovery Program in the Freetown Declaration

In late April 2009 at the spring meeting of the Development Committee of the IMF and the World Bank, the president of the African Development Bank warned that the sub-Saharan countries would be severely affected by the global financial crisis that had begun the previous year.[4] When the African finance ministers met in Freetown in mid-August 2009 his warning had been realized. In this context the ministers and their representatives issued a declaration unusual for its clarity, forcefulness and break with prevailing policy.

Unlike previous declarations that had pledged the governments to orthodox policies of macro stability and institutional reform,[5] after noting the need for sound policy and social 'safety nets', the Freetown Declaration issued a bold declaration,

---

[2] This is an annual meeting of finance ministers to discuss the issues which would arise at the subsequent IMF-World Bank meeting, which in October 2009 was held in Istanbul.

[3] The declaration was adopted on 12 August 2009, by the Caucus of African Governors of the IMF, World Bank and African Development Bank; henceforth cited as (CAG 2009).

[4] The warning included the prediction that, "It will certainly take African countries a longer time to emerge from the crisis than other countries.", http://www.afdb.org/en/news-events/article/world-bank-imf-spring-meetings-africa-needs-a-rapid-response-to-crisis-says-afdb-president-4520/

[5] For example, the declaration of October 2007 referred to a "wide array of far-reaching reforms to achieve macroeconomic stability".

> We, the African Governors to the Bretton Woods Institutions (BWIs) and the African Development Bank (AfDB), commit to...
> Implement fiscal stimulus measures where appropriate to weather the impact of the global economic downturn;
> Expand high-growth yielding public investments...to restore and raise our countries growth and employment potential as well as crowd-in private investment;
> Implement monetary policies that support the short-term fiscal stimulus measures...
> Remain prepared to exit from the countercyclical fiscal stimulus policies as soon as the macroeconomic conditions permit. (CAG 2009)

These commitments, if implemented, would represent a break with the standard IMF macroeconomic framework that stresses minimizing fiscal deficits and keeping a tight monetary stance to achieve low inflation, usually single digit. The commitment to a fiscal stimulus would imply a lower fiscal surplus for a few countries and for most countries it would mean a larger deficit. More fundamentally, the commitment to a stimulus implies using the deficit as part of an active fiscal policy rather than as a problem to be reduced.

The commitment to increase public investment has three policy implications that are potentially inconsistent with orthodox macro policy. First, it asserts the public sector as an active driver of growth rather than merely establishing the framework for private sector-driven growth. Second, the IMF and World Bank's view that public borrowing 'crowds out' private investment is explicitly reversed: the Freetown Declaration asserts that public investment, which would by necessity be financed through borrowing, can 'crowd-in' private investment.[6] Third, it provides an implicit strategy for an active fiscal policy: countercyclical intervention will be used to stabilize output near potential, and public investment will foster higher growth rates through increased productive capacity.

A further break with Washington Consensus macro policy is made by the commitment to use monetary policy to support the active fiscal policy. While policy consistency requires that fiscal and monetary measures be coordinated, an accommodating monetary policy contradicts one of the basic tenets of most IMF programs, inflation targeting, as well as associated limits on money growth. Even more fundamental, committing monetary policy to support fiscal policy renders it derivative from fiscal policy, a return to so-called Keynesian macro management. Finally, the commitments explicitly

---

[6] A case for public investment as a driver of poverty reducing growth is found in Roy and Weeks (2004).

emphasize the fiscal stimulus as countercyclical and short term by specifying the need to exit from it as economies recover.

After stating the recovery program, the Freetown Declaration presents a list of 'requests' for the multilateral development agencies of which the ministers are governors,

> To this end [the fiscal stimulus], African International Monetary Fund and World Bank Group (IMF/WBG) Governors urge the International Monetary Fund to
> - Support our policy frameworks [and give] us the needed policy space…to leverage [external] resources…
> - Facilitate expeditious access to the newly created financing instruments;
> - Mobilize additional resources to allow an increase in concessional lending while ascertaining that these new instruments are fully funded;
> - Promptly activate the precautionary component of the SCF [Special Credit Facility].
>
> We ask the World Bank Group to introduce a more flexible and adaptable budget support instrument that is capable of responding quickly to crisis.

The second, third and fourth requests of the IMF are derivatives from the first, allowing governments the flexibility, the "policy space", to design and to implement their programs. The request of the IMF for "expeditious access" and of the World Bank for a "more flexible and adaptable budget support" reflects a general view among the officials at the Caucus of tardiness by the Fund and the Bank in their response to the impact of the global crisis on African countries.

The Freetown Declaration represented a clear break from the macro policy framework common to most African countries prior to the international financial crisis of 2008. The macroeconomics of this framework was combined with a cautious monetary stance and a neutral fiscal policy in the context of market deregulation. This policy approach, based on a "price constrained framework", has as its prerequisite that the world economy operates near its potential.[7] From mid-2008 it was clear that aggregate demand was insufficient to permit the world economy to achieve its potential. In response

---

[7] An early use of this terminology is in Liejonhufvud (1968, Section 2). The theoretical and the policy difference between "price constrained" and "quantity constrained" economies is discussed in Weeks (1989). The recently revised edition of that book can be found at http://jweeks.org.

governments of the major industrial countries introduced “stimulus packages” designed to replace the fall in private demand with public expenditure.

In this demand constrained world economy, African governments have two general policy options. They could pursue a “business-as-usual, hope-for-the-best” option in which they continue with the policy framework designed for a robust world economy and await international recovery. This would follow advice to place primary emphasis in macro policy on “stability”, which in IMF terminology means preventing inflation, reaching targets for fiscal deficits, and maintaining a free-floating exchange rate.[8] It does not mean stabilizing output by policy intervention.

However, the crisis may have brought a degree of change in IMF policy advice. A January 2009 IMF report on the world economy (IMF 2009c) called for a “firm commitment” to a “timely implementation of fiscal stimulus across a broad range of advanced and emerging economies”. In line with this commitment, a May 2009 press release reported that the IMF recommended a fiscal stimulus for a low income country, Mozambique.[9] In its survey of the impact of the financial crisis, the World Bank also recommended that governments “assess their ability to undertake countercyclical poli-

---

[8] A clear statement of this approach is found in an IMF report on the global financial crisis,

> Countries should focus on macroeconomic stability. In some countries with falling inflation rates there may be scope for monetary easing; others, however, still experience continued or renewed price pressures. Those with flexible exchange rates should allow them to move, so that they function as shock absorbers. (IMF 2009a, viii)

[9] The complete IMF statement on fiscal policy reads as follows,

> In current circumstances, the timely implementation of fiscal stimulus across a broad range of advanced and emerging economies must provide a key support to world growth. Given that the current projections are predicated on strong and coordinated policy actions, any delays will likely worsen growth prospects. Countries that have policy room should make a firm commitment to do more if the situation deteriorates further. Fiscal stimulus packages should rely primarily on temporary measures and be formulated within medium-term fiscal frameworks that ensure that the envisaged build up in fiscal deficits can be reversed as economies recover and that fiscal sustainability can be attained in the face of demographic pressure. (IMF 2009c, 1)

A press release titled “IMF Mission Calls for Fiscal Stimulus in Mozambique” states, “In the short term, given Mozambique’s low level of public debt, the [IMF] mission sees scope to at least partly offset the impact of the global economic crisis on Mozambique with somewhat more expansionary fiscal and monetary policies.” (IMF 2009d) The IMF approved higher deficit limits for El Salvador and Ethiopia (BWP/Bretton Woods Project 2009, 9) cies".[10] The African Development Bank as well has recommended countercyclical fiscal intervention.[11] Without explicitly mentioning countercyclical measures, in 2009 the IMF recommended for Sierra Leone that the country's fiscal deficit be allowed to increase to respond to the impact of the financial crisis on import prices.[12] None the less, a commitment to the pre-crisis orthodoxy remains among professionals in the Bretton Woods institutions.[13]

3 Countercyclical Fiscal Policy: Analytical Framework
3.1 Countercyclical Deficit Finance

Countercyclical policy is increasing in demand when the economy grows below its long run potential, and decreases in demand when output encounters resource scarcities that provoke inflationary pressure. This output stabilization policy maintains an economy as close to its potential as is consistent with other goals of policymakers. It is not a growth policy, which would involve public investment to contribute to increasing productive capacity.

To be relevant for the low income countries of sub-Saharan Africa, countercyclical policy intervention requires concrete specification. Reducing taxes would be relatively ineffective because of the nature of the revenue generation. In low income countries personal income taxes are rarely important, with most revenue coming from taxes on internal commerce, international trade, and corporations.[14] Almost all the company tax is collected from for-

---

[10] It reads: "The challenge for policymakers in this environment is to assess their ability to undertake countercyclical policies given the resources available to them as well as their institutional and administrative capacity to rapidly expand and adapt existing programs." (WB 2009, 10)

[11] The African Development Bank's 2009 report calls on donors and lenders to "[Focus] on results, rather than prescribing rigid policies and actions, allowing countries space to respond according to their particular needs and circumstances". More specific, it recommends that donors and governments "[i]ncrease flexibility in macroeconomic frameworks to allow more scope to balance macroeconomic stability and the need to stimulate domestic demand". (AfDB 2009, 2)

[12] "[IMF] Staff is proposing that the primary fiscal deficit be revised upward by 0.4 percentage points of GDP to accommodate the unanticipated budget impact of the rise in world oil prices." (IMF 2009b, 5)

[13] In his personal blog in early 2010 the World Bank chief economist for Africa, Shanta Devarajan, argued against a fiscal stimulus "for Africa" on the grounds that increasing a fiscal deficit would result in inflation or a reduction in private investment ("crowding out") or both.

[14] The World Bank data base *World Development Indicators* gives disaggregated tax statistics for twenty sub-Saharan countries in the 2000s. For all but two trade taxes were at least twenty percent of revenue. The exceptions were South Africa and the

eign enterprises engaged in extractive activities, and reducing their taxes would have little impact on their domestic investment decisions.

The alternative to tax reduction, enhancing demand by public expenditure, requires that the increases are flexible enough to be initiated quickly when there is a demand shock, and that they are terminated with similar dispatch as the economy approaches its potential. Public investments do not meet this condition because of their relatively long and inflexible construction time. Much of current expenditure is also inflexible. For example, it might be possible to increase the number of school teachers if trained people were available, but it might not be rational to terminate them when the economy approaches its potential. If it were judged rational from an educational point of view, it might prove politically difficult.

Because of the inappropriateness of capital expenditure and much of current expenditure for countercyclical intervention, government could base stimulus programs in the sub-Saharan countries on temporary employment schemes, 'cash for work', etc. Appropriate projects would be rapidly-completed activities using employment-intensive techniques that have a large component of repair and maintenance.[15] Examples of such programs are digging sanitation ditches, repair of public buildings, environmental improvement measures through erosion reduction, and clearing of rural footpaths. These activities were implemented in 2009 throughout Sierra Leone by the National Commission for Social Action (NCSA) as part of a countercyclical intervention policy (Weeks 2009d). The projects would make a contribution to community welfare, though their primary purpose is to increase aggregate demand through the expenditures of those directly and indirectly employed. To be effective, the employment schemes would have the following characteristics:

1) They are identified and "stock-piled" prior to the need for them, with accounting procedures in place to reduce the likelihood of misuse of funds;
2) they are easily initiated and quickly terminated, implying that they should be implemented by the central government in order to

---

Republic of Congo. Sales taxes accounted for thirty percent or more for eleven of the twenty countries. Personal and company taxes brought in twenty percent or more of revenue in only four of the countries (Ghana, Kenya, South Africa and Zambia). The source provides no information for the major petroleum exporters, Angola, Cameroon, Chad, Equatorial Guinea, Gabon, and Sudan.

[15] The International Labor Organization calls such projects as "labor-intensive public works". The ILO website provides further information on short term employment programs.

avoid delays due to the limited administrative capacity of local governments; and

3) wages and salaries are the major element of expenditure of such schemes, with a low capital component.

Some issues that plague public works projects with controversy need not be relevant for the ones whose purpose is countercyclical intervention. For example, the wage at which workers are paid is a secondary consideration because these are not long term or even medium term employment schemes. The appropriate wage will vary across countries and regions, guided by the principle that the primary purpose of the projects is to increase demand quickly. This would be best achieved by hiring as many people as possible, which implies paying wages at or below prevailing rates. These programs would be introduced when the labor is in excess supply, thus being unlikely to affect prevailing wage rates. A ministry of finance study in Sierra Leone recommended this type of employment program as a policy measure to counter the effects of the financial crisis (MoFED-EPRU 2009).[16]

Clear rules should be established for the initiation and termination of countercyclical projects. A "countercyclical" expenditure that becomes permanent negates its purpose. Initiation and termination could be triggered by a policy rule based on appropriate macroeconomic indicators. The specific indicator that is used will vary by country, and is determined by the development and the structure of the economy. Among sub-Saharan countries, only in South Africa are employment statistics sufficiently current and reliable to serve as a trigger indicator. In other countries, almost all of which lack quarterly data on aggregate output, a proxy based on trade statistics could be constructed.[17]

As shown in the next section, external support in addition to current aid levels would be required to support a stimulus in some countries. It is unfortunate but the case that donor funding does not lend itself to countercyclical programs because of the fixed, but often unreliable, schedule of allocation and disbursement.[18] To make their funding more appropriate for countercyc-

---

[16] In Sierra Leone the most important "cash for work" project in 2009 was supported with US$ 4 million by the World Bank. It employed about 14,000 people in infrastructure maintenance.

[17] In a study for Sierra Leone data on quarterly export revenues and government expenditures were used to estimate the quarterly GDP (Weeks 2009d).

[18] At the annual Caucus of African governors of the IMF, World Bank and the African Development Bank held in Freetown in August 2009, a frequent criticism held by ministers of the IMF and World Bank's operational practice was the slow-disbursing nature of lending and grant programs. This criticism was directed specifically at three programs of the IMF, the Extended Credit Facility (ECF), the Stand-by Credit Facility

lical programs, donors should accelerate disbursement and adjust their allocation procedures to allow for an "aid fund" analogous to national mechanisms created for resource booms. Money could be drawn from such a fund when the economy is below potential, and can be "hoarded" when the economy is near full potential. Donor grants ear-marked for investment could not be used for countercyclical expenditures, for reasons explained above. As a result, domestic public borrowing would be necessary to fund a stimulus, the practicality of which is discussed in the next section.

Two technical arguments are presented to justify abandoning fiscal policy for economic management: the possible inflationary effect of deficits, and the putative tendency for public borrowing to "crowd out" private investment by causing interest rates to rise. We first consider if the relationship between public deficits and inflationary pressures is analytically straight-forward, and then we look at the crowding out issue.

An increase in spending from any source results in a reduction of expenditure of another type if an economy is at full potential. If the expenditure is made by the public sector, its inflationary impact will depend on how it is financed. The expenditure can be financed through borrowing by sales of government securities to the private sector ("open market operations") or by the ministry of finance when borrowing from the central bank ("monetizing the deficit"). An increase in a public deficit is not inflationary if financed by bond sales to the private sector, because the net change in the money supply is zero. The government takes money out of circulation by the bond sale, and returns the same amount to circulation through its increased public expenditures. Assuming that the private sector holds its desired amount of bonds before the additional public borrowing takes place, the government must offer the bonds above the prevailing interest rate. If the increased bond rate transmits to private financial markets and when investment is sensitive to interest rates, then "crowding out" results. In contrast, if the government borrows directly from the central bank, the money supply increases and inflation results, but with an important exception. In an open economy part of the increased money in circulation will be spent on imports, reducing the inflationary impact, but creating or increasing a trade deficit.

If the economy is operating at less than full potential, neither type of deficit financing should generate more than minor and transitory inflation, though "crowding out" could occur. More government expenditure as financed by bond sales to the private sector would bring a net increase in aggregate demand. As before, no change in the money supply occurs. Also as before, if the public held their desired amount of government debt prior to the

---

(SCF) and the Rapid Credit Facility (RCF). The ECF has replaced the Poverty Reduction and Growth Facility (PRGF).

bond sale, the new issues must be at a higher interest rate, creating an upward pressure on private interest rates, and depressing private investment expenditure. The net change in aggregate demand would be positive and less than the increase in public expenditure unless private investment is extremely interest rate elastic, which is extremely unlikely in the sub-Saharan region. Financing the expenditure by direct borrowing from the central bank would not require a higher bond rate. The increase in aggregate demand would equal the increase in public expenditure, and monetizing the deficit generates an increase in the money supply sufficient to circulate the increased output that results from more public expenditure.

Few sub-Saharan countries have sufficiently developed bond markets to allow for effective open market operations. In the absence of an effective secondary bond market the major motivation of commercial banks to hold public bonds is statutory requirements on the composition of reserves. This implies that high interest rates are required to induce banks to purchase bonds beyond their legal obligation. The absence of a secondary market and the prevalence of high yields on public bonds mean that financing deficits by bond sales has the perverse effect of discouraging commercial banks from funding productive investments, which are riskier than holding government securities.[19] A second major effect of high interest rates is to increase the cost of servicing the domestic public debt.

With the economy well below its potential, monetizing the deficit is an effective tool for the expansion of aggregate demand, generating neither inflation nor "crowding out" of private expenditure. The government's expenditures on infrastructure could be consciously designed to "crowd in" private investment by lowering costs of transport, electricity and water supply.[20] In many African countries, Zambia for example, the increased cost of servicing the public debt as a result of bond sales should be a greater concern than inflation or "crowding out".

---

[19] This process is discussed in detail for Zambia (in Weeks et. al. 2006). This effect represents what might be called "bank squeezing out". The typical use of the term "crowding out" refers to a fall in private investment resulting from government borrowing that pushes up interest rates. More relevant in sub-Saharan countries is the decision by private banks not to lend because the risk-adjusted return on public bonds is greater than that for lending to private non-financial borrowers. The return on public bonds is high because of the oligopsonistic power of private banks in sub-Saharan countries.

[20] An example is the repair of the Bumbuna hydroelectric site, which could greatly reduce power cuts and the need for private generators in Sierra Leone, especially in Freetown.

3.2 Exchange Rate Management

Fiscal expansion, by increasing output and private demand, will increase imports and generate a trade deficit or make an existing deficit larger. This is one of the problems that undermined the use of active fiscal policy in developing countries in the past and has discredited it as an instrument of macro management, especially in Latin America in the 1970s. Exchange rate depreciation or devaluation can be used to counter the tendency of fiscal expansion to create an unsustainable trade balance.

Thus, depreciation or devaluation is an intended part of a countercyclical policy, and it causes a rise in the domestic price level equal to at least the "pass-through rate" (marginal propensity to import) times the change in the nominal exchange rate. While necessary and intended, this exchange rate-induced increase in the price level creates the risk of destabilizing inflation if the nominal devaluation is large. Managing this risk is an essential part of a successful active fiscal policy.

As fashion moved against active fiscal policy over the last three decades, there was a shift to a view that "flexible" exchange rates were the only practical policy choice for governments. Therefore, it is necessary to explain why exchange rate management by African governments would be both feasible and possible as part of policy to counter the global crisis.[21] In practice almost all governments intervene in foreign exchange markets.[22] The policy choice is not between "fixed" and "flexible" exchange rate regimes, but in the selection of the most appropriate point on a range of forms and degrees of intervention in the context of the characteristics of the economy (Fischer 2001). Governments and central banks repeatedly shift between "flexible" and "fixed" exchange rates.[23] Any time a central bank intervenes to moderate the

---

[21] An argument in favor of a return to managed exchange rates is found in Rolnick and Webber (1989), who write, "[W]e maintain there is a convincing case that a fixed exchange rate system is feasible and should be established. Theory shows it feasible, and overlooked empirical evidence shows it possible."

[22] The IMF categorizes countries by the exchange rate regime, and the Annual Report for 2007 lists only thirty-five out of over 150 as having an "independently floating" exchange rate. Only two were in the sub-Saharan region, Democratic Republic of Congo and Somalia. The listing of the latter seems an anomaly because Somalia has no government and no currency. Another anomaly is the absence of Sierra Leone from the table.

[23] Exchange rate management is treated in Rolnick and Webber (1989) and in Bartolini and Prati (1997). An IMF Staff Paper from the 1970s shows how much the conventional wisdom has moved against exchange rate management (Lipschitz 1978).

rise or fall of the national currency it is "fixing" the exchange rate, however briefly.

The exchange rate management that would be part of the proposed stimulus package would not seek to maintain a "fixed" rate for the domestic currency against any foreign currency. The purpose of the intervention would be to control the rate of depreciation of the national currency against the currencies of major trading partners in order to prevent a widening of the trade gap as the economy expanded and to prevent an excessive weakening of the domestic currency that would stimulate unmanageable inflation. The exchange rate managers would face two possible contexts, one in which the fiscal expansion is not accompanied by a "weakening" of the currency and another in which fiscal expansion automatically provokes depreciation.[24]

The *devaluation case* occurs if there is no market pressure to weaken the national currency as public expenditure increases. The government must act directly on the exchange rate to raise the price of tradables, which will reduce import demand and raise the return to exporters. The mechanism for exchange rate management will differ with the characteristics of financial and foreign exchange markets in each country. In effect, the government would temporarily be implementing a "crawling peg" exchange rate regime. The *depreciation case* occurs if the fiscal expansion is accompanied by market pressure with the effect to weaken the currency. While the market pressure to weaken the exchange rate serves the government's purpose of increasing competitiveness, intervention is potentially necessary to prevent the currency from depreciating at a rate that generates unmanageable inflation pressures.[25]

In summary, the exchange rate can be an effective policy instrument for supporting a fiscal stimulus, being especially important if monetary policy is ineffective. This effectiveness is limited by potential inflationary effects. However, for many governments in the sub-Saharan region exchange rate policy is precluded by currency arrangements, as discussed in the next section.

---

[24] The well-known Fleming-Mundell model predicts that a fiscal expansion would result in exchange rate appreciation. That analysis is not relevant to most of Africa because the countries have no significant level of portfolio flows due to lack of the necessary financial institutions. Theoretical problems in the model are discussed in Weeks 2009b.

[25] Exchange rate management in Zambia is discussed in detail in Weeks *et. al.* (2007)

4 Feasibility of a Fiscal Stimulus

If a government could effectively use all its policy instruments the design of the stimulus package would follow the standard textbook prescription: an increase in expenditures or a reduction in taxes would provide the principle demand stimulus; the exchange rate would be managed to prevent deterioration in the external current account; and the fiscal deficit would be financed in part or entirely by public bond sales to the private sector to prevent excessive money growth. For countries that export exchange rate-inelastic commodities, such as petroleum, currency adjustment would affect only imports.

However, the policy options facing the governments of the sub-Saharan countries are considerably more restricted than this, as Annex Tables 1-4 show. If we ignore the restrictions set by donors and lenders, policy space in the sub-Saharan region is restricted by two types of constraints, institutional and economic ones. As the first column of Annex Table 1 shows, very few countries in the region have the basic institutions to implement monetary policy. As summarized in Annex Table 2, seventeen countries were part of a common currency zone (fourteen) or operated with an inflexible link to the South African Rand (three). Of the twenty-nine countries with national currencies, in eighteen of these governments did not issue bonds, or have issued bonds but no formal bond market existed.[26] For the region as a whole, only eleven of almost fifty countries had secondary bond markets, and only South Africa had an effective and relatively efficient bond resale market.[27] For practical purposes, monetary instruments are of little use in the sub-Saharan region except for a few countries.

Though less limited than monetary policy, exchange rate adjustment is not available to a substantial number of sub-Saharan governments, because, as noted above, fourteen have a common currency (Franc CFA). Three more have chosen to maintain a strict link to the Rand within the Common Monetary Area (CMA). Of the remaining twenty-seven countries, eight operated with adjustable fixed exchange rates and nineteen with managed or "flexible" rates. The majority of these twenty-seven had no bond markets in which sterilization operations could be implemented. For several of the twenty-seven

---

[26] The most accessible source for information on monetary institutions and financial markets in Africa is the Wharton Financial Institutions Center of the University of Pennsylvania, which provides recent reports on almost all countries. See http://fic.wharton.upenn.edu. For countries in Africa not covered in Wharton studies, websites of central banks were used.

[27] For example, the government of Zambia issues bonds and the Bank of Zambia conducts open market operations. However, the market for these bonds is narrow, limited to a few expatriate banks (Weeks, *et. al.* 2006, Chapter 6).

countries, exports would be exchange rate-insensitive (e.g., Angola and Nigeria, as petroleum exporters).

With regard to fiscal policy (Annex Table 3), the countries of the West African Economic and Monetary Union (WAEMU) and of the Central African Economic and Monetary Community (CAEMC) (together forming the so-called CFA zone) had restrictions on fiscal operations that required the governments to balance the annual current budget. The capital budget could be in deficit if the method of finance were specified. While this arrangement does not exclude a fiscal stimulus, in practice it greatly restricts it. The *sine qua non* of countercyclical intervention is that it can be initiated and terminated quickly in response to demand shocks. Capital expenditures lack this flexibility.

In addition to these primary institutional constraints on policy tools, there are the secondary ones stressed by the IMF, such as the performance indicators. Some initial conditions would be so unfavorable as to render a stimulus package unwise because it would generate macro instability rather than recovery. In general, a stimulus policy should be consistent with a sustainable fiscal balance, manageable external current account, and an inflation rate which is not destabilizing. The initial values of these variables, which are consistent with macroeconomic stability, will be dependent on the structural and behavioral characteristics of each economy and the size of the stimulus to be implemented. In this context, the most important behavioral characteristics are the exchange rate elasticity of trade, the propensity to import, the income elasticity of public revenues, and the degree of structural inflation.

On the basis of the average import propensity and the inflation rates for the region, and assuming low elasticities of trade and public revenues, the following performance guidelines are proposed. Prior to the implementation of the stimulus package,

1. The fiscal balance, after concessional finance (Official Development Assistance/ODA), should not exceed five percent of GDP;
2. The external current account deficit should be covered by ODA, and the foreign exchange reserves should be at least at the level of three months of imports; and
3. The inflation rates should not exceed fifteen percent per annum except in the case of a fiscal surplus.

Annex Table 4 combines these performance constraints with the previously discussed institutional limits on policy implementation to identify the stimulus packages that would be feasible in the sub-Saharan region. Whether it would be appropriate to do so requires individual country analysis. For eighteen countries it would be feasible to implement a combined fiscal expansion and exchange rate management package. Despite its high inflation rate of eighteen percent, Angola is included in this group because of the country's large fiscal and current account surpluses.

In most of these countries it would be possible to finance the increased public expenditures by bond sales because of functioning financial markets. For some, for example Angola, Comoros, Gambia, and Tanzania, it would be necessary to monetize the increase in the fiscal deficit. With the exception of South Africa, in none of the countries is it likely that foreign exchange operations by the central bank would be a safe method of exchange rate management.

The practicality of implementing a stimulus is verified by three of these countries initiating such packages in 2009 or 2010.[28] The IMF supported the countercyclical intervention in Mozambique, even though the government's fiscal deficit was over three percent of GDP and the external current account balance was almost minus nine percent of GDP. Almost all the countries in Annex Table 1 that would use both fiscal policy and exchange rate instruments had smaller negative balances after considering ODA inflows.

For six countries exchange rate management would not be possible due to currency arrangements, but their fiscal and current account balances allow for fiscal expansion (see Annex Table 4). Fiscal expansion would threaten neither internal nor external stability. In ten countries a fiscal expansion would require external concessionary finance because of limits on deficit financing. In ten other countries the performance indicators do not justify a stimulus policy.

To summarize, in twenty-four of the forty-four countries, over half, a domestically financed fiscal stimulus package would be feasible and justified by the most recent performance indicators. The performance indicators for ten more countries do not preclude a stimulus, but it would require external assistance because of the current account impact in the context of exchange rate inflexibility. Ten countries require stabilization programs to move towards internal and external balance before a stimulus would be sustainable.

5 Conclusions and Policy Recommendations: Acting on and Overcoming the Constraints on Macro Policy in the Medium to Long-Term

In this contribution the potential of fiscal stimulus packages had been outlined, by analyzing the framework for more independent macro policies and effective recovery programs in Africa (section 2), by highlighting the policy

[28] These are Sierra Leone (Weeks 2009d), Mozambique (IMF 2009c), and Nigeria (Alabi and Adams 2010).

constraints of countercyclical fiscal policy and the analytical base for fiscal stimulus packages (section 3), and by identifying the feasibility of countercyclical fiscal action in countries of the Africa region.

There are severe constraints. The low level of development of financial institutions renders monetary policy ineffective in the vast majority of the sub-Saharan countries. Common currency arrangements further limit the policy options of many governments. In some countries policy options are further limited by the size of the fiscal deficit, the current account imbalance, the low level of foreign exchange reserves, and the high inflation rate.

However, as the Freetown Declaration of African finance ministers stated, these constraints limit but do not preclude purposeful policy in which governments of the region assert themselves as agents of short term recovery and of long term development. For a few governments active policy intervention can be done through a balance of all the standard instruments, fiscal, monetary, and exchange rate policy. For a majority of countries fiscal policy with domestic deficit financing can be used to re-commission the public sector as an agent of change. In three-quarters of the countries purposeful action is consistent with macro stability.

However, the governments need donors and the IMF to grant "policy space" through the following measures, specified in the Freetown Declaration:

1) Elimination of the pro-cyclical conditionalities and "benchmarks" for deficit limits, inflation rates, external borrowing, and foreign exchange holdings (all explicit in the Declaration);

2) Donor reliability on delivery of assistance is needed because the stimulus policies will be "finely tuned", and late or non-delivery of assistance could provoke macroeconomic instability; and, more generally,

3) a suspension of the "business as usual" approach to negotiations over development assistance is needed which emphasizes "reform" issues that the current external crisis has rendered of less immediate importance.

The combination of a carefully calibrated stimulus policy and of donor flexibility offers the firm prospect of overcoming the potentially serious effects of the external shocks from the international financial crisis. While a stimulus package involves risks, they are minor compared to the certain effect of the global recession on poverty and public welfare. By managing the crisis in this way, lessons for the future can be learned.

References

Alabi, Reuben Adeolu and Oshobugie Ojor Adams (2010), 'Achievement of the Millennium Development Goals and the Global Financial Crisis', paper presented to the International Conference on The Impact of the Global Financial Crisis on Economic Reform Processes in Africa, Bremen, January 2010

AfDB/African Development Bank (2009), Impact of the Crisis on African Economies – Sustaining Growth and Poverty Reduction: African Perspectives and Recommendations to the G20, A Report from the Committee of African Finance Ministers and Central Bank Governors established to monitor the crisis, Tunis-Belvedère: African Development Bank/AfDB

Bartolini, Leonardo, and Alessandro Prati (1997), 'Soft versus Hard Targets for Exchange Rate Intervention', in: Economic Policy 12, pp. 13-52

BWP/Bretton Woods Project (2009), 'IMF advice paradox: increase social spending, but contain deficits', Bretton Woods Update 67

CAG/Caucus of African Governors to the Bretton Woods Institutions, CAG (2009), Freetown Declaration, Freetown, Sierra Leone, August (document available from the web site of the Ministry of Finance and Economic Development of Sierra Leone)

Fischer, Stanley (2001), 'Exchange Rate Regimes: Is the Bipolar View Correct?', in: Finance and Development 38, 2, pp. 1-26

International Monetary Fund (2007), Annual Report 2007, Washington: IMF.

International Monetary Fund (2009a) The Implications of the Global Financial Crisis for Low-Income Countries, Washington: IMF

International Monetary Fund (2009b), Sierra Leone: 2008 Article IV Consultation, Third Review Under the Three–Year Arrangement Under the Poverty Reduction and Growth Facility, Financing Assurances Review, and Requests for Waivers of Non-observance of Performance Criteria, Augmentation of Access, and Modification of Performance Criterion — Staff Report; Public Information Notice and Press Release on the Executive Board Discussion; and Statement by the Executive Director for Sierra Leone, IMF Country Report No. 09/2 (Washington D.C.: IMF)

International Monetary Fund (2009c), World Economic Outlook Update, Washington: IMF

International Monetary Fund (2009d), IMF Mission Calls for Fiscal Stimulus in Mozambique, Press Release No. 09/165, May 13

Leijonhufvud, Axel (1968), On Keynesian Economics and the Economics of Keynes, New York: Oxford University Press

Lipschitz, Leslie (1978), Exchange Rate Policies for Developing Countries: Some Simple Arguments for Intervention, IMF Staff Papers 25, 4, pp. 650-675

MoFED-EPRU/Ministry of Finance & Economic Development, Economic Policy & Research Unit Sierra Leone, MoFED-EPRU (2009), IMF PRGF - 4th. Review: Note on Impact of the Financial Crisis & Global Recession on Sierra Leone, Freetown: MoFED

Rolnick, Arthur J., and Warren E. Webber (1989), Case for Fixing Exchange Rates, The Federal Reserve Bank of Minneapolis Annual Reports, Minneapolis: FRB of Minneapolis,

http://www.minneapolisfed.org/publications_papers/pub_display.cfm?id=677

Stiglitz, Joseph (1998), More Instruments and Broader Goals: Moving Toward the Post-Washington Consensus, Helsinki: WIDER

United Nations (2009), World Economic Situation and Prospects 2009, New York: United Nations

Weeks, John (1989), A Critique of Neoclassical Macroeconomics, New York and London: St. Martins and Macmillan, revised 2010 as False Paradigm: A Critique of Neoclassical Macroeconomics, forthcoming

Weeks, John (2009a), Enhancing the effectiveness of fiscal policy for domestic resources mobilization, paper prepared for the United Nations Economic Commission for Africa, Ad-hoc Expert Group meeting on Financing for Development and Fiscal Policy in Africa, Abuja, Nigeria, February 2009

Weeks, John (2009b), The Effectiveness of Monetary Policy Reconsidered, PERI Working Paper 202 (Amherst, Mass: Political Economy Research Institute/PERI)

Weeks, John (2009c), Global Crisis and Africa - Responses, Lessons Learnt and the Way Forward, Keynote address to the African Governors of the IMF, World Bank and African Development Bank, Freetown, 12-13 August 2009

Weeks, John (2009d), The Impact of the Global Financial Crisis on the Economy of Sierra Leone: A Report for UNDP Freetown and the Ministry of Finance and Economic Development, Republic of Sierra Leone, Freetown: United Nations Development Programme/UNDP

Weeks, John (2009e), How Fiscal Policies in Africa Can Respond to the Global Financial Crisis, Development Viewpoint 37, London: Centre for Development Policy and Research/CDPR

Weeks, John, Victoria Chisala, Alemayehu Geda, Hulya Dagdeviren, Terry McKinley, Alfredo Saad-Filho, and Carlos Oya (2006), Economic Policies for Growth, Employment and Poverty Reduction: Case Study of Zambia, Lusaka: UNDP and Mission Press

Weeks, John, Shruti Patel, Allan C. K. Mukungu, and Venkatesh Seshamani (2007), Kwacha Appreciation, 2005-2006: Implications for the Zambian Economy, Lusaka: UNDP

Weeks, John, and Rathin Roy (2003), Making Fiscal Policy Work for the Poor, New York: UNDP

WB/World Bank (2009), Swimming Against the Tide: How developing countries are coping with the global crisis, Background Paper prepared by World Bank Staff for the G20 Finance Ministers and Central Bank Governors Meeting, Horsham, United Kingdom, held on March 13-14, 2009, Washington D.C.: World Bank

WB/World Bank, Various years, World Bank data base World Development Indicators, Washington D.C.: World Bank

Annex Table 1a: Policy Tools, Late 2000s

Country	Monetary policy	Fiscal policy	Exchange rate pol.
Angola	NSM		Managed
Benin	NCB	Constrained	WAEMU
Botswana	NSM		Managed
Burkina Faso	NCB	Constrained	WAEMU
Burundi	NSM		Managed
Cameroon	NCB		CAEMC
Cape Verde	LSM		Fixed (Euro)
Cen Afr Rep	NCB		CAEMC
Chad	NCB		CAEMC
Comoros	NSM		Fixed (Euro)
Congo DR	NSM		Managed
Congo, Rep	NCB		CAEMC
Cote d'Ivoire	NCB	Constrained	WAEMU
Eq Guinea	NCB		CAEMC
Eritrea	NSM		Fixed (US$)
Ethiopia	NSM		Managed
Gabon	NCB		CAEMC
Gambia	NSM		Managed
Ghana	LSM		Managed
Guinea	NSM		Fixed (US$)
Guinea-B	NCB	Constrained	WAEMU
Kenya	LSM		Managed
Lesotho	CMA		CMA (rand)
Liberia	NSM		Fixed (US$)
Madagascar	LSM		Managed
Malawi	LSM		Managed
Mali	NCB	Constrained	WAEMU
Mauritania	NSM		Managed
Mauritius	LSM		Fixed (basket)
Mozambique	NSM		Managed
Namibia	LSM		CMA (rand)
Niger	NCB	Constrained	WAEMU
Nigeria	LSM		Managed
Rwanda	LSM		Managed
Senegal	NCB	Constrained	WAEMU
Seychelles	NSM		Fixed (basket)
Sierra Leone	NSM		Managed
South Africa	ESM		Managed
Sudan	NSM		Managed
Swaziland	NSM, CMA		CMA (rand)
Tanzania	NSM		Managed
Togo	NCB	Constrained	WAEMU
Uganda	LSM		Managed
Zambia	LSM		Managed
Totals	Feasible monetary policy 12/44	Feasible fiscal policy 37/44	Feasible exchange rate policy 27/44

Annex Table 1b: Macroeconomic Indicators, Late 2000s

Country	Fiscal deficit	Crr Acc deficit	Forex reserves	ODA/ GDP	Inflation
Angola	6.5	19.3	4.2	0.9	18.2
Benin	-0.2	-5.0	7.0	8.3	4.5
Botswana	11.4	18.4	21.3	0.7	14.5
Burkina Faso	-5.0	-11.2	na	13.9	2.1
Burundi	-1.9	-13.7	4.1	46.8	13.5
Cameroon	4.1	-1.7	5.0	9.4	1.8
Cape Verde	-2.2	-10.2	3.3	11.7	4.3
Cen Afr Rep	-0.5	-8.2	na	8.8	3.6
Chad	-1.9	-2.0	na	6.5	10.7
Comoros	-2.0	-5.0	na	7.8	3.7
Congo DR	-2.0	-26.4	na	21.5	18.1
Congo, Rep	6.0	-8.0	3.4	3.3	7.5
Cote d'Ivoire	-1.1	1.1	2.8	1.3	5.4
Eq Guinea	21.0	5.7	na	0.6	19.9
Eritrea	-30.0	-12.0	na	17.4	17.5
Ethiopia	-7.6	-8.2	2.1	13.7	16.8
Gabon	14.8	11.0	2.4	0.5	9.7
Gambia	0.5	-10.5	4.3	14.3	3.8
Ghana	-7.3	-11.3	3.2	8.5	5.8
Guinea	-3.3	-8.0	na	5.4	18.0
Guinea-B	-19.1	2.4	na	28.9	5.8
Kenya	-2.6	-3.5	3.7	4.5	9.0
Lesotho	8.7	8.5	4.8	4.7	7.9
Liberia	0.3	-28.5	0.6	80.2	12.8
Madagascar	-2.6	-10.0	2.7	14.8	12.3
Malawi	-2.5	-5.5	na	21.0	13.4
Mali	8.0	-6.2	4.6	14.2	6.1
Mauritania	-5.0	-20.0	na	10.2	15.1
Mauritius	-2.7	-8.8	3.5	0.6	7.3
Mozambique	-3.4	-9.9	3.8	23.5	8.5
Namibia	-4.5	11.2	3.2	2.1	10.6
Niger	12.5	-8.0	3.3	14.1	5.1
Nigeria	0.9	-5.3	9.5	1.7	9.6
Rwanda	-0.2	15.0	6.8	22.2	11.7
Senegal	-1.5	-10.4	3.6	8.2	4.9
Seychelles	-1.8	-16.3	0.9	0.8	4.2
Sierra Leone	-5.0	-8.6	4.3	29.4	11.7
South Africa	1.5	-7.4	na	0.3	9.0
Sudan	-0.4	-10.1	1.5	6.1	10.4
Swaziland	-2.8	-4.8	2.8	1.8	6.2
Tanzania	-3.5	-9.6	5.3	13.7	10.9
Togo	-3.4	-15.3	2.1	4.2	1.8
Uganda	-1.0	-5.9	6.9	14.7	3.6
Zambia	-1.1	3.8	3.1	14.2	13.3

Sources: Monetary institutions: Wharton Financial Institutions Center of the University of Pennsylvania, all but Mauritius, Namibia, Nigeria and Seychelles, and http://www.afdb.org/en/news-events/article/donor-workshop-on-african-bond-market-4443/. Economic indicators: World Bank, World Development Indicators 2009 and IMF country reports.

Notes to Table 1: Countries omitted due to incomplete data: Djibouti, Sao Tome and Principle, Somalia, and Zimbabwe. Shaded cells indicate values or characteristics that restrict policy options. Indicators (2006-07 or last two years that were available): Fiscal deficit is the cash deficit as a percentage of GDP. Crr Acc deficit is the current account of the balance of payments as percentage of GDP. Forex reserves are central bank holdings of foreign exchange, measured in months of imports. ODA/GDP is official development assistance (OECD definition) as percentage of GDP. Inflation is the annual rate of change of the GDP deflator. The final row in 1a gives the number of countries out of the total for which each policy instrument is feasible. Fiscal expansion is judged as not feasible if: the fiscal deficit exceeds the share of ODA in GDP by more than five percentage points; the current account deficit exceeds the ODA share by more than five percentage points; foreign exchange reserves are less than three months of imports; and/or inflation rate exceeds fifteen percent.

Acronyms: The so-called CFA franc zone is the West African Economic and Monetary Union (WAEMU, with the countries being member Benin, Burkina Faso, Cote d'Ivoire, Guinea-Bissau, Mali, Niger, Senegal, and Togo). In addition to a common currency the governments of these countries are constrained to balance the current account of the public budget. The capital account can have a deficit if the method of funding the deficit is specified. The Central African Economic and Monetary Community (CAEMC, with the countries being member Cameroon, Central African Republic, Chad, Republic of Congo, Equatorial Guinea, and Gabon) also has a common currency with a fixed parity to the euro. Both currencies are commonly called the CFA franc. They are not freely interchangeable, except via euro convertibility that is guaranteed by the French Treasury, which holds at least sixty-five percent of the pooled reserves of each area. CMA is the Common Monetary Area, with the currency Rand (South Africa, Lesotho, Namibia, and Swaziland). NCB is for a country with no central bank, including countries sharing a common central bank. NSM is meaning that there is "no secondary market", which includes cases in which the government does not issue bonds, issues them but does not sell them on the open market, or sells them but there is no secondary (or resale) market. LSM is meaning "limited secondary market" and refers to the number of buyers and sellers. ESM is meaning "effective secondary market". Fiscal deficit includes grants and other revenue on income side.

Annex Table 2: Sub-Saharan Countries, Monetary Institutions, 2010

Category	Notes
Common Currency	(17) WAEMU, CAEMC/BEAC, CMA
National currency	(27) fixed or managed
No bond market	(16) no bonds or no re-sale market
Bond market	(11) formal re-sale market
Narrow	(10) usually commercial banks only
Effective	(1) South Africa

Note: Franc BEAC (Banque Des Etats De L'Afrique Centrale)

Annex Table 3: Sub-Saharan Countries, Exchange Rate Regimes, 2010

Category	Notes
Common Currency	(17) WAEMU, CAEMC/BEAC, CMA
Single currency, fixed	(8) US$ (3), Euro (2), basket (3), 3 with bond market
Single currency, managed	(19) 8 with bond market

Note: Franc BEAC (Banque Des Etats De L'Afrique Centrale)

Annex Table 4: Sub-Saharan Countries, Fiscal Policy Summary, Late 2000s

Category	Countries
1. Excluded from domestic financing because constrained to balance current budget	(14) Benin, Burkina Faso, Cote d'Ivoire, Guinea-Bissau, Mali, Niger, Senegal, Togo, Cameroon, Central African Republic, Chad, Republic of Congo, Equatorial Guinea, Gabon
2. Excluded by fiscal deficit (Fiscal deficit - ODA) < (-5% GDP)*	(2) Eritrea, Ethiopia
3. Excluded by current account deficit (Current account - ODA) < zero*	(4) Guinea, Mauritania, Seychelles, Togo
4. Excluded by forex reserves (forex reserves) < (3 months of imports)	(3) Liberia, Madagascar, Sudan
5. Excluded by inflation rate (Inflation over 15%)*	(2) Angola, Congo DR
<u>Feasible</u>: Domestically financed fiscal expansion with exchange rate management	(18) Angola, Botswana, Burundi, Cape Verde, Comoros, Gambia, Ghana, Kenya, Malawi, Mauritius, **Mozambique**, **Nigeria**, Rwanda, **Sierra Leone**, South Africa, Tanzania, Uganda, Zambia
<u>Feasible:</u> Domestically financed fiscal expansion, no exchange rate management (fiscal surplus, strong current account)	(6) Cameroon, Eq Guinea, Gabon, Lesotho, Namibia, Swaziland
<u>Feasible:</u> Externally financed fiscal expansion, no exchange rate management	(10) Benin, Burkina Faso, Central African Republic, Chad, Congo Rep, Cote d'Ivoire, Guinea-Bissau, Mali, Niger, Senegal
<u>No stimulus feasible:</u> excluded by fiscal deficit, current account deficit, or inflation rate	(10) Eritrea, Ethiopia, Guinea, Mauritania, Seychelles, Togo, Liberia, Madagascar, Sudan, Congo DR

Notes: Countries in "bold" initiated fiscal stimulus programs in 2009 or 2010.
*Countries in previous categories excluded.

The Implications of the Global Financial Crisis for African Countries' Export volumes and Value

Mareike Meyn and Jane Kennan*

Abstract

The global financial crisis (GFC) has not only resulted in downward growth rates and recession tendencies all over the world but also reduced global demand for African country products. African countries are heavily affected by trade as a transmission mechanism of the GFC since most of them are trade-dependent, open economies that export only a small range of products to few markets. In addition to declining prices and lower demand for some commodities, the GFC also aggravated the price volatility which has further increased the revenue uncertainty.

Even more heavily affected are those African countries hit by multiple effects of the crisis, many of which also fall into the first category of undiversified and highly export dependent economies. Other African ace multiple commodity shocks for more than 50% of their total export revenue and are also affected by declining revenue from tourism and remittances.

Although falling commodity prices have severe consequences for commodity-dependent exporters, they benefit importing African countries. Thus, the financial crisis has smoothed the effects of peaking fuel and food prices.

---

* Dr Mareike Meyn works as a Consultant on trade and private sector development for the GFA Consulting Group in Hamburg. Previously, she worked for two years as a Research Fellow in the area of international trade for the Overseas Development Institute (ODI) in London. She is specialized in the evaluation of regional and international trade agreements for trade in goods and trade in services.

Jane Kennan works as Research Officer for the International Economic Development Group (IEDG) of the Overseas Development Institute (ODI) in London. She is specialized in trade data analysis.

The paper is an updated and Africa-focussed version of the ODI Working Paper "The implications of the global financial crisis for developing countries' export volumes and values" by Mareike Meyn and Jane Kennan, June 2009, ODI: London.

Moreover, lower prices help to reduce inflation and to improve the competitiveness of producers, as the low value of the local currency might further stimulate consumption of domestically produced products at the expense of imports. At the same time, the depreciation of most African countries' currencies vis-à-vis the dollar has increased costs of external debts in the past months. Some countries that are dependent on trade tariffs for revenue also fear that the decreased demand for imports will severely affect resource mobility.

The paper discusses the different trade effects of the GFC and their implications for African economies. It further assesses African countries' options for national policy responses and pledges for a development-oriented international policy response to mitigate the effects of the GFC on African economies.

1 Introduction

The global financial crisis (GFC) has resulted in the deepest global recession since World War II. Past financial crises affecting developing countries have often been regional (with speculative attacks affecting a few countries and contagious effects spreading little beyond their neighbours), but the effects of the latest crisis are much more global: nearly all countries had been affected. For African countries, trade is a key a transmission mechanism, linking them to markets that are heavily affected by the financial crisis via changed terms of trade and export demand. The immediate trade effects visible in late 2008/early 2009 were that the resultant slump in demand had seriously affected main commodity prices, which have been reduced dramatically since their peaks in the first half of 2008.

This paper investigates which African countries and products had been affected most as a result of the global financial crisis (GFC) and what are possible national and international trade policy responses to mitigate the effects. After a secondary literature review of how trade is expected to respond in a crisis (Section 2), we undertake an empirical analysis of African countries' most relevant export products (Section 3). Price and volume trends were analysed to assess which products and countries have been most affected by the economic downturn. Section 4 analyses the policy implications for the most affected products and countries and discusses possible mitigation strategies on a national and international level.

2 Trade effects on prices and volumes in times of crises

In order to assess the implications of the GFC for African countries' trade it is important to start by asking what we should expect to see happening and to examine the extent to which these theoretical predictions proved correct in past crises.

Most African countries depend on the export of few commodities for the bulk of their export revenue. The elasticity of the commodity's demand in the importing country is therefore an essential element of how an economic crisis affects their export revenue.

Fuel and mining products are highly responsive to global GDP changes. A lower utilisation of production capacities translates directly into reduced demand for these products. Since the production of fuel and mining products is fixed in the short run, the oversupply depresses the price further.

Agriculture products are generally income inelastic; the more the good is a basic necessity, the lower its income elasticity of demand. This applies to agricultural products generally.

Many traditional agricultural exporters have diversified into non-traditional agricultural exports, such as exotic fruits and fresh vegetables, which are generally perceived to be less affected by volatility in terms of trade and to reap higher export revenues (AfDB, 2004). Similarly, traditional food items where value had been added, such as 'fair trade coffee' or 'organic cocoa', are less affected by volatile commodity prices. However, in times of crisis, the income elasticity for these 'luxury' agricultural items is higher than for basic crops and they are likely to be substituted by domestic goods or canned products. The deeper the crisis, the more likely it is that traditional agricultural products will also be affected by decreasing demand. Thus, the Asian crisis resulted in reduced demand for coffee, palm oil, rice, sugar, rubber, cocoa and tea (Boorman et al., 2000).

As for fuel and mining products, African countries' possible volume response for agricultural products is slow. Because of the nature of production countries are only able to respond to lower prices at the next harvest, which bears the risk of depressing prices further through supply overhangs.

African country manufactured goods, such as clothing, show an income elasticity of demand >1, i.e. a certain percentage decline of income in the export market will lead to a larger percentage decline in demand for manufactured goods. As discussed by UNCTAD (2002), the concentration on an outward-oriented industrialisation strategy based on simple manufactured exports carries a similar risk of fluctuating and deteriorating terms of trade, as the export of primary products because developing countries with large supply capacities are able to produce labour-intensive high-quality products at lower cost than are small developing countries. Subsequently, global competition for simple manufactured goods is very high, exerting a downward influence on prices and terms of trade.

An economic crisis affects developing country manufactured exports not only because of the high income elasticity of demand for manufactured products but also because of their high dependency on imported inputs. The sourcing of inputs for manufactured exports might be severely constrained by depreciated currencies and restrictive trade finance conditions, as experienced by South East Asian exporters of computer and electronic equipment during the 1997 crisis (Ernst, 1999; Boorman, 2000).

It needs to be borne in mind that the income elasticities of developing country exports depend not only on the composition of their export products but also on their destination. Virtually all fuel and mining exports go to unspecified world markets and are heavily dependent on changes in world GDP. For agricultural exports, however, it depends: Least Developed Countries (LDCs) and most ACP countries (to which all African countries belong) enjoy duty- and quota-free market (DFQF) access to the EU, where the agricultural market is regulated by the Common Agricultural Policy (CAP). Most EU agricultural products have price levels that are considerably above those on the world market and are stabilised by interventionist policies, which makes the EU an attractive export destination for LDC and ACP agro-exports.

In order to assess to what extent agro-commodity exporters are affected by a crisis it is therefore important to review the preferential price conditions they might enjoy for selected products (and volumes) in their main export market. Countries that do not enjoy any preferences and are directly affected by lower world market prices for their main commodities might respond by higher export volumes. However, as noted above, exporters of fuel/mining and agricultural products cannot expand their volumes immediately. And the ability of manufactures exporters to expand export volumes might be constrained by producers' high dependency on imported inputs. Generally, the expansion of export volumes in times of crisis runs the risk of resulting in a further worsening of the terms of trade. This is the case not only for primary commodities but also for simple manufactured products (UNCTAD, 2002).

Another possible policy response to declining commodity prices and lower demand would be the devaluation of the domestic currency vis-à-vis that of the major competitor in order to improve the export competitiveness of the commodity-exporting country and to raise the domestic value added of exports. This, however, also increases the price of imports and the costs of external debt.

3 Past, current and future effects: an empirical analysis of trade prices, volumes and values

Most African countries are highly dependent on few commodities for their export revenue. This section assesses how commodity prices developed in the past decade, how major African country exporters of these commodities responded to changing prices and how their unit prices developed. Based on these considerations and price projections for the near future, an analysis has been made of the commodities and countries most affected by the crisis.

3.1 Methodology

According to UNCTAD (2008), developing countries' main exports cover 242 products at the Standard International Trade Classification (SITC) 3-digit level. Selecting from these products only those that account for the bulk of African countries' total exports (such as the 'top 10') would run the risk of excluding small African countries which do not contribute significantly to total exports – but which are highly dependent on the respective commodity for total export revenue.

We therefore chose a range of mineral, agricultural and manufacturing products that form a significant proportion of total African country exports and contribute significantly to the total export revenue of individual African countries according to secondary literature sources. [1] These products are:

- metals and minerals: aluminium, copper, gold and crude oil;
- other raw materials: natural rubber;
- traditional agricultural commodities: cocoa, coffee, cotton, palm oil, rice and sugar;
- non-traditional agricultural products: vegetables and vegetable products, fruit and nuts, and flowers
- labour-intensive manufactured products: female woven clothing.

Based on this selection the section identifies:

a. which African countries are the main exporters of these products, and
b. which African countries are highly dependent on the export of these products.

---

1 UNCTAD (2008); WTO (2008); World Bank (2009a).

In a second step, we look at these countries' export volumes, export values and unit price developments for the specified products for the period 1998-2007. [2]

Unfortunately, it is not possible to assess monthly export volume and value trends by this exercise since countries report to the UN's Comtrade database only on an annual basis. However, by identifying (a) the latest price developments for major commodities; (b) the main developing country exporters and the most dependent developing country exporters; and (c) their export volumes, values and unit prices, we have been able to assess which countries are most at risk.

3.2 Metals and mineral: aluminium, copper, gold and oil

Demand for metals and minerals increased in the past decade due to global growth. However, the driving factor for increased prices was the lack of supply in these sectors. Mineral and oil companies have not invested in new capacities and have met the growing demand largely by reviving their idle capacities. When demand increased further at the beginning of the century supply could not keep up and prices increased (World Bank, 2009).

3.2.1 Aluminium

Aluminium prices increased by more than 30% in the period 2005 to 2007 to US$2,638/metric ton. Up to 2007 prices declined and the World Bank projected in early 2009 further price declines as a result of the GFC. However, this has not materialised. The current price[3] for aluminium is $2,235/metric ton and forecasts have been corrected, expecting new price peaks (see Figure 1).

China accounted for more than a third of global aluminium exports in the period 2005–7. South Africa is Africa's biggest and the world's third largest aluminium exporter accounting for 11% of global exports. Mozambique, the fourth most important exporter, is by far the most dependent exporter – with aluminium accounting for more than 60% of its total export revenue.

---

2 Where possible three-year average figures have been used. Where only one or two years' data were available, that was all that could be used.

3 All latest figures relate to January 2010 if not specified otherwise.

Figure 1. Aluminium: price developments 1997–Jan 2010 (US$/metric ton)

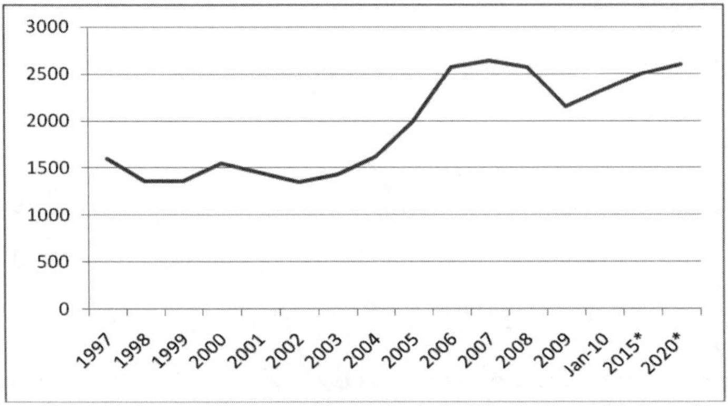

Sources: IFS data (up to 2005) and World Bank (2008, 2009, 2010) (including forecasts).

Mozambique was able to expand its export quantities in the period 2000–07 by an annual average of 49%; thus, heavily benefitting from the price increases. This boosted its export revenue by almost 400% every year (from just over US$4 thousand in 1999 to US$1,516 million in 2007). South Africa increased its volumes only slightly, which suggests that it was unable to respond to the booming aluminium prices. China, however, the largest aluminium producer and a net exporter, had the capacity to increase its supply by over 20% p.a., thus multiplying its benefits from high aluminium prices.

3.2.2 Copper (SITC 682)

Copper prices peaked in 2007 at US$7,118/metric ton, a 120% increase over the 2005 level. In the period 2007-2009 prices declined drastically and the World Bank expected the 2007 price to decline by 50% in 2010. However, global demand from the car and construction sector did not decline as projected and copper even reached a new price peak in January 2010 (see Figure 2). This high price is, however, not regarded as sustainable since China as the major consumer has stockpiled the commodity and its reduction in purchase will result in lower metal prices.

Chile, China and Peru are the biggest copper exporters in the world. The fourth biggest exporter, Zambia, is by far the most dependent economy: almost 68% of its export revenue is earned from copper.

Figure 2. Copper: price developments 1997–Jan. 2009 (US$/metric ton)

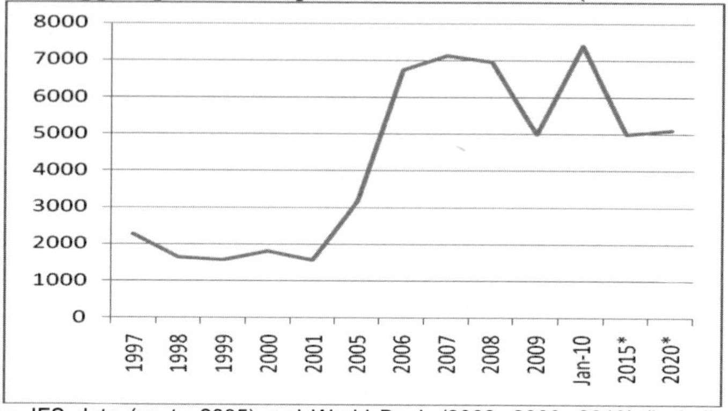

Sources: IFS data (up to 2005) and World Bank (2008, 2009, 2010) (including forecasts).

To date, the exporting countries' response to the commodity boom was limited. Despite the doubling of prices and very large increases in their unit values, both the major exporter (Chile) and the most dependent exporter (Zambia) increased their export volumes only moderately (by 4% and 6% p.a. respectively) in the period 1998–2007 which suggests capacity problems.

3.2.3 Gold (SITC 971)[4]

Gold prices reached their annual highest level in January 2010 at US$ 1,118/troy ounce – almost one third higher than at the start of the GFC. This new peak, which nobody expected, might be explained by investors' concerns about currency volatilities. For the future, prices are predicted to fall slightly but to remain at very high levels (see Figure 3).

Hong Kong and Peru are the main developing country exporters, accounting together for about 42% of global developing country gold exports. The least developed countries (LDCs) Mali, Burundi, Tanzania, and Ghana are the most dependent exporters, with gold accounting for between 32% (Ghana) and 72% (Mali) of their total export revenue.

While Peru and Hong Kong were able to respond to the price boom with increased volumes, Mali's and Ghana's exports declined. Burundi, Guinea and Niger also increased their export volumes (albeit from a very low level),

4 SITC 971 = Gold non-monetary excluding ore.

which suggests that African countries' ability to expand their gold exports is currently limited.

Figure 3. Gold: price developments 1997–Jan. 2010 (US$/troy ounce)

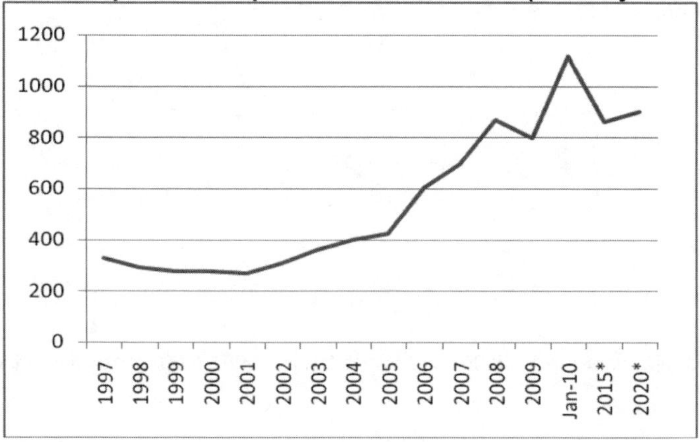

Sources: IFS data (up to 2005) and World Bank (2008, 2009, 2010) (including forecasts

3.2.4 Crude oil (SITC 333)

The price for crude oil increased by 100% in the period 2005–8, peaking at over US$140/barrel in mid-2008 (see Figure 4). The price decline in October 2008 due to falling US demand was only temporary; prices recovered to about US$ 77/barrel in January 2010 and are expected to stay at about this level. The main explanatory factors for this forecast are continued high demand, high production costs of new supplies and political instabilities in the major supplying countries (World Bank, 2008c: 52). So far we have not seen sufficient policy and technological changes that would have made alternative energy resources sufficiently competitive and would have a lasting negative impact on the price for crude oil.

Angola and Nigeria are the fifth and sixth largest oil exporters respectively. Both are highly dependent on oil, which accounts for 93% of total export revenue in case of Nigeria. [5] There are also some small African oil exporters, which are, however, still very dependent on oil as export revenue, such as Gabon, Algeria and Cameroon.

[5] Angola does not report its trade to Comtrade.

Figure 4. Crude oil: price developments (average spot) 1997–Jan. 2010 (US$/barrel)

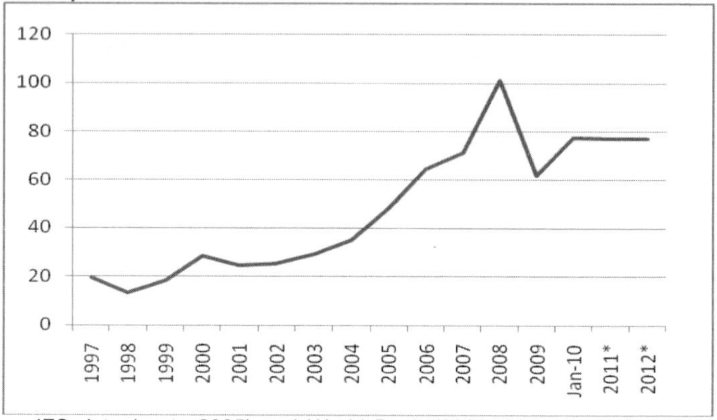

Sources: IFS data (up to 2005) and World Bank (2008, 2009, 2010) (including forecasts).

3.3 Traditional agricultural commodities: Cocoa, coffee, cotton, and sugar

3.3.1 Cocoa (SITC 072)

Cocoa prices have experienced two recent peaks: one in 2009 at US$2.89 and one in January 2010 at US$3.52. Both price peaks were driven by speculations and port disruptions in Côte d'Ivoire. The main producers have responded to the high prices by expanded production. The World Bank forecasts that production will expand more rapidly than demand. Thus, prices are expected to decline to 2006 price level in 2015 (see Figure 5).

The biggest exporters, Côte d'Ivoire and Ghana, are (together with the small exporter São Tomé) also the most dependent ones with cocoa accounting for about 30% of total export revenue (and almost 90% in case of São Tomé). For the other two large cocoa exporters, Indonesia and Malaysia, cocoa accounts only for a marginal share of total export revenues.

While Ghana and Indonesia took advantage of increasing cocoa prices and expanded their export volumes this was not possible for Côte d'Ivoire due to political instability.

Figure 5. Cocoa: price developments 1997–Jan. 2010 (US$ cent/kg)

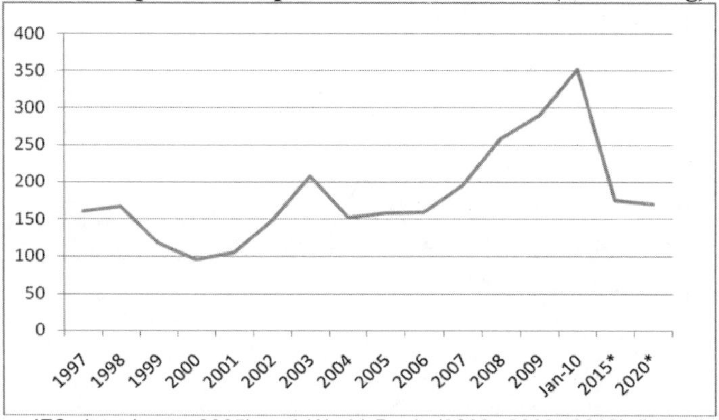

Sources: IFS data (up to 2005) and World Bank (2008, 2009, 2010) (including forecasts).

3.3.2 Coffee (SITC 071)

Coffee prices increased by more than 50% (Arabica) and almost 100% (Robusta) in the period 2005–8 (Figure 6). The price increase reflects a decrease in global production due to poor weather conditions for the main producers, Brazil and Vietnam, during the harvest 2006/07. However, global crop production has recovered in the meanwhile and is expected to increase constantly. As a result of this increased production output, the World Bank expects prices to fall to about the 2006 level by 2020.

Brazil, Colombia and Vietnam account together for almost 60% of developing country coffee exports. The countries that are highly dependent on coffee exports are largely (very) small exporters from Africa, namely Sierra Leone, Ethiopia, Rwanda, Burundi and Uganda. For these countries, coffee exports account for between 23% (Uganda) and 86% (Sierra Leone) of total export revenue.

Figure 6. Coffee: price developments 2000–Jan. 2010 (US cent/kg)

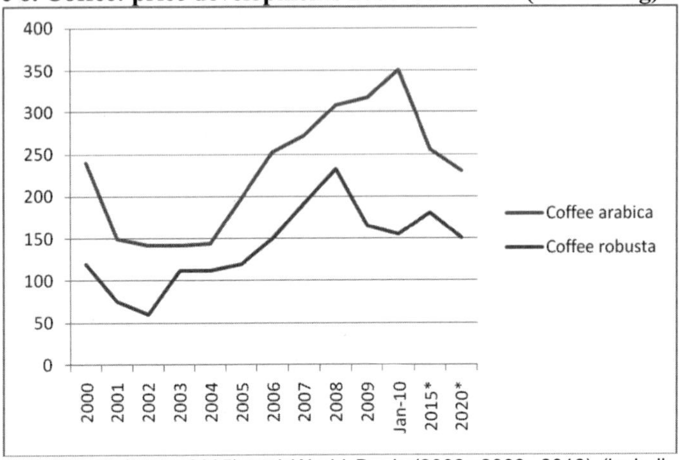

Sources: IFS data (up to 2005) and World Bank (2008, 2009, 2010) (including forecasts).

3.3.3 Cotton (SITC 263)

Cotton prices have been more volatile than most other commodities in the past decade and have also increased less markedly in the period 2005–8. The price increase (from about US$0.80/kg in 1997 to US$1.57 in 2008) can be explained by a 40% reduction in US plantings, and thus exports. The US is the world's second largest cotton producer (after China) and exports around half of its heavily subsidised production.

Global cotton production is expected to decrease due to a decline in cotton producing areas. However, the reduced production will meet a stagnant supply so that the World Bank expects prices to decline slightly further (see Figure 7).

West African cotton producers supply only about 20% of developing country cotton exports but the commodity is of great importance for them, accounting for almost 70% of the total export revenue of Burkina Faso and Benin. However, traditional West African cotton producers have been hardly able to benefit from rising prices, for Togo and Mali export volumes have even decreased. India and Brazil on the other hand increased their cotton exports more than tenfold in the period 2004–7, thus becoming the biggest developing country cotton exporters in one decade, each having exported virtually no cotton in 1998.

Due to the increasing growing of genetically modified (GM) cotton by India and Brazil (and the US), these countries were able to expand exports and to achieve higher unit prices than West African countries which have to rely on conventional production and are therefore more dependent on external conditions. The increased use of GM technology is expected to increase the outputs of the largest cotton exporters further, which will contribute to the downward pressure on cotton prices (World Bank, 2008a).

Figure 7. Cotton: price developments 1997–Jan. 2010 (US cent/kg)

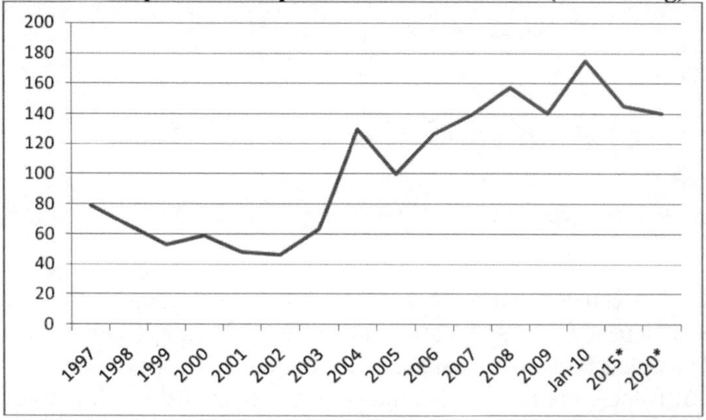

Sources: IFS data (up to 2005) and World Bank (2008, 2009, 2010) (including forecasts).

3.3.4 Sugar (SITC 061)

The free market sugar price has been greatly affected by global subsidies and protectionist measures. Still, the free market sugar price showed an 88% increase in the period 2005–8 and a further 48% price increase in the period 2008-January 2010, reaching a new peak of US$0.58/kg (see Figure 8). This reflects declining production in the EU as well as the rising oil prices which encouraged Brazil (the world's largest sugar producer) to shift some production from cane sugar to ethanol. With the falling oil price, it is expected that the demand for ethanol will decrease, which might result in increased sugar production by Brazil, thus depressing the sugar price. However, the World Bank expects the stabilisation of sugar prices at 2009 level in the medium term, though future policy processes (such as the reform of the EU Common Sugar Market) might distort these forecasts.

Figure 8: Free market raw sugar: Price developments 2000–Jan. 2010 (US$ cent/kg)

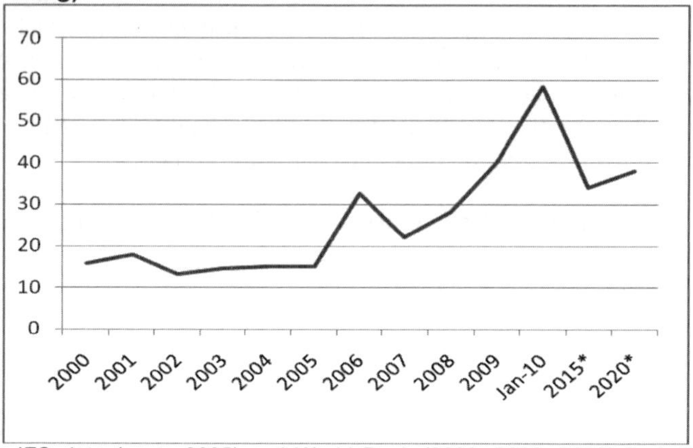

Sources: IFS data (up to 2005) and World Bank (2008, 2009, 2010) (including forecasts).

Brazil accounts for more than 45% of developing country sugar exports. The most dependent sugar exporters are all ACP countries that benefited from the EU's Sugar Protocol which guaranteed fixed prices for an allocated sugar quota. It is therefore not the free market sugar price that is relevant for most African countries but the EU sugar Protocol price. For Mauritius and Swaziland sugar accounts for about 17% of total export revenue, for Malawi, it accounts for about 7%

3.4 Non-traditional agricultural exports: vegetables, fruit, flowers

3.4.1 Vegetables and vegetable products (SITC 054)

Non-traditional agricultural exports such as fresh and frozen vegetables and fruit and flowers generally show a lower price volatility than traditional agricultural exports (UNCTAD, 2002). Mexico and China are the largest developing country fresh, chilled and frozen vegetable producers, accounting together for about 56% of total developing country exports. However, for none of them do vegetable exports account for a significant export share. Some African countries, on the other hand, depend significantly on vegetables as an export revenue earner. Thus, vegetables account for 12% of Gambia's, 6% of Kenya's and Ethiopia's and 5% of Zimbabwe's and Eritrea's total export revenue.

Though, African producers export their vegetables largely to the EU market (their traditional export destination), they do not benefit from higher unit prices than the big exporters. Instead prices are highly volatile which can be explained either by declining product quality or by increased competition in the export market where countries with less static export volumes managed to benefit from economies of scale.

3.4.2 Flowers (SITC 292) [6]

Cut flowers are an important export product for Ethiopia, Kenya, and Zimbabwe, accounting for between 9 and 14% of their total export revenue. Kenya and Zimbabwe are also among the main developing country exporters, with a share of about 6% each.

The unit prices obtained differ greatly from country to country and show, particularly among the African suppliers, large fluctuations which might be explained by weather conditions. Colombia and India show much more stable unit prices, which might be a result of the more extensive use of fertilizers.

Both the main exporters and the most dependent exporter were able to expand their export volumes between 5% p.a. (Colombia) and 16% p.a. (Kenya) in the reported time periods (see Figure 9).

3.5 Labour-intensive manufactured goods

The 'Fallacy of Composition' problem, according to which primary products face not only the problem of fluctuating and deteriorating terms of trade but also an unfavourable international constellation of supply and demand, has been expanded to cover simple manufactured products. Since developing countries with large supply capacities, such as China, India or Brazil, are able to produce labour-intensive high-quality products at lower costs than small developing countries, the international competition for simple manufactured products is high. This can exert a downward influence on prices and the terms of trade for basic manufactured goods. If again exporters face significant and sustained declining terms of trade, their export activities may even result in 'immiserizing growth' (Bhagwati 1958), which means that increased export quantities do not fully compensate for terms of trade losses but contribute to a further deterioration of terms of trade, thus increasing developing countries' dependency on exactly these export activities. It is argued that the export of

6 SITC 292 = Crude vegetable materials (including flowers).

simple labour-intensive manufactured goods can be compared to that of primary commodities rather than technology-intensive manufactures.

Figure 9: Flowers: selected developing country exports (kg million)

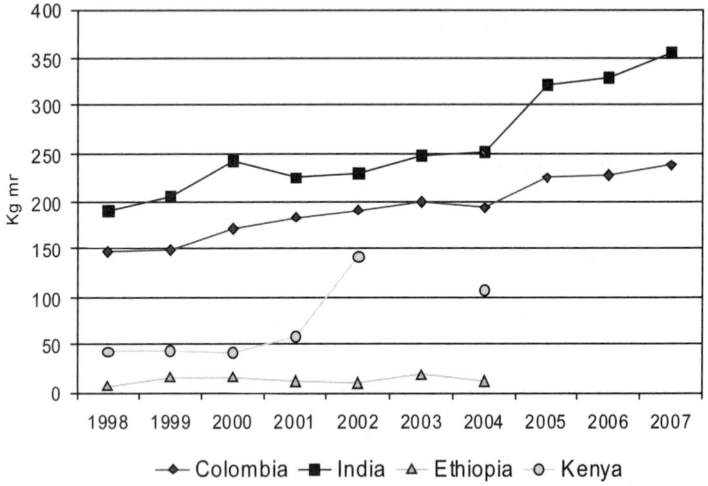

Note: An anomalous 'outlier' (931 kg million for Kenya in 2003) omitted.
Source: UN Comtrade database (data downloaded February 2009).

3.5.1 Woven clothing

As a result of the US-AGOA initiative that guaranteed free market access, many African countries re-started with the production of woven clothing. Woven clothing is an extremely competitive product that is largely supplied by South East Asian countries, with China and India leading, together accounting for more than 66% of total developing country exports. African exporters like Madagascar, Lesotho and Swaziland supply only tiny quantities but have become increasingly dependent on the production of woven clothing for their export revenue.

With respect to unit prices, huge discrepancies between countries are again evident. The unit values for woven clothing are much lower in Asian than in African countries, for which the duty and quota free access to the US and the EU market that African countries enjoy is the possible explanation. In other words: African countries can only compete because of DFQF in their main markets.

4 Policy implications and mitigation strategies

Differently to what had been predicted at the start of the GFC commodity prices have not shrunk considerably and it did not take long for them to recover at historically very high level. However, the GFC has aggravated the problem of highly fluctuating commodity prices which affects particularly African countries since most of them show a high economic dependency on a small range of commodities.

So far we have seen the following effects of the GFC on commodity prices and demand.

- Construction materials such as aluminium and copper have been less affected by the GFC than originally predicted. Depending on China's production surplus and its building boom prices can, however, depress in case of further economic downturn which would have dramatic consequences for metal-dependent exporters such as Zambia and Mozambique.
- Oil exporters have been heavily affected, with the price of crude oil declining sharply since October 2008 as a result of falling US demand. However, prices have in the meanwhile reached US$77/barrel again and are expected to stabilise at this high level.
- Gold prices are expected to remain high, reflecting investors' concerns about currency volatilities. This is good news for the most dependent gold exporters, Mali and Ghana.
- Demand and prices for traditional agricultural commodities, such as cocoa and coffee, have been little affected by the crisis. Their income elasticity of demand is low, so that reduced income in developed countries is not expected to have significant effects on consumption. However, the position of cocoa and coffee producers in the global value chain might worsen as a result of the crisis. This is particularly likely to affect conventional producers that do not serve valued-added markets (such as fair trade or organic products).
- Non-traditional agricultural products like fruit and nuts, vegetables and flowers, show a higher income elasticity of demand than traditional agricultural commodities. It might, however, be the case that importing countries substitute imports with domestic horticultural products as a response to the GFC. Moreover, non-traditional agricultural products might suffer from increased protectionism, e.g. in the form of more stringent product standards, 'carbon labelling' and

other non-tariff barriers. [7] As reported by the World Bank, 17 of the G-20 countries have increased/introduced protectionist measures since the beginning of the GFC – with non-tariff border measures prevailing (Newfarmer and Gamberoni, 2009).

- Simple manufactured exports, such as clothing, are heavily affected by the crisis since their income elasticity of demand is high. Global competition for simple manufactured products is very stiff, with China leading in most product categories.

A huge problem for African countries is that, due to their low diversification degree, they are either heavily dependent on a single commodity or face multiple commodity shocks affecting a large proportion of their total export revenue (see Table 1).

4.1 Country-specific trade strategies to mitigate the effects of the GFC

The expansion of export volumes is, in theory, one policy option to compensate for price losses. It carries a risk, however, of depressing prices even further if expanded volumes meet a stagnant demand. An additional risk is increased protectionism in the import market as a result of increased exports. Large commodity exporters are well aware of the risks of expanding volumes in an economic downturn. The low-price periods for sugar, cotton, palm oil and cocoa (2000/01) were hardly accompanied by expanded exports from the major exporters. The price boom periods, on the other hand, were largely met by increased volumes, e.g. for aluminium, copper, cocoa and coffee. This procyclical response appears to be the best strategy to benefit from commodity resources. It appears, however, hardly possible for most African commodity exporters due to various constraints of expanded production. In fact, many African countries struggled to manage booming commodity prices in a sustainable way and to gradually diversify their economies and instead have increased their dependency on the commodities in question. This makes them particular vulnerable for crisis situations.

Since expanded exports are neither the right nor a feasible response to compensate for low commodity prices in an economic crisis, African countries might divert their commodity exports to the domestic market, which is

---

[7] This would also affect EU preference-dependent exporters of non-traditional agricultural products, such as Belize, Côte d'Ivoire, Dominica, Dominican Republic, Ethiopia, East Timor, Kenya, São Tomé, Sierra Leone, Tonga, and Uganda,

likely to require increased protectionist measures. Likely candidates are commodities that are largely managed by parastatals, such as sugar or coffee. To compensate for export revenue losses producers may call for subsidies or protectionist measures to direct surpluses to the domestic market (such as increased tariffs/minimum prices). Such policy response would harm poor consumers and might have negative consequences for the export competitiveness of the commodity in the medium term.

Table 1: African countries most affected by commodity price changes

Country	Products affected	Combined share of total exports (three latest years reported)
Countries affected by multiple commodity price changes		
Burundi	Gold, coffee	77.9%
Cameroon	Crude oil, cocoa, cotton, aluminium	61.2%
Côte d'Ivoire	Cocoa, crude oil, natural rubber, fruit and nuts, cotton	46.9%
Ethiopia	Coffee, flowers, veg., gold	61.1%
Ghana	Gold, cocoa	61.1%
Kenya	Flowers, vegetables, coffee	20.3%
Tanzania	Gold, coffee, cotton	42.8%
Uganda	Coffee, gold, flowers, cotton	39.2%
Countries heavily dependent on a single commodity		
Algeria	Crude oil	55.2%
Angola	Crude oil	n.n.
Benin	Cotton	68.6%
Burkina Faso	Cotton	68.7%
Cameroon	Crude oil	42.9%
Gabon	Crude oil	81.8%
Mozambique	Aluminium	60.2%
Nigeria	Crude oil	93.0%
São Tomé e P.	Cocoa	88.7%
Sierra Leone [a]	Coffee	86.5%
Zambia	Copper	67.6%

Note:

(a) Based on one year's data only (2002 – the only year for which Sierra Leone has reported to Comtrade).

Further possible trade policy responses could be increased most-favoured-nation (MFN) tariffs (possibly up to the rates bound at WTO), which countries might want to undertake to offset for decreased export revenues. The risks of such a policy approach depend on whether tariffs are selectively increased for revenue-sensitive items or across the board (which is likely to have a negative impact on poor consumers and can harm producers that source inputs for re-exports). Other possible negative implications are decreased investments (as a result of increased prices for capital goods) and inflationary tendencies. Moreover, it needs to be considered that the response of tariff increases is not only limited by the WTO but, for most countries, also by bilateral and regional treaties.

Some countries have already applied 'beggar thy neighbour' policies as a response to the crisis.[8] The depreciation of currencies of large economies like South Africa and Nigeria vis-à-vis the US dollar is at the expense of small neighbouring countries which have neither the fiscal policy space to devalue their currencies nor an independent fiscal and monetary policy (e.g. members of the West African Economic and Monetary Union that have a common currency tied to the Euro).[9] Moreover, we see that various countries have raised several forms of protectionist measures – including tariffs, non-tariff barriers and subsidies.

In addition to these defensive trade policies many countries have also pursued offensive policies such as credit guarantees to support exports and minimise the risk for banks[10] or the introduction of fiscal stimuli programmes. However, in most African countries fiscal stimulus programmes are constrained by their weak fiscal position and high debt levels. Additional aid flows are needed to support the countries but not all of them have the institutional capacity to absorb increased spending. However, African countries with low institutional capacities are those with the highest poverty levels and

---

8 "Beggar thy neighbor", describes a policy that seeks benefits for one country at the expense of others. It usually takes the form of (1) restricting imports by quotas or by raising tariffs, (2) currency devaluation that makes imports more expensive and exports cheaper, or (3) currency appreciation that reduces domestic inflation but makes its products more expensive in the importing country.

9 The West African Economic and Monetary Union (UEMOA) is the continuation of previous regional arrangements dating back to 1945, under which member countries have a common currency, the CFA Franc, tied to the French Franc (today the Euro).The French Treasury (today the European Central Bank) guarantees free convertibility at a fixed parity between the Euro and the CFA Franc.

10 Governments could make use of the World Bank's Global Trade Finance Program (GTFP); through which the IFC can guarantee the payment risk of issuing banks up to the full value of a transaction.

are thus, in most critical need of financial and technical support to cope with the effects of the crisis.[11]

Low fiscal space, high external debts and high aid inflows require fiscal prudence which limits the interventionist policy options for many African countries. The African Development Bank expects the economic crisis to worsen the continent's macroeconomic balances further by decreased revenue from exports and tourism as well as declining remittances, capital inflows, and domestic and foreign investment (AfDB, 2009). Given these unfavourable external conditions it is recommended that African countries concentrate on the promotion of domestic growth drivers, i.e. on supporting those industries that are responsible for a large share of employment and economic growth.

4.2 International trade policy responses

While it is acknowledged that the successful conclusion of the WTO Doha Development Round would be desirable to discipline the maximum application of tariffs and subsidies, it needs to be borne in mind that the WTO offers no insurance against the application of protectionist measures such as domestic subsidies or restrictive product standards. Moreover, the Doha Round has an ambitious agenda which is unlikely to be achieved in the current economic climate (see Meyn et al., 2009). Instead of pushing for a minimalistic consensus, which runs the risk of damaging the institution of the WTO, policy makers should instead concentrate on ***fighting any forms of new protectionism*** at home that would additionally harm African exporters, such as:

- avoiding the introduction of new formal or informal product standards, labelling requirements and so on, intended to encourage discrimination against imports;
- supporting the surveillance process that the WTO has put in place to track the new protection measures applied by members and encouraging it to cover a broad range of potentially distorting measures;
- coordinating fiscal stimuli programmes with the objective of disciplining trade-distorting impacts and avoiding discrimination against foreign firms.

---

[11] The IMF (2009) identified Burundi, CAR, Comoros, DRC, Gambia, Guinea, Guinea-Bissau, Côte d'Ivoire, Liberia, and Togo as highly and medium exposed countries that have low institutional capacities and limited fiscal space.

The importance of trade finance differs significantly among developing countries and sectors, depending on their position in international value chains. For most African countries we do not have much evidence that exporters are affected by a lack of trade finance (te Velde, 2009, Humphrey, 2009). This is explained by the fact that the (foreign-owned) firms are operating in well-established global chains and are considered as 'good risks' by banks. Still, it is important ***that trade finance be available and that, if necessary, international organisations step in to secure*** it. However, this should be the case only where exporters' access to trade finance is a serious problem; otherwise such action is likely to crowd-out domestic banks.

The GFC is increasing African countries' need for effective and timely Aid for Trade (AfT). Many countries are being affected by a combination of falling export volumes and prices and depreciation of their currencies, and for many the consequence will be worsening trade deficits, fiscal challenges and increased foreign debt levels. Though additional aid should be provided to protect social expenditure and progress in reducing poverty, it is critical to ensure that assistance is also given to countries' productive and institutional capacities and trade infrastructure. The G-20 need to renew their AfT commitments and make clear that such funds will be increased without reducing other aid commitments. This requires a consistent definition of AfT to avoid the danger of existing aid activities, such as infrastructure projects, simply being re-labelled as AfT. In particular for the wider AfT agenda it is often questionable whether a specific project is related to trade or not. It is therefore important to improve the definition and measurement of AfT projects following the WTO Task Force on Aid for Trade, according to which 'Projects and programmes should be considered as Aid for Trade if these activities have been identified as trade-related development priorities in the recipient country's national development strategies' (WTO, 2006). In addition to ensuring that *additional* funds are available it is necessary to ensure that these funds respond *adequately* to countries' needs. This will require African countries to exercise strong leadership and donors to give centrality to national development plans. The AfT framework needs to be tightened up to ensure that the aid is adequate, and made available in an appropriate and timely way to deal with the actual, new costs resulting from the GFC.

Most African countries enjoy DFQF access to the EU market and significant preferences in the US market. However, African country exports are to a large extent still constrained by restrictive origin rules. While important improvements have taken place in the past decade with respect to manufactured products (such as the US's AGOA, which resulted in increased Asian investment in the African apparel industry and a consequent 'boom' in African exports to the US, or the recent EU decision to allow the import of single transformation garments from selected trading partners), this is not yet the case for all goods. Agro-processed exports in particular face restrictive rules of origin that make it difficult for developing countries to access the EU and US markets (Stevens and Kennan, 2007).

Granting African countries more generous rules of origin for agro-processed products would be a powerful signal that the EU and the US could send to African countries. It could help to stimulate investment and expand and diversify exports, which in turn would help to mitigate the negative implications of the GFC. Given the powerful agricultural lobbies, particularly in the EU market, it might only be politically feasible to start with a few products. However, as the examples of the US AGOA initiative or the EU's permitting Pacific EPA states to process fish outside their waters without losing originating status have shown, a few product lines can make a big difference.

5 Conclusions

The GFC affects African countries' trade through price and volume effects. Open economies, which are highly trade-dependent and export only a small range of products to few markets, are affected most by the trade transmission mechanism. Such a characteristic applies to most African countries.

- In Zambia, Ghana, Mozambique, Nigeria, Botswana and Namibia 20-40% of GDP is earned by exporting one commodity. In most of these economies more than 80% of total exports destined for two markets: the US and the EU (WTO, 2008).
- In Botswana, Mozambique, Namibia, and Zambia more than 80% of exports are derived from mining and related activities, notably diamonds, aluminium, and copper. Declining demand and prices translate directly into decreased investment, currency depreciation and unemployment.

Even more heavily affected are those countries hit by multiple effects of the crisis, many of which also fall into the first category of undiversified and highly export dependent economies.

- Nigeria has been hit both by the rapidly declining oil price (68% within one year) and by a decrease of more than 45% in share price, resulting in a depreciation of the Naira and drastically worsened terms of trade.
- Various countries such as Burundi, Cameroon, Ethiopia and Ghana face multiple commodity shocks for more than 50% of their total export revenue. Many of these small economies are additionally affected by declining revenue from tourism and/or remittances.

South Africa as a major commodity exporter is less affected due to its comparably high degree of diversification. Moreover, South Africa has a large domestic market and effective institutions. Thus, the gravity of the effects of the GFC also depends on countries' institutional conditions which determine possible responses.

However, national trade policy options to mitigate the effects of the crisis are limited. The expansion of exports is often not possible due to limited capacities and further unlikely to compensate for revenue losses as it risks accelerating price declines. Directing exports to the domestic market and regional markets might be an option for some countries but would often require the application of increased protectionist policies – which risk harming producers and reducing the international competitiveness of the product in the medium term. Some countries have already raised tariffs and non-tariff barriers on imports and introduced subsidies for domestic production. Such policies are, like the devaluation of domestic currencies *vis-à-vis* the US dollar, at the expense of neighbouring countries, thus, undermining their ability to export.

Moreover, many African countries are incapable of applying interventionist policies (such as fiscal stimuli programmes, supporting trade finance, or subsidising companies) due to high current account deficits, debts and double-figure inflation rates. Additional financial and technical support that goes beyond the current aid levels is therefore required to help African countries to mitigate the effects of the GFC. Furthermore, G-20 countries should do their outmost to ensure that their markets remain open for developing countries' exports and resist domestic pressures to apply protectionist and trade distorting measures.

References

AfDB (African Development Bank) (2009): 'Impact of the Financial Crisis on African Economies – An Interim Assessment.' Paper presented at the Meeting of the Committee of Finance Ministers and Central Bank Governors, Cape Town, 16 January 2009.

AfDB (2004): 'African Development Report 2004: Africa in the Global Trading System.' Oxford: Oxford University Press.

Bhagwati, J. (1958): 'Immiserizing Growth: A Geometric Note.' In: Review of Economic Studies vol. 25, pp. 201-205.

Boorman, J. /Lane, T. /Schulze-Ghattas, M. /Bulir, A. /Ghosh, A. /Hamann, J. /Mourmouras, A. /Phillips, S. (2000): 'Managing Financial Crises: The Experience in East Asia.' IMF Working Paper WP/00/107 http://www.imf.org/external/pubs/FT/Weo/weo1297/pdf/1297ch2.pdf, accessed 04/02/10.

Ernst, Dieter (1999): 'Responses to the crisis: constraints to a rapid trade adjustment in East Asia's electronic industry.' DRUID Working paper No. 99-2.

IFS (International Financial Statistics): International Monetary Fund (IMF) Data and Statistics, 1995-2002, CD-Rom.

Humphrey, J. (2009): 'Trade credit', in IDS In Focus Policy Briefing, Issue 07, Policy Responses to the Global Financial Crisis, pp. 15–16, March 2009 (online): http://www.ids.ac.uk/UserFiles/file/publications/in_focus/If07/IFPB7_FullSet.pdf, accessed 04/02/10.

IMF (2009): 'The Implications of the Global Financial Crisis for Low-Income Countries.' March 2009, IMF: Washington D.C.

Meyn, M./Cali, M./Hewitt, A./Page,S./te Velde, D.W. (2009): 'Pursuing a Doha Trade Deal is a low priority.' ODI Opinion no. 126, February 2009, ODI: London.

Newfarmer, R. and Gamberoni, E. (2009): 'Trade Protection: Incipient but Worrisome Trends." Trade Notes No. 37, 02 March 2009, The World Bank: Washington D.C.

Stevens, C. and Kennan, J. (2007): 'Temporary Cotonou+ Preferential Rules of Origin.' ODI: London.

te Velde, D.W. (2009): 'Workshop on the Global Financial Crisis and Developing Countries.' 11 February 2009, ODI: London.

UN Comtrade (United Nations Commodity Trade Statistics Database) available at: http://comtrade.un.org/db/

UNCTAD (United Nations Conference on Trade and Development) (2008): 'UNCTAD Handbook of Statistics 2008.' Geneva: UN (available online): http://www.unctad.org/Templates/webflyer.asp?docid=10193&intItemID=2068&lang=1, accessed 04/02/09.

UNCTAD (2002): 'Trade and Development Report 2002.' UN Publication: Geneva and New York.

World Bank (2010): 'Commodity forecasts (current US prices)' (available online): http://web.worldbank.org/WBSITE/EXTERNAL/EXTDEC/EXTDECPROSPECTS/EXTGBLPROSPECTS/0,,contentMDK:20675357~menuPK:627723~pagePK:2904583~piPK:2904598~theSitePK:612501,00.html, accessed 06/02/10.

World Bank (2009): 'Commodities at the crossroads. Key findings from Global Economic Prospects 2009.' The World Bank: Washington D.C.

World Bank (2008): 'Commodity Market Briefs. Global Economic Prospects 2008. Prepared November 10, 2008' (available online): http://web.worldbank.org/WBSITE/EXTERNAL/EXTDEC/EXTDECPROSPECTS/EXTGBLPROSPECTS/0,,contentMDK:20659291~menuPK:1691529~pagePK:2904583~piPK:2904598~theSitePK:612501,00.html, accessed 04/02/09.

WTO (2006). 'Recommendations of the Task Force on Aid for Trade' (http://docsonline.wto. org/imrd/directdoc.asp?DDFDocuments/t/WT/AFT/1.doc, accessed on 19 January 2009).

WTO (2008): 'World Trade Profiles.'(available online): http://www.wto.org/english/res_e/publications_e/trade_profiles08_e.htm, accessed 20/01/10.

The Strategy of the G 20 to Overcome the Impact of the Global Financial Crisis on Africa

Karl Wolfgang Menck*

Abstract

There is available a vast set of publications which reflect the impact of the Global Financial Crisis (GFC) on the world economy, on the developed countries, and on a number of developing countries. However, these studies do not reflect intensively the fact that the GFC has identified inefficiencies in the African financial industry, and the necessity to extend reforms to these sectors is not emphasized.

Propositions are circulated to overcome the impact of the GFC on the banking sector, mainly to be read in the G20 declarations and in the proposals by the IMF and related bodies. Referring to regional co-operation also the EU discusses measures to be undertaken. The propositions are perceived as a tool box for all the countries being inflicted by the GFC. As the main policy instruments those actions are recommended which may help to regulate the financial markets as well as to adapt monetary policy to the situation and thereby to stabilise the macro-economy, the real economy, and the capital accumulation. Furthermore, it is proposed to stick to trade liberalisation and to foster the flexibility of markets so as to eradicate unemployment. Monetary policy is requested as a key instrument to avoid the beginning of deflationary as well as inflationary processes, and so there is a need to restructure the international monetary system to avoid such a danger.

The paper focuses mainly on the impact of the GFC impact on Sub-Saharan African (SSA) countries excluding South Africa, and especially on the African banking industry. The contribution refers to the major studies which report on the impact of the GFC on SSA and on the proposed strategies to adjust the regulation of the financial markets to the crisis conditions

* Menck, Karl Wolfgang, Ph.D., Lecturer, Research Fellow, Hamburgisches Welt-Wirtschafts-Institut, Hamburg, Germany

and to install additional and improved mechanisms for the functioning of finance and the monetary policy. The paper also outlines proposals for the needed reforms in the banking industry in SSA, taking into consideration specifically the G20 and EU approaches to overcome the GFC. The paper concludes with an outline of policy measures proposed by multilateral financial institutions and/or by SSA countries.

1 Africa South of the Sahara: The Impact of the Global Financial Crisis (GFC)

1.1 The Economic "footprint" of the GFC

Rather few studies are directing the attention to the impact of the GFC on the SSA countries. It is argued that the globalisation and the liberalisation of financial markets have enlarged the worldwide trade flows and the production of goods and services especially after the year 2000. However, SSA countries have participated to a smaller extent than developed countries and emerging countries in this growth trend. Concomitant it is assumed that the GFC will have a more limited impact on the SSA countries either through the reduction of trade flows, or the curtailment of private foreign investment and a reduced provision of official development assistance (Teunissen 2007, pp. 1; African Union 2008, paragraph II; African Governers 2009; Assembly of the African Union 2009, paragraphs. 1; IMF 2009, pp. 2; Fosu/ Naudė 2009, pp. 1; Macias/Massa 2009, pp. 2; Spratt 2009, pp. 150; Bibow 2010, pp. 2, IMF 2010, pp. 41). Other studies however claim that the volatility of the SSA countries has been severely enlarged and that the resilience to external crises has been considerably weakened by the GFC. Thereby the credit risks have increased and the capital flows are affected negatively, including that capital flight from SSA is accelerated (Naudé 2010, p. 8). Resources to generate investment, employment, and social welfare will therefore not be available in the SSA countries (Macias/Massa 2009; Fosu/Naudé 2009, p. 5). Another position indicates that the increase in volatility and the loss in resilience in SSA countries are the outcome of protracted reforms and of inadequate economic policies. It is concluded that the GFC draws the attention to the need to enhance the commitment of the SSA countries to speed up internal economic reforms.

1.2 The GFC "footprint" in the Financial Sectors of Africa

One of the consequences of the GFC is that the issue of the efficiency of the banking industry in Africa has become a subject of a wide-reaching and deep analysis. Reforms for the sector are discussed much more intensively now and with large public concern. Observations indicate that the impact of the GFC on the SSA banking sector is assessed in an ambiguous manner. A more positive evaluation concludes: "… African banks hardly ever take their loans and then turn them into other instruments, break them into mortgage securities and trade them …it's a simpler system and therefore it's less prone to the particular kind of downfall that the American financial system has been facing." (Cortez 1999, p. 202) It is assumed that these countries which have complained in the past about an inappropriate inflow of capital are protected in a "shelter" from the inflow of private capital flows coming from the worldwide financial markets, due to the expectation of low returns which are explained among others by the limited economic size as well as by a financial sector being not adapted to participate in the international financial flows (Yartey/Adjasi 2007, pp. 6; IMF 2009 p. 9)

Other studies underline that there is an interrelationship between the existing political and social structure, the weak economic performance, and the exposure of the banking sector in Africa south of the Sahara. Various research findings stress that in Africa south of the Sahara the banking sector only in a very few countries has the potential to participate in the international financial markets, due among other factors to weak supervision and regulation, lack of professionals, inadequate expertise to screen and monitor borrowing, poor loan documentation, poor internal controls, and insider lending. It is said: "…politicians who were shareholders often received loans in return for deposits from parastatals or other favors." Political power structures enabled some "to obtain bank licenses or prevent actions by regulators, reducing constraints to imprudent lending and worsening moral hazard problems." Another indicator to describe the weakness of the banking industry in many SSA countries is the large amount of capital flight (Report of the Feasibility Study 2008, paragraph 41, p. 10). Additionally, the macroeconomic policies being implemented in Africa south of the Sahara did not contribute to the generation of a well functioning financial industry (Okeahalam/Afful 2006, pp. 39; Degefe 1999, p. 209).

The GFC may have had an ambiguous impact on the banking sector in those countries which have reformed the sector in the past. Reforms which had been undertaken will be interrupted, and capital flight is enlarged. Adjustments which are now envisaged to match the impact of the GFC on the global banking sector will however encourage further and additional reforms.

Banking reforms have been initiated among others in Ghana, Mauritius, and in the Franc-Zone countries, as well as in Uganda, Malawi, Nigeria and Tanzania (Camara 1998; Joseph 2002, pp. 10; Beck/Fuchs/Uy 2009, p. 4; HWWI 2010, pp. 64; Kabango7Paloni 2010, pp. 12). Banking reforms have also supplemented structural adjustment commitments in SSA (Report of the Feasibility Study 2008, paragraph 43). Policies implied are the liberalisation of the capital market, balance-sheet restructuring, restoration of distressed markets, and a decrease of the number and the size of the government-controlled or government-owned banks. Capital markets were extended, and opportunities were created to channel savings to long-term investments at reasonable conditions (Obstfeld 2008, pp. 12). This process has started mainly in the years after 2000 (Brownbridge/Maimbo 2003, pp. 47).

Regarding Uganda it is observed that "the sector now comprises well-managed and solvent institutions. The interbank market in both local and foreign exchange has been expanded, while the credibility of the regulators has been greatly enhanced….The reforms also provided the institutional framework necessary for the conduct of market based monetary policy, with equivalent development in capital markets." (Byarohanga/Henstridge/ Kasakende 2010, pp. 75) "The general direction of reforms undertaken is in many ways similar across African countries adopting SAP (Structural Adjustment Programs), but the sequence and pace differed, as did the initial financial conditions, such as banks' and borrowers' net worth and the scale of fiscal imbalances preceding financial sector reforms. Thus, the nature and scope of financial reforms was influenced by the portfolio position and the asset quality of financial institutions, as well as by government financing requirements and the general fiscal profile. These variations have had a critical bearing on the effects of reforms." (Nissanke 2002, p. 135)

The cases of Ghana, Malawi, and Tanzania underline the necessity of macro-economic stability and of adequate supervision during the process of liberalisation. Another critical point refers to the timing and the "abruptness" of reforms. In Tanzania the balance-sheet restructuring implied a large-scale accumulation of non-performing loans of the banks when the reform process was started. The Nigerian experience denotes that the deregulation of interest markets and entry requirements - when reaching the financial industry - added to the instability; these reforms necessitated further reforms which initiated short-term corrective actions and have undermined the long-term credibility of reforms (Nissanke 2002, pp. 143). Foreign investors were attracted by the abundant liquidity, the allocation efficiency of the capital market, and by the rewards in the market. The increase of income through higher commodity prices, the decrease of government debts (supported by international financial institutions), and a liberalisation of the entry conditions for foreign investors were appreciated by depositors and by investors (Report of the Feasibility Study 2008, paragraph 125). Macroeconomic policies have gradually proceeded in some countries as in Ghana and Malawi, whereas in other countries such as in Nigeria there was no progress. Degefe (1999) concludes: "Vulnerability to external shocks, poverty, undeveloped technical capacity and a heavy external debt burden can be easily evoked when characterizing the region. It is precisely these characteristics that need to be faced and addressed in the course of developing a sufficiently robust economic policy. To this end, the current policies need to be revised and a more appropriate and robust strategy put in place. Two basic lessons to be learned from these countries are that there is a need for a strong and visionary state and that the market must be assisted in the allocation of the limited resources in the region." (Degefe 1999, p. 211)

Regional stock markets have not yet been sufficiently developed in SSA. In 1998, a regional stock exchange was installed in Mauritius, and about the same time it was intended to set up a bourse in Gabon in close collaboration with Cameroun, Central African Republic, Chad, Congo Republic, and Equatorial Guinea. Another regional stock exchange was founded in Abidjan. Botswana, Lesotho, Malawi, Zimbabwe and Zambia envisaged to collaborate with the Mauritian bourse and to extend in the region the financial trade flows. Since May 29, 2009 the Grand Towers Africa Fund PCC (GTA) is listed on the Stock Exchange of Mauritius. The investment objective is to promote privately negotiated equity investments in commercial properties in SSA (Listing of Grand Towers Africa Fund 2010). However, considerable progress has not been realized and the size of financial flows at regional level still remains low. As main reasons are identified the lack of political will, which is documented among others by national monetary and economic policies, and an inadequate harmonisation of the legal and fiscal policies. Also, there was no consensus about the application of mutual acceptance of listing procedures and of regulatory rules. Furthermore, the institutions in the SSA countries did not provide the institutional and staff capacities which are required to set up a regional stock market. The SSA countries hesitated for a long time to encourage the cooperation with multilateral financial agencies as well as with bilateral donors to install regional stock markets (Report of the Feasibility Study 2008, paragraphs 31). It is argued that for such stock exchanges to succeed "...basic requirements for the establishment are

- Regulators and supervisors have sufficient skills and resources to perform their role and be relatively remunerated.
- Regulatory and supervisory agencies should be free of political influence, with appointments on merit.
- The supervisory approach - ...- should be tailored to the circumstances of each individual country.

- Regulations should be consistent and transparent and supervision conducted according to similar standards of consistency and transparency." (Spratt 2009, p. 159)

Inefficiencies of the supervision of the financial sector and a lack of adequate liberalisation of the financial markets were identified during the GFC as weaknesses and have to be removed (Spratt 2009, pp. 27). It is concluded that a main requirement to implement sustainable reforms is a fundamental upgrading of the regulation mechanism (Fosu and Naudé 2009, p. 9). Regional efforts have to be enhanced in this context.

Also, a sound macroeconomic environment has to create conditions being conducive to enhance resilience and to reduce volatility of the capital markets (Whitworth/Williamson 2010, p. 25). Specifically, it is proposed to reduce the budget deficits, to reduce the amount of government bonds sale through public-owned banks, and to balance the demand and supply in the goods and services markets. Currency and monetary policy have to provide a sound macroeconomic environment (Spratt 2009, pp. 229).

1.3 The Propositions of SSA countries to reform the Banking Sector

Representatives of SSA countries have underlined their commitment to foster efforts which may reform the financial industry. The African Governors to the Bretton Woods Institutions agreed in the Freetown Declaration on a comprehensive set of policies to improve the regulation and to create an adequate macroeconomic environment. A programme was also envisaged by the 2008 Partnership Forum for Making Finance Work (see on the recommendations by these initiatives the Box 1 below).

These proposals indicate that the GFC has already involved broader governmental and non-governmental circles in Africa to speed up economic and banking reforms.

2 Strategies to Reform the African Finance Industry

2.1 The Elements of the G20 Approach

The economic impact of the GFC immediately has initiated a debate in the G20 countries, in the G20 Club, and in other international financial institutions as well as in other national governments and regional associations how to remove the origins of the GFC and how to develop strategies which in the future may avert further crises. The recommendations have been summarized among others by the OECD and provide a guideline for actions being envisaged (OECD 2009; BMF 2009, pp. 69). It is argued that measures should be implemented not only in the G20 countries, but in all countries being hurt by the GFC, and so they are felt to be useful also for SSA countries (see Box 2 on the G20 statements being of relevance for Africa).

Box 1: Recommendations by African Representatives

The recommendations prioritise an improved legal, regulatory, and judicial environment, the set-up of a better financial infrastructure, the implementation of adequate governmental actions, information and documentation, the extension of the financial sector as a service agent in agriculture activities and rural development, and among low-income segments of the population; the introduction of innovative financial products is also recommended. Furthermore, regional activities such as joint stock markets should be established. Also, additional consultancy services should be made available through international financial institutions. Finally, the flow of resources being channelled to Africa through trade liberalisation in developed countries, through foreign direct investment, and through official development assistance has to be enhanced.

Forum Proceedings 2008, pp. 5; African Governors 2009

The proposals of the G20 meetings to SSA countries may enable African states to share insights and to participate more fully in the overall development of the global financial architecture. This may enable SSA countries to create a banking system and structure which attracts foreign capital by reducing transaction costs and by minimizing risks due to diverging rules and procedures in the national African financial industries. An improved performance may also help to curtail capital flight and may enable banking system supervisors in SSA countries to identify illegal capital movements out from the SSA countries. However, the financial environment and its degree of flexibility as well as the state of macroeconomic reforms in SSA should be reviewed carefully before implementing the reforms of the finance industry. This would be the first step to change the situation with regard of banking and finance industry in Africa.

Box 2: G20 statements regarding the GFC

Declaration of the Summit on Financial Markets and the World Economy (2008), Washington, D. C.

Declaration on further steps to strengthen the financial system (2009)

Pittsburgh Summit (2009), Leaders' Statement: The Pittsburgh Summit, September 24 – 25

2.2 The Reform of the African Finance Industry and the G20 Approach

The major proposals of the G20 concept which should be implemented in SSA countries are to strengthen the regulatory framework, to improve the integrity in finance industry and at financial markets, and to enlarge the capitalization base of the banking industry. Furthermore, the G20 approach which has to be applied also in SSA countries stresses the need for a redesign of the macroeconomic framework and especially of the tax policies, as well as the need for financial education and awareness programmes and a higher level of consumer protection. The SSA countries may find of importance for their economies additional valuable proposals from the G20 such as to strengthen the competition among banks, steps towards the privatisation of banks, and measures towards the recovery from bad assets (OECD 2009, pp. 5). To clarify all these proposals and their relevance for Africa some further explanations are needed.

Transparency is closely related to the accountability of the management of financial institutions. Because of the extent of inefficiencies of the financial industry in SSA countries the recommendations by the G20 are important – especially the suggestion to strengthen corporate governance in African countries (OECD 2009, pp. 51; Bundesbank 2009, pp. 53) It is proposed by the G20 that the banks are controlled more efficiently by the shareholder. Also, decisions on the bank operations should be taken only by those who are remunerated for operating and completing these tasks. This should be done without transferring risks to others who are not able to assess and to transfer insecure positions and who are then ultimately forced to take over the losses. Deposit insurance schemes and guarantees have to protect deposits and may help to create a business culture which avoids moral hazard situations. It is recommended also to enlarge considerably the share of capital that is deposited. The costs of guarantees should be adequate to the level of risks and these costs should be made transparent with regard of the returns for financial products. The banking industry is called upon to set up rescue funds which may protect the deposits, and thereby it would become possible to prevent that taxpayers' money is the only source of emergency operations.

It is requested in SSA countries – along the G20 proposals - to enhance the supervision in terms of strengthening the transparency of the whole financial system. Taking into account the need for banking reforms in SSA countries, the scope of auditing should be extended considerably and oversight procedures are to be performed regularly, without being announced by the supervisory bodies and in quite short intervals. Creating independent rating agencies outside of the range of the existing credit rating agencies are debated as a possible solution, or alternatively – if it is not possible to set up such institutions - a strong control of independence and reliability of the existing credit rating agencies is recommended by the G20. A harmonization of national accounting standards is also felt as being necessary (OECD 2009, pp. 36) The responsibility of supervisory agencies should be strengthened and additional resources are needed for their staffing, but as well a mechanism is required which initiates a co-operation between the national supervisory authorities in a global context (OECD 2009, pp. 29).

Referring to the default cases of the banking sector in SSA due to mismanagement and because of its huge impact on the overall economy as well as the high cost governmental rescue operations which had to be undertaken in the past, additional measures are needed. The respective recommendations which are discussed in the G20 circles should be taken into consideration also by SSA countries. In addition to the micro-prudential supervision as proposed in the G20 approach and denominated as the "too big to fail" problem in the course of rescue operations, a further step towards enhanced macro-prudential supervision is required (see Box 3).

Box 3: Macro-prudential Surveillance

"First, it aims to limit the distress of the the entire financial system rather than distress to individual institutions.

Second, its chief aim is to avoid large and burdensome costs to the economy – such as expensive bank bailouts – rather than aiming to protect more narrowly the depositors of an individual bank.

Third, it is based largely on the assumption that at least some of the risks faced by the banking system collectively differ from those faced by individual banks.

And, fourth, it aims to examine risks that arise from the interaction of banks as part of the financial system rather than on a bank-by-bank basis."

Rabeck 2006, p. 3; Sachverständigenrat 2009, pp. 140

Although the origins of bank defaults in SSA countries may be different from the situation in G20 countries, the impact of failures in African countries of only one of the few banks in a country may be similar to those problems which were created in the G20 countries due to losses of single large banks. Micro-prudential and macro-prudential supervisory policies are therefore requested not only in the G20 countries, but also in African countries, and these instruments have to be combined adequately.

The details of the macro-prudential approach have not yet been designed: there is however a consensus to extend the supervisory mechanism of the central banks and of the supervisory institutions. Mainly, the needed operations and activities should include "the formalisation of payments and settlement system oversight, the publication of financial stability reports, stress testing and scenario analysis, and concern with the financial condition of non-bank financial intermediaries and the health of corporate and household balance sheets." (Rabeck 2006, pp. 7) The implementation of these operations and activities is perceived as the "genetic code" of the central bank, and this term denotes the capability and the further extension of the capacities to implement a macro-prudential approach.

The GFC has underlined that the capital requirement ratios and the leverage ratios being defined among others in the Basle Accord should be adjusted and accepted worldwide. The SSA banking industry needs therefore also measures which strengthen the capital basis. The regulatory and supervisory regimes in SSA countries should define harmonized risk weights and should give definitions of the various forms of capital supply to the banks and of credit provision to the non-banking sector. Government bonds in this context should be valued at preferential risk assessment. A fair weight is also recommended regarding real estate lending (OECD 2009, p. 43). Banks in SSA countries should also be enforced to observe secure liquidity standards in relation to the structure of the credit exposure (OECD 2009, pp. 42). It is also necessary to define capital requirements according to the real cost of potential rewards and risks, which are determined by the overall portfolio structure and by the losses which have been materialized by accounting for charges on the income on a regulatory basis (OECD 2009, p. 44).

In the follow-up of the GFC there is a widespread perception that the institutional set-up of supervisory agencies is not adequate with regard to those standards which were required to avoid the international financial turmoil (OECD 2009, pp. 29). The SSA case shows that improvements in the supervision of banks are urgently needed. A comprehensive adjustment of the legal status, the responsibility of staff, the staffing modalities, and of the procedures is required, and a simple reformulation of the guiding principles of the past would not be sufficient. An independent, single and well-staffed agency with far-reaching responsibilities should be installed, which has the power to provide stability of the individual financial institutions and of the overall financial industry.

The tasks of the envisaged institution are mainly to organize and to implement a continuous flow of information between the financial institutions and the supervisory agent, and to create capacities which enable it to identify early-warning rescue operations. The supervision has to include sanctions against and closures of financial institutions which did not obey the rules. "Institutionally, greater accountability for performance would work to combat the problem by concentrating the attention of the chief executive and by influencing the bureaucratic culture….The counterpart to greater accountability is sufficient autonomy to achieve specified objectives. In particular, this points to the desirability of direct funding and the absence from governing boards of government and other agency representatives where conflicts in policy objectives may be present." (OECD 2009, p. 35) The staff's qualification and its dedication are to be promoted so as to create and develop "... remuneration packages better designed to offer attractive long-term career prospects and to retain staff who can realistically regard the financial sector as a viable career alternative as well as tighter restrictions on mobility between supervisory agencies and institutions being supervised" (OECD 2009, p. 35).

The G20 recommendations furthermore propose to adjust the macroeconomic policy in order to strengthen the financial industry. For the SSA countries it is recommendable firstly, to provide a tax policy that strengthens market-based incentive elements and to control risk assessments, and secondly, to create a sustainable macro-economic environment which is conducive to private activities (OECD 2009, p. 23).

2.3 Reforming the Banking Sector in SSA countries through International Cooperation

In addition to these actions central banks and international financial institutions need to enhance international cooperation (Bundesbank 2009, pp. 53). The SSA capabilities to manage the supervision of the financial industry may benefit from border-crossing institutions being set up to form a joint control mechanism. The G20 group agreed to enhance international cooperation "to implement the FSF (Financial Stability Forum) principles for cross border crisis management immediately, to see that home authorities of each major financial institution should ensure that the group of authorities with a common interest in that financial institution meet at least annually; to support continued efforts by the IMF, FSB (Financial Stability Board), World Bank, and the BCBS (Basel Committee on Banking Supervision to develop an international framework for cross-border resolution arrangements; to see the importance of further work and international cooperation on the subject of exit strategies; and to see that the IMF and the FSB should together launch an Early Warning System at the 2009 Spring Meeting". (Declaration on Strengthening the Financial System 2009, p. 2)

Also, the SSA countries should participate in actions being recommended "which will ensure a robust and comprehensive framework for global regulation and oversight." (Declaration on further steps to strengthen the financial system 2009, p. 19) The supervisors in SSA countries will benefit if the border-crossing financial industry pursues, as the G7 formulates, risk avoiding strategies: "Systematically important financial firms should develop internationally-consistent firm-specific contingency and resolution plans. Our authorities (central banks and related national regulatory bodies) should establish crisis management groups for the major cross-border firms and a legal framework for crisis intervention as well as to improve information sharing in times of stress. We should develop resolution tools and frameworks for the effective resolution of financial groups to help mitigate the disruption of financial institution failures and reduce moral hazard in the future…" (Pittsburgh Summit 2009, paragraph 13).

The IMF may assist SSA countries by activities that contribute to macroprudential risk assessment in the course of the surveillance mechanism: "The IMF, with its focus on surveillance, and the expanded FSF, with its focus on standard setting, should strengthen their collaboration, enhancing efforts to better integrate regulatory and supervisory responses into the macroprudential policy framework and conduct early warning exercises. The IMF given the universal membership and core macro-financial expertise, should, in close coordination with the FSF and others, take a leading role in drawing lessons from the current crisis, consistent with its mandate." (Declaration of the Summit on Financial Markets and the World Economy 2008, p. 5)

2.4 Financial Facilities to Developing Countries through the IMF

The SSA countries have to acknowledge that reforms of the financial industry are a necessary input to match the GFC impact and to reduce the volatility and to strengthen the resilience of all economies being inflicted. When improving the efficiency of the national banking industry capital markets will be restored and enabled to enhance economic growth. However, regarding developing countries it is widely accepted that additional resources may be conducive to mitigate the impact of the GFC and to create an environment being conducive to reforms of the banking industry and the restoration of macroeconomic stability and resilience.

SSA countries will benefit from proposals which provide additional resources to those developing countries which were hurt by the GFC. The G 20

Declaration of the Summit on Financial Markets and the World Economy proposed actions such as these: "We should review the adequacy of the resources of the IMF, the World Bank Group and other multilateral development banks and stand ready to increase them where necessary. The IFIs (International Financial Institutions) should also continue to review and adapt their lending instruments to adequately meet their members' needs and revise their lending role in the light of the ongoing financial crises. We should explore ways to restore emerging and developing countries' access to credits and resume private capital flows which are critical for sustainable growth and development, including ongoing infrastructure investment. In cases where severe market disruptions have limited access to the necessary financing for counter-cyclical fiscal policies, multilateral development banks must ensure arrangements are in place to support, as needed, those countries with a good track record and sound policies." (Declaration of the Summit on Financial Markets and the World Economy 2008, p. 5) A similar proposal has been also accepted at the Pittsburgh Summit which contains a separate part on the reform of the mandate, of the mission, and of the governance of the IMF: "We have delivered on our promise to treble resources available to the IMF: We are contributing over $ 500 billion to a renewed and expanded IMF New Arrangements to Borrow (NAB) Facility. The IMF has made Special Drawing Rights (SDR) allocations of $ 283 billion in total, more than $ 100 billion of which will supplement emerging market and developing countries' existing reserve assets. Resources from the agreed sale of IMF gold, consistent with the IMF's new income model, and funds from internal and other sources will more than double the Fund's medium-term concessional lending capacity." Additionally it is promised: "Our collective response to the crisis has highlighted both the benefits of international cooperation and the need for a more legitimate and effective IMF. The Fund must play a critical role in promoting global financial stability and rebalancing growth. We welcome the reforms of IMF's lending facilities, including the creation of the innovative Flexible Credit Line. The IMF should continue to strengthen its capacity to help its members cope with financial volatility, reducing the economic disruption from sudden swings in capital flows and the perceived need for excessive reserve accumulation. As recovery takes hold, we will work together to strengthen the Fund's ability to provide even-handed, candid and independent surveillance of the risks facing the global economy and the international financial system. We ask the IMF to support our effort under the Framework for Strong, Sustainable and Balanced Growth through its surveillance of our countries' policies frameworks and their collective implications for financial stability and the level and pattern of global growth." (Pittsburgh Summit 2009, paragraphs 19 and 20)

2.5 Stabilisation of the Global Economic System and Sound Economic Policies

The G20 approach argues in a comprehensive manner that banking reforms as well as the provision of additional resources are a necessary, but not sufficient steps to regain growth after the GFC. A sound macroeconomic policy has to be provided at the national level as well through international cooperation. Referring to the needs of the SSA countries it is requested to reduce government budget deficits in developed countries and to enhance savings as well as investment. Benefits are expected to SSA from the stabilisation of the international monetary system, as it is formulated by G20 and international financial institutions. Actions are defined as "durably anchoring fiscal, monetary and financial regulatory policies of the main reserve issuers…and the international monetary system…could be made even more resilient if countries' appetite for self-insurance - and hence their demand for reserves – could be reduced. This demand, which is expected to rise further in the wake of the crisis, is at the heart of a recurring source of instability of the international monetary system…sound economic policies clearly can reduce the need for insurance over time as policy credibility is enhanced and confidence in currencies is strengthened. At the global level, we should seek ways to reduce the impact of volatile capital flows and hence their potential to disrupt financial systems. Third-party insurance should in theory be the most efficient alternative, but pricing uncertainties and significant counterparty risks have prevented the emergence of a market for this." (Strauss-Kahn 2009, p. 10) To provide a sustainable growth in developing countries, developed countries are called upon to foster trade liberalisation, to encourage the flow of long-term capital to developing countries, and to extend official development assistance to heavily indebted countries and to eradicate poverty. Reforming the IMF is an important task ahead, and various proposals are discussed (Box 4).

Box 4: Reform proposals concerning the international monetary system

John Williamson: "The IMF needs a rulebook that commits it to active surveillance of the macroeconomic policies of its systemically important members, based on regular calculation of a set of mutually consistent reference exchange rates believed to be compatible with a generally acceptable set of current account balances."

Henk Brower: "This would not only require frequent policy negotiations among the major countries, it will also be very difficult to reach an agreement on the level of this reference exchange rate, let alone doing so regularly."

Jane D' Arista: ...to create a public international investment fund for emerging economies..."to provide flows that are stable, in amounts appropriate to the size of a country's economy and directed towards the goals of development rather than solely toward the short term profits of investors." The proposal focuses on changes in the financial structure of the IMF (contributions of the member countries as a limit to extend the lending facility, and the permit to intervene in private markets).

Henk Brower reminds us that this proposal has been rejected at the Bretton Woods Conference in 1944, and since then there was no acceptance on reforms.

Source: Teunissen 2007, pp. 7

2.6 Regional Actions

Simultaneously with the G20 the European Union has started deliberations on how to implement actions to regain stability and to reduce the volatility of the financial markets. The frame of actions was designed according to the structure of the G20 approach. However, European member states as well as the European institutions defined joint agencies which should be responsible to collect data on markets, and to coordinate and to complement actions done by the member states. Although the proposals relate mainly to the further progress of European integration and towards enhancing the organisational and staffing capabilities in Europe, the SSA countries should examine these experiences when establishing their own regional efforts to strengthen the financial industry. Summarising, it is proposed in Europe to establish at a regional level an early warning system, a macro- prudential supervision system, and to develop technical standards and a legal empowerment framework to ensure that the banks operate in a manner which is consistent with the rules (see Box 5). Furthermore, joint rescue operations are envisaged which would force banks to contribute to mutual funds and by additional taxes which are imposed on bank transactions and/or on rewards of the banking staff (bonus payments). European agencies may also get competencies to settle disagreements between national supervisory authorities. In the course of an assessment of the reliability of rating agencies European Union members discuss the viability of the establishment of an independent rating agency which is to be based in Europe.

The challenges which arise when implementing such agencies are made obvious by the lengthy process of discussions and the differing preferences among the member states, the banks and the governments. However, the program outlines various options which may be conducive to support a deeper regional co-operation on such issues in Europe, and there may be interest of those countries heading for a deeper regional integration in SSA.

Box 5: Joint European institutions to supervise the European banking industry
European Systemic Risk Board
European System of Financial Supervisors
European Supervisory Authorities
European Banking Authority
European Securities and Markets Authority
European Insurance and Occupational Pensions Authority

Source: COM 2009-499; COM 2009-503; Group on Financial Supervision in the EU

3 Policy Proposals and Conclusions

3.1 The G20 approach as a Tool Box for Policy Makers

When elaborating policy measures to be addressed to policy makers in SSA and in international financial institutions working with and for Africa, it has to be kept in mind that the G20 focuses on measures to reinstall an efficient financial industry in developed countries. The purpose of the G20 debates and proposals is it to remove the consequences of a far-reaching economic crisis with impacts on the credit supply of those countries. The approach of the G20 may also be perceived as an adjustment of the liberalisation policy for the finance industry. It is discussed how to remove the severe disadvantages of the deregulation policy in the banking industry of developed countries, a policy that was implemented in recent decades to enlarge the global capital supply and thereby to provide the resources for further global growth, not only in the developed, but also in the developing countries. The G20 approach is perceived as a means to find a badly needed equilibrium between banking sector regulation and the liberalization of the finance industry in developed and in developing countries.

SSA is called upon to adjust the respective actions to the conditions in their countries. It is within the responsibility of the policy makers to understand "that one size does not fit for all", and that a continuous adaptation is needed. For SSA additional actions are required to improve the existing banking infrastructure and to remove the deficiencies of the local financial industry; providing services to the rural areas and disseminating more quickly and effectively micro-credits to small producers are felt as pressing needs.

The reform needs for SSA in the policy proposals of the G20 are not defined in specific details. Some elements of the package are still on the agenda of a quite controversial discussion. Governments and international financial institutions have yet not been able to decide on concrete actions. The concept of the G20 for Africa is not clearly defined. Macroeconomic adjustment in Africa - to quote only one example - is not dealt with extensively. Reforms of the international monetary system, further progress in the trade liberalisation, and measures to enhance private capital flows and the flow of ODA to developing countries and also to SSA seem so far to be of minor importance in the G20 approach. Regional activities are not outlined yet what means that specific guidelines of action for Africa including SSA cannot be deducted for policy makers. However, there is an urgent need to develop such concrete guidelines for action as the finance industry in Africa is so important for the future development of the continent.

3.2 Ensuring Transparency and Supervision

To insulate SSA countries from crises like the GFC these countries should establish a sound system to ensure transparency and supervision. SSA is therefore urgently requested to install a mechanism which enables it to create transparency and supervision. Rules have to enforce the financial industry to inform the general public. The supervisory agents should check the risk assessment continuously. Liquidity regulations have also to be installed and controlled. Regular reports as financial stability analysis and stress tests have to be provided by the banking sector. These standards should be in conformity with international norms, referring to "asset classification, provisioning and income recognition mandatory for banks. Secondly, the regulators should impose meaningful penalties on banks which fail to comply with these mandatory standards, and on their auditors." (Brownbridge/Maimbo 2003, p. 62) Referring to the capitalization of the financial industry, the adjusted Basle rules should be applied in SSA. Criteria for intervention should include the efficiency of capital allocation, the definition of incentives for compliance with the rules, and the minimisation of transaction costs of credit provision. Banks' regulations should be done in such a way as to reduce the administrative costs being incurred by the rules.

With regard to the dissemination of banking services in SSA countries supervision is to be designed in a manner which avoids the discrimination of investors in rural areas or in the informal sector (Sacerdoti 2005, pp.20). Also, bank regulations should be harmonized in line with the liberalisation of markets for goods and services as well as with social requirements (Von Drachenfels/ Krause 2009, pp. 30).

SSA is also called upon to organise for the independence and strength of all regulatory institutions. Their responsibility and capacity to act has to be defined in a comprehensive manner: "...regulatory orders, cease and desist orders, on banks and provide for strong penalties when banks fail to comply with these orders...explicit authority to take over a bank, to remove its management, to suspend shareholders' rights, to close it and to put into liquidation, based on the regulators' assessment of that bank's net worth. The regulators must have the legal authority to close and resolve an undercapitalised bank even if its regulatory capital is still positive, provided that this is in the best interests of its depositors. The bank should grant the regulators immunity from legal action in carrying out their statutory duties, provided the regulators have acted in "good faith"." (Brownbridge/ Maimbo 2003, pp. 63) Political interference has to be removed through clear and published rules to intervene. Costs of political actions against the rules have to be clarified by the regulators to the banking sector and to the general public. In addition, independence is even enlarged if there are (regional or international) autonomous institutions which supervise the regulators. Political leaders should refrain from actions against the regulators when fulfilling their duties. International financial institutions and bilateral donors are recommended to support these actions in SSA by technical consultancy and training (IMF 2009, pp. 9).

3.3 Macro-prudential Supervision and Macroeconomic Improvements

As the G20 approach referring to the macro-prudential supervision is not yet fully clarified, the international financial institutions as well as the central banks and the financial regulation bodies are well-advised to define the scope and the content of the actions being intended under the heading of macro-prudential supervision. SSA is called upon to participate in these ongoing discussions and to implement those measures which have been considered as important to create the operational and institutional capacities to elaborate macroeconomic financial stability reports and stress tests for the whole banking system. Central banks in the developed countries and international financial institutions have to provide training and consultancy services for those countries where there is an urgent need, especially to SSA countries.

Policy changes in SSA countries should therefore include fiscal reforms, especially the reduction of budget deficits, and the creation of a "fiscal space". It is recommended among other proposals to enlarge the domestic resources base through tax reforms and appropriate measures with regard of public expenditure reduction (IMF, Implications, pp. 30). Fiscal stimuli to generate growth in periods of slackening growth have to be adapted to the absorptive capacity of the local bond market and to the needs of the other investors. Countries which had been supported by the debt relief initiatives of international institutions have to create conditions for the long-term debt sustainability of local capital markets (IMF 2009, pp. 7).

Policy-makers in SSA countries and in international financial institutions have to find out whether the GFC is the starting point of a reform of the international monetary system and they have to agree on reform options which are considered as promising for SSA in the future. Various controversial plans have already been formulated, and the African position is awaited. Some recommendations request changes in the policy of the IMF on surveillance. Other recommendations focus on a more regulated global financial and monetary architecture and on the extension of the IMF facilities to be provided for those developing countries which are hurt by international monetary imbalances. Other policy proposals imply it to install a "managed floating plus" system which is intended to mitigate the impact of exchange rate fluctuations on the borrowing capacity of developing countries, and to support the development of local and regional bond markets in and among developing countries. However, in the past there was neither a consensus about this policy proposal nor were there efforts to establish local currency bond markets. International investors were not attracted and so there was no real impact on the local economies. Therefore it is concluded that policy options should provide for a liberalisation of the financial markets and for measures in developing countries such as the SSA countries which develop the domestic financial sector by macroeconomic and institutional reforms on the basis of good governance (Obstfeld 2008, pp. 28).

An alternative policy approach geared to the needs of SSA contains the provision of financial support to those countries being inflicted by the GFC, either by additional financial facilities and/or technical consultancy services. Main points on the consultancy agenda should be the macroeconomic management, reforms of the financial industry, the policy framework for setting-up of a strong business community, and specific actions to eradicate poverty (IMF 2009, p. 10; Spratt 2009, pp. 244). Developed countries' policies should also consider trade liberalisation as a means to match the impact of the GFC on developing countries and SSA, and ways to shift resources which may be spent to generate "fiscal space" and local resources so as to increase the capital supply to financial markets (Bibow 2010, pp. 34).

Referring to the lack of sustainable regional efforts to set up joint stock markets in SSA, the World Bank and other donors should undertake additional efforts to strengthen the African Development Bank as a partner and supporter of African regional efforts (Spratt 2009, pp. 269). Existing stock markets have to establish an improved administration, the agreement on a central depositary system, and a profit-based ownership system through legal and organizational changes at the regional level (Yartey/Abjasi 2009, pp. 18). A comprehensive program to establish a pan-African stock exchange is proposed, and there are efforts to formulate joint instruments for the stock market operations, a system for the exchange of information and comprehensive supervision, a joint listing and quoting of securities, and regular meetings between the stakeholders as issuers, brokers, banks, investors, central banks, and supervisory agencies. Also, tax policies and other regulations pertaining to the efficiency of the capital markets have to be harmonized (Report of the Feasibility Study 2008, paragraphs 225).

3.4 Conclusions

The paper focuses on the GFC impact on the Sub-Saharan African (SSA) countries, excluding South Africa; it is especially investigating on the repercussions of the GFC on the banking industry. The paper outlines proposals for reforms in the banking industry in SSA taking into consideration specifically the G20 and EU approaches and proposals.

The approach of the G20 may be perceived as a timely adjustment of the liberalisation and regulation policy in the global financial industry. The G20 approach is a means to find a new equilibrium between enforcing effective banking regulations and continuing with the liberalization of the finance industry in developed and in developing countries. It is within the responsibility of the policymakers in the SSA countries to understand "that one size does not fit for all", so that the African governments and the African subregions have to formulate their own solutions and have then to implement these proposed and agreed upon measures. A continuous adaptation of measures to regulate and to liberalize financial markets and banking systems in their countries is needed and marks the profile of a wise policy-making. Referring to the situation in SSA additional actions are required so as to improve the existing banking infrastructure, especially in order to provide better services in rural areas and to disseminate more micro-credits to small producers. SSA is also urgently requested to install a mechanism that enables it to create better conditions of transparency and supervision in the African finance industry. Rules have to enforce the financial industry to inform the general public about the situation and the trends. Bank capitalization in Africa should also be adjusted according to the newest Basle standards. SSA is called upon to organise for the independence of all regulatory institutions and for the banking institutions itself. The responsibility of the African regulatory institutions has to be defined in a comprehensive manner. Political interference has to be removed through clear, transparent and published rules and rights to intervene. Independence can be enhanced if there are regional and/or international autonomous institutions which have the capacity to supervise the national regulators. Political leaders should refrain from actions against the regulators when they are fulfilling their duties. SSA should participate in discussions and deliberations on a more effective macro-prudential surveillance system. Policy changes in SSA should therefore include fiscal reforms, especially the reduction of budget deficits and the creation of a "fiscal space" which enables the extension and the deepening of a sustainable banking system. International financial institutions and donors are invited to support the recommended actions by training and consultancy.

References

African Governors (2009), African Governors to the Bretton Woods Institutions, Freetown Declaration, http://www.mofed.gov.sl/index?phpoption=com_contentsdu_ pdf=18id=99, approached 12. 5. 2010

African Union (2008), Presentation by The Commissioner for Economic Affairs on Global Financial Crisis, http://www.africaunion.org/UA/Conferences/2009/Jan/Summit_Jan_2009/doc/CONFERENCE/Financial%20Crisis%20final%20MM.doc approached 14. 5. 2010

Assembly of the African Union (2009), The African Development Bank Group, Statement at the Assembly of the African Union Twelfth Ordinary Session 1 – 3 February 2009, Addis Ababa, Ethiopia, Economic Impact of Financial Crisis, Dr. Donald Kaberuka, President, African Development Bank Group, February 3, http://www.africa-union.org/root/UA/Conferences/2009/Jan/Summit_Jan_2009/doc/CONFERENCE/ASS-FIN-CRISIS_ADB_030209/DOC approached 12. 5. 2010

Beck, Thorsten/Fuchs, Michael/Uy, Marilou (2009), Finance in Africa, Achievements and Challenges, Finance and Private Sector Development Department, World Bank, Africa Region, Policy Research, WPS 5020, Washington D. C.

Bibow, Jörg (2010), Global Imbalances, the U.S. Dollar, and How the Crisis at the Core of Global Finance Spread to "Self-insuring" Emerging Market Economies, Working Paper No. 591, Levy Economics Institute of Bard College, Annandale-on-Hudson, March

BMF/Bundesministerium für Finanzen (2009), Ergebnisse der Treffen der G20-Staats- und Regierungschefs sowie der Jahrestagung von IWF und Weltbank und des G7-Finanzminister-Treffens, in: Monatsbericht des BMF, Oktober, pp. 69 - 76

Bossone, Biagjo/Honohan, Patrick (2003), Coping with a Small Financial System: Policy Issues for Africa, in: African Business Finance and Development Policy, co-published as Journal of African Business, Volume 4, Number 2, Haworth Press, New York, London, Oxford, pp. 5 – 20

Brownbridge, Martin/Maimbo, Samuel Munzele (2003), Can Prompt Corrective Action Rules Work in the Developing World? in: African Business Finance and Development Policy, co-published as Journal of African Business, Volume 4, Number 2, Haworth Press, New York, London, Oxford, pp. 47 – 68

Bundesbank, Deutsche (2009), Internationale Zusammenarbeit auf dem Gebiet der laufenden Bankenaufsicht, in: Deutsche Bundesbank, Monatsbericht, 61. Jahrgang, Nummer 12, pp. 53 - 64

Byaruhanga, Charles/Henstridge, Mark/Kasakende, Louis (2010), Exchange Rate, Fiscal, and Monetary Policy, in: Florence Kuteesa/Emmanuel Tumusiime-Mutebile/Alan Whitworth/Tim Williamson, Eds., Uganda's Economic Reform, Insider Accounts, Oxford University Press, Oxford, pp. 52 - 88

Camara, Modibo Khane (1998), Die Finanzsektorreform in Afrika, Das Beispiel der Franc-Zone, Entwicklung und Finanzierung, Development and Finance, Bd./ Vol. 5, Lang, Frankfurt am Main, Berlin, New York, Paris Wien

COM 2009_499, Commission of the European Communities, (COM2009) 499 final, 23. 9. 2009, Proposal for a Regulation of the European Parliament and of the Council on Community macro-prudential oversight of the financial system and establishing a European Systemic Risk Board

COM 2009_503, Commission of the European Communities, (COM2009) 503 final, 23. 9. 2009, Proposal for a regulation of the European Parliament and of the Council establishing a European Securities and Markets Authority

Cortez, Ana (1999), Introduction – Africa, in: Global Financial Turmoil and Reform: A United Nations Perspective, Barry Herman, Supervising Editor, United Nations University Press, New, York, Tokyo, Paris 1999, pp. 201 - 204

Declaration of the Summit on Financial Markets and the World Economy (2008), Washington, D. C., http://www.whitehouse.gov/news/releases/2008/11/print/20081115-1.html, approached 16. 11. 2008

Declaration on Strengthening the Financial System (2009), G-20 Meeting of Finance Ministers and Central Bank Governors, London, 4-5 September 2009, http://www.g20org/Documents/FMCBG_Declaration_-_Final.pdf, approached 1. 1. 2010

Declaration on further steps to strengthen the financial system (2009), Department of Finance, Canada – News Release 2009 – 83, 9. 4. 2009, http://www.fingc/ca/n08/data/09-083_eng.asp, approached 1. 1. 2010

Degefe, Befekadu (1999), South-East Asia's Economic Crisis and Africa: A View from the African Region, in: Global Financial Turmoil and Reform: A United Nations Perspective, Barry Herman, Supervising Editor, United Nations University Press, New, York, Tokyo, Paris 1999, pp. 205 - 212

Von Drachenfels, Christian/Krause, Matthias (2009), Fostering Economic Development in Sub-Saharan Africa: What Role for Reforming Business Regulations?, in: CESifo Forum, 4, München, pp. 30 – 35

Forum Proceedings (2008), 2008 Partnership Forum for Making Finance Work in Africa, Accra, Ghana, June 17 – 18, 2008, http://www.afdb/fileadmin/uploads/Documents/Kadinga%20Finance%20Work %20for % Africa%20Proceedings.pdf approached 14. 5. 2010

Fosu, Augustin Kwasi/Naudé, Wim (2009), The Global Economic Crisis, Towards Syndrome-Free Recovery for Africa, World Institute for Development Economics Research, WIDER Discussion Paper WDP 2009/3, Helsinki, June

Group on Financial Supervision in the EU, The de Larosière Group: The High-Level Group on Financial Supervision in the EU Chaired by Jacques de Larosière, Report, http://ec.europa.eu/internalmarket/finances/docs/ delarosiere_report_en.pdf approached 16. 5. 2010

HWWI (2010), Afrika, Strategie 2030, Vermögen und Leben in der nächsten Generation. Eine Initiative des Hamburgischen Welt-Wirtschaftsinstituts und der Berenberg Bank, Berenberg Bank, HWWI Hamburgisches Welt-Wirtschaftsinstitut, Hamburg

IMF (2009), Impact of the Global Financial Crisis on Sub-Saharan Africa, Washington, D. C.: IMF, http://www.imf.org/external/pubs/ft/books/2009/afrglobfin/ssaglobalfin.pdf Approached: 10/7/2010

IMF (2010), International Monetary Fund: Sub-Saharan Africa Back to Growth?, World Economic Outlook, World Economic and Financial Surveys, Regional Economic Outlook, April, http://www.imf.org/external/pubs/ft/reo/2010/afr/eng/sreo0410.pdf approached 16. 5. 2010

Joseph, Anne (2002), La réforme du secteur financier en Afrique, OECD Development Centre, Technical Paper 190, OECD, Paris

Kabango, Grant P./Paloni, Alberto (2010), Financial liberalisation and industrial development in Malawi, March, http://www.gla.ac.uk/media_145952_en.pdf, approached 15. 5. 2010

Listing of Grand Towers Africa Fund (2010), Listing of Grand Towers Africa Fund PCC on the Stock Exchange of Mauritius, http://www.stockexchangeofMauritius.com/downloadsGrandTowers.pdf approached 10/7/2010

Macias, José Brambila/Massa, Isabella (2009), The global financial crisis and sub-Saharan Africa, The effects of slowing private capital inflows on growth, ODI Working Paper 304, London, June

Naudé, Wim (2010), Fallacies about the Global Financial Crisis Harm Recovery in the Poorest Countries, in: CESifo Forum, 4, München, pp. 3 - 12

Nissanke, Machiko (2002), African Experiences with Financial Sector Reforms: What Has Been Achieved So Far?, in: Deregulation and the Banking Crisis in Nigeria, A Comparative Study, Edited by Howard Stein/Olu Aajakaniye/Peter Lewis, Eds., International Political Economic Studies, Houndmills, Basingstoke and New York, ISBN 0-333-72142-X, pp. 129 – 167

Obstfeld, Maurice (2008), International Finance and Growth in Developing Countries: What Have We Learned?, Working Paper No. 34, Commission on Growth and Development, Australian Government, AusAID, Department for International Development, Dutch Ministry of Foreign Affairs, The William and Flora Hewlett Foundation, SIDA, The World Bank, Washington D. C., http://www.growthcommission.org/storage/cgdev/documents/gcwp03wed/pdf approached 16. 5. 2010

OECD (2009), The Financial Crisis, Reform and Exit Strategies, OECD, Paris

Okeahalam, Charles, Afful, K. B. (2006), Stock markets, development indicators and investment in Sub-Saharan Africa, in: African review of money and finance, Milan, pp. 39 -60

Pittsburgh Summit (2009), Leaders' Statement: The Pittsburgh Summit, September 24 – 25, http://www.pittsburghsum mit.gov/mediacenter/129639.htm, approached 26. 09. 2009

Report of the Feasibility Study (2008), African Union, Report of the Feasibility Study on the Establishment of the Pan African Stock Exchange, Department of Economic Affairs, December, http://www.africa-union.org/root/ua/Conferences/2009/Jan/EA/11-14jan/EA622-ENG-STOCK%20EXCHANGE%20STUDY%2016122008%accept%20changes.doc approached 18. 5. 2010

Rabeck, William A. (2006), Macro Prudential Policy: A new name for some old ways of thinking?, Korea Financial Supervisory Commission/Financial Supervisory Service, International Monetary Fund, Macro Prudential Supervision Conference: Challenges for Financial Supervisors, 7 November 2006, Seoul, http://imf/org/external/up/seminars/eng/2006/macropr/pdf/ryback/pdf approached 2. 3. 2010

Sacerdoti, Emilio (2005), Access to Bank Credit in Sub-Saharan Africa: Key Issues and Reform Strategies, IMF Working Paper WP/05/166, Washington D. C.: International Monetary Fund

Sachverständigenrat (2009), Sachverständigenrat zur Begutachtung der gesamtwirtschaftlichen Entwicklung, Jahresgutachten 2009/ 2010, Die Zukunft nicht aufs Spiel setzen, http://www.sachverstaendigenrat-wirtschaft.de/gutacht/ga-content.php?gaid-55, approached 1. 1. 2010

Spratt, Stephen (2009), Development Finance, Debates, dogmas and new directions, Routledge Advanced Texts in Economics and Finance, Routledge, Milton Park and New York

Strauss-Kahn, Dominique (2009), Beyond the Crisis: Sustainable Growth and a Stable International Monetary System, Speech by Dominique Strauss-Kahn, Managing Director of the International Monetary Fund at the 6th Bundesbank Lecture in Berlin, September 4, 2009, in: Deutsche Bundesbank, Auszüge aus Presseartikeln, Nr. 38 vom 9. 9. 2009, pp. 7

Teunissen, Jan Jost (2007), Introduction, in: Teunissen, Jan Jost/Akkerman, Age (editors): Global Imbalances and Developing Countries, Remedies for a Failing

International Financial System, Forum on Debt and Development (FONDAD), FONDAD, The Hague, pp. 1 – 7

Whitworth, Alan, Williamson, Tim (2010), Overview of Ugandan Economic Reform Since 1986, in: Florence Kuteesa/Emmanuel Tumusiime-Mutebile/Alan Whitworth/Tim Williamson, Eds., Uganda's Economic Reform, Insider Accounts, Oxford University Press, Oxford, pp. 1-34

Yartey, Charles Amo, Adjasi, Charles Komla (2007), Stock Market Development in Sub-Saharan Africa: Critical Issues and Challenges, IMF Working Paper WP/07/209, Washington D. C.: International Monetary Fund

Unit 2: Regional and Country Cases

Building Infrastructures for Macroeconomic Stability of the West African Monetary Union in an Environment of the Global Financial Crisis (GFC)

A. B. Amadasun[1] and Sam Guobadia[2]

Abstract

This paper outlines the relevant incentives and fundamental measures that would help in stabilizing the West African economies in the light of the Global Financial Crisis (GFC) as they strive to achieve full monetary integration. The paper posits that there is a high level of under-development and of macro-economic instability in the ECOWAS Zone. If the problems identified were allowed to scale up within the context of the current global financial crisis, then they could lead to devastating consequences for fiscal sustainability and other critical components of the formative stages of a monetary union. The paper examines inadequacies in forging a common regional policy as a convergent platform since the sub-region suffers from chronic macroeconomic instability, and the drive for macroeconomic management of all relevant institutions is bedeviled by divergent policies. Specific examinations of the macroeconomic and financial infrastructures in the sub-region were done, including an analysis of performance score card on the macroeconomic convergence criteria. These are examined in light of the goal of achieving a full macroeconomic delivery in the ECOWAS Zone, a pre-curser for an effective and viable region-wide West African Monetary Union (WAMU). The fundamental set of solutions will emerge from quick policy convergence and the

[1] A. B. Amadasun , Ph. D, is a lecturer in the department of Political Science and Public Administration, Benson Idahosa University, Benin City, Nigeria

[2] Sam Guobadia, Ph. D, is a Senior Lecturer and Head of Department, Economics, Banking and Finance, Benson Idahosa University, Benin City, Nigeria

deepening of essential reforms in order to avert the negative contagion effects of the GFC in the drive to realize the established primary and secondary convergence targets and to achieve full economic and monetary integration for the region.

1 Introduction

The Economic Community of West African States (ECOWAS) was established as a sub regional economic group in the Treaty of Lagos of May 28, 1975. The major aim was the accelerated economic growth and development of the sub region, and ultimately, to create a common market or monetary union. From inception to date, the ECOWAS is made up of two major groups: (1) The Francophone (French speaking) Group, which comprises Benin, Burkina Faso, Cote d'Ivoire, Guinea Bissau, Mauritania, Niger, Senegal and Togo. Mauritania opted out of the group in 2002. (2) The Anglophone (English speaking) group consists of Cape Verde, the Gambia, Ghana, Guinea, Liberia, Nigeria and Sierra Leone (Guinea left the Francophone group to join the Anglophone countries in monetary cooperation and programs). The Francophone group has progressed faster than the Anglophone group in terms of efforts in setting up a monetary union – as typified in the Union Economique Monetaire de l'Ouest Africain (UEMOA). Therefore, monetary integration in the sub region is discussed from two perspectives: The non – UEMOA (Non CFA) or WAMZ (West African Monetary Zone) and the UEMOA (CFA) perspectives.

The Union Economique Monetaire de l'Ouest Africain (UEMOA) dates back to 1962. This group adopts a common currency, the CFA, issued by Banque Centrale des Etats de I' Afrique de l' Ouest (BCEAO), with the backing of the French treasury and having a fixed convertibility rate with the Euro. The Anglophone countries had a common currency prior to their independence. This was administered by the Common Currency Board of British West Africa for commercial transactions. With the granting of independence, each country adopted its own currency and conducted its national trade policies to suit its own development strategy and needs. Due to the historically divergent policies of the two groups on monetary issues, the challenge of achieving a single monetary union for the entire ECOWAS Zone requires dedication and the retained interests of the stakeholders. In 1999, it became obvious that the implementation of the ECOWAS Monetary Cooperation Program (EMCP) that was adopted in 1987 was either failing or moving at a very slow pace. Consequently, at the 22nd Summit in Lome, Togo (December 1999), the Authority of the Heads of State and Government of ECOWAS adopted a "Fast Track" approach for economic and monetary integration. Specific objectives of the EMCP include:

- Improvement and strengthening of sub-regional payments systems under the West African Clearing House (now West African Monetary Agency - WAMA);
- Introduction of limited Currency convertibility;
- Establishment of a single monetary zone (merger of the French and English speaking countries' monetary programs);
- Creation of a common central bank; and
- Ultimately, the introduction of a single common currency.

In December 2000 in Bamako, Mali, the ECOWAS Heads of State and Government have agreed to the establishment of the West Africa Monetary Zone (WAMZ), comprising the Anglophone countries, including Guinea; the establishment of a common Central Bank; and the introduction of a single common currency in 2003, and eventually to merge with UEMOA in 2004 under an ECOWAS monetary integration program. It was on this premise that the West African Monetary Institute (WAMI) was established in January 2001 to commence preparatory work for the introduction of a single currency and a common central bank in the WAMZ. Under WAMZ, primary and secondary convergence criteria were established.

The ECOWAS Zone has, in the past decade, been subjected to significant economic reforms in the macroeconomic and financial sectors with a view of achieving a viable monetary union within the context of globalization and GFC. However, the GFC has presented the region with new challenges. Data (see Table 5) for the WAMZ countries show that the average GDP growth rate has dropped from 6.44% to 5.3% between 2008 and 2009. The UEMOA group also has experienced a slight drop from 3.5% to 3.3% during the period. In the ECOWAS Zone (WAMZ and UEMOA), the GDP growth rate in 2009 was 4.9%., down from 5.8%, the figure recorded for 2008. A drop in commodity prices during the GFC has affected all the countries in the region; exports dropped from 6.8% (2008) to 3.3% (2009)[3]. The challenges in the ECOWAS Zone in the context of the current global financial crisis are, therefore, significant. They are to be tackled both at the individual Member States' level and at the sub-regional level. However, because of the complex and multi-dimensional nature of these challenges, this paper only attempts to provide broad policy guidelines for achieving full monetary integration for the region. Questions are: What macroeconomic and financial policies and

[3] See WAMA (2009:10)

programs does the sub region need to put in place in order to sustain monetary integration drives in a GFC environment? Will the liberalization of the capital markets across the sub-region be helpful to weathering the GFC? Will transparency and accountability provide additional layers of protection for the sub-region in times of crises? How important are the convergence criteria performances of the various countries in the region?

Tables 5 and 6 provide economic indicators reflecting some overall macroeconomic performance results of the region. The major challenge is however building the necessary sub-regional macroeconomic and financial infrastructures which will enhance full economic and monetary integration of the ECOWAS Zone. Therefore, one of the main objectives of this paper is to provide rigorous arguments for the building of effective macroeconomic infrastructures in the ECOWAS Zone which will insulate the region from the most devastating effects of a GFC as the region strives to achieve both full economic and monetary union. To achieve this goal will involve a complete assessment of the countries' convergence criteria performances which is carried out in Section 4. Central to the forming of any economic union is monetary integration which, if properly established, can result in regional stabilization and growth of the region during or after crises. As has been demonstrated in Europe, the goal of any monetary union is to formulate monetary and financial policies for a region and to institute the issuance of a single currency or to establish fully convertible currencies at exchange rates which are irrevocably fixed. Although the difficulties in the attempts to integrate ECOWAS Zone are quite pronounced within the WAMZ as well as the convergence problems between WAMZ and UEMOA, it is interesting to note that the benefits of monetary integration have been captured in the economic and financial progress within the UEMOA. For example, UEMOA's regional economic and financial cooperation programs have strengthened the countries' global competitiveness in a crisis or non-crisis environment as rooted in a unified external tariff system, common regulatory frameworks, periodic reviews of macroeconomic convergence, a single stock exchange (the BRVM), harmonization of consumer price indices, etc.

The efficacy of monetary integration is not in doubt. Despite the difficulty of achieving monetary integration, the practical success of a West African Monetary Union (WAMU) for the entire ECOWAS Zone depends on the willingness of the stakeholders to critically review the issues of macroeconomic convergence, but also on improved within-bloc trade, capital market liberalization, and the institution of a common currency. It also will mean the full integration of all financial and investment instruments with a single monetary authority. It thus follows that with determination at both the national and regional levels, a new West African Monetary Union (WAMU) for the ECOWAS Zone will undoubtedly stabilize the region in monetary and fiscal matters due to economies of scale, which is the ultimate goal of stakeholders, and the increased ability to achieve sustainable growth in times of crisis or non-crisis.

The paper will consider as its review period 2001 - 2009, analyzing the relevant macroeconomic convergence performance data for the period and stating the implications of key indicators for a sustainable drive for monetary union. Subsequent sections of this paper support the view that fiscal convergence will result in constraints on national fiscal policies, a reduction in nations' trade with non-bloc countries and more intra-regional trade development, a subjugation of the nations' central bank activities in favor of a single monetary authority for the whole region, and also, the loss of power over exchange rate policies. But under monetary integration, the benefits outweigh the costs of integration. These benefits include removal of hedging costs in exchange rate transactions, transparency in pricing and accounting procedures, economies of scale, increased competiveness in both the input and product markets, and the benefits of a single currency which this paper prescribes. Specifically, the rest of this paper breaks down as follows: Section 2 outlines and analyzes key macroeconomic infrastructures. This is followed by critical comments on the financial infrastructures in Section 3. Section 4 provides a detailed analysis of macroeconomic convergence performances of the various countries in the WAMZ and UEMOA groups. The paper ends with conclusions and recommendations in Section 5.

2 Macro Economic Infrastructures

The macroeconomic development of the ECOWAS Zone is best analyzed in terms of performances at the national level, group level, zonal level, and the level of macroeconomic convergence criteria, which are established for the countries in the region throughout the review period. It thus follows that the macroeconomic performance *score cards* reflect the countries' ability or inability to meet the established convergence criteria, and hence the success of monetary integration is contingent on the depth of macroeconomic convergence among the member states. These criteria are similar to the euro convergence or Maastricht criteria[4]. These criteria established the process and targets that the European countries must pass through in stages in order to achieve macroeconomic convergence for the European Monetary Union (EMU). The success of the European Union can be attributed to the established criteria and the commitment of the countries to satisfy set benchmarks.

---

[4] Duff, et al (1996: 19-53)

Presented below (Table 1) are the initial convergence criteria established for both the WAMZ and UEMOA blocs. The 1999 revised criteria were accompanied by a multilateral surveillance framework for the harmonization of macroeconomic policies. For WAMZ, the countries were expected to meet the convergence criteria by 2003/2003 because the overall convergence for the entire zone was set for 2004. The countries in the UEMOA group were expected to achieve their own convergence criteria in 2002 because the WAMZ was to fully converge in 2003.

Table 1: Convergence Criteria (1999)

Primary Criteria	Secondary Criteria
1. Budget Deficit/GDP Ratio ≤ 4% 2.Inflation rate ≤ 5% 3.Central Bank Financing of Budget Deficit ≤ 10% of Previous Year's Tax Revenues 4.Gross External Reserves ≥ 6 Months Imports Cover	1. Elimination of Domestic Arrears and Non-Accumulation of New Arrears 2. Tax Revenue/GDP Ratio ≥ 20% 3. Wage Bill/Total Tax Revenue Ratio ≤ 35% 4. Public Investment Financed Through Internal Sources/Total Tax Revenue Ratio ≥ 20% 5. Maintenance of Real Exchange Rate Stability 6. Maintenance of Positive Real Interest Rates

Source: Macroeconomic Convergence Report First Half, WAMA, 2009

We can observe from Tables 2 and 3 below that both WAMZ and UEMOA recorded mixed results in the implementation of the established 1999 Convergence Criteria for selected variables (see the highlighted convergence criteria rows in the tables). While The Gambia, Guinea and Liberia met the target in 2002 and 2003, Ghana, Nigeria and Sierra Leone failed to meet the targets for 2002 and 2003 (with the exception of Nigeria who met only the 2002 target) for the inflation criterion. For the reserves/months of imports ratio, the 2002 results were better than the 2003 performance. In 2006, none of the WAMZ countries met the 2003 benchmark. Poor performances are also recorded across board for the ratios of the central bank advances to tax revenues and the fiscal deficit to gross domestic product criteria. The UEMOA countries did not perform any much better as evidenced in Table 3.

Table 2: Revised 1999 Convergence Criteria for WAMZ Countries

	Inflation (%)	Reserves/ Months of Imports	Central Bank Advances/ %tax Revenues	Fiscal Deficit/ GDP
Gambia	1.7	5.7	32.0	4.8
Ghana	13.8	1.5	8.2	8.2
Guinea	4.6	2.6	29.6	5.1
Liberia	4.0	0.0	0.0	0.4
Nigeria	6.6	4.5	55.0	7.7
Sierra Leone	34.1	2.0	70.9	14.9
Convergence Criteria by 2002	**<10**	**>3**	**-**	**<5**
Convergence Criteria by 2003	**<5**	**>6**	**<10**	**<4**

Source: IMF Staff Estimates [see also IMF (2001: 4 -5)]

Table 3: Revised 1999 Convergence Criteria for UEMOA Countries

	Fiscal Balance/ GDP	Infl. (%)	Outstanding Debt/ GDP	Wage Bill/ Total Tax Rev.	Invest. Financed by dom. Sources	Tot. Rev./ GDP
Benin	0.5	0.3	59.3	33.0	11.3	13.7
Burkina Faso	-0.6	-1.1	70.5	37.1	19.3	14.0
Cote d'Ivoire	-1.7	1.6	118.8	33.4	15.9	17.0
Guinea-Bissau	-7.2	-0.9	364.4	66.3	43.5	7.6
Mali	0.1	-1.1	116.8	27.7	22.2	14.1
Niger	-3.1	2.9	92.2	60.2	3.6	7.7
Senegal	2.0	0.8	94.0	34.0	2.1	16.6
Togo	-1.7	-0.1	116.0	51.0	2.5	13.3
Convergence Criteria by 2002	**≥0**	**≤3**	**≤70**	**≤35**	**≥20**	**≥17**

Source: IMF Staff Estimates [see also IMF (2001: 4 -5)]

Note: The Wage Bill includes only public wages and all other personnel costs absorbed by the State

A new set of criteria[5] has, since 2002, been established for the whole ECOWAS Zone. Most of the targets in the first set of convergence criteria were retained with slight adjustments for Wage Bill/Tax revenues and Exchange Rate Stability, which are respectively adjusted such as $\leq 30\%$ and 5%. The Primary criteria, which include the specified variables, are very crucial for the achievement of macroeconomic convergence, and the targets were retained under the new set of criteria.

Fiscal Sustainability

For several reasons, fiscal sustainability is a critical tool for building infrastructures and for withstanding the GFC. Fiscal imbalances of the ECOWAS member countries have resulted in fewer investments and the build-up of government debts, which have threatened macroeconomic stability as well as monetary integration drives. The attendant higher interest rates necessitated by deficit borrowing have often compounded the problems. The transmission channels of the various countries' monetary policies become difficult to achieve[6]. ECOWAS Member Countries have experienced fiscal challenges due to the decline in performance of the external sector which resulted from the GFC of 2008 onward.

The period under review has been accompanied by shifting deadlines based on the outcomes of the earliest reviews to the most recent ones. The inability of countries to satisfy both the primary and secondary criteria has resulted in numerous shifting deadlines delaying full monetary integration of the ECOWAS Zone. This explains the deadline shift from 2003 for WAMZ and from 2004 for UEMOA, choosing July 1, 2005 for example as the new date for a common currency in WAMZ. This is what has further informed the stakeholders in WAMZ to postpone, yet again, the commencement of the monetary union in the WAMZ to 2009[7] , repositioning WAMI to achieve the newly set target date. 2009 has come and gone with a new proposed date of 2015. Hopefully, this new deadline will provide sufficient time for the WAMZ (as well as the UEMOA) countries to satisfy all the convergence criteria benchmarks. According to Jameh (2009*)*[8], "the overall progress of the convergence scale was still insufficient despite some progress made toward meeting the primary criteria; only the Gambia met the four primary criteria for the three consecutive years of 2006, 2007, and 2008" Other WAMZ countries' performances include Nigeria's ability to meet four primary criteria in

---

[5] See WAMA (2009: 4)

[6] See WAMI (2008: 24 -26)

[7] Banjul Declaration of 2005 (WAMZ DOC 2005: 1-4)

[8] Speech delivered by President Yahya Jameh, Chairman of the Heads of State of WAMZ, 2009, Abuja.)

2006 and 2007, but it was only able to meet three criteria in 2008. Guinea satisfied only two criteria in 2007 and 2008; Sierra Leone satisfied two in 2004. For Ghana, its record position in this respect was meeting two criteria between 2002 and 2007, but it failed to meet any criterion in 2008. These were the results before the effects of the GFC set in.

Several factors critically constrain fiscal sustainability in the ECOWAS Zone. The factors include unfavorable terms of trade, weak revenue base, overdependence on foreign grants, excess expenditures, and the dependence on one-export commodities. These factors often explain why negative external shocks can easily destabilize the fiscal program of ECOWAS economies, and other genuine attempts at achieving full economic and monetary integration. Also, the GFC led to a reduction in foreign direct investments, further compounding fiscal management efforts. In this kind of environment, the move towards convergence remains a difficult task in the region – requiring hard decisions and choices, particularly because macroeconomic policy coordination in the sub-region is very weak. Many ECOWAS members do not set their macroeconomic targets in consonance with the regional benchmarks to which they have committed themselves, and there is no effective mechanism for the sanctioning of member states that consistently miss the set targets. This may have, inadvertently, encouraged the trend of shifting deadlines. Onwioduokit (2004: 21 - 48) found that overall fiscal imbalances can be identified with trade and financial shocks; weak revenue base; overdependence on foreign grants; excessive expenditure; and so on.

Intra-Regional Trade

It is fair to state that full economic integration is a necessary condition for monetary integration. The ECOWAS Trade Liberalization Scheme (ETLS) and the protocol on the free movement of goods and services came into force on January 1, 1990; the aim being to establish a common union among ECOWAS member States over a 15-year (1990 – 2005) period. It represents a formidable tool established by ECOWAS for the facilitation of trade towards achieving economic integration. It specifies the free movement of citizens and goods among ECOWAS States. However, 20 years after, these protocols have not worked and the full implementation of the scheme faces several challenges, which include the lack of adequate information on the availability of products, inadequate trade facilitation and poor infrastructural development (including problems with power, transportation, and road networks). Other barriers include protection laws instituted by the various countries, corruption, the non-convertibility of the sub-region's currencies, and the lack of a common currency that could help with the facilitation of trade (Alawode, 2009: 30).

Trade among the French speaking countries has progressed faster because of the monetary integration efforts they have made under UEMOA and the adoption of a common reserve currency, CFAF. They have free internal trade and a common external tariff, free movement of products, capital and people, and the harmonization and mutual recognition of technical standards. Trade policy in most of the UEMOA countries is seen as instrument of national development. In the case of the Anglophone group, the countries opted for their individual currencies and conducted national trade policies to accommodate their individual development strategies, with numerous tariff policy variations among its members. Overall, the sub-region suffers from a low value of intra-regional trade; the countries are highly open to trade with the rest of the world at the expense of trade integration within the region. The low values and volumes of intra-ECOWAS Zone trade have been unhelpful to the regional integration process. Intra-regional trade remains at less than 15% of overall trade figures (while 70% of the European Union trade happens within the EU). The leading economies in the region; namely, Nigeria, Ghana, Cote d'Ivoire, and Senegal are sustaining respective national development agendas and thus prefer linkages with developed countries outside the region. The existence of many currencies in the sub-region is a key drawback to its trade and integration drives. In order to be able to compete globally, ECOWAS countries ought to liberalize their economies and to avoid imposition of protectionist trade laws, and so to enjoy more economies of scale.

Capital Accounts Liberalization

Capital accounts liberalization which represents the systematic removal of administrative and legal control on international capital transactions is very critical in the policy reforms for ECOWAS Zone's monetary union in the context of the GFC. Ojo[9], citing a study carried out by the West African Monetary Agency (WAMA), West Africa Monetary Institute (WAMI) and the ECOWAS Secretariat, found that in the region of the UEMOA countries, capital movements were liberalized but capital movements between UEMOA and WAMZ were regulated. Overall, ECOWAS presents a case of a sub-region with an above average level of controls on capital movements which situation is not good for monetary union drives, particularly within the context of developing a capital market for the region and enhancing capital resourcefulness which could shelter the region from the effects of contagion. Capital account liberalization in the ECOWAS sub-region assumes complexities that involve action in several economies with diverse features and management practices. Against this background, for ECOWAS to be able to weather the current financial crisis and future ones, it must address the mini-

[9] Paper presented at Central Bank of Nigeria Seminar Series, 2006

mum conditions for effective capital account liberalization. These conditions include: 1. Stable macroeconomic environment that is free of high domestic inflation rates, fiscal and monetary instability, and external imbalances of its member countries. 2. Strong prudential guidelines and adequate supervisory frameworks that would checkmate excessive financial market risks. 3. Stable political environment in the sub-region. 4. The financial sector must be sound and fully integrated within the context of a monetary union. 5. Determination and execution of a well sequenced liberalization program. This is important because the ECOWAS Zone is made up of a number of countries that are likely to be at different stages of economic and financial development, evolution of institutional structures as well as legal and business practices.

Exchange Rate Mechanism and Common Currency

There are about eight different currencies in the ECOWAS, of which the CFA Franc (now simply referred to as CFA) – the common currency of the French speaking West African Economic and Monetary Union - is one of them. The ECOWAS Monetary Cooperation Program (EMCP) adopted in 1987 continues to pursue the realization of a common currency for the sub-region. In order to make the ECOWAS payment system more efficient and to pave the way for the emergence of a single monetary zone, the West African Monetary Agency (WAMA) was established in 1995. The adoption of a single currency is to be facilitated by a transitional Exchange Rate Mechanism (ERM) in the WAMZ. This is designed to encourage exchange rate stability and to assist the process towards merging with the CFA Zone and towards the monetary convergence of the entire sub-region. In the drive to achieve a single currency for the sub-region, two options have been debated within WAMZ; namely, fixed parities relative to a regional/zonal basket of currencies and each participating currency would have a par value against the other currency allowing for fluctuation within a band of $\pm$15%. The current prescribed band is $\pm$5. When an exchange rate approaches the upper or lower limit of its fluctuation range, the WAMZ zone's central banks would be obligated to intervene in the market. In addition, the need for countries to hold reserves in the zone's currencies will allow them the leverage to intervene to support the bilateral exchange rates, but there is the problem of the Zone's currency not being internationally traded. And the implementation of this option requires meeting the guidelines for efficient convertibility system. The alternative option available to WAMZ in the transition to a single currency is to provide for fixed parities relative to an international reserve currency or a basket of foreign currencies. WAMI has recommended a fixed adjustable peg of the zone's currency to an outside-the-region reserve currency similar to the CFA Franc/Euro arrangement under UEMOA. This option has the advantage of simplicity, transparency and consistency for trade partners of the zone, and so would support external trade. Furthermore it would focus exchange rate policy on promoting external competiveness and make transition to a common currency with the CFA zone easier as the CFA is pegged to the Euro[10]. The option has, at least, two disadvantages; pegging to an external currency will mean that Central Banks would need to have sufficient currency/reserves to undertake intervention, and the option lacks appeal to nationalistic sentiments. Currently, there are two parallel exchange rate systems in the ECOWAS Zone; a fixed exchange rate system for the UEMOA group and a flexible (±5% band or fluctuation margin) exchange rate regime for the WAMZ group.

3 Financial Infrastructures

Financial Reporting and Accounting Standards

The globalization of financial and product markets has raised the interest of market participants and regulators in the quality of financial reporting worldwide due to the rise of stock returns and the spread of bubble assets. Questions are: Would greater transparency in financial statement information reduce volatility and produce more accurate stock value within the context of the current global financial crisis in the ECOWAS sub-region? Would more transparent financial statements improve lending and credit evaluation decisions and contain banking crisis in the ECOWAS Zone (or banking crises that emanate elsewhere)? These are important questions for the stakeholders and all the financial system participants in the ECOWAS Zone, particularly within the context of assessing the impact of the current global financial crisis.

Market participants seek high quality financial information because it mitigates information asymmetry between management of firms and outside investors. The salient institutional factors are the nature of corporate governance, the legal system, and the existence of laws governing protection and disclosure standards[11]. But there is a persistent weakness in these factors in the ECOWAS financial system. There is no doubt that high quality financial reporting is important for efficient financial systems. Within the ECOWAS sub-region and in the context of the global financial crisis, there seems to be a consensus for the need for a high quality financial reporting system. Since the financial system remains a critical nerve center of the ECOWAS monetary/economic system, sound financial reporting and its importance cannot be overstressed.

[10] See Obadan (2002: 149 – 165)

[11] see Alashi (2002: 86 -102)

Banking Sector Supervision

UEMOA has established the Banking Commission as a supra-supervisory agency in the Union. The Commission is funded by the Central Bank of West African States (BCEAO) and it carries out both on-site and off-site supervision of 64 banks and 24 other financial institutions in the Union. As of December 21, 2001, the UEMOA banking system has total assets of US$ 7billion (Alashi, 2002). Banking activities in UEMOA are governed by a Uniform Act for all member States within a community-based framework. As a result, the UEMOA Council of Ministers determines the general framework and ensures the overall cohesion of the community-based mechanism. Consequently, the banks and the financial institutions are answerable to a Triple Authority in varying degrees. These include the Ministry of Finance in the country of location; the Central Bank of West African States (BCEAO), the issuing authority which manages the common currency (CFA) and which drafts relevant regulations particularly in the area of banking; and also the UEMOA Banking Commission, which is responsible for the regulation and monitoring of the banking systems. The framework is constantly reviewed in light of the UEMOA developments and in response to global financial systems requirements, and development and growth trends. In addition, since 1998 the Union has in place a single licensing mechanism, and the BCEAO is the licensing authority.

In WAMZ, the Central Bank in each Member State is the apex regulatory institution with the exception of Nigeria where the Nigeria Deposit Insurance Corporation (NDIC) complements the efforts of the CBN in supervising banks. The coverage of supervision varies from one Member State to another. For instance, the Central Bank of The Gambia also supervises insurance companies, whereas in Nigeria insurance companies are supervised by the National Insurance Commission of Nigeria. This kind of variation is certainly bound to produce opposition to a proposal for a unified banking regulatory agency in the WAMZ. Only Nigeria has an effective financial safety net that includes an Explicit Deposit Insurance Scheme (EDIS); the other member states in the WAMZ operate only on the basis of Implicit Deposit Protection Schemes (IDPS).

The major issue is the role defined for the ECOWAS banking sector in terms of economic development in the sub-region, particularly in times of crises. The desire would be to establish a financial system that is efficient, competitive and stable, providing diversity of choice; macroeconomic stability; economic development; and accomplishment of other social objectives. The importance of the banking sector supervision in the sub-region cannot be over-emphasized, especially as indications point to a weak banking sector in terms of performance, structure and regulation. Many of the supervisory agencies lack sufficient independence from special interest groups and the political process, thus rendering them ineffective. Any viable banking sector reform for the sub-region will have to include prudential guidelines, efficient information gathering systems, and enhanced liquidity management.

Capital Market Development in the ECOWAS Monetary Integration Agenda

Undoubtedly, the GFC has had a direct impact on the ECOWAS Zone. Capital flight, collapse of the stock markets, and the overall deterioration of financing conditions dealt a severe blow to investment growth and GDP growth, as we see in the tables presented in this paper. For this and other reasons, the stakeholders in the region must speed up full development of the capital markets. A key component of the sub-regional drive to achieve a comprehensive economic and monetary integration is the setting up of a common investment and capital market superstructure. A capital market integration involves perfect capital mobility, and the sub-regional investment projects are then financed by a pool of capital; free movement of capital assets with minimal costs of doing so; all participants in the capital markets are free to transact financial businesses throughout the region without any hindrance. In recognition of this, the moves toward full integration of the three major stock exchanges in the ECOWAS sub-region received a boost on December 4, 2009 at the conclusion of the 13th Annual Conference of the African Securities Exchanges Association that was held in Abuja, Nigeria. The representatives of the two major WAMZ stock exchanges (Nigerian and Ghana stock exchanges) as well as the Bourse Regionale des Valeurs Mobilieres (BRVM) signed a Memorandum of Understanding (MOU), expressing their commitment to integrate the stock exchanges in the region. The BRVM is a regional stock exchange for the Francophone West African countries and serves Cote d'Ivoire, Benin Republic, Burkina Faso, Mali, Niger, Senegal, Togo, and Guinea-Bissau. The ultimate goal for the stakeholders is to have a common stock exchange serving the entire sub-region by instituting a regional platform which addresses differences in currencies, language, and laws guiding securities regulations.

There are many benefits from capital market integration. An integrated capital market signifies deeper capital markets for all participants. It creates and supports a situation where huge capital resources are mobilized for investment purposes. It also encourages competition and a more efficient allocation of resources among competing alternatives. Above all, capital market integration yields other dividends in the form of investment opportunities, economies of scale, bigger stock markets, longer listings, higher yields, industrial transformation of markets, improved macroeconomic performance, and so on. The foregoing definition and the benefits of capital market integration inform the keen mind why the stakeholders in the ECOWAS Zone are desirous of achieving full capital market integration despite the odds. In a globalizing world with heavy emphasis on private sector-led approaches to development in open economies and regional economic blocs, capital market integration would seem to be a strategic solution for the monetary and financial challenges of the region. The ECOWAS Zone is increasingly becoming an intricate part of the globalizing world which is still largely rooted in market fundamentals.

The West African sub-region boasts of a vibrant private sector modeled on the basis of market orthodoxy. Many of the private companies are officially listed and traded at the Nigerian Stock Exchange, the Ghana Stock Exchange, and the BRVM. Also, the activities of several banking and non-banking financial institutions due to regulatory shocks and actions have further deepened the capital markets. Some of the investment and financial institutions have started to develop global outreach as a result of the huge financial mobilization credited to the stock markets. Since globalization is pervasive, it is important to acknowledge that the growth and the changes in capital markets worldwide can be traced to the increasing interactions among global capital market participants, including investment banks and issuers; and to the competition among brokers, investors, and exchanges. Furthermore, the growth in demand for capital market instruments is in the upswing; the increase in the supply of financial resources on a border-less basis have spurred fresh competition, whereby the exchanges and economic blocs that survive will be those benefitting from the assessments measured by the relative sizes of the market and the depth of trading activities. It is necessary that the ECOWAS Zone develops quickly and liberalizes its capital market sector in order to compete globally on the one hand. On the other hand, deep and effective mobilization of financial resources for development of the real sector is also a great motivating factor. To speed up this development, policy guidelines will include lowering of costs of financial transactions, reduction of associated risks in cross-border capital transfers, and a faster integration of the capital markets, etc. The willingness and readiness of the Zone on this subject is captured in the setting up of the Common Investment Market Initiative (CIMI), adopted by the Authority of the Heads of state in the sub-region.

The drive to achieve one regional capital market has resulted in the setting up of the ECOWAS Common Investment Code (ECIC), the ECOWAS Investment Policy Framework (EIPF), and the ECOWAS Bank for Investment and Development (EBID). The code and the framework contain guidelines on competition and investment rules, and they have sufficiently laid the foundation for the take-off of the sub-regional Investment Market Process. The challenge in this regard does not rest on the formats of the codes and frameworks, but rather, on the accomplishment of agreements on convergent positions, the peculiarity of the divergent views, and the streamlining of convergence criteria in all aspects of capital market institutions. The EBID, which was transformed from the ECOWAS Fund, has, as its main goal, the facilitation of business, investment, and financial transactions in the ECOWAS Zone. This bank (EBID) has contributed to financial and capital market developments throughout the sub region. As the principal financial institution of ECOWAS, its increasing activities are designed to encourage the achievement of full economic and monetary integration of the region. The private sector focus of EBID includes adopting the private sector as the engine of sustainable growth and development. It also takes the financing of cross-border investment projects and the marrying of UEMOA and WAMZ as its primary objectives.

Deepening Effects of Capital Markets Development in the ECOWAS Zone

Many banking reforms in the sub-region have triggered the deepening effects of the capital markets, and most of the financial institutions view the capital markets as the preferred source of raising capital. The development of the capital markets and the interest in equity financing have already yielded huge benefits - for the small savers, for the companies, as well as for the development of the capital market sector itself. A vibrant capital market sector will encourage the public to provide investible funds by purchasing securities as part of their investment choices. This leads to economies of scale in all the sectors of the sub-regional economy, encourages the citizens of ECOWAS to be more inclined to save and to invest by way of equity. The growth of the capital markets is best captured by the ratios of Market Capitalization to GDP (MC/GDP) for Ghana, Nigeria, and the BRVM, as shown in Table 4. The trends established in table 4 are encouraging, and they represent the deepening effects of the capital markets. While the ratio of market capitalization to GDP was quite low in the 1980's and 1990's, there has been a significant improvement on the market capitalization as shown in the numbers recorded for the years 2000 to 2008, prior to the GFC. Although there are no figures for 2009 on the table 4, the weakening global economy had started to show some strain in the market as reflected in the drop for market capitalization between 2007 and 2008.

Table 4: Ratio of Market Capitalization to Gross Domestic Product for Ghana, Nigeria & the BRVM

Countries	Years										
	1988	1989	1990	1991	1992	1993	1994	1995	1996	1997	1998
Ghana	-	-	-	1.2	1.3	2.0	34.4	25.5	21.5	16.5	18.5
Nigeria	4.2	4.2	4.8	6.9	3.7	4.8	11.5	7.2	10.1	10.1	9.0
Cote'Ivoire /BRVM	4.3	5.4	5.1	5.2	4.3	3.7	5.1	7.9	7.5	10.9	14.2

Countries	Years									
	1999	2000	2001	2002	2003	2004	2005	2006	2007	2008
Ghana	11.9	10.1	9.9	12.0	18.7	29.8	15.5	25.4	15.9	21.1
Nigeria	8.5	9.2	11.3	9.7	14.0	16.5	17.2	22.3	52.0	23.5
Cote'Ivoire/BRVM	12.1	11.4	11.0	11.6	12.0	13.5	14.2	23.9	42.2	30.2

Source: World Development Indicators, (WDI 2009 Database) World Bank

To fully maximize the gains from a comprehensive sub-regional integration this will require harmonization in monetary policies, financial services policies, investment policies, corporate tax policies, and the intensification of capital market integration and development. This suggests that to achieve a viable common capital market may essentially result in some loss of sovereignty, because success will require a considerable amount of policy cooperation and harmonization. A common sub-regional Investment and Capital Market must contain the following essential components:

(a) Free movement of capital assets;
(b) Access to Commercial Credit throughout the ECOWAS Zone;
(c) Ease of opening an account with brokerage firms as well as other financial institutions; and
(d) Ease of transfers of dividends, capital gains and other profits from financial services.

4 Analysis of Score Cards on Macroeconomic Convergence Criteria

This section contains an analysis of the most recent trends in macroeconomic performance and the satisfaction of convergence criteria for all the fifteen countries of the ECOWAS Zone. While the tables 5 and 6 give trends in growth and inflation, the tables 7 through 12 reveal that the movement of the countries towards macroeconomic convergence remains mixed, with some countries doing better on the macroeconomic and convergence scales than others.

Table 5: Trends in Economic Growth within ECOWAS, 2002 – 2009

	2002	**2003**	**2004**	**2005**	**2006**	**2007**	**2008**	**2009**
ECOWAS	3.7	6.8	5.1	5.7	5.4	5.6	5.8	4.9
UEMOA	1.3	3.1	2.8	4.2	3.1	3.1	3.8	3.5
BENIN	**4.4**	**3.9**	**3.1**	**2.9**	**3.8**	**4.6**	**5.0**	**3.8**
BURKINA FASO	**4.6**	**8.0**	**4.6**	**7.1**	**5.5**	**3.6**	**5.0**	**3.5**
COTE D'VOIRE	**-1.6**	**-1.7**	**1.6**	**1.8**	**1.2**	**1.5**	**2.3**	**3.7**
GUINEA BISSAU	**-7.1**	**0.6**	**3.2**	**3.5**	**1.8**	**2.7**	**3.3**	**2.9**
MALI	**4.3**	**7.6**	**2.3**	**6.1**	**5.3**	**4.3**	**5.1**	**4.1**
NIGER	**5.8**	**3.8**	**-0.8**	**8.4**	**5.8**	**3.3**	**9.5**	**3.0**
SENEGAL	**1.2**	**6.7**	**5.6**	**5.6**	**2.3**	**4.7**	**2.5**	**3.1**
TOGO	**-0.2**	**4.8**	**2.5**	**1.2**	**3.9**	**2.1**	**1.6**	**2.5**
WAMZ	4.6	8.8	6.3	6.4	6.0	6.35	6.44	5.3
GAMBIA	**1.3**	**7.4**	**6.6**	**6.9**	**7.7**	**6.9**	**6.1**	**3.6**
GHANA	**4.5**	**5.2**	**5.6**	**5.9**	**6.4**	**6.3**	**7.3**	**5.9**
GUINEA	**4.2**	**1.2**	**2.3**	**3.0**	**2.4**	**1.8**	**4.9**	**1.2**
NIGERIA	**4.6**	**9.6**	**6.6**	**6.5**	**6.0**	**6.5**	**6.4**	**5.3**
SIERRA LEONE	**6.5**	**10.7**	**9.6**	**7.6**	**7.2**	**6.4**	**5.6**	**5.9**
Others	6.1	2.4	1.9	4.2	8.1	7.7	6.3	4.3
CAPE-VERDE	**5.3**	**4.7**	**4.3**	**5.6**	**8.2**	**6.7**	**5.9**	**4.0**
LIBERIA	**7.8**	**-1.9**	**-2.8**	**1.4**	**7.8**	**9.5**	**7.1**	**4.9**

Source: WAMA, Central Banks, and ECOWAS Member States (EMCP Macroeconomic Convergence Report First Half, 2009)

For ease of analysis, the countries' score cards will be assessed based on the established primary and secondary criteria. Firstly, as we have seen in Tables 5, the economic growth rates shrunk from 5.8% to 4.9% for the whole region due to GFC. This also explains the difficulty of many countries to satisfy the convergence criteria established for the region. The following countries, Republic of Benin, Burkina Faso, Guinea-Bissau, Mali, and Niger, have recorded weaker economic results among the UEMOA countries. Only Cote d'Ivoire, Senegal and Togo show signs of an improved growth after the initial effects of the GFC.

Table 6: Trends in End of Period Inflation in ECOWAS, 2002 - 2009

	2002	2003	2004	2005	2006	2007	2008	2009
ECOWAS	9.0	15.3	8.3	9.0	7.1	6.3	13.6	7.8
UEMOA	2.9	-0.7	3.8	2.9	2.7	2.9	8.5	2.5
BENIN	**2.4**	**1.5**	**0.9**	**3.8**	**5.2**	**0.3**	**9.9**	**3.4**
BURKINA FASO	**2.4**	**1.5**	**0.9**	**4.5**	**1.5**	**2.3**	**11.6**	**3.9**
COTE D'VOIRE	**3.1**	**3.3**	**1.4**	**2.6**	**1.5**	**1.5**	**8.9**	**3.0**
GUINEA BISSAU	**3.9**	**-3.5**	**0.9**	**0.3**	**2.0**	**9.3**	**8.7**	**3.8**
MALI	**5.0**	**-1.3**	**-3.1**	**3.4**	**3.2**	**2.2**	**7.8**	**2.6**
NIGER	**2.6**	**-1.6**	**0.2**	**4.2**	**3.6**	**4.7**	**13.6**	**3.9**
SENEGAL	**2.3**	**0.0**	**0.5**	**1.4**	**0.3**	**6.1**	**4.3**	**3.6**
TOGO	**3.1**	**-0.9**	**0.4**	**5.5**	**4.0**	**3.4**	**10.2**	**4.3**
WAMZ	12.1	23.4	10.5	12.1	1.5	7.3	15.3	9.4
GAMBIA	**13.0**	**17.6**	**8.0**	**1.8**	**9.2**	**6.0**	**6.8**	**5.0**
GHANA	**15.2**	**23.6**	**11.8**	**13.9**	**10.9**	**12.8**	**18.1**	**29.8**
GUINEA	**6.1**	**12.9**	**27.6**	**29.7**	**39.1**	**12.8**	**13.5**	**7.7**
NIGERIA	**12.1**	**23.8**	**10.0**	**11.6**	**8.5**	**6.6**	**15.1**	**7.7**
SIERRA LEONE	**-1.3**	**11.3**	**14.4**	**13.1**	**7.3**	**13.8**	**13.2**	**10.0**
Others	5.8	0.2	5.3	3.5	6.1	6.9	7.7	6.4
CAPE-VERDE	**3.0**	**-2.3**	**-0.3**	**1.7**	**4.7**	**4.4**	**6.8**	**5.0**
LIBERIA	**11.1**	**5.0**	**16.1**	**7.0**	**8.9**	**11.7**	**9.4**	**9.1**

Source: WAMA, Central Banks and ECOWAS Member States (EMCP Macroeconomic Convergence Report First Half, 2009)

The WAMZ countries of Cape Verde, Gambia, Ghana, Guinea, Liberia, Nigeria, and Sierra Leone recorded mixed performance results. Nigeria's economic growth dropped to 5.3%, and the other countries did equally poorly apart from Sierra Leone which recorded a slight improvement. Liberia's strong performance for 2006, 2007 and 2008 is noteworthy before its growth path was derailed by the GFC. As regards inflation (Table 6), the UEMOA group of countries, on average, performed better than the WAMZ countries with several flash points in Guinea-Bissau, Ghana, Guinea, and Nigeria.

Tables 7 and 8 below show the number of countries that are compliant with the convergence criteria as well as the number of criteria satisfied by each country. Five (5) of the fifteen (15) countries in the ECOWAS Zone met the budget/GDP ratio criterion of ≤ 4%, down from 8 countries recorded for 2008. Throughout the period, 2001 to 2009, there is evidence of weak performance results as shown in Table 7 on all the convergence targets with the exception of central bank financing of budget deficits and real exchange rate stability, in which the majority of the countries met the targets. In 2009, 14 countries met the target for central bank financing and 15 countries met the target for real exchange rate stability.

Table 7: Number of Countries that met the Convergence Criteria in ECOWAS (2001-2009)

	01	**02**	**03**	**04**	**05**	**06**	**07**	**08**	**09***
Budget deficit	6	5	5	4	4	6	7	8	5
Inflation	9	10	10	9	9	9	7	1	10
Reserves	10	9	9	9	1	1	9	1	9
Central Bank Financing	13	11	11	14	15	13	15	14	14
Domestic Arrears	5	4	5	5	4	5	5	6	8
Tax Reserves	0	0	0	2	2	2	3	2	3
Salary Mass (Wage Bill)	6	5	8	6	7	8	9	7	5
Public Investments	6	5	6	8	6	6	7	7	6
Real Interest Rate	6	8	9	7	7	6	6	0	3
Real Exchange Rate	11	12	7	12	10	11	12	6	15

Source: WAMA (EMCP Macroeconomic Convergence Report First Half, 2009) * = Projection

As evidenced in the Table 8 below, no country in the ECOWAS Zone has yet been able to satisfy all the primary and secondary criteria established for the region. As at the end of 2009, only Senegal achieved seven (7) targets, followed by Nigeria, Niger, Mali, Cote d'Ivoire, and Republic of Benin (6 targets each).

Table 8: Number of Primary & Secondary Criteria Met by Each Country (2001-2009)

	01	02	03	04	05	06	07	08	09*
BENIN	6	7	6	6	4	3	8	4	6
BURKINA FASO	5	5	6	6	5	5	6	2	5
CAP-VERT	3	3	4	4	4	4	4	3	4
COTE D'VOIRE	4	4	4	5	4	5	5	2	6
GAMBIA	2	0	1	4	4	6	3	3	4
GHANA	1	0	2	3	3	3	4	2	2
GUINEA	5	3	1	1	3	2	4	4	3
GUINEA BISSAU	4	4	3	5	3	4	2	1	4
LIBERIA	4	4	3	2	3	4	4	4	4
MALI	4	6	7	7	6	5	7	2	6
NIGER	5	4	6	5	4	6	6	4	6
NIGERIA	4	4	4	5	5	5	6	5	6
SENEGAL	8	8	8	7	6	4	4	5	7
SIERRA LEONE	3	3	0	1	1	0	2	1	2
TOGO	4	5	6	6	2	4	6	3	4
UEMOA	4	6	5	5	5	5	6	2	6
WAMZ	4	5	5	5	4	4	6	5	6
ECOWAS	3	4	4	5	6	6	6	5	6

Source: WAMA (EMCP Macroeconomic Convergence Report First Half, 2009)

In the rest of this section, specific analysis is provided for each criterion with emphasis on the 2007 – 2009 periods, which helps us to assess the probable effects of the GFC on the economies of the ECOWAS Zone and on the convergence criteria established for the countries. The score cards for the primary criteria will be presented first, followed by a brief assessment of the secondary criteria score cards for the region.

<u>The Score Card for the Budget Deficit/GDP criterion (≤ 4%)</u>

Between 2007 and 2009, the ratios of budget deficit to GDP deteriorated overall for the countries, with the WAMZ group recording a relatively better average result than the UEMOA group - with 1.9% for WAMZ and 5.7% for UEMOA region countries. While 7 countries met the target in 2007, there was a slight improvement to 8 countries in 2008; the number of countries satisfying the criterion dropped to 5 in 2009 due to the effects of the GFC (see table 9).

Table 9: ECOWAS Zone Convergence Performance Score Card on the Budget Deficit/GDP Criterion (2001-2009)

	01	02	03	04	05	06	07	08	09*
BENIN	2.6	3.1	4.4	3.6	4.6	2.5	1.4	3.4	4.4
BURKI-NA FASO	6.7	9.1	8.2	8.6	9.1	11.3	12.4	8.7	10.5
CABO-VERDE	11.4	10.5	9.1	8.4	11.0	9.7	6.1	5.8	6.2
COTE D'VOIRE	0.4	2.0	3.2	2.6	2.7	1.5	1.4	2.1	1.7
GAMBIA	-9.8	-9.1	-7.6	-10.2	-8.4	-2.7	-1.1	-4.2	-4.3
GHANA	13.2	8.3	7.5	8.1	6.9	12.9	14.5	19.5	18.0
GUINEA	3.4	6.2	8.8	5.9	1.6	2.0	0.9	1.7	2.9
GUINEA BISSAU	24.7	13.6	23.0	30.1	24.2	19.9	26.0	23.3	19.3
LIBERIA	1.9	1.0	3.7	4.4	0.9	-3.0	3.4	2.0	2.0
MALI	9.6	6.9	5.3	7.0	7.3	7.6	8.1	5.9	9.7
NIGER	8.0	8.5	7.8	8.4	9.6	6.8	6.8	4.0	11.7
NIGERIA	5.8	5.9	2.8	1.7	1.3	0.6	1.2	0.2	0.4
SENE-GAL	3.8	1.8	3.2	5.5	4.7	7.3	6.2	4.9	4.6
SIERRA LEONE	16.7	16.5	19.4	14.3	9.5	8.5	5.0	8.6	8.1
TOGO	2.3	1.0	1.8	-0.6	4.1	4.2	2.9	2.8	5.6
UEMOA	4.3	3.8	4.4	4.8	5.2	5.1	5.1	4.3	5.7
WAMZ	6.4	6.1	3.4	2.3	1.8	1.6	2.2	1.8	1.9
ECOWAS	5.7	5.4	3.7	3.2	2.9	2.8	3.2	2.6	3.1
No. of countries	6	5	5	4	4	6	7	8	5

Source: WAMA and Central Banks (EMCP Macroeconomic Convergence Report First Half, 2009)

The Score Card for the Inflation Criterion (≤ 5%)

Overall, the UEMOA countries enjoyed a much lower projected average rate of inflation (2.5%) than the WAMZ group countries which recorded a rate of 9.4%. Between 2007 and 2009, the number of countries meeting the target increased from 7 (2007) to 9 (projected for 2009), after a very poor result of one country recorded for 2008 during the heat of the GFC, when high inflationary pressures were felt due to fuel and food crises (see table 10).

Table 10: ECOWAS Zone Convergence Performance Score Card on the Inflation Criterion (2001-2009)

	01	02	03	04	05	06	07	08	09*
BENIN	4.0	2.4	1.5	0.9	3.8	5.2	0.3	9.9	3.4
BURKINA FASO	4.0	2.4	1.5	0.9	4.5	1.5	2.3	11.6	3.9
CABO-VERDE	4.2	3.0	-2.3	-0.3	1.7	4.7	4.4	6.8	5.0
COTE D'VOIRE	4.3	3.1	3.3	1.4	2.6	2.0	1.5	8.9	3.0
THE GAMBIA	8.1	13.0	17.6	8.0	1.8	1.4	6.0	6.8	5.0
GHANA	21.3	15.2	23.6	11.8	13.9	10.9	12.8	18.1	29.8
GUINEA	5.2	6.1	12.9	27.6	29.7	39.1	12.8	13.5	7.7
GUINEA BISSAU	3.3	3.9	-3.5	0.9	0.3	3.2	9.3	8.7	3.8
LIBERIA	19.4	11.1	5.0	16.1	7.0	8.9	11.7	9.4	9.1
MALI	5.2	5.0	-1.3	-3.1	3.4	3.6	2.2	7.8	2.6
NIGER	4.0	2.6	-1.6	0.2	4.2	0.3	4.7	13.6	3.9
NIGERIA	16.4	12.1	23.8	10.0	11.6	8.5	6.6	15.1	7.7
SENEGAL	3.0	2.3	0.0	0.5	1.4	4.0	6.1	4.3	3.6
SIERRA LEONE	3.4	-1.3	11.3	14.4	13.1	7.3	13.8	13.2	10.0
TOGO	3.9	3.1	-0.9	0.4	5.5	1.5	3.4	10.2	4.3
UEMOA	4.1	2.9	-0.7	3.8	2.9	2.7	2.9	8.5	2.5
WAMZ	16.4	12.1	23.4	10.5	12.1	9.2	7.3	15.3	9.4
ECOWAS	12.3	9.0	15.3	8.3	9.0	7.1	5.8	13.0	7.1
No. of countries	9	10	10	9	9	9	7	1	10

Sources: WAMA, Central Banks (EMCP Macroeconomic Convergence Report First Half, 2009)

<u>The Score Card for Central Bank Financing of Budget Deficit/Previous Year's Tax Revenue Criterion (≤10%)</u>

The entire ECOWAS Zone continues to record its best performance on meeting the target of budget deficit financing by central banks as evidenced in Table 11. Prior to the GFC of 2008, the countries performed relatively well under this criterion, and this performance extended to the period of the GFC. In 2009, 14 countries met the target, with the exception of Ghana.

Table 11: ECOWAS Zone Convergence Performance Score Card on the Budget Deficit Financing by Central Banks Criterion (2001-2009)

	01	02	03	04	05	06	07	08	09*
BENIN	0.0	4.6	0.0	0.0	0.0	0.0	0.0	0.0	0.0
BURKINA FASO	0.0	0.0	0.0	0.0	0.0	0.0	0.0	0.0	0.0
CABO-VERDE	0.1	20.7	6.3	0.2	0.0	0.0	0.0	0.0	0.0
COTE D'VOIRE	0.0	0.3	0.0	0.0	0.0	0.0	0.0	0.0	0.0
THE GAMBIA	80.7	22.0	63.1	0.0	0.0	0.0	0.0	0.0	5.4
GHANA	0.0	12.1	0.0	1.6	0.0	0.0	0.0	17.3	15.5
GUINEA	-0.7	24.5	14.6	26.2	-8.8	54.0	0.0	5.8	0.0
GUINEA BISSAU	0.0	0.0	0.0	0.0	0.0	0.0	0.0	0.0	0.0
LIBERIA	0.0	0.0	0.0	0.0	0.0	0.0	0.0	0.0	0.0
MALI	0.0	0.0	0.0	0.0	0.0	0.0	0.0	0.0	0.0
NIGER	4.9	0.0	0.0	0.0	0.0	0.0	0.0	0.0	0.0
NIGERIA	29.3	0.0	19.7	0.0	0.0	0.0	0.0	0.0	0.0
SENEGAL	0.0	0.0	0.0	0.0	0.0	0.0	0.0	0.0	0.0
SIERRA LEONE	8.9	0.0	26.4	0.0	0.0	13.3	0.8	0.3	0.5
TOGO	0.0	0.0	0.0	0.0	0.0	0.0	0.0	0.0	0.0
UEMOA	0.0	0.0	0.0	0.0	0.0	0.0	0.0	0.0	0.0
WAMZ	26.4	1.5	18.3	0.6	-0.2	1.1	0.0	1.4	1.2
ECOWAS	17.5	1.1	12.1	0.4	-0.1	0.8	0.0	1.0	0.8
No. of countries	13	11	11	14	15	13	15	14	14

Source: WAMA and Central Banks (EMCP Macroeconomic Convergence Report First Half, 2009)

The Score Card for Reserves ≥ 6 Months Imports

Gross foreign exchange reserves' accumulation performance for the entire region stood at an average of 9 countries meeting the target during the period. The eight UEMOA countries and Nigeria met the target during the period, but with the exception of 2008. From the Table 12 one can see that, apart from Nigeria, no country in the region met this target in 2008, the year of the onset of the GFC, when most of the countries scrambled to draw down on their foreign exchange reserves to fight off many effects of the GFC.

Table 12: ECOWAS Zone Convergence Performance Score Card on the Reserves ≥ 6 Months Imports Criterion (2001-2009)

	01	02	03	04	05	06	07	08	09*
CABO-VERDE	1.5	2.0	1.8	2.4	3.4	3.6	4.1	4.1	4.0
THE GAMBIA	7.2	2.9	3.1	4.7	5.2	4.9	4.4	4.3	5.3
GHANA	1.2	2.3	4.1	4.1	4.0	3.7	3.9	2.2	2.3
GUINEA	2.8	2.3	1.6	1.6	1.1	0.8	0.4	1.1	1.8
LIBERIA	2.6	0.0	-0.2	0.2	0.1	0.1	0.7	0.7	0.7
NIGERIA	11.3	9.9	8.5	16.1	11.8	15.1	17.4	15.3	14.6
SIERRA LEONE	2.3	3.1	1.7	3.3	4.8	4.9	5.1	4.2	4.6
UEMOA	6.7	7.6	6.0	6.8	5.7	5.6	6.0	5.7	6.0
WAMZ	10.3	9.1	8.0	14.7	10.9	13.8	15.9	13.9	13.3
WAMZ less Nigeria	2.0	2.4	3.1	2.9	3.2	2.9	2.9	2.1	2.4
ECOWAS	9.0	8.5	7.2	12.0	9.1	11.0	12.5	11.1	10.8
ECOWAS less Nigeria	5.4	6.1	5.1	5.7	5.0	4.8	5.1	4.7	5.0
No. of countries	10	9	9	9	1	1	9	1	9

Source: WAMA and Central Banks (EMCP Macroeconomic Convergence Report First Half, 2009)

Score Card Performance on Secondary Criteria

A summary of score card performance analysis on some of the established secondary criteria is useful for some of the conclusions drawn in this paper. With respect to the Tax revenue/GDP Ratio (≥ 20%), the ECOWAS Zone has recorded a poor performance due to the overall difficulty of maximizing tax revenues which is tied to inefficient tax codes that are established in the various countries in the region. Not more than three countries have ever satisfied this criterion throughout the review period. In 2009, only Cape Verde, Ghana and Senegal met the target (WAMA, 2009: 23 – 24). There are mixed results for Wage Bill/Total Tax Revenue Ratio (≤35%) criterion. Throughout the period, not more than 9 countries have ever met the target, with the WAMZ group generally performing better than the UEMOA group (WAMA 2009: 24) The Public Investment financed through Internal Sources/Total Tax Revenue Ratio (≥ 20%) criterion has suffered a similar fate as the tax revenue criterion. Mixed results are recorded for the entire region, with an average of 6 countries being able to meet the target throughout the review period. In 2009, Republic of Benin, Burkina Faso, Guinea, Nigeria, and Senegal (5 countries) met the criterion, as against 7countries respectively for in 2007 (pre-GFC year) and in 2008 (onset of GFC)[12]. The last two secondary criteria; namely, maintenance of real exchange rate stability and maintenance of positive real interest rates, reveal a strong performance by the countries on one and a weak performance by the countries on the other. In 2009, 15 countries were projected to meet the real exchange rate criterion; this was up from the 6 countries recorded for 2008 and the 14 countries recorded for the first half of 2009. While most of the countries have recorded overall positive performance under the real exchange rate criterion, the majority of countries have experienced negative real interest rates; this being largely due to high inflationary pressures. Overall, UEMOA performance was better (1.0%) than WAMZ's (-6.6%) The entire ECOWAS Zone average of -4.1% is a far cry from the target set for the convergence criterion (WAMA, 2009, 26 – 27).

4 Conclusions and Recommendations

The paper has examined a number of issues regarding economic and financial developments within the context of GFC, with a view of providing policy guidelines being necessary for the formation of a monetary union for the ECOWAS Zone. Particularly, it analyzed several key issues, processes and procedures affecting the macroeconomic and financial architecture in the region. As the performance results which were detailed in the preceding sections show, building a sub-regional monetary integration framework among a diverse group of national, political, economic, and cultural interests is, no doubt, a difficult task. But the stakeholders must strive to refine important processes and procedures as well as to improve on their macroeconomic developments in an environment of globalization and GFC. The globalizing world has necessitated increased competition which requires large scale

---

[12] See WAMA (2009: 24 - 27)

economies, which are achieved through economic and financial integration programs

Undoubtedly, member countries of ECOWAS are faced with the challenges of meeting the agreed convergence criteria. It is obvious that the political and cultural difference between the Anglophone and Francophone countries partly explains the protracted policy divergence. But each time genuine efforts have been made to integrate many economic and financial aspects of the sub-region, the resulting outcomes have been quite laudable. This partly explains the sustained drive toward integration in times of crisis or non crisis. The paper presents the view that an unchecked set of deficiencies in inter-regional trade, capital accounts liberalization, exchange rate determination, financial reporting and accounting standards, banks' surveillance and supervision of the capital markets would, undoubtedly, have consequences at two levels; a) in blocking the drive for monetary integration and b) enlarging the effect of contagion which results from the GFC.

This paper strongly recommends, in addition to quick policy harmonization, a continuation of financial reforms which are already taking place in the region, and a speedy development of necessary infrastructures, such as in telecommunication and road networks. Also strongly recommended is the implementation of legal and institutional frameworks to support the financial sector liberalization. Other recommendations include:

- The various monetary authorities in the region are to speedily develop frameworks and procedures for successful implementation of a single monetary policy. These frameworks of necessity would include operational monetary policy transmission guidelines.
- For macroeconomic convergence, the achievement of deadlines and the success of a monetary integration would depend on how quickly the nations can achieve macroeconomic convergence. It would also depend on the effectiveness of monitoring the convergence performance of member states. Thus a comprehensive program of surveillance would be necessary for meeting the primary and secondary convergence criteria. The WAMI and the WAMA would have to actively compile region-wide statistical data on all macroeconomic variables for more frequent deliberation of the region's stakeholders.
- Development of aggressive sensitization programs will speed up the move toward monetary integration and acceptance by the citizens of the region.
- The WAMZ group is urged to get its act together and put an end to the shifting deadlines, expedite the ratification of WAMZ legal instruments, and achieve the group's common currency on or before the latest deadline of

2015, to pave the way for the ECOWAS Zone's monetary union, and introduction of a new Zonal common currency ***(eco*).**

- Rather than encourage more shifting deadlines, the majority of countries in the region should strive to achieve better convergence results and move ahead and fully integrate. The relatively non-performing countries can join the monetary union on the basis of specially/separately established deadlines for the weaker countries – since the ultimate goal is to carry every nation in the region along in the drive for full economic and monetary integration programs. The deadlines are a bit becoming too many.
- Accounting standards and financial reporting that meet international standards must be the goal of the financial system, taking into consideration ECOWAS' peculiar social, economic and political features and its environment.
- Structures for extensive consultation with relevant stakeholders must be established. Besides that, extensive consultation with all stakeholders and participants in the financial system (accounting, banking, and taxation bodies inclusive) is needed before standards are set. This is because to act contrary will not be in the interest of the financial system.
- There should be wide publicity and constant review of accounting standards after they have been set.
- There should be in place a speedy process for the criminal persecution of auditors who collide with management to window dress financial reporting with the intention of helping to maintain the false quality of financial reports.
- Put in place mechanisms for ensuring that financial reports comply with legal regulatory and disclosure requirements.
- Ensuring that regulatory agencies create incentives for increased capitalizations. In addition, consolidated supervision and specific regulations for bank holding companies should be required with a view to averting the risk of conglomerate designs which are used to channel low quality assets into banks.
- Providing for a sound and sustainable macroeconomic policy environment in the sub region. This is particularly important in the WAMZ where there is a large level of policy inconsistency, and an inadequate coordination of monetary and fiscal policy, all of which tends to encourage divergence in many of the sectors.
- Installing an effective financial market premised on a culture of financial transparency and effective corporate governance discipline in the financial institutions.
- Establishing a proper credit culture in the sub-region that would foster the honoring and enforcement of financial contracts, on the one hand.

On the other hand, the enthronement of the best practice of ethical standards in financial dealings is needed.

- In order to achieve the full effects of the capital markets, the different institutions must be carefully organized for efficiency and oversight. Accordingly, there would be a need for an ECOWAS Securities Exchange Commission (ESEC), and an ECOWAS Securities Insurance and Protection Commission (ESIPC). The primary responsibility of each of these Commissions will, respectively, be for oversight and protection of participants in the sub-regional capital market sector. Other processes and procedures for success include, the creation of subzones in the sub-region for the physical location of stock-exchanges; the listing of all stocks in the ECOWAS ZONE stock-exchanges; the establishment of a Zonal Average Daily Index System to track daily volumes traded for the entire region; and the development and implementation of an educational and sensitization program for the benefits of potential participants in the sector.

In conclusion, the trends of new global competition and increasing global interdependence which have been so clearly demonstrated in the GFC should forge the basis for a new action on the part of all stakeholders in the sub-region. By achieving full monetary integration, broad-based monetary assets would be developed to withstand the challenges of a GFC. This need must be of paramount importance with respect to policy guidelines. The weaknesses in the region's infrastructures partly explain the poor convergence criteria score cards for every country. The countries' macroeconomic performances during the review period (particularly 2007 to 2009) indicate the countries' inability to completely weather the effects of the GFC compared with the resilience demonstrated by their counterparts in East and South East Asia. Since the GFC has had a disruptive effect on the region's integration drives, all post-crisis developments must emphasize macroeconomic harmonization, speedy establishment of key financial infrastructures, and satisfaction of established convergence criteria. These efforts are bound to be boosted by the signs of economic rebounds in the various countries in the region.

Finally, and for emphasis, every progress made in the drive to fully integrate the region will be contingent on the depth of macroeconomic policy harmonization among Member States. The critical areas include, but are not limited to, broad-based monetary issues, fiscal issues, financial services issues, investment and corporate tax issues as well as incentives policy issues. Above all, harmonization of domestic responses to the effects of contagion, due to globalization and international financial crises, would be necessary. In terms of the establishment of new deadlines for fully integrating, the ECOWAS Zone must wait until a large majority of the counties in both the WAMZ and UEMOA groups are compliant with the established convergence criteria for a future effective and viable monetary union.

References

Alashi, S. O. (2002), "Banking Sector Supervision under the West African Monetary Zone", *Central Bank of Nigeria Economic and Financial Review*, Vol. 49, No. 4, December

Alawode, O. (2009), "Brainstorming on Free Trade", Business Day, Monday, October 12

Bergsten, Fred C. (1999), "Exchange Rate Choices: Discussion", in: Rethinking the International Monetary System, Little, J. S. and Giovanni, P. O. (Eds.), Boston: Federal Reserve Bank of Boston, pp. 124 – 128

Cooper, C. A. and B. F. Massell (1965), "Towards a General Theory of Customs Union for Developing Countries", in: *Journal of Political Economy*, Vol. 73: 73: 461-476

Duff, A., Pinder, J. and Pryce, R. (Eds.) (1996), Maastricht and Beyond: Building the European Union, Routledge Publishers, New York

Foroutan, F. and L. Pritchett (1993), "Intra-sub-Saharan African trade: Is it too little?", in: *Journal of African Economics*, Vol. 2, No. 1: 74-105

Iyoha, M. A. (2004), "African economic integration: Are there lessons for the West African Monetary Zone?", in: *West African Financial and Economic Review*, Vol. 2, No. 2

IMF (2001), "Monetary Union in West Africa (ECOWAS): Is It Desirable and Could It Be Achieved?", Masson, P. and Pattillo, C., Working Paper 204, IMF, Washington, D. C.

Kreinin, M. E. (1964), "On the dynamic effects of a customs union", in: *Journal of Political Economy,* Vol. 72: 193-95

Mailafia, O. (2006), *Keynote Address* presented at the Executive Seminar of the Central Bank of Nigeria, on Capital Accounts Liberalization: Issues, Problems and Prospects, Central Bank of Nigeria, Abuja

Nnonna, J. O. (2002), "The West African Monetary Zone (WAMZ) Convergence or Divergence: Which Way Forward?", in: *Central Bank of Nigeria Economic and Financial Review*, Vol. 40, No. 4, December

Pownall, G. and Schipper, K. (1999), "The Implications of Accounting Research for SEC's Consideration of International Accounting Standards for the US Securities Offerings", in: *Accounting Horizons,* SEC, pp. 259 - 280

Obadan, M. I. (2002), "Exchange Rate Mechanism under the West African Monetary Zone (WAMZ)", *Central Bank of Nigeria Economic and Financial Review*, Vol. 40, No 4, December

Ojo, M. O. (2006), "Capital Account Liberalization: The ECOWAS Experience", presented at the Executives Seminar of the Central Bank of Nigeria, on Capital Accounts Liberalization: Issues and Prospects

Onwioduokit, E. A. (2004), "Fiscal Sustainability in the West African Monetary Zone", *Economic and Financial Review*, Volume 42, No. 3, September

Onyewuenmi, N. A. (2005), "ECOWAS Trade: Progress, Challenges and Prospects", *Central Bank of Nigeria Bullion*, Vol. 29, No. 4, Oct/Dec, pp. 65 – 74

Walker, J. L. (2000), "Building the Legal and Regulatory Framework", in: Building Infrastructures for Financial Stability, Federal Reserve Bank of Boston, Rosengren, E. S. and John S. J. (Eds.) Conference Series, No 44, June, pp. 31 – 67

WAMA (2009), Macroeconomic Convergence Report First Half 2009, ECOWAS Monetary Cooperation Programme, Freetown, Sierra Leone, November, WAMA

WAMI/West African Monetary Institute (2004), Assessment of Country Performance in the WAMZ Programme, Accra, Ghana

WAMI (2008) Annual Report, Accra, Ghana

WAMZ (2009), 25th Meeting of the Convergence Council of Ministers and Governors of Central Banks, WAMZ, Accra, Ghana

World Development Indicators (WDI 2009 Database), World Bank, Washington, D. C., USA

Effects of the Global Financial Crisis on the Diamonds Market and Government Responses: The Case of Botswana

David Sebudubudu[1] and Brothers W. Malema[2]

Abstract

Botswana is a diamonds export- dependent country. Diamonds are the mainstay of Botswana's economy, affecting its governance and development. Being one of the leading diamonds producers in the world, Botswana is of interest as a case study. This paper argues that the Global Financial Crisis (GFC) impacted on the world diamonds market and thus has demonstrated the vulnerability of minerals export-dependent economies. It examines the role of minerals, particularly of diamonds, in African development by using the case of Botswana. The paper first examines the impact of the GFC on Botswana's economy. Secondly, it assesses the policy measures that were put in place to alleviate the effects of the crisis. It concludes by arguing that the GFC offers a key lesson for Botswana and for other minerals export-dependent countries too - to diversify their economies away from minerals exports, in particular from diamonds.

1 Introduction

The focus of this paper is on the role of minerals exports, particularly diamonds, in African development by using the case of Botswana. It assesses

[1] Dr. D. Sebudubudu, Associate Professor in Political Science and Head, Department of Political and Administrative Studies & Coordinator, Democracy Research Project (DRP), Faculty of Social Sciences, University of Botswana P/Bag 00705 Gaborone, Botswana

[2] B. W. Malema, Senior Lecturer, Department of Economics, Faculty of Social Sciences, University of Botswana, P/Bag 00705 Gaborone, Botswana

the impact of the GFC on Botswana's economy and the policy measures that were put in place to alleviate the effects of the crisis. It concludes by arguing that GFC offers a key lesson for Botswana and also for other minerals export-dependent countries to diversify their economies away from minerals exports, in particular diamonds.

Using a case study approach to explain the role of minerals in African development, this paper relies on secondary sources (literature review) and on primary sources (official reports). The paper is divided into seven sections. The first section is the introduction. It states the focus of the paper and what the next different subsections seek to do. This is followed by the section two on the Political economy of Botswana. This gives a background of politico-economic conditions in Botswana, and highlights its economic performance, the improvements in infrastructure as well as advances in human development - save for some exceptions. Section three examines the issues of the GFC, the tendencies of the world market for diamonds, and the prospects of African development. It emphasises the impact of the GFC on the world diamonds market as well as the role of diamonds in African development. In this way, this section focuses on the mineral sector in Africa and how the GFC has affected the mineral-dependent economies in Africa. Section four considers the impact of the GFC on Botswana – a diamond-dependent economy. The section shows that Botswana's over-reliance on minerals, especially diamonds, makes its economy very vulnerable. Section five assesses Botswana's policy responses to the crisis. That is, it examines the policy measures to alleviate the effects of the GFC on the country and its people. Section six analyses the lessons learnt from the GFC. Lastly, the paper presents the conclusion and policy recommendations. Having said this, it is the political economy of Botswana that we now turn to.

2 The Political Economy of Botswana

The minerals sector, particularly diamonds extraction, plays a central role in Botswana and in some African countries' development. For example, out of the 18 diamond-producing countries in the world, 12 are found in Africa (Olsson, 1997). Diamonds, by and large, facilitate development in a number of African countries like Botswana, Namibia, and South Africa. Diamonds constitute a tiny fraction of South Africa's economy, but in Botswana diamonds have been the main pillar of development and were responsible for driving economic growth. Botswana provides a positive lesson on how minerals – legally exploited - can facilitate development. However, there are a number of countries in Africa that are rich in diamonds, but diamonds have been the source of domestic conflict and of violence. These countries include Angola, Sierra Leone, and the Democratic Republic of the Congo. Instead of driving development, diamonds were used to fuel conflict in those countries – giving rise to the issue of 'conflict diamonds'. Hence, "conflict diamonds" (or illegal diamonds) became a major problem for diamonds export-dependent countries in Africa. It is in this sense that minerals are regarded as a 'curse' for a number of countries (Iimi, 2007). That is, instead of fueling development, they have facilitated underdevelopment. Botswana is one of the few exceptions where diamonds extraction has led to impressive economic growth and to development. In spite of the impressive resource management in Botswana, the country has so far failed to reduce its over-dependence on diamonds extraction.

At independence in 1966, Botswana was a poor agrarian economy with agriculture contributing around 40% to Gross Domestic Product (GDP). The country was one of the poorest in Africa with a per capita income of around US$ 60. At independence, the country had only about 22 university graduates and only 13 kilometers of paved road, largely due to British colonial neglect (Edge, 1998; Sebudubudu and Lotshwao, 2009). The discovery of minerals, especially diamonds, a few years after independence, has changed Botswana's economy. Minerals have since replaced agriculture as the major contributor to GDP with a share of 40.9% in the year 2000 and of 28.3% in the year 2009 (see table 1). Agriculture however was left an insignificant role in the economy; manufacturing also has a very small share in the GDP.

Table 1: Sectoral Contribution to GDP (Percentages, 2000-2009)

	Agr.	**Mining**	**Man.**	**W/E**	**Cons.**	**Tr./H**	**Trans/ Com.**	**B/Ins.**	**GG**
00	2.6	40.9	3.8	2.2	5.2	9.4	3.4	10.0	14.8
01	2.4	41.1	3.8	2.2	4.7	9.7	3.4	10.3	15.1
02	2.0	42.0	3.4	2.2	5.8	9.5	3.2	10.0	15.6
03	2.2	42.2	3.3	2.2	4.7	10.0	2.9	9.5	15.8
04	1.9	40.5	3.3	2.2	4.9	9.8	2.9	9.3	16.1
05	1.8	40.7	3.5	2.2	4.5	9.1	3.2	10.0	16.6
06	1.7	41.7	3.4	2.2	4.4	9.5	3.4	10.2	15.6
07	1.7	39.0	3.8	2.2	4.8	10.1	3.6	10.5	15.5
08	1.7	36.5	3.8	2.2	4.7	10.4	1.0	11.7	16.2
09	2.3	28.3	3.9	2.4	5.7	11.4	4.7	13.0	17.9

Key: Agr. = Agriculture; Man. = Manufacturing; W/E Water/Electricity; Cons. = Construction; Tr./H = Trade/Hotel; Trans/Com. = Transport/ Communication; B/Ins. = Bank/Insurance; GG = General Government.
Source: Bank of Botswana (2009)

However, the annual growth rates of mining have changed dramatically in the recent years, with declining growth rates since 2004 and negative rates since 2007 (see table 2). The drastic market changes become visible in the data for 2009 with a rate of decline of 27.1 per cent, affecting considerably also the overall GDP growth rate.

Table 2: Share of Mining to GDP, Annual Growth Rates of Mining and the GDP Growth Rate (Percentages)

Year	Share of Mining to GDP	Annual Growth Rate of Mining	GDP Growth Rate
2000	40.9	13.8	5.9
2001	41.1	3.9	3.5
2002	42.0	11.5	9.0
2003	42.2	6.7	6.3
2004	40.5	1.8	6.0
2005	40.7	1.9	1.6
2006	41.7	7.9	5.1
2007	39.2	-2.0	4.8
2008	36.7	-3.7	3.1
2009	28.3	-27.1	-6.0

Source: Bank of Botswana (2009)

Table 3: Growth Rates of GDP and Non-Mining GDP (Percentages)

Year	**GDP**	**Non-Mining GDP**	**GDP per Capita**	**Non-Mining GDP per Capita**
2000	5.9	1.0	4.7	-1.4
2001	3.5	3.2	2.3	2.0
2002	9.0	7.2	7.7	6.0
2003	6.3	6.0	5.1	4.8
2004	6.0	9.0	4.8	7.8
2005	1.6	1.4	0.8	0.6
2006	5.1	3.2	4.3	2.4
2007	4.8	9.7	4.1	8.9
2008	3.1	7.5	2.4	6.7
2009	-6.0	6.1	-6.6	5.4

Source: Bank of Botswana

Obviously, the non-mining sector has – parallel to the minerals sector crisis - captured higher growth rates in recent years, so that also the non-mining GDP growth per capita has recorded considerable gains (see table 3).

The share of mining revenue to overall government revenue is still high, around 30% in 2009, but also declining as there were shares of around 60% in 2000, and this trend is valid both for the share in tax revenues and in overall government revenues (see table 4).

Table 4: Share of Mining Revenue to Tax Revenue and to Government Revenue

Year	Share of Mining Revenue to Tax Revenue (%)	Share of Mining Revenue to Government Revenue (%)
2000	69.3	59.3
2001	66.1	55.0
2002	61.2	52.4
2003	57.7	50.4
2004	53.4	48.3
2005	54.9	49.6
2006	52.0	47.9
2007	47.7	38.5
2008	40.9	33.4
2009	32.3	28.0

Source: Bank of Botswana (2009)

Unlike most countries that depend on minerals, Botswana has used its minerals to transform the country and the social conditions of its people (see Gaolathe, 1997; Hillbom 2008). The transformation is reflected on improved human development records such as reduced mortality rates, increased basic literacy rates, and access to clean water. However, the low and even declining life expectancy at birth with 48.1 years in 2005 (see UNDP 2007, p. 231) is a serious signal post to review health policies and even overall development policies. The economic performance has improved, with increased per capita incomes and improvements in infrastructure, but the human development advances are – with some exceptions - as well impressive (as shown in Tables 5 and 6).

The improvement of the adult literacy rates in Botswana since 1970 is quite considerable (see table 6).

Table 5: Social Indicators

Year	1970	1990	2008	1970-1990	1990-2000	2000-2008
Population growth rate	-	-	-	3.3	2.4	1.4
Crude Birth Rate	46	35	25			
Crude Death Rate	13	7	12			
Life Expectancy	55	64	54			
Total Fertility Rate	6.6	4.7	2.9			
Under 5 mortality	142	50	31			
Infant Mortality		39	26			

Source:UNICEF http://www.unicef.org/infobycountry/botswana_statistics.html

Table 6: Adult Literacy rates by sex 1970-2003

Year	15 – 65+ Years		
	Male	Female	Total
1970	-	-	41
1971	-	-	40
1991	66.8	67.7	67.3
1993	66.9	70.3	68.9
2001	69.9	73.6	71.8
2003	80.4	81.8	81.2

Source: Hanemann (2005)

It is on this basis that Samatar (1999: 188) considers Botswana as 'an African Miracle' in the light of its deviancy from most African countries in realizing a positive and impressive development trajectory. Owing to this, the country is today regarded as an upper middle income country by the World Bank with a per capita income of US$ 6, 982 by 2008 (The World Bank, 2010). Thus, the windfall from minerals revenues has been used to transform the economy and the peoples' lives positively in Botswana. In this context, diamonds have been seen widely as Botswana's 'best friend' (Niemann, 1993).

Faced with limited resources at independence, the Botswana political elite applied some policy strategies with the aim to transform the economy. First, it brought key natural resources under the control of the central government as opposed to the local state. Initially, mineral resources were under the control of chiefs, private individuals and white settler farmers. As a result of good leadership, management of resources was transferred from the original owners to the central government. Second, the Botswana state entered into a strategic partnership/ alliance with the De Beers Diamond Mining Company. Both parties formed a jointly-owned company called De Beers – Botswana Mining Company (DEBSWANA) on the basis of a 50/50 split of the diamond revenues. DEBSWANA, which manages diamonds mines in Botswana, has equal membership and a rotating chairmanship between De Beers and the Government of Botswana. This partnership has been regarded as the best to be entered between a government of a developing country and a multinational company. The agreement was highly favorable to Botswana as the government gained more revenues from De Beers through taxes. These policy strategies demonstrate that responsible leadership played a pro-active role in economic development (Sebudubudu and Molutsi, 2009). The success story of the strategic alliance between De Beers and the Government of Botswana remains a basic lesson for other natural resource-dependent economies in Africa.

Even then, minerals alone are not the only factor that propelled Botswana's development success. There are other factors that also contributed to Botswana's development success. Amongst them included are sound economic management (Salkin, 1997) and good leadership (Samatar, 1999; Tiruneh, 2004; Sebudubudu and Molutsi, 2009), driven by a committed and competent public service (Wallis, 1989 and Tiruneh, 2004). As Samatar puts it, "a key force that distinguishes successful states from failed states is the social chemistry of the dominant class and the discipline of its leadership". (Samatar, 1999: 6) For further details see also Sebudubudu and Molutsi (2009) on the origins of the Botswana ruling elite and its role in development. Sebudubudu and Molutsi (2009) noted that these achievements were a result of sound policies and of solid political and institutional foundations established at independence. The political elite established institutions that facilitated development. It is in this sense that Leith (2000) concluded that "the growth of the Botswana economy is not simply a story of a mineral enclave …" (Leith, 2000: 4). Thus, a committed leadership, sound policies, and good management were the critical factors to Botswana's success.

3 The GFC, the World Market for Diamonds, and African Development

This section focuses on the minerals sector in Africa and how the GFC has affected the minerals-dependent economies in Africa. As noted above, minerals play a central role in some African countries' development. The impact of the GFC is such that some of these countries lost substantial revenues, also from diamonds exports. The impact was also severe because of the suspension or cancellation of ongoing development projects. It was becoming difficult to finance health care, education and infrastructure development in the region. The impact of the GFC was mostly felt in the African countries because of the structure and the nature of their economies. The African economy is largely a mono-export sector economy. The economy is either dependent on one mineral or one agricultural commodity – which are all vulnerable to world market and price fluctuations. Consequently, any external shock of such a magnitude like the GFC will have negative effects on the regional economy.

Analysts presented two divergent views on the possible effects of the GFC and of the global changes on African economies and on African development. One view perceives Africa as marginalized so that changes in the world economy will have modest consequences on the performance of its economies. The other view regards Africa as significant in global terms so that changes in the world economy will result in major consequences on African economies, i. e. in earnings from commodity sales and in capital flows (Lawrence, 2009). The latter position seems to be true for African economies, especially for the mineral-dependent economies. The GFC of the years 2008 and 2009, which started in the United States of America (USA), attest to this. The United States of America (USA) and the European Union (EU) remain the major markets for African commodities. In fact, the USA is the biggest diamonds market in the world. In recent years, China and India are emerging markets for African commodities.

Figure 1 shows the significance of diamonds production to the African economy. Africa accounted for 61 percent of global diamonds production in 2005, with Botswana and the Democratic Republic of Congo (DRC) each accounting for 21 percent of the global production. The two countries were followed by Russia, Australia and South Africa at 15, 14 and 10 percentage points respectively (see figure 1 for the source).

On the demand side, the United States of America has been the largest market of diamonds, followed by Japan. However, Yang (2010) reports that China has overtaken Japan as the global second largest consumer market for diamonds in 2009. India has been the largest world polisher of diamonds, accounting for 60 percent of the world diamonds, and exporting most of them to the USA, being the world's largest finished jewellery consumer. However, China is emerging strongly as a contender to replace India as the largest diamond processing country (Dudu 2010).

Figure 1: World Diamonds Production by Country for 2005

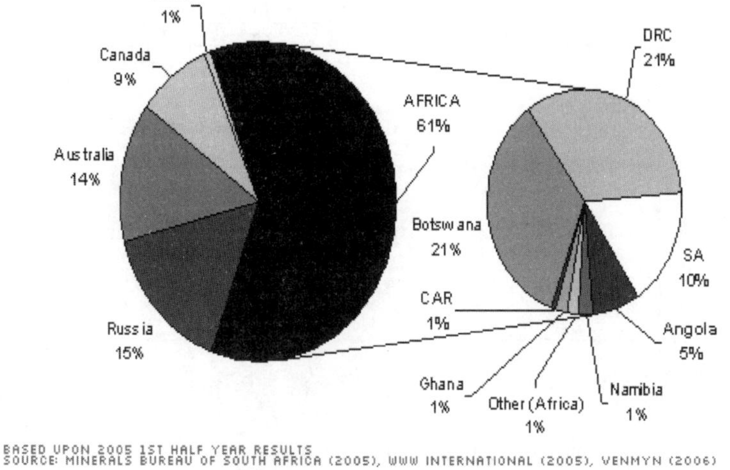

Source: http://pangeadiamondfields.com/diamond-sector.htm

The projected supply and demand for diamonds, as shown in Figure 2, has serious implications for the prices of the diamonds. With demand exceeding supply it is expected that the prices will increase due to the insufficient supply which falls short of demand (see figure 2 for the source). The dominance of De Beers in the diamonds industry has been accountable for the favorable prices for diamonds which have shown a tendency to increase over time. This has been attributed to De Beers' ability to stockpile output during times of excess production in order to control prices.

The entrance of new players into the diamonds industry, not controlled by De Beers, has strengthened the competition within the industry. The companies which are in the forefront in successfully competing with De Beers are Rio Tinto and BHP Billiton, even though there are others which have intensified global competition (Diamine Explorations, 2010).

In 2009, however, diamonds output fell from 160 million carats to 120 million carats and rough diamond prices fell by between 30 and 50 percent, as the GFC took its toll on the global diamonds industry (Kohler, 2009). Diamonds producers, including De Beers which controls 40 percent of the global market, decided to cut down on their supply in line with a call by the World Federation of Diamond Bourses (WFDB). The WFDB considered the move to be in the interest of rough diamonds-producing countries, the diamonds industry, the banking system, and the diamonds-mining companies.

Figure 2: Industry Supply versus Demand (2005 – 2015)

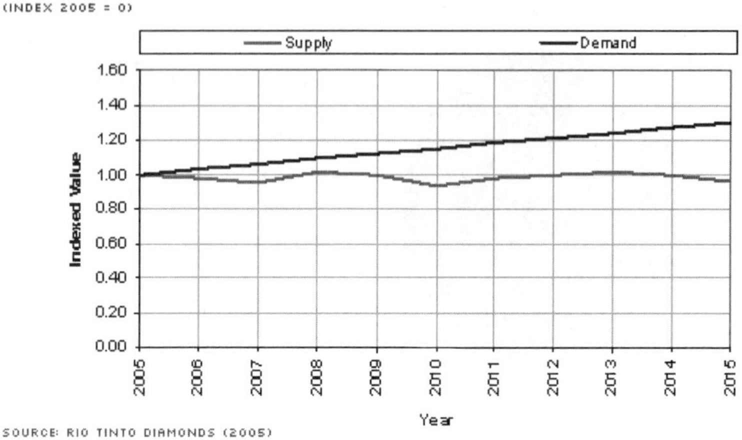

Source: http://pangeadiamondfields.com/diamond-sector.htm

There is no doubt that the GFC led to a crush of the world commodity prices, and of the world diamonds market in particular. In this way, the GFC has ruined to some extent African development because it resulted in significant losses of revenue through commodity earnings, mainly from exports to the USA and EU markets. The GFC has revealed the vulnerability of mineral-dependent countries that have so far failed to diversify their economy. Owning to the lack of diversification of the export products and export destinations, the collapse of commodity prices in the second half of 2008 and at the beginning of 2009 led to a shrinking of the African trade (African Economic Outlook, 2010). Approximately 80% of the African exports are oil, minerals, and agricultural goods, with fuels and mining products accounting for the largest part.

The USA and the European Union (EU) markets account for almost two-thirds of Africa's exports and as such Africa was negatively affected by the GFC via the shrinking of those markets. Moreover, intra-regional trade, which contributes just about 10% of the total trade for Africa, failed to cushion the effects of the crisis. Africa has been affected strongly through the trade avenue. Export prices declined by 50 percent for crude oil and by more than 20 percent for coffee, sugar, cotton and copper between February 2008 and February 2009. In addition to the decline in prices, the volume of African exports has also declined, resulting in low export earnings. The slow economic recovery in Europe and in the United States of America has contributed to persistence of Africa's weak exports. According to the African Economic Outlook (2010) the export volumes for Africa fell by 2.5% and the import volumes fell by roughly 8%, owing to the effects of the GFC. Consequently, this has led to the depreciation of the terms of trade for Africa with export values falling by above 30% and import values by roughly 20% (African Economic Outlook, 2010). Broadman (2009: 2) sums up the impact of this crisis on Sub-Saharan Africa as follows:

The US and the EU are the major export destinations, accounting for 60 percent of the African exports. Given that the import volumes in both the US and the EU had declined in 2009 by two percent and five percent respectively, African economies were adversely affected. The problem was compounded by the decline in commodity prices as prices for both oil and copper declined by 15 percent. Declines in commodity prices for coffee, cocoa and cotton were also observed. The inflow of finances into Africa – of foreign investment and of remittances - has declined; while foreign investment has declined because of the direct effects of the GFC, remittances have declined as workers employed in developed countries lost their jobs.

These changes have serious ramifications on the economies of African countries and for African development. The effects of the GFC on the world diamonds market and on African development can be classified as both direct and indirect. The direct effects were losses in terms of minerals export revenues and lower financial inflows because of the crisis in the financial sector. The stock market indices declined by around 67 percent in Egypt and Nigeria, with Botswana, Kenya, Mauritius and Zambia also experiencing significant declines (United Nations Economic and Social Council/Economic Commission for Africa, 2009). Indirect effects have followed (disruption of the African banks and financial systems, budgetary problems, unemployment and poverty increases, etc.). Having said this, we now consider the impact of the GFC on Botswana.

4 Impact of the GFC on Botswana

The Botswana economy is predominantly a minerals export economy, and the minerals sector share to total Gross Domestic Product (GDP) has averaged around 40 percent in the past 10 years. Within the mining sector, diamonds have been the major driver of Botswana's economy relative to other minerals, such copper, nickel and gold. Tables 1 and 2 give the share of the minerals sector to the Gross Domestic Product (GDP) of the Botswana economy. The share of the sector to GDP has even been in excess of 40 percent prior to 2006. It has fallen below 40 percent since 2007 and has been declining. However, its share to the GDP remains above thirty three percent, and this serves to illustrate its significance to the economy. The table 2 also gives the rate of growth of both the mining sector and of the GDP, while table 3 gives the growth rates of the non-mining sectors.

The revenues from the minerals sector have been a major source of overall government revenues, contributing in excess of 50 percent of total tax revenues from 1998/1999 to 2006/2007 and an average of 50 percent to total government revenues and grants over the same period (as shown in Table 4). Since 2007, the mineral revenue shares have fallen below 50 percent, and both the share in tax revenues and the share in total revenues and grants have been falling sharply in 2009. However, the rate of decline in minerals revenues has been greater than that of total tax revenues and total government revenues. The minerals revenues in 2009 were almost half its 2006 and 2007 levels due to the GFC. With the exception of 2009, both tax revenues and government revenues have been on the rise even though the minerals revenues were declining. This is due to some other sources of government revenues, which have gained prominence over time, namely non-mineral sector income taxes, general sales tax/VAT, and customs and excise duties, which have been on the rise for the past decade (Bank of Botswana, 2009a).

As the aggregate demand dwindled as a result of the GFC, the world market prices and the global demand for diamonds fell significantly. Gaolathe (2009) pointed out that Botswana's major export destinations, namely America, Europe, Japan, and India, experienced severe impacts of the financial crisis. This led to a decline in both the price and the demand for diamonds, leading to a sharp decline in the government revenues. Both the USA and Europe have experienced the worst financial crisis since the 1930s. Given that the USA accounted for 41 percent of the global demand for jewellery, such a decline undermined diamonds production, employment, and export receipts in Botswana. In addition, some mining companies, in particular those in diamonds mining, shelved their plans to invest (Kamidza, 2009). The impact of the decline in diamonds revenues was aggravated by the rising food and oil prices, particularly given the fact that Botswana is a net importer of food and fuel which drains the country's foreign exchange reserves (Gaolathe, 2009; Kamidza, 2009). The mining sector experienced a decline in employment of 8.9 percent (1,039 persons), and quarrying had a decline of 2.6 percent (970 persons) between September 2008 and March 2009 (Benza, 2010).

During the first to the third quarter of 2008, the country experienced a steady decline of GDP and of exports due to the global financial crisis. This is indicative of the relationship between trade and the global financial crisis (Kamidza, 2009). Gross Domestic Product (GDP) contracted by 6 percent in 2009, leading to the lowest GDP growth since 1975. In the same financial year, mining sector and manufacturing sector growth rates were negative at 27 percent and 5 percent respectively. The other economic sectors registered positive rates of growth, with the agricultural sector being in the lead at around 25 percent of positive growth. Despite the fact that only two sectors shrank over the year, and that eight other sectors had growth, of which 50 percent of them grew at rates in excess of 10 percent, Botswana's aggregate economy contracted by 6 percent (Jefferis, 2010: 3).

The GFC has affected the mining sector adversely in Botswana with a negative growth rate of 27 per cent in 2009. Given the significance of mining on the Botswana economy, particularly its contribution to government revenues, it is no surprise that the government has registered a substantial budget deficit.

5 Botswana's Response to the Crisis

The budget situation for the year 2009/10 was difficult, with an envisaged budget deficit following many years of surpluses as the government battled to provide stimulus to maintain growth and employment within the economy. In order to avoid depleting the foreign exchange reserves, Botswana borrowed from amongst others the African Development Bank (AfDB) to finance the deficit. The government was of the view that programs and projects with high propensity for economic diversification were to receive greater financial preference and emphasized financial discipline in addressing the crisis (Gaolathe, 2009). The AfDB approved a US$ 1.5 billion loan for Botswana in line with its commitment to provide support for countries being affected by the GFC. This is the largest loan ever granted by the bank. It was meant to finance the 13.5 percent of GDP budget deficit caused by a decline in diamond prices (African Development Bank, 2009).

The government also introduced *Ipelegeng*, a labour-intensive public works programme, which was conceived as a social safety net mechanism for the poor (see Table 7).

The programme is a poverty eradication strategy spearheaded by the president. The programme was initially allocated a vote of BWP 60 562 500. 00, but the figure was latter revised to BWP 320 562 500. 00[3]. The revision was made effective as a result of a presidential directive that able-bodied destitutes should be removed from the destitute programme and be enrolled in the *Ipelegeng* programme (Lute, 2009).

---

[3] US$ 1 roughly equals 7 Botswana Pula

Table 7: Economic Policies/Programs

Policy /Program	Objectives/ Principles	Key Policy Actions/Strategies	Comments
Ipelegeng*, 2008	▪ Employment support for unskilled and semiskilled labor	▪ Provide temporary employment on a rotational basis	▪ Addresses poverty by providing short term employment to those with limited or no income ▪ Key Challenges o Sustainability of the programs o Short term solution to the biggest problem o Value addition of the program
ISPAAD, 2009**	▪ Increase grain production ▪ Promote food security ▪ Commercialize agriculture ▪ Facilitate access to inputs and credit ▪ Improve extension outreach	▪ Cluster fencing ▪ Provision of portable water ▪ Provision of seeds ▪ Provision of fertilizers ▪ Facilitation of access to credit ▪ Establishment of agricultural service centers	▪ Addresses poverty through provision of wage and self-employment opportunities in the agricultural sector ▪ Key Challenges o Performance monitoring o Sustainability of the program o Capacity of farmers to graduate from traditional to commercial farming o Access to credit o Access to land

Sources: *Republic of Botswana (2009a) ** Republic of Botswana (2009b)

The *Ipelegeng* programme is reported to have substantially increased national employment by 21.8 percent from September 2008 to March 2009 (Benza, 2010). During this period, the local government sector, within which *Ipelegeng* falls, experienced a 233.5 percent (66, 488 persons) increase in employment. The programme employed 38, 000 persons per month since its inception in July 2008, and by October 2009 it had cumulatively employed 397, 494 persons. The program's target is it to employ 40, 000 people (Benza, 2010). The central government, on the other hand, only has realized a 2.2 percent (2,046 persons) growth in employment, while the private sector employment remained constant.

Also as an attempt to diversify the economy away from minerals, the government has introduced the Integrated Support for Arable Agricultural Development (ISPAAD) program as shown in Table 7. The programme aims to boost production in the agricultural sector. This is a government programme, which assists farmers by providing free and subsidised seeds and fertilizers, free plugging, planting, fencing, portable water for domestic use, and with loans at reasonable interest rates (Botswana Gazette Online, 2008). It should be noted that in the year 2009, the agricultural sector experienced a remarkable growth. Notwithstanding, crop production shrank by 14 percent (Jefferis, 2010), despite the government's heavy investment into this sector through ISPAAD.

It is important to note that most of the initiatives undertaken by the government were not specifically to address the GFC. Those initiatives were to address the structural shortcomings of the economy, which were in existence long before the onset of the GFC. The GFC helped to expose the limitations of the narrow diamonds-based economy. Having noted these shortcomings, which have been an integral part of the economy, the government embarked on numerous initiatives. The president in his State of the Nation Address spelled out most of these initiatives. He pointed out that the country will need to diversify the economy through 'focused hubs' and through a range of important initiatives. There were six established Hubs[4], namely the Diamonds Hub, the Transport Hub, the Agricultural Hub, the Health Hub, the Education Hub, and an Innovation Hub (Khama, 2009). The other initiatives, amongst others, include promotion of FDI which focuses on mining, tourism, agriculture and manufacturing sectors, construction, information technology, local procurement preference, import substitution, and the promotion of government schemes.

GFC's effect on the Botswana economy was profound because of the heavy reliance on the diamonds sector. The country had to put in place measures to mitigate the effects of the GFC on the citizenry, although at a cost by increasing the national debt. Whereas the overall value addition potential of *Ipelegeng* and of ISPAAD to the economy is questionable, they both provided social security, particularly to the vulnerable members of the society, thus mitigating the effects of the GFC. With the recovery of the global economy, and in turn the mining sector, it is projected that GDP will grow in

---

[4] These are established centers.

Botswana by 5 percent in 2010. This is as a result of the increased demand for minerals, particularly diamonds, in the industrialized countries.

6 Possible Lessons Learnt from the GFC

The effects of the GFC on the Botswana economy have been very profound on the mining sector. The mining sector has remained the mainstay of the economy despite of almost three decades of government efforts to diversify the economy. Given that mining has accounted for almost 50 percent of the government revenues, it may be difficult for the Botswana economy to remain resilient in the phase of a shrinking mining sector. This is more so considering the fact that the private sector is still small, rudimentary and dependent on the government for its existence. In light of the centrality of the mineral sector to the Botswana economy, a decline in this sector negatively impacts on government, and by extension also on the private sector. Despite this crisis, the non-mining GDP continued to grow (see again table 3). This is attributed to government-increased expenditure on agriculture, social safety nets (see table 7: Ipelegeng program), and infrastructure amongst others.

It would have been of interest to know what the trend would have been had this crisis remained steadfast for a longer period. The government failure to sustain its expenditure in the long-term would have had catastrophic effects on the non-mining sector. More importantly, the GFC has exposed, beyond doubt, the volatility of the Botswana economy's dependence on the mining sector. It is in this sense that the current budget speech has had "*Transforming Our Economy after the Crisis: 2010 and Beyond*" as its theme, thus underlining the urgency for the government to deal with the diversification of the Botswana economy in a more practical and productive way.

It is also worth noting that the agricultural sector was the fastest growing sector in 2009, due to cattle, pigs, poultry, small stock, forestry, bee keeping and other sub-sectors, even though crop production has declined in the same period (Jefferis, 2010). Crop production shrank by 14 percent contrary to expectations, despite government-increased expenditure in the arable sector through the ISPAAD program (see table 7). The recurring droughts undermine this programme. This puts into question the suitability of ISPAAD, given that it fails to address the problems facing the arable agricultural sector. One of the key challenges facing this sector is recurring droughts.

While measures as Ipelegeng aimed at improving the income of the poor by targeting productive public works, the government avoids it to engage private businesses to do such works. While economic theory enthusiasts may consider such a move as of a 'crowding out' nature, the private sector's promotion should not be done for the sake of it without being driven to higher innovativeness. A typical example is the case of tenders for bush clearing along the highways. Such an undertaking is of great value as it minimizes the risk of accidents whereby cars hit animals, thus leading to loss of lives and repair costs. Such undertakings as bush clearing could be done through the public works programs and will give those working in them an opportunity to earn better wages. This will also have the effect of reducing government expenditure through these tenders. If an enterprise that could have tendered for bush clearing is crowded out, then there would be no significant economic cost incurred by this sector. It is important that the government should strive to get value for expenditure on productive programs. Failure to do that will put a constraint on the government resources and will render the diversification drive untenable.

The government of Botswana is committed to the private sector as the engine of economic growth as espoused in the 1994 budget speech (Mogae, 1994). The insufficient inflow of FDI into the country is the major impediment to the attainment of this objective. Though Botswana is an upper middle-income country, the government is the major shareholder to the overall economy along with mining. Taking into account the existence of a number of parastatals, we observe that the share of government activity to the national economy is much greater than that directly provided for by the national income accounts. Furthermore, the government is a major shareholder in mining. These factors make the government the most significant player in the economy endowed with the greatest resources. If the private sector is to be robust, particularly in the light of limited FDI, the government will have to take a lead. The government has done this on a number of occasions through the establishment of agencies meant to provide financial assistance to potential entrepreneurs. The Financial Assistance Policy (FAP) and the Citizen Entrepreneurial Development Agency (CEDA) are some of the organs the government has established as finance and incubation vehicles towards private sector development, economic empowerment and diversification of the economy, albeit with limited success. To encourage the spirit of entrepreneurship and enterprise, the Local Enterprises Authority (LEA) was established in 2004. It offers specialized advice and support services aimed at the facilitation of business planning, access to finance, adoption and diffusion of technology, access to markets, provision of mentoring, training and advisory services, identification of business opportunities for existing and future small and medium scale enterprises (SMEs), and the promotion of general entrepreneurship and SMEs amongst others. It does not provide finance even though it facilitates access to finance and provides support services to SMEs before and after funding (LEA, 2010).

The government has established the Public Enterprises Evaluation and Privatization Agency (PEEPA) in 2001 as an autonomous agency of the government to spearhead the privatization of some of the parastatal sector enterprises. The agency has until now not been able to practically realize its objectives, with the privatization of Air Botswana having had to be stalled because it was clouded in controversies. The privatization of the Botswana Telecommunications Corporation (BTC) is currently at an advanced stage. The privatization of parastatals in itself does not diversify the economy but changes ownership of such entities. In this sense, privatization does not provide solutions to the narrow economic base of the economy. Export diversification policies are of central importance for Botswana, and the government has a guiding role in it as well as in private sector development.

7 Conclusions and Policy Recommendations

Some Conclusions

The paper has shown that the GFC has had a negative effect on the Botswana economy – an economy that is heavily dependent on minerals, and particularly on diamonds. The GFC has demonstrated that Botswana's economy is fragile to external shocks because of its structural nature. As a way of alleviating this crisis, the government has introduced a stimulus package. This has entailed that the government increased its expenditures what has resulted in a huge budget deficit that was financed largely through borrowing and by the use of its foreign exchange reserves. The lesson for Botswana is to diversify its economy away from minerals.

Measures taken by the government to diversify the economy should have the potential to add significant value to the economy. Public works programs, though short term measures, have the potential to reduce unemployment and to contribute to the infrastructure upgrading in the economy if used productively. To realize the productive growth of the agricultural sector, ISPAAD needs revision in order to address the specific problems deterring the sector. This will ensure efficiency of use of the limited resources and will provide scope for further economic expansion. It is important that the problem of drought be addressed either through ground water or dams so as to utilize irrigation for efficient agricultural production. This will give some certainty in agricultural output and employment creation.

The new economic order laid emphasis on the market fundamentalism. This approach is accountable for the recent GFC. The order calls for limited government involvement particularly in productive investment. The government of Botswana has attempted to attract substantial foreign direct investment (FDI), but without much success as most of it had been directed to the capital- intensive mining sector (Malema, 2008). The approach to rely on FDI to diversify the economy and to create employment has been futile. In light of the substantial resources the country has, this paper argues that it will be necessary for such resources to be used to expand the productive capacity of the economy. By using the resources to engage them in productive investments, the government will have to broaden the economic base, so as to create employment and wealth, thereby minimizing the effect of economic shocks and ensuring that the productive capacity is expanded to generate more income.

The paper recommends that government should assist farmers to drill underground water and to acquire irrigation equipment to engage in irrigation farming. This could be done through the provision of loans at low interest rates. The construction of dams for irrigation purposes will go a long way in helping the economy diversify into agriculture.

The government should use its resources to facilitate productive ventures that go beyond infrastructural development. This is informed by the fact that previous attempts by the government to render financial assistance for the promotion of private engagement in productive investments have not borne sufficient or significant fruits. A think tank mandated with identifying feasible and profitable possible investment ventures should be put in place. Efforts to avoid crowding out of the private sector should be core to the identification process. This recommendation is driven by the recognition that there is insufficient inflow of FDI into the country, yet the government is a major player in the economy with massive savings in the form of foreign exchange reserves.

Lastly, we would like to point out that even though the recent GFC adversely affected the Botswana economy, the impact has been mainly through the mining sector. The Bank of Botswana has however taken an initiative to ensure that the financial sector remains solid and effective. This initiative entails the establishment of a Financial Stability Division, which was necessitated by the recent global financial crisis. It aims at strengthening the central bank's capacity to monitor economic and financial developments with a view to ensure stability of the financial system (Bank of Botswana, 2009b, 2010). Maintaining financial stability is necessary for an effective undertaking of the central bank's mandate of maintaining monetary stability and financial conditions conducive to the balanced and sustained development of Botswana (Bank of Botswana, 2009b). This will minimize the danger of a crisis of this nature arising from the collapse of the domestic financial system.

Summary of Policy Recommendations

There is need for the government to make diversification of the economy a practical reality. This can be realised through amongst others:

- ISPAAD should be revisited so as to identify major impediments to the agricultural sector. This will allow for the government to come up with measures aimed at addressing the identified loopholes, and this may lead to increased arable production and help realise food sufficiency, employment creation and diversification of the economy.
- In light of the narrow economic base of the economy and the budget constraints, it is our view that the resources available should be utilized optimally to ensure a maximization of economic returns. To this end the public works programmes such as *Ipelegeng* should not only be used as social safety nets but should be sources of economic growth by being used in an economically productive way.
- In light of insufficient inflows of FDI into the country, particularly to non-mining sectors, and given that the country has substantial foreign exchange reserves, it is important that the government should use them to expand the economic base of the country. This calls for an identification of viable investment and productive opportunities for which the reserves could be invested into. A think tank mandated with identifying feasible and profitable possible investment ventures should be put in place. Such an organ should further advice on how the reserves could be productively utilized.
- More organs along the lines of the Financial Stability Division should be set up to help avoid economic shocks. Such organs should be spread across the economy to address specific economic needs and identify possible sources of economic shocks.

References

African Economic Outlook (2010), "Adverse Effect of Commodity Prices and Export Volumes", www:africaneconomicoutlook.org/en/outlook/macroeconomic-situation-and-prospect; accessed 16 June 2010

African Development Bank (2009), "AfDB Approves US$ 1.5 Billion Budget Support for Botswana to Help Country Cope with the Financial Crisis", http://www.afdb.org/en/news-events/article/afdb-approves-us-1-5billion-budget-support-; accessed 26/04/2010

Bank of Botswana (2009a), Annual Report 2009, Gaborone: Bank of Botswana

Bank of Botswana (2009b), Financial Stability, http://www.Bankofbotswana.bw/index.php/content/2009111814047-financial-stability; accessed on 03 August 2010

Bank of Botswana (2010), Financial stability Division. http:/www.Bankofbotswana.bw/index.php/content/2010063014012-financial-stability-division; accessed on 03 August 2010

Benza, B. (2010), Botswana: *Ipelegeng* Boosts Formal Employment Figures – CSO, *Mmegi,* January 2010, http://allafrica.com/stories/printable/201001070742.html; accessed 2 June 2010

Benza, B. (2008), "Botswana: Diamond Exports Threatened By World Financial Crisis", Mmegi, 31 October 2008, http://allafrica.com/stories/200811040819.html; accessed 26/04/2010

Botswana Gazette Online (2008), "What is ISPAAD?, Any Better than ALDEP, ARAP, etc.?", http://www.gazettebw.com/index.php?view=article&catid=15%3Aeditorial&id=1343%3; Accessed: 3 June 2010

Broadman, H. (2009), *The Impact of the International Financial Crisis on Sub-Saharan Africa*, Panel Discussion prior to the meeting of the Sub-Saharan Advisory Committee (SAAC) of the Export-Import Bank of the United States (EX-IM Bank), 25 March 2009.

Diamine Explorations, Inc., World Diamond Market, Global Diamond Supply, in http://www.diamineexplorations.com/web/index/.php?id=147, Accessed 23/06/2010.

Dudu, China May Replace India as the World's Largest Diamond Processing Country; see: http:/www.articlesbase.com/organizational-articles/china-may-replace-india-as-the-world039s-largest-diamond-producing-country-2130559.html; Accessed 23/06/2010

Edge, W. (1998), 'Botswana: A Developmental State' in Edge, W. and Lekorwe, M. (Eds.), *Botswana Politics and Society,* Pretoria: Van Schaik

Gaolathe, B. (2009), Statement by the Governor of Botswana, Fourty-Fourth Annual Meeting of the Board of Governors and the Thirthy-Fifth Annual Meeting of the ADF Board of Governors, Held at the Palais Des Congres, Hotel Meridien President Dakar, Senegal on 13 and 14 May 2009

Gaolathe, N. (1997), "Botswana's Boom and Recession Experience: A Discussion", in: Salkin, J. S, Mpabanga, D., Cowin, D., Selwe, J and Wright, M. (Eds.) *Aspects of the Botswana Economy – Selected Papers,* Oxford: James Currey, pp. 37-52

Hanemann, U. (2005), Background paper prepared for the Education for All Global Monitoring Report 2006 *Literacy for Life* Literacy in Botswana, UNESCO Institute for Education Hamburg, Germany March, 2005 http://unesdoc.unesco.org/images/0014/001460/146005e.pdf, accessed 30 July 2010

Hillbom, E. (2008), "Diamonds or Development?, A Structural Assessment of Botswana's forty years of success", in: *Journal of Modern African Studies*, 46, 2, pp.191-214

Iimi, A (2007), "Escaping from the Resource Curse: Evidence from Botswana and the Rest of the World", *IMF Staff Papers*, 54, 4, pp. 663-699

Jefferis, K. (2010), *Economic Review,* Bifm Economic Review, Gaborone: Bifm Botswana Limited, 1st Quarter, pp. 1-7

Kamidza, R. (2009), Social Impact of the Financial Crisis on Botswana, Economic Justice Network with support from the Open Society Initiative for Southern Africa (OSISA), Policy Series No. 4/2009

Khama, S. K. I. (2009), BW: State of the Nation address by the President of Botswana, on Empowering the Nation through Democracy, Development, Dignity and Discipline

Kohler, S. (2009), Global diamond market expected to worsen. http://www/ miningweekly.com/article/globl-diamond-market-2009-06-05. Accessed 23/06/2010.

Lawrence, P. (2009), "What will the World Financial Crisis do to Africa", in: *Review of African Political Economy* No. 120, pp. 283-300

LEA, (2010), About Us, http://www.lea.co.bw/article.php?id_mnu=1 ; accessed 16 July 2010

Leith, C. (2000), "Why Botswana Prospered", Unpublished Paper, November

Lute, A. (2009), "Massive Boost for *Ipelegeng*", in: *The Botswana Gazette*, 8 December 2009

Malema, B. W. (2008), 'Botswana's International Investment Position: The Role of Direct Foreign Investment', in: *Asian-African Journal of Economics and Econometrics,* Vol. 8, No 1: pp. 45-54

Mogae, F. (1994), Making the Private Sector an Engine of Economic Growth, Budget speech 2004, Gaborone: Government Printer

Niemann, M. (1993), "Diamonds are a State's best friend: Botswana's Foreign Policy in Southern Africa", in: *Africa Today* 40, 1, pp. 27-47

Olsson, O. (2007), "Conflict Diamonds", in: *Journal of Development Economics* 82, pp. 267-286

Republic of Botswana (2009a), Guidelines for the Implementation of Ipelegeng Programme, Ministry of Local Government, Gaborone, Botswana

Republic of Botswana (2009b), ISPAAD, Ministry of Agriculture, Gaborone, Botswana

Salkin, J. S. (1997), "Introduction", in: Salkin, J. S, Mpabanga, D.,

Cowan, D., Selwe, J. and Wright, M. (Eds.), *Aspects of the Botswana Economy – Selected Papers*, Oxford: James Currey Publishers

Samatar, A. I. (1999), *An African Miracle: State and Class Leadership and Colonial Legacy in Botswana Development*, Portsmouth: Heinemann

Sebudubudu, D. and Lotshwao, K. (2009), *Managing Resources and the Democratic Order: The Experience of Botswana*, South African Institute of International Affairs, Johannesburg, Occasional Paper No. 31

Sebudubudu, D. and Molutsi, P. (2009), *Leaders, Elites and Coalitions in the Development of Botswana,* Leaders, Elites & Coalitions Research Programme (LECRP), World Bank Research Paper No.2 (April 2009)

Tiruneh, G. (2004), 'Democratic Development in Botswana and Tunisia: A Comparative Analysis', in: *Journal of Contemporary African Studies*, 22, 1, pp. 13-28

UNDP (United Nations Development Programme), (2007), Human Development Report 2007/2008, Fighting Climate Change: Human solidarity in a divided world, New York, USA: UNDP 2007

United Nations Economic and Social Council/Economic Commission for Africa (2009), *The Global Financial Crisis: Impact, responses and way forward*, Meeting of the Committee of Experts of the 2nd Joint Annual Meetings of the AU Conference of Ministers of Economy and Finance and ECA Conference of Ministers of Finance, Planning and Economic Development, 2-5 June 2009, Cairo

UNICEF Botswana Statistics, http://www.unicef.org/infoby country/botswanastatistics.html; accessed 30 July 2010

Wallis, M. (1989), *Bureaucracy: Its Role in Third World Development*, Hong Kong: MacMillan

World Bank (2010), GDP per capita (current US$), http://data.worldbank.org/indicator/NY.GDP.PCAP.CD; accessed 30 July 2010

Yang, C. (2010), China becomes second largest diamond market, http://business.globaltimes.cn/industries/21010-01/500580.html; accessed 23 June 2010

Achievement of Millennium Development Goals and Global Financial Crisis in Nigeria

Alabi, Reuben Adeolu[#] and Adams Oshobugie Ojor[*]

Abstract

The Millennium development goals (MDGs) were launched at the beginning of the 21st century to help developing countries eradicate extreme poverty and hunger, achieve universal primary education, reduce infant and maternal mortality rates, promote girl child education, combat HIV/AIDS, malaria and other diseases, among others. The available information indicates that Nigeria has appropriated over N340 billion (2.27 billion US dollars) for MDGs in the last three years and that over 24 trillion naira (160 billion US dollars) will be needed in the next five years to meet the MDGs by 2015. We inferred in this paper that Nigeria will not be able to raise this huge amount of money and that the progress in achieving MDGs may be hindered due to global financial crisis which induced a decrease in export prices (oil and cocoa prices), decline in international remittances from developed countries, a slowdown or even withdrawal of Foreign Direct Investments (FDI) as well as increased inflation and taxation. Apart from these afore mentioned factors that can hinder the achievement of MDGs in Nigeria, the corruption in the use of MDGs fund and lack of proper coordination of the MDGs activities are also implicated as some of the problems that may hinder the achievement of MDGs in Nigeria. We concluded the paper by recommending diversification of the economic base, lowering of the interest rate for the real sectors of

[#] Associate Professor in the Department of Agricultural Economics, Ambrose Alli University, Ekpoma, Nigeria and Alexander von Humboldt Fellow (AvH, Bonn, Germany. E-mail: bayobimb@yahoo.com.

[*] Doctoral Student in the Department of Agricultural Economics, Ambrose Alli University, Ekpoma, Nigeria. E-mail: adamsosbhogue@yahoo.com,

the economy, targeted bailout for farmers' loans, rural employment and social security programmes. Besides, proper coordination of MDGs projects and programmes among the three tiers of Government is a necessary condition for Nigeria to make faster progress in achieving these desirable goals. We stressed that all the public funds meant for MDGs should be transparently and prudently used for the purpose they are set aside for. In addition, meeting the MDGs will require partnership between donor agencies, government, civil societies, the public and the private sectors.

1 Introduction

At the millennium summit in September 2000, the largest gathering of world history, the world leaders adopted the UN millennium Declaration, committing their nations to a new global partnership to reduce poverty, improve health, and promote peace, human rights, gender equality, and environmental sustainability. Soon after, world leaders met again at the March 2002 International Conference on Financing for Development in Monterrey, Mexico, establishing a landmark framework for global development partnership in which developed and developing countries agreed to take joint actions for poverty reduction. Later that same year, UN member states gathered at the World Summit on sustainable development in Johannesburg, South Africa, where they reaffirmed the Millennium Development Goals (MDGs) as the World's Time bound developmental goals (UN, 2002a). If the MDGs are achieved by 2015, it means that more than 500 million people will be lifted out of extreme poverty. More than 300 million will no longer suffer from hunger. Rather than die before reaching their fifth birthdays, 30 million children will be saved, so will be lives of more than 2 million mothers (UK, 2005). Achieving the goals will mean safe drinking water for another 350 million people, and basic sanitation for 650 million, allowing them to lead healthier and more dignified lives. Women and girl will lead their lives in freedom, with more security and more opportunity (MDG Report, 2005). Therefore, any effort aimed at achieving these noble targets will be for the good of all and sundry. However, the financial commitment to meet these goals are great, for example the UN Millennium Project (2005) estimated that household contribution to meet MGDs needs in Africa will increase from \$79 per capita in 2006 to \$100 and \$141 per capita in 2010 and 2015 respectively. The MDG financing gap alone in 2006 was \$48 per capita out of which official development assistance provided about \$14 per capita, leaving the gap of about \$34 per capita (ERA, 2005). According to Sanchez and Vos (2009), the cost of achieving the MDGs will rise by about 1.5 to 2% of GDP as additional spending per year between 2010 and 2015 as compared to a non- global financial crisis situation. The available information indicates that Nigeria has appropriated over N320 billion (2.27 billion US dollars) for MDGs in the last three years and that over N24 trillion (160 billion US dollars) will be needed in the next five years to meet the MGDs by 2015. The issue is that Nigeria may not be able to raise that amount of money in this period of global financial crisis. We imply that global financial crisis will have impact in Nigeria and by implication, the achievement of MDGs through the decline in prices and revenue from exports, through declined foreign direct investment, international remittances, increases in inflation and taxes which will culminate in declined economic growth and inability to raise sufficient funds necessary for achieving the MDGs.

The rest of the paper is divided into five sections. Section two presents the progress of MDGs in Nigeria before the global financial crisis, section three deals with impact of global financial crisis on Nigeria and establishes its implications on MDGs, section four links corruption with spending on MDGs in Nigeria, section five elaborates on Nigerian government responses to Global Financial Crisis (GFC), section six concludes the paper with policy recommendations.

2 Progress in MDGs in Nigeria before the Global Financial Crisis

The goals of millennium development include those dedicated to eradicating poverty, achieving universal primary education, promoting gender equality and empowering women, reducing child mortality, improving maternal health, combating HIV/AIDS, malaria and other diseases, ensuring environmental sustainability and developing a global partnership for development. The progress MDGs in Nigeria is assessed in this section based on eight main targets. Using 1990 as the baseline, the targets are:

a. Eradicate extreme poverty and hunger

2015 target: Halve proportion of people living on less than $1 a day, and those suffering hunger.

b. Achieve universal basic education

2015 target: Achieve universal primary completion.

c. Promote gender equality

2005/2015 target: Eliminate gender disparities in primary and secondary education enrolment by 2005, and achieve equity at all levels by 2015.

d. Reduce child mortality

2015 target: Reduce by two thirds the child mortality rate.

e. Improve maternal health

2015 target: Reduce by three quarters the proportion of women dying in childbirth.

f. Combat AIDS, malaria and other diseases

2015 target: Halt and begin to reverse the incidence of HIV-AIDS, malaria and other major diseases.

g. Ensure environmental sustainability

Integrate the principles of sustainable development into country policies and programmes and reverse the loss of environmental resources.
2015 target: Reduce by half the proportion of people without access to clean drinking water and basic sanitation. By 2020 achieve a significant improvement in the lives of at least 100 million slum dwellers.

h. Develop a global partnership for development

They are not measurable, but goal 8 commits north and south to working together to achieve an open, rule-based trading and financial system, more generous aid to countries committed to poverty reduction, and relief for the debt problems of developing countries. It draws attention to the problems of the least developed countries and of landlocked countries and Small Island developing states, which have greater difficulty competing in the global economy.

2.1 Progress in Eradication of Extreme Poverty and Hunger in Nigeria

Globally, poverty is decreasing in the world (including Sub Sahara Africa (SSA) as indicated in Table 1); however, the level of poverty in Nigeria has increased from about 43% in 1990 to 54.4% of population in 2005. The implication of this is that in 1992 about 39 million Nigerians were poor, which increased to more than 76 millions in 2005 and has since continued to increase. In terms of poverty reduction, Nigeria is lagging behind the Sub-Sahara Africa average in the millennium development goal of halving poverty by 2015. According to 2005 MDG report in Nigeria, if the current efforts at poverty reduction in Nigeria is maintained (without global financial crisis), the poverty incidence in Nigeria would reduce to 43% as opposed to 21.4% by 2015.

Table 1: Progress in MDGs in Nigeria and Sub Sahara Africa between 1990 and 2007.

	Nigeria		Sub-Sahara Africa	
	1990	2007	1990	2007
Poverty Level (head count)	42.7	54.4	57.4	50.7
Malnutrition Prevalence (weight for age (% of Children under 5)	35	26	31	28
Literacy rate %	74	57	53.7	62.2
Primary school net enrolment (%)	58	62	53.5	73.5
Ratio of girls to boys in primary and secondary schools (%)	0.79	0.82	0.83	0.90
Immunization against measles (percentage of children ages 12-23 months)	54	35	56	73
Mortality rate [infant (Per 1000 live births)]	91	76	107	88
Mortality rate [under 5 (per 1000)]	230	194	183	145
Maternal mortality (per 100,000 live births)	800	704	920	900
Incidence of tuberculosis (per 100,000 people)	106	282.6	150	234
Total Debt service (% GDP)	23	16	17.6	4.2
Improved sanitation facilities (% of population with access)	39	44	26	42
Improved water source (% of population with access)	49	48	49	58
Fertility rate (births per woman)	6.7	5.5	-	-
Contraceptive prevalence (% of women ages 15-49)	6	13	12	21.5
Life expectancy at birth (years)	46.4	43.0	-	-
Trade (% of GDP)	72.2	88.4	-	-
Forest area (% of land area covered)	19	12	29.2	26.5
HIV prevalence (% 15-49 years)	1.8	4.4	2.1	4.9
Co_2 emission (metric tone per capita)	0.5	0.5	0.9	0.8
Birth attended by skilled health staff (%)	30.8	35.2	42	44
Aid per capita (current US$)	2.9	49	-	-

Sources: Millennium Development Goals Report (2009), MDG Report (2005)

2.2 Progress in Achievement of Universal Basic Education in Nigeria

There is improvement in education sector in Nigeria. The primary school net enrolment rate has increased from 58% to 62% in 2007. According to Igbuzor (2006), the efficiency of primary education has equally improved, as the primary six completion rate increased steadily from 65% in 1998 to 83% in 2006. However, the achievement in net primary school enrolment in Nigeria which stood at 62% in 2007 is below the SSA average of about 74%. The literacy rate also declined from 74% in 1990 to 57% in 2007.

2.3 Progress in Promoting Gender Equality in Nigeria

At the primary, the number of girls is still lower than the numbers of boys. The ratio which was 0.79 in 1990 rose to more than 0.82 in 2007. However, the ratio of girls to boys in primary and secondary school in Nigeria is however lower than the average for SSA of 0.83 and 0.90 in 1990 and 2007 respectively. Nevertheless, the national average in Nigeria conceals the regional gender disparity as noted by Alabi (2009). He indicated that we have more girls than boys in the primary and secondary schools in the South-eastern part of the Nigeria while the reverse is the case in the Northern part of the country.

2.4 Progress in Reducing Child Mortality in Nigeria

Infant and under five mortality rates declined from 91 and 230 in 1990 to 76 and 194 in 2007 respectively. This is one of the MDG goals that Nigeria has the chance to achieve without the financial crisis scenario. In fact, the infant, mortality rate in Nigeria in 2007 is lower than the average of 88 estimated for the SSA. However, the under five mortality of 194 is higher than the average of 145 estimated for SSA. The fact that under five mortality rate of 194 estimated for Nigeria is higher than the average for SSA can be attributed to the decline in immunization between 1990 and 2007. The measles immunization declined from 54% to 35% within the period, while it increases from 56% to 73% between 1990 and 2007 in SSA.

2.5 Progress in Improvement in Maternal Mortality in Nigeria

Nigeria has improved in the area of maternal mortality from 800 to 704 per 100,000 live births between 1990 and 2007. The improvement is greater than the average for SSA that has declined from 920 to 900. However, the disparity between the maternal mortality in the rural area is significant as indicated by Igbuzor (2006). He noted that the maternal mortality in rural areas is more than twice as high as in the urban areas. The improvement in maternal mortality rate among women in Nigeria can be attributed to the increase in the use of contraceptive for family planning in Nigeria. The contraceptive prevalence rate increased from 6% to 13% between 1990 and 2007, (117% increase) this is higher than the improvement of 12% to 21.5% in SSA (79% increase). The fact that the birth attended by skilled health staff has increased from about 31% to 35% between 1990 and 2007 can be an important factor that contributed to improved safe delivery and reduction in maternal mortality in Nigeria. The increase in the proportion of birth attended to by the skilled health staff in the Nigeria was also higher than the average for SSA. The increment was 13% for Nigeria, while it was 5% for SSA between 1990 and 2007. The reduction in birth rate as a result of use of contraceptive methods can also explain decline in fertility rate from 6.7 to 5.5 per woman between 1990 and 2007.

2.6 Progress in Combating AIDS, Malaria and Other Diseases in Nigeria

Since the identification of the first HIV-AIDS case in mid 1980s in Nigeria, the HIV prevalence rate has continually been on the increase. According to MDGs report (2005), it increased from 1.8 to 5.8% in the period between 1991 and 2001 and decreased to 5% in 2003. The HIV prevalence rate in Nigeria in 2007 stood at 4.4%. This is lower than 4.9% estimated for SSA in 2007. The fact that HIV prevalence rate increased from 1.8% to 4.4% between 1990 and 2007 implies that the incidence of HIV-AIDS is not being reversed in Nigeria. Apart from the increase in HIV prevalence rate, there is also increase in the incidence of tuberculosis(TB), which has increased from 106 to about 283 per 100,000 people between 1990 and 2007. The rate of incidence of TB in Nigeria in 2007 which stood at about 283 is till higher than the SSA average of 234 per 100,000 people. The increase in the incidence of TB and prevalence of HIV might have contributed to reduction in life expectancy at birth in Nigeria which has reduced from 46 years to 43 years between 1990 and 2007.

2.7 Progress in Ensuring Environmental Sustainability in Nigeria

There was an improvement in access to sanitation facilities, which has increased from 39% to 44% between 1990 and 2007. However, the accessibility of improved water source declined from 49% to 48% within the period under consideration. The country is endowed with abundant environmental resources; however, high population growth rate and increasing demand for these resources threaten environmental sustainability. This is supported by the fact that the area covered by the forest in Nigeria decreased from 19% to 12% of total land area in Nigeria. The forest area cover of 12% is lower than about 27% forest area cover estimated for SSA in 2007. The carbon dioxide emission of 0.5 metric tonne per capita is however; lower than 0.8 metric tonne per capita for SSA. Although, while the Co_2 emission in Nigeria remain 0.5 metric tonne per capita between 1990 and 2007, the SSA $C0_2$ emission decreased from 0.9 to 0.8 metric tonne per capita between 1990 and 2007.

2.8 Progress in Developing a Global Partnership for Development in Nigeria

The level of official development assistance has increased from 2.8 to about 49 US dollar per capita in Nigeria between 1990 and 2007. This increment can be attributed to improved democratic environment within the period. Another area where Nigeria has improved significantly is in the area of debt services. Debt service as ratio of GDP reduced from 23% to 16% between 1990 and 2007. Nigeria has enjoyed debt forgiveness within the period and the money saved as a result of debt forgiveness forms major component fund used for executing the MDGs projects. However, the financial crisis may lower the future chance of achieving this goal as it may lead to decline in the official aid and that Nigerian government may incur more debt in order to finance critical project for which they may not have enough fund. In fact, MDG report (2009) has indicated that share of OECD/DAC Aid in Gross National Income declined from 0.33% to 0.30% between 1990 and 2008. The GFC may threaten this further.

3 Impact of GFC on Nigeria and its Implication on MDGs

If pre-crisis trends had continued unabated, Nigeria would likely be able to attain the MDGs of net enrolment in primary education, gender equality in education and possibly also combat HIV/AIDS and other diseases. The speed of progress for achieving the goals for extreme poverty reduction and hunger has been insufficient, though pre-crisis progress however is assessed on the basis of linear projections, even though the path towards the goals need not follow a linear pattern (Vos and Sachez, 2009). However, the incidence of the GFC has affected and will affect the chances of MDGs in several ways.

In Nigeria, the debate was intense on whether the global financial crisis will affect the country or not. Most commentators were of the opinion that the banking sector would weather the storm due to the fact that (i) the financial system is not strongly integrated into the international financial architecture, (ii) the relatively simple nature of the financial products and (iii) the strong capitalisation and liquidity of Nigerian banks. The reality is that the global crisis has affected Nigeria through sharp declines in the value of oil exports, rapid depreciation of exchange rate, worsening investor sentiments in the banking sector, fall in foreign direct investment and remittances. In addition, as foreign investors divested from the Nigerian stock exchange, market capitalisation plunged drastically (Babatunde and Busari, 2009). This section explains in details how the GFC has affected Nigeria and the impact it will have on the achievement of MDGs through various transmission channels.

3.1 International Remittances

Remittances are a way by which the global financial crisis can affect African economies. Remittances are a component of international capital flows mostly used for consumption and investment purposes. Many economists argue that large amounts of remittances can substitute financial underdevelopment and promote economic growth. If remittances are channeled to productive investments, then the potential for increased growth will be high (Giuliano and Arranz, 2005). In Africa, remittances can boost growth in countries where the financial systems are less developed by providing an alternative way to finance investment and help overcome liquidity constraints (Amusa, 2009). The use of remittances includes improvement in the health and education sectors and by extension improvements in human capital, alleviation of infrastructure bottlenecks as well as reduced volatility of GDP growth (Amusa, 2009). The loss of income migrant workers will experience will result in a decline in their consumption and will worsen the poverty conditions for those who are already impoverished. According to the World Bank Report (2009) on growth rate of remittances in Sub Saharan Africa (SSA), a significant decline of about 8.3% in the growth rate was expected for 2009.

In the case of Nigeria, the Nigerians in Diasporas remitted $10 billion in 2008, indicating a 10 per cent increase to amount remitted in 2007 (World Bank Report, 2009). The $10 billion inflow represents 5 per cent of the nation's gross domestic product (GDP) and puts Nigeria at number six among the top ten recipients of migrant remittances in the world (Nurudeen and Obi, 2009). The report shows that despite the global economic meltdown which peaked in 2008, remittance to Nigeria by migrant workers have been increasing steadily in the past six years from $1.2 billion in 2002 to $10.8 in 2008. This improvement according to the World Bank is due to the fact that remittance flow to Nigeria is diversified in terms of destinations and sectors. The World Bank report also indicates that remittances are expected to fall in 2009 due to the biting effect of the global crisis, with remittances to Nigeria declining slightly to $9.58 billion in 2009 (Komolafe, 2009)[1]. Moreover, informal remittance to Nigeria, which is estimated as 50% of formal transfer, is expected to be more affected by GFC than the formal remittance. The implication of this is that the household who relied on remittance to finance their education and health care will not be able to do that, thereby hampering the progress on attainment of school enrolment and health goals. This is important because the household contribution as investment in attaining MDGs is about 9% (UN Millennium Project, 2005). So if this percentage is missing, the chance of achieving the MDGs may be bleak, particularly for the MDGs

---

[1]The Nigeria receives nearly 65 percent of officially recorded remittance flows to Africa and 2 percent of global flows. Underreporting of remittance flows to Nigeria is common because of data collection deficiencies and the prevalence of informal transfer mechanisms. The latter account for 50 percent of total flows to the country (UK-Nigeria Remittance Corridor, 2009). Although several formal financial institutions for transferring money exist in UK, Europe and USA, several people choose to send money informally. The most common method is to give a person traveling to Nigeria cash to deliver to beneficiaries. Sometimes, remittances are in kind, for example, sending clothes or cars, or purchasing a phone card and sending the PIN by e-mail. In Nigeria, with over 3000 commercial bank branches, a dual financial environment comprising formal and informal service providers competes for clients. This environment exists due to Nigerians' distrust of the formal institutions, poor transport and communications infrastructure outside urban areas, and an inefficient payment system in which over 90 percent of transactions are in cash.

that require substantial contribution from the households such as health and education.

3.2 Taxation and Inflation

As the controversy of the Federal Government's deregulation policy in Nigeria rages on (which was triggered by GFC), the 36 state governors have unanimously resolved to impose more taxes. The indication that Nigerians are to face harsher economic realities is further reinforced by the latest report of the National Bureau of Statistics (NBS, 2009), that the surge of inflation in the country is likely to lead to increase in the prices of food and other products. As a way to shore up their dwindling revenue bases, governors of the 36 states of the federation have agreed on the need to promulgate new tax laws, review existing ones, as well as ensure that they are enforced to reflect the existing realities. These decisions formed part of the 14-point communiqué issued at the end of the three-day 1st National Roundtable Strategy Session on Internally Generated Revenue (IGR). The communiqué noted with concern the dwindling revenue base of the federal, state and local governments, owing to fluctuation in the price of oil, stressing the need to explore and identify alternative sources of revenue so as to forestall the dire consequences of an over-dependence on oil and attain fiscal autonomy (Usigbe and Omankhanlen, 2009). Even before the Governors' Roundtable Strategy meeting, Governors of Edo and Lagos states have imposed some taxes and levies on the populace to soar up their revenue base which has dwindled since the inception of the GFC. Moreover, in a bid to raise the government revenue base, the federal government decided to increase the tariff rate (proposed electricity tariff rate is to increase by 10%). All these are bound to reduce the people purchasing power and further worsen the chance of eradicating poverty and hunger.

Meanwhile, against the promise of the Central Bank of Nigeria (CBN) governor, Mr. Sanusi Lamido Sanusi, that the nation's inflation will fall below 10 per cent by the end of 2009 (Sanusi, 2009), the rate has continued to rise. Latest report by the National Bureau of Statistics NBS (2009) indicated that consumers' inflation rose to 11.6 per cent year-on-year in October, 2009, from 10.4 per cent the previous month. The growth in food prices, which form the bulk of the inflation index basket, rose to 13.5 per cent from 12.5 per cent in September, 2009. The rise in the index was caused by an increase in the prices of food items like meat, fish, sea food and fruits (Usigbe and Omankhanlen, 2009). These increases in prices of food items and inflation will definitely affect the progress on poverty and hunger reduction goals of MDGs.

3.3 Foreign Direct Investment

Another transmission channel of the crisis is through its impact on foreign direct investments (FDI). Given that corporate profits are going to fall due to the crisis, their ability to invest in other countries will be negatively affected. FDI is considered to be one of the consequences of globalization and its advance is led by Multinational Cooperation's (MNCs) or Transnational Cooperation's (TNCs) in the hope that FDI will transfer superior technology and management skills, stimulate investment and growth, generate efficiency spillovers and enhance job creation (Accenture, 2009). In the 1990s, the promotion of FDI became popular especially amongst developing countries. The realization of FDI's contribution to economic growth and sustainable development led to policies for attracting FDI becoming an integral part of national policies. The main source of FDI into Africa is the United States and European Union. Between 2004 and 2007, FDI inflows into Africa increased from 13 to 33 billion dollars, with Nigeria and South Africa accounting for 55% of the inflows (UNCTAD, 2009). While FDI inflows have been more stable compared to other forms of private capital throughout the worst part of the crisis, FDI inflows will not remain unaffected. According to UNCTAD, the pattern of continued FDI inflows is going to change. In Nigeria, the reduction among the capital inflows which include, foreign direct investment and portfolio investments, bilateral and multilateral aid resources, amongst others, would result in sharp reduction in investment. It is projected that the FDI in Nigeria will fall and this will jeopardize the country's hope of realizing $600 billion in FDI before 2020 to further its vision of being one of the world's top 20 economies by 2020. To further endanger Nigeria's FDI prospects is the negatively volatile nature of oil prices since the last quarter of 2008. It is interesting to note that most FDI inflows to the country are directed at the oil sector (Obi, 2009).

3.4 Declined Export

The recent economic slowdown being witnessed can however be attributed to the declining trade flows. The dependency on (narrow range of) primary commodities for export is largely responsible for the impact of the slowdown on African countries. For example, Nigeria's investment, output and government revenues have fallen significantly due to declining prices for hydrocarbons (oil and gas). Oil and gas extraction account for 30 percent of the economy's GDP, over 90 percent of its exports and a large share of government revenues (Babatunde and Busari, 2009). Table 2 indicates that the current account deficit in Nigeria was by -9.05 % of GDP in 2009 and is expected to be -6.44 % of GDP in 2010. The effect of the fall in the revenue and current account balance on MDGs can be noticed in the ability of the government to execute MDGs projects and programme. The deterioration of the current account may also hinder the ability of the government to import machineries that may be used to boost productivity in the economy that may positively impact on the livelihood of the populace (Laishley, 2009).

Table 2: Export Revenue and Current Account Balance in Nigeria in 2009 and 2010

Before Crisis		During Crisis		Estimated Short Fall		Current Account Balance (% of GDP)	
2009	2010	2009	2010	2009	2010	2009	2010
89.08	99.47	50.40	55.31	38.68	44.16	-9.05	-6.44

Source: Extracted from Babatunde and Busari (2009), 2009 = expected, 2010 = estimate

3.5 Fall in commodity prices and exchange rate depreciation

Oil export remains Nigeria's major revenue earner. The current global economic crisis has brought about a radical decline in crude oil prices. The severe fall in crude oil price from a peak of $147 in 2008, has brought about intense pressure on the exchange rate. The foreign exchange market came under enormous pressure at the onset of the crisis in the country. The naira declined by 10 percent and increased the cost of imported intermediate inputs with great consequences for production, output and employment. With the depreciation of currency and Nigeria being a net importer of food which is a major component of consumer price index, domestic prices of consumer goods in the country will increase with a reduction in access to food by the vulnerable groups. Exchange-rate depreciation will also increase exchange-rate risks faced by domestic firms and increase the likelihood that they will default on loans owed to domestic banks, thereby increasing the vulnerability of these banks. According to the Central Bank of Nigeria, the official exchange rate was N150.6/US$ on 28 August, 2009 against N119.30/US$ in 2008.

Table 3 indicates that the prices of Brent crude oil and cocoa, which are the major exports from Nigeria, decreased by 56% and 2% respectively in the international market between December, 2007 and December, 2008 in Nigeria. With about 90% of government's revenue coming from crude oil export, the free fall in oil prices implies that government must revise its budget to be in line with current reality. Thus, in March 2009, it finally adopted on the basis of an oil price of USD 45/barrel and supply rates of 2.29 million/bpd (Switzerland, 2008). The reality is that the current financial crisis would have a negative effect on both short-term and long-term programmes of government. Indeed, the shortfall in oil revenues might lead to abandonment, postponement or outright cancellation of large investment projects. This would have negative multiplier effects on employment, poverty reduction, achieving MDGs. Also, revenue contraction could lead to a decline or inability to achieve infrastructural development which would in turn worsen the infrastructure-finance gap; thereby making it difficult to actualize the Nigeria's various development goals e.g. the lingering problem of electricity (Hassan, 2009).

Table 3: Changes in some commodity prices between January, 2007 and December, 2009

	Brent(US dollars per barrel)	Cocoa beans(US dollars per metric ton)
January, 2007	53.7	1702.0
December, 2007	92.1	2113.1
December, 2008	40.3	2067.7
% change Jan, 07 and Dec, 07	71.6%	24.2%
% change Dec, 07 and Dec, 08	-56.2%	-2.1%

Source: Extracted from AfDB (2009)

3.6 A Downturn in the capital market

The current financial crisis has affected the capital market in Nigeria. Starting from August, 2008, share trading value of the capital market drastically reduced from about N13 trillion down to about N5 trillion. The worsening economic climate has made investors to be cautious, resulting in significant divestment (flight of capital) back to their home economies. This resulted in foreign investors withdrawing some $4 billion from the Nigerian capital market in 2008 (Laishley, 2009). With about 65% of the value of the entire Nigerian stock market being held by banks, they are the most affected by the crisis in the stock market. Having lost an estimated N1 trillion from their exposure to the stock market, banks are now frantically sourcing for money as this has affected their balance sheet with increased build-up of bad debt and decreased profitability. It has been shown that market capitalization fell, from N10.18 trillion in January 2008, to N6.957 trillion January 2009 and further to N5.02 trillion on 7th May 2009. A huge loss of about N3 trillion was recorded by the market on August 22, 2008 and this is larger than the total budget of the government for 2008.

3.7 Fall in Nigeria's Foreign Reserves

Mordi (2009) has shown that Nigeria's foreign reserve has declined from $53 billion in 2008 to about $47 billion in 2009. This is not unconnected with the fall of oil price at the international oil market. Further depletion could be experienced if political pressure persists to spend the excess crude oil fund[2]. The fall in value of the external reserves may be due to frequent and large intervention to smoothen volatility of the Naira which increases drawdown and un-curtailed withdrawal by the fiscal authorities as well as servicing of foreign commitments. The outcome of course would be reduced accumulation of external reserves due to the fall in crude oil prices. In fact, income generation and safety concerns on external reserves will set in. The likelihood of renewed external debt build-up and the resultant effect of debt servicing on the external reserves cannot be ruled out.

3.8 Declined Economic Growth

Nearly all the region experienced a marked reduction in GDP growth. Nigeria, for instance, had its output down in the first quarter of 2009 to 4.85 per cent from 5.75 per cent estimated for 2008. The decline in economic growth which the current global financial crisis portends for Nigeria would likely reverse the progress that has been made in the economy the past decade. Available statistics indicate that GDP growth rate projection for Nigeria as at March 2008 was 5.30 % for the year 2008 and 3.30% for the year 2009 (Accenture, 2009). Of course, these are all below the required ratio for pover-

---

[2] Excess crude oil fund is the money set aside by Government during the oil price wind fall to be used in time of financial crisis.

ty reduction[3]. The latest estimates of economic outlook of Sub-Saharan Africa shows that a lower rate of output growth is expected in 2009. In the case of Nigeria, Table 4 indicates that GDP growth declined by 2.2% between 2008 and 2009 as a result of GFC. Indeed, a lower economic growth would slow down the fight against poverty, unemployment and inequality. Thus, the prospects of meeting the MDGs target of halving the number of the poor people by 2015 would remain a mirage.

Table 4: Real GDP Growth (%) in Nigeria before and during the GFC

Before the Crisis		During the Crisis		
2008(e)	2009(p)	2008(e)	2009(p)	GDP growth change
6.2	6.1	6.1	4.0	-2.2

Source: Committee of African Finance Ministers and Central Bank Governors (2009), P = projection, e = estimate

4 MDGs Spending and Corruption in Nigeria

After the US$19,293,207,575 debt owed by Nigeria to the Paris Club was successfully written off by the creditors, the deal was to direct the savings that the country would make from not having to pay for the debts to pro-poor projects and programmes which would, in turn, assist in attaining the Millennium Development Goals (MDGs). To achieve results, what is later known as debt relief grant is appropriated annually in the budget to expand the existing high-impact MDG-related interventions. In fact, the move to achieve a strong mechanism to drive home this initiative culminated in the appointment of a Senior Special Assistant to the President on MDGs in 2005. As it were, since 2006, the Federal Government has been incorporating the use of the debt relief gains for MDG goals into the budget. The MDGs office is responsible for setting up a Virtual Poverty Fund (VPF) under which the Debt Relief Funds (DRF) falls. The allocation of the VPF between sectors has varied over time as it has consistently reflected pressing priorities. To that effect, the chunk of funds has been directed to health, education, agriculture and water. The argument has on its own been that the sectors have much more impact on

[3] It requires an annual GDP growth rate of 7-8% in order to halve the number of people in poverty by 2015, and this translates to an investment rate of more than 30% per annum. Currently, the country grows at about 3 percent and the national savings rate is about 15 percent (Babatunde and Busari, 2009).

the eight goals. Unarguably, at the inauguration of the use of DRF in achieving MDGs in 2006, a sum of N100 billion was allocated to Federal ministries, departments and agencies to boost attainment of MDGs goals, though from 2007 till date, the volume of fund allocated has dropped to 40 per cent (which can be attributed to GFC). However, it is on record that the sum of N430 billion was appropriated between 2006 and 2009 to achieve investment results in MDGs. There is also a conscious effort to improve service delivery through conditional grants to states, community health insurance scheme, quick wins and conditional cash transfers. Details of the DRF allocation for 2009 as presented in Table 5 shows that the total sum of N9,486,000,000 was allocated to education; N15,960,000,000 to health; N4,016,000,000 to youth empowerment; N1,742,200,000 to women affairs; N1,789,776,779 to water resources and N4,496,706,923 to housing. Others are N1,000,000,000 to defence and police each; N3,800,000,000 to capacity building; N2,000,000,000 to mine and energy; N32,600,000,000 as conditional grant scheme and N19,700,000,000 as quick wins.

In the agriculture and water sector, the MDGs office claimed that it constructed Challawa-Karaye, Jato-Aka and Galala irrigation projects. It also rehabilitated Doma and Batsari dam and sunk tube wells in Katsina –Ala. In the health sector, the MDGs office claimed that it established 12 blood banks in six new satellite centres and provided starter packs and laboratory consumables to designated new centres as well. A total of 2,500 midwives were recruited and deployed to 625 facilities. Contract was awarded for the supply of midwifery kits. It also provided funds to National Primary Health Care Development Agency (NPHCDA) for the procurement of some routine polio vaccines. On the other hand, an average of 45 million and 27 children were vaccinated just as the strengthened health system in six selected local government areas. The office purchased 48 ambulances with complete accessories and some essential supplies and they were distributed to three local governments per senatorial district in 12 states. The states are Ogun, Ekiti, Edo Plateau, Abia, Kogi, Adamawa, Gombe, Akwa Ibom, Kebbi, Kaduna and Yobe. It also claimed that it equally completed the report on baseline studies on maternal/child health, persons with disabilities and other vulnerable groups. In the defense and police sector, the MDGs office in 2009 claimed that it rehabilitated schools and health centres in 22 armed forces barracks. Out of the figure, eleven are in army barracks, seven in naval barracks while four are in air force barracks. The beneficiaries included Maiduguri Cantonment, Odogbo Cantonment, Army Barracks, Zuru, NN Barracks, Okurho-Oghara and Nigeria Air Force (NAF) Base, Yola. It supplied furniture and medical equipments and recreational facilities. Boreholes and generators were in addition provided for the barracks. Twelve police primary schools, two per zone were claimed to be upgraded (Okeke, 2009).

The sum of N430 billion said to have been expended by the Federal Government in the last three years on the implementation of the Millennium Development Goals (MDGs) must have shocked many Nigerians, especially rural dwellers who are the targets of the MDG projects. Those who thought that funding must have been the cause of the inaction must thus be as stunned as we were told that N430 billion has been pumped into MDG-related projects in the last three years. The figure popped up in a report said to have been submitted to the House of Representatives by the Senior Special Assistant to the President on MDGs. The report shows that a substantial part of the N430bn went to state governments under the Conditional Grant Scheme (CGS) for them to supplement their 50 per cent counterpart funding of the MDGs projects.

According to Awofadeji (2009), major challenge towards the achievement of the MDGs in Nigeria is the corruption that is said to have defined the spending of the DRF funds. Across the states, there are reports of contracts for projects that were not executed, leading to the discovery of no projects during site visits. Yet, the contractors were fully mobilized. In other instances, contracts were awarded for the supply and distribution of drugs when there were no health facilities available for the drugs. A visit to Amuwo Odofin Health Centre, in Festac Lagos as well as that in Agege is revealing enough (Nwokeoma, 2009). Sadly enough, in spite of the deluge of complaints that trailed the expenditure towards the MDGs so far, no audit of the expenditure has been undertaken by government, much less finding and prosecuting contractors and agencies that might have fleeced the nation. Strangely, these sad developments notwithstanding, an analysis of government posturing tend to show that its emphasis seems not to be on the evaluation of the impact of the DRF spending on the targeted communities, leading to the achievement of the MDGs, as it is on the quantum of funds disbursed. Reeling out statistics of funds released when there is nothing on ground to show for such expenditure is not a sure way of achieving the MDGs (Nwokeoma, 2009). For example, in Bauchi state, the realisation of the Millennium Development Goals [MDGs] might not be possible as the state government has frozen the account of the Office of Millennium Development Goals on the allegation that money allocated to that office has been misappropriated (Awofadeji, 2009).

Table 5: Details of the Debt Relief Funds (DRF) Allocation for 2009

Serial Number	Sector	Amount
1	Education	N9,486,000,000
2	Health	N15,960,000,000
3	Youth Empowerment	N4,016,000,000
4	Women Affairs	N1,742,200,000
5	Water Resources	N1,789,776,779
6	Housing	N4,496,706,923
7	Defense	N1,000,000,000
8	Police	N1,000,000,000
9	Capacity Building	N3,800,000,000
10	Mine and Energy	N2,000,000,000
11	Conditional Transfer Grant	N32,600,000,000
12	Quick Win Project	N19,700,000,000
	Total	N9,486,000,000

Source: Okeke (2009)

The fact that implementation of MDGs is not transparent is evident by the case of Niger state in Nigeria. The Governor of Niger State was worried by the grim reality evident in his state, ordered the probe of all the contracts awarded under the MDGs in the state since 2006. According to him, in spite of the huge sum totaling N3.7bn claimed to have been spent by the Federal Government on MDGs- related projects in Niger state, there was nothing on ground to show that such amount was committed to development projects in the state (Edet, 2009).

The Senate, which reviewed the performance of the Federal Government in the Millennium Development Goals (MDGs) projects, lamented that they were characterised by corruption, inefficiency and waste (Jimoh and Daka, 2009). It was said that the process of selecting contractors for the MDG projects has been hijacked by the senior special assistant and her members of staff, who fabricate company names and pre-qualify them for the job in many instances. Nearly all the companies awarded the MDG jobs in one state are traced to one person and one address, though they appear to be different companies (Jimoh and Daka, 2009). The result is that the jobs are undone because the companies lack capacity, and were never interested in doing these jobs in the first instance.

Generally, Corruption has increased in Nigeria with the country currently ranking 130th out of 180 countries surveyed in the 2009 Corruption Perceptions Index (CPI) released by Transparency International (TI). Last year Nigeria scored 2.7 points and took 121st position out of 180 countries, but in 2009 the country's CPI score dropped to 2.5 ranking at the same position with Lebanon, Libya and Mauritania (Edet, 2009). This suggests that Nigeria scored 2.5 out of maximum mark of 10 in the transparency index. The implication of this score may have a far reaching implication on the achievement of MDGs. The available information indicates that Nigeria has appropriated over N340 billion (2.27 billion US dollars) for MDGs in the last three years in Nigeria. This may explain non- existence of some claimed projects and the slow pace in achieving MDGs in Nigeria. The high corruption level in the country will rob on the over 24 trillion naira (160 billion US dollars) needed in the next five years to meet the MDGs by 2015. If the corruption level persist, it is possible that most of money will go into private pockets even if the money is made available. The high corruption level will also corrode the impact of stimulus packages on the economy during GFC. This made the Chair of Transparency International (TI), Huguette Labelle, to say that at a time when massive stimulus packages, fast-track disbursements of public funds and attempts to secure peace are being implemented around the world, it is essential to identify where corruption blocks good governance and accountability, in order to break its corrosive cycle (Udo, 2009)

The other reality about the MDGs projects in Nigeria is lack of proper coordination among the tiers of the government. During a recent advocacy visit to a top official of the Lagos State government with an international Non Governmental Organisation (NGO) engaged in monitoring the utilization of the DRF towards poverty eradication in the country, the delegation was shocked to discover that the state government was almost in the dark about the various MDGs-related projects financed in some council areas by the Federal Government (Nwokeoma, 2009). It was therefore not uncommon to find out, as many monitors observed, that at the same location or locality, same type of projects, say primary healthcare centres, were sited and funded both by the Federal Government and states as well as multilateral donor agencies, with attendant cost implications, at a time when with proper coordination and institutional collaboration, this duplication would have been avoided and eliminated. But, beside the extant lack of collaboration among the various tiers of government is the subsisting absence of needs- assessment by the implementing agency, this time the Federal Government, before contracts were awarded. The resultant effect of this development is that projects were located in localities where they were not needed by the beneficiary communities. This was the case because the projects were designed, conceptualized and contracts awarded in Abuja, without the input, and/or taking cognisance of the peculiar needs, of the supposed beneficiaries at the local levels. For instance, in a community where a primary health centre was needed, a water project was instead awarded and sited. And, because the project sited was not the need of the community, the project, even when completed, suffered from poor patronage thereby leading to wastage of funds. In many other cases, contractors mobilized on site without the knowledge of the critical stakeholders in the communities resulting in needless altercations and frictions.

5 Nigeria Government Responses to the Global Financial Crisis

The Nigerian government used the 2009 budget and the country's foreign exchange reserves (which now stands at less than US$50 billion) as stimulus package to reduce the impact of the crisis and to promote economic growth. The federal and state governments were expected to borrow N1.6 trillion (stimulus) to meet their expenditure for the 2009 fiscal year. Besides, in February 2009, the government injected 70 billion naira into the textile industry to revive ailing companies. Nigeria Government (through the Central Bank of Nigeria) announced a bail out of 420 billion naira to save five commercial banks with huge debt and non- performing loans[4] (Nurudeen and Obi, 2009). In addition, the former management executives of the respective banks have been sacked, the new ones have been appointed. Also, Soludo (2009) reported that, in response to the global financial crisis, the monetary authorities have adopted various measures for proper supervision and regulation, as well as ensure soundness of the financial (and banking) system. For instance, in an attempt to manage liquidity within the economy, the Central Bank of Nigeria (CBN) reduced the Monetary Policy Rate (MPR) from 10.25 % to 9.75 % and now to 8.0 % (below inflation rate), Retail Dutch Auction System (CRR) from 4.0 % to 2.0 % and now to 1.0 %, and the liquidity ratio from 40.0 % to 30.0 % and now to 25.0 %. Also, the CBN has embarked on the restructuring of the Bureaux de Change (BDC) operations by categorizing them into Classes 'A', 'B' and 'C'. In addition, is the sale of cash Foreign exchange only through bank operated BDC, and the revision and enlargement of transactions that are eligible under the Retail Dutch Auction System (RDAS) window. In order to properly regulate and supervise the banks, the CBN has deployed resident examiners to the banks with effect from January 2009. There are also 'standby teams' of target examiners that may be deploy to any bank at any time to fish out those that do not observe the code of cor-

[4] Indications have emerged that many banks in Nigeria are not financially sound as projected, the position which is further threatened by GFC. Many of them have started restructuring which include sacking of their employees.

porate governance, in order to inject discipline and restore confidence in the system. The CBN is rendering advisory service to banks on risk management. This includes extra conservation during time of crisis, capital conservation, cost minimization, de-emphasis on size, salaries and or bonuses, to mention just few. Furthermore, the CBN is also strengthening institutional coordination through the Financial Sector Regulatory Coordinating Committee (FSRCC). The CBN has continued to emphasis the use of e-FASS as a tool for banks' returns analysis for speedy identification of early warning signals. Henceforth, 'Consolidated teams' rather than the current fragmented one are to examine and supervise the financial sector in 2009, while a common accounting year end has been adopted for all banks with effect from end-December 2009. The objective here is to improve data integrity and comparability of the status and soundness of every bank, as well as the adoption of International Financial Reporting Standards (IFRS). Finally, the CBN will continue to review the BOFIA in order to strengthen regulatory capacity. In an attempt to reduce pressure on inter-bank rates, the CBN reduced the Expanded Discount Window (EDW) rate to a maximum of 500 basis points above MPR beginning from March 16, 2009. This measure is expected to help reduce the problems of banks facing temporary liquidity crisis. Moreover, the bankers' committee has pegged the maximum deposit and lending rates at 15 % and 22 % respectively, effective from April 1 2009 until end of 2009, so as to promote the growth of real sectors of the economy. In the area of confidence building, CBN has repeatedly emphasized that Government and the monetary authorities will ensure that all banks remain sound and no bank would be allowed to fail. In fact, the CBN has disbursed over N700 billion to banks facing liquidity problems.

The 2.8 trillion naira (22.6 billion dollar) 2009 budget submitted to the National Assembly is noticeably heavy on recurrent expenditure and light on capital spending and investment. The government launched a Presidential Steering Committee on the Global Economic Crisis in January 2009. The Committee is responsible for developing a framework to respond to the global crisis. Government announced plan to suspend the 5 percent excise duty on some goods manufactured such as juices, instant noodles and nonalcoholic drinks, aiming to support its distressed industry and avert job losses. Nigerian government imposed foreign exchange controls to stem off the slide in the Naira. These measures include that foreign exchange purchases from the central bank window are only to be used for customers, and not on the inter-bank foreign exchange market.

6 Conclusion and Policy Recommendations

The problem of development is a global challenge and the MDG is a response by world leaders to that effect. The MDGs provide a platform to engage the development process. The situation in Nigeria indicates that there are challenges in meeting the goals by 2015 which is threatened by GFC. Generally, for Nigeria to meet the goals in 2015, despite the GFC, there is the need to formulate and implement policies that will promote transparency and accountability; overcome institutional constraints; promote pro-poor growth; bring about structural change and enhance distributive equity.

6.1 Recommendations for Weathering the GFC

To achieve the MDGs and to scale through the period of global financial crisis, Nigeria need to change the structure of the economy in such a way that the economy is not dependent on only one product but diversified economy and expanding the industrial sector. For Nigeria to weather the liquidity problem during the global financial crisis, the commercial banks have to reduce their benchmark prime lending rates. This will allow flow of fund to real sector of the economy and promote economic growth. The stimulus packages should not concentrate on banking sector but should be diverted towards farmers' loans, rural employment and other social security programmes as done in India (Singh, 2009). Export sector and infrastructure sector can be offered financial aid as part of bail-out packages. For example, pre and post-shipment export credit can be made available for labour intensive exports, i.e., textiles (including handlooms, carpets and handicrafts), leather, gems and jewellery, marine products and small and medium enterprise (SME) sector. These SME can be made more attractive by providing an interest subvention subject to minimum rate of interest of 7 percent per annum. The bail out money should be deducted from excess crude oil account and Debt Relief Gain, not resulting to excessive borrowing this time around.

6.2 Recommendations for Achieving MDGs in the Period of GFC

Constitutionally, implementation of MDGs activities fall within the purview of sub-national governments, hence significant progress cannot be made unless states and local governments are committed to and coordinated in implementing MDGs related activities. The need to address the weak database for effective monitoring of MDGs in the country is vital for substantial progress to be made. Deliberate efforts and policies must be put in place to redistribute income. The MDGs will be met if the poor and the excluded in society are empowered to meet their basic needs. In addition, meeting the MDGs will require partnership between government, donor agencies, civil societies, the public sector and the private sector.

Members of the National Assembly must demand details of the disbursement of the money spent on MDGs and should go out of their way to verify the claims that the funds have been applied to projects. Indeed, there ought to be a public hearing on the matter to allow Nigerians to come forward and testify of how they have not yet felt or felt the impact of the debt relief funds. The President from whose office Senior Special Assistant on MDGs operates should also review the progress of the country towards attaining the MDGs with a view to re-strategising to ensure the success of the programme.

If the state governors have been misusing the funds, a new strategy must be evolved to stop such. If it is confirmed that the MDGs' office in the presidency cannot cope with the execution of constituency projects, alternative arrangements must be made to ensure that these grassroots based projects are executed to bring relief to the people who need them most. The debt relief funds, and every other income of the country, must be prudently and transparently applied for maximum effect and those in authority at all levels must ensure this.

References

Accenture (2009): The Challenges of global financial crises. Paper presented at the Information Technology Retreat. Central Bank of Nigeria, Abuja, Nigeria.

AfDB (2009): African Development Bank response to financial crisis. Available on the internet at http://www.afdb.org/en/news-events/article/afdb-response-to-financialcrisis- economic-impact-4362/

Alabi, R. A (2009): Redistribution of education and redistributive effect of education spending in Nigeria. A Paper Presented at the Nigeria Country Workshop on New Researches on Development in Nigeria organised by Institute for World Economics and International Management, University of Bremen, Bremen, Germany. 29th July, 2009.

Amusa, K (2009): Global Economic and financial crisis: Transmissions channels and impacts on African economies. A paper presented at the African Economic Research Consortium (AERC). *Rethinking African Economic Policy in Light of the Global Economic and Financial Crisis Conference*. Nairobi, Kenya.

Awofadji, S. (2008): Corruption: Bauchi freezes MDGs accounts. Available on the internet at http://www.thisdayonline.com/nview.php?id=127662

Babatunde, M.A and D.T Busari (2009): Global economic slowdown and the African Continent: Rethinking export-led growth. A paper presented at the African Economic Research Consortium (AERC) *Rethinking African Economic Policy in Light of the Global Economic and Financial Crisis Conference*. Nairobi, Kenya.

Committee of African Finance Ministers and Central Bank Governors (2009): Impact of the crisis On African economies –sustaining growth and poverty reduction: African perspectives and recommendations to the G20. *A report from the Committee of African Finance Ministers and Central Bank Governors established to monitor the crisis.* March 21.

Edet, B (2009): Nigeria: The country slips on corruption index. Available on the internet at http://allafrica.com/stories/200911180190.htm

ERA (2005): Our common interest. Report prepared for Commission for Africa. Department of International Development, London.

Giuliano, P and M. Arranz (2005): Remittances, financial development and growth. IMF working paper. Available on the internet at www.worldbank.org

Hassan, T (2009): Global economic crisis: The need for African government interventions for rapid economic recovery and stability. A paper presented at the African Economic Research Consortium (AERC) Rethinking African Economic Policy in Light of the Global Economic and Financial Crisis Conference. Nairobi, Kenya.

Igbuzor, O (2006): The MDGs: Can Nigeria meet the goals in 2015. A paper presented at a symposium on MDGs and Nigeria: Issues, challenges and prospects organised by the Institute of Chartered Accountants of Nigeria (ICAN), Abuja district on 27th July, 2006 at Sheraton Hotel and Towers, Abuja.

Jimoh , A.M and T. Daka (2009): National Assembly uncovers fraud in MDGs, River Nig-
cr projects. Available on the internet at http://www.nigeriamasterweb.com/paper frmes.html

Komolafe, B (2009): Remittance from Nigerians abroad. Available on the internet at http://odili.net/news/source/2009/nov/19/220.html

Lamido, Sanusi (2009): The Speech sacking the five Bank Chief Executives in The Nation Newspaper of Saturday, August 15, 2009.

Laishley, R. (2009): World downturn squeezing Africa. United Nations Africa Renewal. Available on the internet at www.un.org/AR

MDGs Report (2009): United Nations Inter-Agency and Expert Group on the Millennium Development Goals Indicators and MDG Indicators Database. Available on the internet at http://mdgs.un.org.

MDG Report (2005): Nigeria Millennium Development Goals 2005 Report. United Nations. New York.

Mordi, C. (2009): Global financial crisis: country experiences and challenges for central banking in Nigeria. Paper delivered at the Monetary Policy Department Retreat, Kaduna, Nigeria. January 30- 31, 2009.

NBS (2009): CPI and Inflation 2005 to December, 2009. National Bureau of Statistics . Available on the internet at http://www.nigerianstat.gov.ng/uploads/latestRelease/834fc9864587637724cd16549a447bd2b4891c49.pdf.

Nurudeen, Abu and B. Obi (2009): Responses by African governments to the global economic and financial crisis and lessons. A paper presented at the African Economic Research Consortium (AERC) *Rethinking African Economic Policy in Light of the Global Economic and Financial Crisis Conference*. Nairobi, Kenya.

Nwokeoma, J (2009): Why Nigeria may not meet the Millennium Development Goals.Available on the internet at http://www.nigeriansinamerica.com/articles/3530/1/Why-Nigeria-may-not-meet-the-Millennium-Development-Goals/Page1.html.

Obi, I. (2009). Nigerian economy under threat as FDI, remittance inflows drop. Business Day Newspapers, Monday, 10 August 2009

Okeke, Christian (2009): Fighting poverty through MDGs. Available on the internet at ww.tribune.com.ng/18092009/politics_2.html.

Switzerland (2008): Economic Report on Nigeria 2008 / 2009. Embassy of Switzerland in Nigeria.

Singh,S (2009): Global financial crisis and Indian economy: Impact assessment, policy responses and recovery. A paper presented at the African Economic Research Consortium (AERC) *Rethinking African Economic Policy in Light of the Global Economic and Financial Crisis Conference*. Nairobi, Kenya.

Soludo, C. (2009): How we have managed the global financial crisis. Available on the internet at http://www.sunnewsonline.com/webpages/features/money/index.htm

Udo, B (2009): Nigeria failing in corruption war. Available on the internet at http://234next.com/csp/cms/sites/Next/Money/Business/5482576-147/story.csp

UNCTAD, (2009): Trade and Investment Report. United Nations, New York.

UK (2005): The contribution of UK to achieving MDGs produced for HM Government by GWS Group.

UK-Nigeria Remittance Corridor (2009): Bilateral remittances corridor analysis (BRCA). Available on the internet at http://siteresources.worldbank.org/INTAFRSUMAFTPS/Resources/NigeriaRemittanceCorridor(background).pdf

UN (2002a): Unleashing entrepreneurship: Making business work for the poor. United Nations Report of the high level panel on financing for development submitted to the Secretary General of the United Nations. United Nations, New York.

United Nations Millennium Project (2005): Investing in development. A practical plan to achieve the MDGs. United Nations, York

Usigbe, L and Omankhanlen, O (2009): Hard times await Nigerians - As governors agree on new tax laws: Inflation hits 11.6%. Available on the internet at anax1a.pressmart.net/nigeriantribune/.../19_11_2009_001_010.shtml

Vos, Rob and Marco V. Sánchez (2009): Impact of the global crisis on the achievement of the MDGs in Latin America. *UN-DESA Working Paper Series* No. 74, United Nations Department of Economic and Social Affairs, New York.

World Bank Report (2009): Advanced economies have led the world into a severe financial and economic crisis. *The World Bank*, Washington, D. C.

Reinforcing Informal Credit Associations to Support the Informal Sector Against the Impact of Global Financial Crisis in Nigeria

Akinrinola, O. O.[1]

Abstract

The current global economic crisis is leading to a downturn revision of economic sizes worldwide. Nigeria like any of the Sub-Sahara economies is expected to witness reductions in the flow of private capital, as well as significant cut in aids flows and remittances. This might inadvertently lead to contraction in the size of the economy, as a result of close down of companies operations, downsizing of work force and/or production below capacity and lost of considerable revenue owing to reduction in demand for export. The foregoing translates to decline in economic growth vis-à-vis gross domestic product, thereby widening the inequality gap and poverty. In order to mitigate the effect of this adverse economic situation on the poor (who are the key players in the informal sector), there is the need to evolve a broad-base pro-poor growth through institutional and policy reforms that will not only expand economic opportunities, but empower the poor to gainfully participate in and measurably benefit from them. Strong public-private partnerships are needed to accelerate both the expansion of opportunities and the empowerment of the poor. Thus, it is necessary to analyze the critical path by which broad-based growth initiatives can lead to an expansion of GDP, and the resultant increase in savings resulting in poverty reduction through fiscal, financial and various other routes rather than focusing on pro-poor policies. One way of accompany this is re-enforcing informal credit institutions and capacity building. Since the poor are credit constrained, a well funded informal credit institution with good management will provide the needed fund for the poor to embark on sustainable income generating ventures and adequate training will trigger entrepreneurship spirit/effective management. Any policy/intervention approach that leads to increase in

[1] Federal University of Technology, Akure, Nigeria.

income, vis-a-vise savings of the poor has greater propensity to reduce poverty scale and dwarf the inequality gap.

1 Introduction

The term "informal sector" refers to the part of the economy that does not fall under the purview of organized economic activities. It consists of very small enterprises that use low technology models and do not refer to legal status (Webster and Fiddler, 1996). Informal economic activities pertain to non-traded goods in the economy - from small retailers, street traders, vocational trade to domestic help. In Nigeria like many developing and transition economies, the informal sector has become an institution, in its own right generating with it various positive and negative implications effects . For instance, Davies (2006) argues that division of labour becomes greater than optimal in the presence of informal institutions, resulting in greater than optimal complexities and higher growth in the country.

On average, about 70% of the labour force in Nigeria belongs to the informal sector, while the urban informal sector rages from 10 percent to 15 percent compared with 15 percent to 20 percent in Turkey, Slovakia to 80p percent in Zambia and about 83 percent in Myanmar (Marjit and Kar, 2007). More importantly, considering the state of agriculture and rural activities in Nigeria, it is quite obvious that the total share of the informal sector in the Nigeria economy as a whole would be very high (ILO,I999). This is reenforced by the work of Turnham (1993), which provides evidence that in low income countries like Nigeria, Bangladegh, Ivory coast, Indian, the share of the whom informal sector to the overall economy is at least as high as 51 percent . Furthermore, the informal sector has subsequently emerged as an important institution due to competitive wage formation rather than unionized process which characterize formal labour market.

Looking at it from the point of view of "minimum wage" earners in the so–called informal sector, substantive employees in the sector earn less than the minimum wage, typically because of non market clearing downward rigid wages along with other corporate taxes push many private firms to operate in informal sector (Gang and Gangopadhyay 1990). A substantial portion of such employment opportunities is generated to provide means of livelihood to poor households. The majority of this workforce is economically marginalized with high poverty incidence, exposure to difficult and hazardous working conditions, non-existence of social security or health benefit schemes other than poorly functioning state-provided medical facilities. Common features of operators in the informal sector include:

• Easier access to production factors which are derivable from social organisation of family and friends.
• Involves entrepreneurs in virtually all branches of the economy ranging from productive activities, general services and specialized services.
• Technology is determined more by the constraints of the social relations.
• Motivation for production by the operators in the informal sector is becoming more profit oriented. (Ademu, 2006).

2 Informal Economy and Global Financial Crisis

The current global economic crisis is leading to a downturn revision of economic sizes worldwide. Nigeria like any of the Sub-Sahara economies is expected to witness reductions in the flow of private capital, as well as significant cut in aids flows and remittances. This might inadvertently lead to contraction in the size of the economy, as a result of close down of companies operations, downsizing of work force and/or production below capacity and lost of considerable revenue owing to reduction in demand for export. How will all of these affect the informal economy and its contribution to the economic growth? In specific term, the current economic crisis has significant repercussion on the workforce in the informal sector, as workers in the sector are the economic crisis: Price increases that followed the crisis resulted in high cost of living, being poorer; they have fewer buffers available to them in the form savings and suffered from greater income uncertainty. The informal producers usually maintained a lower level of stocks and hence are also adversely affected by hike in input prices. However, the impacts of the crisis on the demand for informal sector products are ambiguous. On one hand, where the cheaper products produced by the informal sector are substitutes for the more expensive formal sector product, demand increases. On the other, where certain goods and services produced by the informal sector were considered to be non-essential (e.g handicraft products) with high income elasticties, demand will be expected to fall (Ademu, 2006).

Equally important, is the direct impact of the economic crisis on the informal labour market. The workers who lost jobs in the formal sector entered the informal sector, increasing the competitiveness within the sector and reducing profit margin. Contrary to conventional belief, it is also witnessed in the recent time in the private sector, especially banks that despite economic prosperity declared by majority of the financial institution, they are entering into informal employment contracts where workers receive contractual tenures and wages with no access to various benefits that earlier generation of workers enjoyed. While this refers to informal practices within the formal institutions, a larger group of workers face more pervasive informalisation with enormous implications on aspects of income volatility, poverty and standard of living for all those inside and outside the informal segment.

The foregoing translates to decline in economic growth vis-à-vis gross domestic product, thereby widening the inequality gap and poverty. It has been argued by Ranis and Stewart (1999) and by Tokman (2001) that when economic growth rates decline, firms in the formal sector tend to contract by retrenching employees in order to reduce costs. This expected high level of unemployment will invariably lead to an expansion of the informal sector. Given the economic trends in the last two years in Nigeria, it is inconceivable that the size of the informal sector would shrink considerably below the existing level and therefore, sustained improvements in the living standards of these groups can only be brought about by capital accumulation, productivity gains, and income increase in this sector. But the extent to which the informal economy is able to offer productive engagement is not clear without adequate intervention and supports that will ensure that key players in the sector are empowered with requisite skills and finances that will enable them exploit their environment to earn sustainable livelihood.

While there may be several mechanisms that can generate such positive economic impact to the players in this sector, the argument here is that one crucial factors in this category is the degree of capital availability to the participants in the informal sector and the level of modern technological compliance skills (capacity building) that increase their competitiveness in spotlighting and exploiting business opportunities around them. The motivation behind invoking the issue of "easily accessible capital" and "capacity building" comes from the observation that the formal financial sector (both money and capital markets) of the Nigeria economy is presently confronted with the credibility challenges. That is, people and corporate bodies have lost confidence in these institutions as a result of their failure to meet the expectations of the teeming populace in terms of provision of adequate credit facilities; mobilizing and pooling savings, producing information ex ante about possible investments and allocating capital; monitoring investments and exerting corporate governance; facilitating the trading, diversification and management of risks and facilitating the exchange of goods and services in the informal sector.

At present, six of the twenty consolidated banks have been adjudged unhealthy by the apex bank while the remaining fourteen classified as safe are hesitant to grant facilities to the poor households who are the key participants in the informal sector (CBN, 2009) . Worst still is that the stock market (though not expected to provide capital for the poor or even small companies (Moss, 2009) has crashed as a result of the global economic crisis. The only viable option for the poor to mobilize working capital for economic activities is through informal credit institutions and/or associations.

3 Informal Financial Institutions, Economic Growth and Poverty Reduction

Informal financial institutions are institutions that embraced all financial transactions that take place beyond the functional scope of various countries' banking and other financial sector regulations. Aryeetey (1998), Chipeta and Mkandawaivre (1991) saw them as institutions that are not directly amenable to control by key monetary and financial policy instruments. These institutions are usually created by organizations and individuals and with no legal status. According to Yusuf et al (2007), informal financial institutions can be classified into three namely:(i) proprietary informal financial entities, such as, money lenders, trader, estate owners, grain millers, smallholder farmers, self-help groups and other businessmen, (ii) staff and social welfare schemes such as those run by employers, friends relatives and neighbours; and (iii) mutual aid entities, such as, Accumulating Saving and Credit Associations (ASCRAs) otherwise known as Cooperative Credit and Thrift Societies; and a Rotating Saving and Credit Associations (ROSCAs) (Chandavarkar 1985 cited in Aredo, 1993; Goodland et al. 1999). Rotating Saving and Credit Associations (ROSCAs) is known as *isusu* in Nigeria, *susu* in Ghana *ko* in Japan. World Bank (2004) defined informal institutions as associations whose members regularly (e.g. weekly or monthly) contribute a fixed amount that is allocated to each member in turn (according to lottery, bidding or other system that the group establishes). Levine (1992) cited in Aredo (1993) saw this fixed contribution as an exchange for privilege of receiving a large sum at some point in the life of the group. Aredo (1993) inferred from these definitions, that in ROSCAs each member agrees to pay periodically a small sum into a common pool so that each, in rotation can receive one large sum. If a member's turn comes early, it is credit mechanism; if it comes late, it is a savings mechanism (i.e. early recipients realize a real net gain, those later a real net loss). The World Bank (1989) identified three types of ROSCAs: common ROSCAs, where the leader receives no special consideration (other than possibly getting the first fund); commission ROSCAs which pays their leaders and who in turn assume liability for defaults; and promotional ROSCAs which are used by merchants to sell their goods, especially consumable durables.

Analysing the importance of Rotating Saving and Credit Associations (ROSCAs), Steel and Aryeetey (1994) observed that they help in mobilizing saving through the people's daily collection of deposits, which are in turn used as working capital to restock supplies which enable them to expand their output and earn a stream of profits, thereby providing a significant source of income to individual household which reduces their level of poverty. Zaman (1999) also observed that credit provided by ROSCAs could increase income and build assets. It increases income when the credit is used for an income-generating activity which brings returns in excess of the credit round payment, while it builds asset when the credit financed investment that does not generate a significant net profit but create an asset that serves as investment for the clients. Richardson and Lennon (2001) also reiterate that ROSCAs provides security for people through the saving facilities provided, thus safeguarding the people's money from incessant appeals from family and friends, while Miller and Northrip (2000) observed that ROSCAs also provide insurance facilities where small premiums are collected from which relatively large payments are made to clients that suffers losses from a specified risky event. Bolnick and Miltlin (1980) asserted that ROSCAs are also used by their clients to finance their finished houses, while Wilson (2001) observed that people join ROSCAs when they are faced by disaster, e.g. asset destruction from either flood or drought. Thus ROSCAs provide loan by allowing clients take loan early in anticipation of a disaster or by waiting until the end of the disaster to salvage the situation. Brass and Henderson (2000) further said that ROSCAs are usually used by subsistence farmers to provide adequate storage facilities to protect their farm produce from seasonal price swing. This enables farmers to store their products in a reliable warehouse/store until prices are high thereby enabling farmers reap the rewards of high profit.

Examining the empirical importance of ROSCAs, the World Bank (1989) reported that in Bolivia, one–third to one-half of all adults living in urban areas often participated in ROSCAs which amounted on the average to about one-sixth of their salaries, and in rural Niger Republic about 398 village households in 1986 indicated that informal credits, most especially ROSCAs accounted for 84 percent of total loans they collect and was equal to 17 percent of their agricultural income. Goodland, et al. (1999) also observed that in Senegal, ROSCAs assisted in equitable distribution and utilization of local resources most especially income and raw materials because credit taken are used to finance income generating activity with returns in excess of the loan, thus reducing the level of poverty of the people. Dia (1996) also said that saving facilities provided by ROSCAs in Senegal are used for financing health care and education, thus increasing the people's access to these social facilities. The findings of Akinrinola and Mafimisebi (2009) also confirm that Cooperative Society is a pivot on which development of micro-business and vocational trades in both rural and urban informal sectors revolves. This was revealed in its enterprise financing, employment generation and wealth creation for members and non-members. Equally important, is the social integration and gender equality encouraged in the appointment of women into leadership positions in the executives of Cooperative Unions and its component cooperative societies.

As significant as the informal credit institutions are in facilitating informal sector economic activities, their capacity to fund investment opportunities in the economy is impaired owing to inadequate capital mobilization for its members, ineptitude on the part of their management to monitor investment and exert corporate governance, dearth of requite skills to facilitate diversification and management of risks and complete absence of technological know-how to facilitate transaction in the economy, both by physically providing the mechanisms to make and receive payment and by reducing transaction and information cost. Suffice to say therefore that any intervention aimed at promoting broad-based growth, stimulating economic activities and creating jobs in the informal sector necessarily needs to partner with these informal institutions as a mean of reaching the economically incapacitated entrepreneurs in the society.

In this present paper, an argument is advanced why mobilization of working capital through informal credit institutions is essential for understanding fully the implications of economic reform on the large informal sector in Nigeria and the paper tries to establish that comprehensive capacity building programme for the players in the informal sectors is *sine qua non* to economic development and poverty reduction in the Nigerian society.

4 Impact of the Global Financial Crisis on Activities of ASCRA/ROSCA in Nigeria: A Case Study of Okitipupa Cooperative Multipurpose Union (OCMU)

4.1 Okitipupa Cooperative Multipurpose Union: A Historical Background

The OMCU is the umbrella body for informal credit/social organizations in Okitipupa Local Government Council of Ondo State, South-west, Nigeria. It is informal in outlook; however, it is characterized by a rather formal organizational framework. The OMCU was formed by agglomeration of nine primary cooperatives with a total of 125 members in the early seventies shortly after the Nigerian civil war to cater for economic empowerment of farmers devastated by the war situation. The 125 members were committed to savings mobilization and advancing credit to members. Five years later, membership grew to 2,066, which spread over 20 primary groups, and the focus expanded to cover input supply, marketing of farm produce and execution of community projects. By 1980, the different primary groups of cooperatives constituting OMCU had increased to 38 and the Union became registered with the

Ondo State Ministry of Commerce and Cooperatives. In 1981, ownership was divorced from management as the Union hired a General Manager, General Secretary, Treasurer, Projects Officer and other officers to manage the affairs of the Union. The management team is responsible to the Union executive committee. This management team established a 25-hectare oil palm plantation in 1982. Twenty-five years after, the hectarage of the plantation had increased to 175. The management further established 10 palm oil/kernel processing plants, apart from those established by members. The production capacity of the palm oil mills and palm kernel plants were 250,000 liters of oil and 45 metric tons of palm kernel cake per day respectively as at December, 2007. Membership had increased to 58 primary groups and 6742 individual members (Akinrinola and Mafimisebi, 2009).

The management of OMCU maintains proper books of records and accounts of the various societies under the union and renders stewardship account at the end of each financial year. Individual members are also assisted to keep proper book of records and accounts. This facilitated easy access to the operations of the OMCU and their members. A two year data set (2008 – 2009) about the activities of the Union with respect to savings by members, loan demanded and amount disbursed and membership was compared with findings of (Akinrinola and Mafimisebi, 2009), using corresponding data in the last five years (2003 – 2007) immediately preceding emergence of GFC. Results of comparative analysis of the two periods are presented below viz: resources mobilization, loan demand and disbursement and membership.

4.2 Resource Mobilization and Credit Disbursement

A characteristic feature of the OMCU was resource mobilization through regular contribution of cash. Contributions are made on meeting days which are usually on fortnight Sundays. The size of contributions made ranged between ₦500 – ₦4,500, ₦750 – ₦6,000 and ₦1000 – ₦7000 for the years under review as shown in Table 1.

Table 1: Savings Mobilization by OMCU (2003-2009)

Year	Savings (₦'000)	Marginal Savings (₦'000)	Percentage Change	Contribution range ₦
2003	15,750	-	-	
2004	17,435	1,685	10.69	350 – 3000
2005	23,460	6025	25.68	500 – 4500
2006	26,450	2,997	12.71	750 – 6000
2007	30,650	4,193	15.85	1000 – 7000

2008*	33,705	2,955	9.64	350 – 3000
2009*	35,650	1,945	5.77	250 – 2650

Source: Akinrinola & Mafimisebi, 2009 * Data extract from OMCU, 2010

It is evident from the Table 1 that prior to the emergence of GFC, savings increased progressively by 10.7% between 2003 and 2004 and by 25.7% between 2004 and 2005. It dropped to 12.7% in the year 2006 and later rose to 15.9% in 2007. The decline in relative percentage change between years 2005 and 2006 may not be unconnected with the political upheavals and uncertainties which characterize periods before and immediately following general elections in Nigeria. At the outset of the Global Financial Crisis, (2008), savings slide to 9.8% from 15.9% in the previous year and declined to 5.98% in 2009. The emergence of the GFC brought about cyclical movement in the saving profile of members. A critical examination of savings movement reveals that savings increased at an increasing rate before the GFC, except for 2006 when it dropped (reason discussed earlier) and during the GFC, it increased at a decreasing rate (in 2008) and declined further in 2009. Though the level of saving seems to be increasing relatively during the GFC, the increase was occasioned by contribution from new members (Table 3) and not as a result of improvement in personal savings of existing cooperators. Individual contributions during the GFC range from ₦350 – ₦3,000 in 2008 and dropped to ₦250 – ₦2,650 in 2009. This gives an average saving of ₦1,675 and ₦1,450 respectively. Comparison of individual contributions during the GFC with the corresponding years before GFC indicates that savings declined by 33 percent and 57 percent respectively (Table 1). Possible reasons for the continued decline in the level of savings of members during the GFC are increase in consumption expenditure due to hike in prices of household consumables, low demand as a result of cash crunch in the Nigeria economy, and reduction in amount of remittances from abroad, that followed the emergence of GFC.

However, the progressive increase in savings mobilization is necessary and conducive for rural development, as the pool of funds are neither hoarded nor banked but rather lent to members to meet their social and economic obligations. The savings mobilized together with loans recovered were disbursed to members, who made requests, as credit leaving only a stipulated proportion for emergency borrowing, union capital projects, social activities and training. In the periods preceding the GFC, a total of 1,150 loans, amounting to ₦18,445,000 (75% of loans demanded) were approved and disbursed in 2003, while credit facilities of ₦20,320,000 and ₦20,950,000) (78% and 83% of loan demanded) were approved and advanced to 1,350 and 1550 members in years 2005 and 2007, respectively. At the inception of GFC, credit demand rose to ₦47,350,000 and ₦63,670.000 in 2008 and 2009 respectively. The OMCU management was able to meet 77% and 72 % of total loan demands during the GFC. This loan performance index of meeting an average of 75% of loan demand (prior to and during GFC), most of which went for agriculture and agro-allied ventures, is far better than the 21% reported by Mafimisebi *et al* (2005) for some rural community banks in Oyo State, Nigeria. The lending rate of seven (7) percent per annum on outstanding balance and a privilege of obtaining 200% of one's total savings as loan, cum favorable three-year repayment period, actually encouraged members to acquire credit. Comparatively, the lending rate of the Union's credit is about 9 percentage points lower than that of the rural Community Banks analyzed by Mafimisebi *et al* (2005). These findings reveal that ROSCA loan is affordable, cheap and it is thus an effective medium for sourcing funds to finance enterprises at the grassroots.

However, this informal credit institution is capital constrained as the credit supply-demand gap before and during GFC ranged from 17% to 33% (Table 2).

Table 2: Credit Supply and Demand Gap

Year	Credit demand ₦'000	Credit Supply ₦'000	Supply-demand gap ₦'000	Shortfall (%)
2003	24,480	18,445	6,035	24.65
2004	26,550	21,650	4,900	18.45
2005	29,750	23,200	6,550	22.01
2006	30,057	20,000	10,057	33.46
2007	35,700	29,500	6,200	17.37
2008	47,350	36,250	11,150	23.55
2009	63,670	45,660	18,010	28.29

Source: Akinrinola & Mafimisebi, 2009

These results stress the need for partnership among public credit institutions, private formal credit institutions and cooperative societies to work out acceptable memorandum of understanding for generating sufficient investible capital to expand cooperatives' resource base and for efficient loan disbursement and repayment. The imperativeness of such cooperation among these three institutions subsists in the recent efforts by the Nigerian Government to transform rural life through micro-credit provision. Hence, this should form an important focus of the policy thrust in the on-going gradual metamorphosis of Community Banks to Micro-Finance Institutions.

4.3 Enhancement of Entrepreneurial Capacity Building

The OMCU organizes special entrepreneurial and record-keeping training programs for members, using their educational reserve funds to meet the training expenses. This training program has a direct effect of inculcating in members the spirit of accountability in business, self-employment and self-reliance through enterprise creation. Prior to the GFC (years 2006 and 2007), two entrepreneurship training programs were organized wherein more than 350 members were trained on different potential trades to encourage diversification of ventures for enhanced income generation by members. In the year 2009, four micro-business development/management trainings were carried, most especially for new members (participants – 70% and 30% new and old members respectively) who joined the Union for a cover from the scourge of lost of employment and dwindling income during the GFC. The participation rate increased to 1005 from 350 witnessed in 2006 and 2007. About 68% of members that had their capacity to run new trades enhanced were women, in accordance with their increased roles at the home front. Members who participated in organized capacity building programs were usually accorded first priority in the loan applications screening exercise following the completion of the training.

4.4 Membership

The strength of any social organization lies in its ability to attract more members and provide them with adequate succor in time of crisis. The OMCU has demonstrated that ASCRA/ROSCA in Nigeria is a form of "Social Safety-Net" to its members. This is evinced in the upsurge of membership during the GFC, as indicated in Table 4. Between 2004 and 2007, membership increased at about 2% on average, however, the trend changed significantly in 2009 where membership rose by over 7%. The rate at which new members joined the Union in the last two years surpassed the rate at which new members were registered in the last three years preceding the GFC. One important factor that makes ASCRA/ROSCA attractive to participants in the informal sector is the swiftness with which it mobilizes fund for its members/provision of capacity building training. This has contributed immensely towards profitability and survival of businesses of ROSCA members.

Table 3 Membership of OMCU from 2005 - 2009

Year	Member	Marginal change	% change
2003	6050	-	-
2004	6115	65	1
2005	6225	110	2
2006	6345	120	1.93
2007	6742	397	6.25
2008	7225	483	7.16
2009	7975	750	10.38

Source: Akinrinola & Mafimisebi, 2009

5 Macroeconomic Framework for Broad-Based Growth in Nigeria

Pro-poor targeted expenditures directly serve the purpose of poverty reduction. In contrast, broad-based (shared) expenditures contribute to GNP growth first and then to poverty reduction by a way of increased savings, which channeled through fiscal resources or banks to particular uses targeted at poverty reduction (Aryeetey 2009). In Nigeria context, the conventional pro-poor policies that are infused in the basic policy package of property rights, fiscal discipline, macro stability and openness to trade to increase the income of the poor households (Klasen, 2001) seems not to have yielded the desired result. As the policy thrusts of government at various levels are not specifically targeted at the poor households.

Achieving pro-poor broad-based growth would entail institutional and policy reforms that not only expand economic opportunities but also empower the poor (many of whom are engaged in the informal economy) to gainfully participate in and measurably benefit from them. Strong public-private partnerships are needed to accelerate both the expansion of opportunities and the empowerment of the poor. Empowering the poor households through the informal credit institutions will require systematic understanding of the *modus operandi* of the activities of these institutions, their challenges, how to mainstream them into public-private partnership agenda. The purpose of such partnership is to design a workable channel through which funds can be transferred to the informal credit institutions in such a way that it will eliminate unnecessary transaction costs to the barest minimum, guarantee adequacy of fund for investment, bring credit source close to the poor households and timely disbursement of fund to meet investment plans.

Considering the significance of the informal credit institutions in transforming the informal sector, the management of such institution though in the hands of elected members, should be closely monitored. Perhaps, institutional arrangement that will mandatorily make their activities accessible to government designated authority has to be put in place. This may be supported with adequate training of the executives of those institutions on the fundamentals of accounts and record keeping, investment appraisal, information management and retrieval and culture of transparency and accountability.

5.1 Approaches to support ROSCA/ASCRA in order to foster growth and reduces poverty among actors in the Informal Sector.

a. Advice and training to strengthen enterprise associations

Enterprise associations can be a valuable support mechanism for businesses during the downturn. They allow members to share ideas and knowledge, provide information on new policies and programs and advocate on behalf of their members vis-à-vis governments. The effectiveness of such organizations varies considerably, depending on the ability to attract members, the level of funding and the leadership and management. The Federation of Small Businesses in the U.K. and the Canadian Federation of Independent Business are two of the many effective organizations around the world. Unfortunately, there are also many small business associations which are less effective and thus the voice of small entrepreneurs it often inaudible. The government reform agenda should incorporate strengthening these associations through training program for small business associations so that these associations can play a more active role during the downturn.

b. Advice and training on business development services

Small enterprises need to cope with reduced demand in their traditional markets and develop products and services for new markets and new opportunities arising during the crisis. For this they need help to 'think outside of the box' and take initiatives to ensure that instead of being 'entrepreneurs in crisis', they are 'entrepreneurial in the midst of the crisis'. Entrepreneurship is a complex issue involving personal attributes, a supporting culture and an enabling policy environment. It can be assisted through training on how to start and manage a business. For many years the National Directorate of Employment (NDE) in collaboration with the ILO has promoted entrepreneurs through its Start and Improve Your Business (SIYB) suite of course, which also includes Generate Your Business Idea and Expand Your Business. These programs have been used for emergency situations, notably in Indonesia and Sri Lanka for tsunami survivors and in China, where the Emergency-SYB program was successful in assisting those whose lives were disrupted by the Sichuan earthquake of 2008. The NDE as a matter of urgency needs to design master trainers programmes for the Management of Informal Credit/Business Associations who in turns will train their members on coping with reduced demand and seizing new opportunities.

c. Public-Private Sector Partnership in Financing Informal Sector
Considering the significance of the informal credit institutions in transforming the informal sector, it is imperative to design a workable memorandum of understanding between Micro Finance Banks (MFBs) and Informal Credit Unions/ tested Non-Governmental organisations so that funds can be channeled through the latter to their members so as to eliminate unnecessary transaction costs to the barest minimum, guarantee adequacy of fund for investment, bring credit source close to the poor households and timely disbursement of fund to meet investment plans. Such partnership is necessary because credits facilities channeled through government agency to the public have very low repayment profile (Olusoji, 2006), and such programmees have not been sustainable in the past. A partnership of this nature will guarantee adequate repayment and recycling of funds, as members will not see the credit as their own share of national cake.

d. Fostering macro-economic stability as a precondition for economic reform, growth and informal sector development
A sound and stable macroeconomic environment that enables economic growth, prevents high volatilities and dampens external and internal shocks not only stimulates the formalization of the informal institutions, but also facilitates business activities in both the formal and the informal sectors. The dynamic of a sound and stable economic environment and increasing demands due to economic growth will also positively affect informal sector activities. The same is true for of a stable political environment and public safety, since high rate of crime and violence disproportionately affect informal sector actors such as street vendors.

6 Conclusion

Evidence suggests that the informal sector is very much a reality in Nigeria like any other developing economy as well as industrialized economy of the world. Evidence also suggests that in times of economic distress this sector works as a buffer and provides a livelihood for the impoverished masses even if the level might be somewhat inadequate. In a sense, the sector itself works as a type of safety net. In view of the role of the sector, leaving it unassisted in times of economic distress would be doing a grave injustice to a large section of poor people who rather than depend on government support are brave enough to fight their way forward when faced by the unfavourable economic environment.

One way of supporting this important sector is re-enforcing informal credit institutions and capacity building. Since the poor are credit constrained, a well funded informal credit institution with good management will provide the needed fund for the poor to embark on sustainable income generating ventures and adequate training will trigger entrepreneurship spirit/effective management. Any policy/intervention approach that leads to an increase in income, vis-a-vis savings of the poor, has greater potential to reduce poverty scale and dwarf the inequality gap.

References

Ademu, W.A (2006) "The informal sector and employment generation in Nigeria: The role of credit". NES 2006 Annual Conference.

Aredo D. (1993):. The Informal and Semi-formal Financial Sectors in Ethiopia - A Study of the Iqqub, Iddir, and Savings and Credit Cooperatives. *African Economic Research Consortium Paper No. 21.*

Aryeetey E 1997. Rural Finance in Africa: Institutional Development and Access for the Poor. In: M Bruno,B Pleskovic (Eds.): *Annual World Bank Conference in Development Economics 1996.* Washington D. C.: The World Bank.

Aryeetey E 1998. Informal Finance for Private Sector Development in Africa. *African Development Bank Economic Research Paper. No. 41.*

Aryeetey E. (2009): The Informal Economy, Economic Growth and Poverty in Sub-Sahara Africa *African Economic Research Consortium Framework Paper on Understanding Links between Growth and Poverty Reduction in Africa*

Akinrinola, O.O. and T.E. Mafiisebi (2009): "Contributions Of Informal Savings And Credit Institutions To Rural Development: Evidence From Okitipupa Multi-Purpose Cooperative Union, Ondo State, Nigeria. Journal of Rural Cooperation forthcoming.

Beecker, Kristina Flodman (2004): "The Informal Economy" A fact Finding Study prepared for the Swedish International Development Agency, Stockholm.

Bolnick J, Mitlin D 1991. *Finance and Empowerment.* South Africa: Shack Dwellers International.

Brass J, Herderson K 2000. Warehouse Receipts - Financing Agricultural Producers. *Technical Note Vol. 5.* Virginia: USAID

Chipeta C, Mkandawaivr MLC 1991. The Informal Financial Sector and Macroeconomic Adjustment in Malawai. *African Economic Research Consortium. Research Paper. No. 4.*

Davis, Lewis S., (2006): "Growing apart: The division of labour and the breakdown of informal institutions. Journal of Comparative Economics, 34, 1, 75-91

Dia M 1996. *Africa's Management in 1990s and Beyond:* INFORMAL FINANCIAL INSTITUTIONS AND POVERTY REDUCTION 81*Reconciling Indigenous and Transplanted Institutions.* Washington DC: The World Bank.

Gang, Ira N and Shubhashis Gangopadhyay (1990): "A Model of the Informal Sector in Development, Journal of Economic Studies, 17, 5, 19-32

Goodland A 1999. *Rural Finance. Policy Series* 1. U.K: Chatham.

ILO (2002a): "Decent Work and the Informal Economy: A Statistical Picture (Geneva International Labour Organisation)

Kar, S & Sugata Marjit, (2001): "Informal Sector in Geneeral Equilibrium: Welfare ERffects of Tade Policy Reforms, International Review of Economics and Finance 10 289-300

Marjit, Sugata, (2003): Economic Reform and Informal Wages – A General Equilibium Analysis. Journal of Development Economics, 72, 371-378

Ranis, G. Stewart. F. (1999): V-Goods and the Role of the Urban Informal Sector in Development, in Economic Development and Cultural Change. Vol. 47, No. 2 pp. 259-288

Turnham, D., (1993): Employment and Development – A New Review of Evidence. Paris Development Centre Studies, OECD

Webster, L., & Fidler, P., (1996): The Informal Sector and Microfinance in West Africa. Washington, DC. World Banks Regional and Sectoral Studies, World Bank.

Wilson, T 2000. *Micro finance during and After Armed Conflict: Lessons from Angola. Cambodia, Mozambique and Rwanda.* Durham: The Springfield Centre for Business in Development. Mount Joy Research Centre.

World Bank 1989. Financial Systems and Development.*World Development Report 1989.* New York: Oxford University Press. World Bank 1990. Poverty. *World Development Report 1990.* New York: Oxford University Press.

World Bank 2004. *Micro and Rural Finance in Ghana: Evolving Industry and Approaches to Regulation Findings*. Washington D.C: The World Bank. World Bank (2005a) *African Development Indicators 2005.* New York: Oxford University Press. World Bank. 2005b. *World Development Indicators 2005.* New York: Oxford University Press.

Yaron J et al. 1997. Rural Finance: Issue, Design and Best Practices. *The World* Bank Environmentally and Socially Sustainable Development Studies and *Monographs Series.* No. 14.

Yusuf N. Gafar T. Ijaiya and Muftau A. Ijaiya (2009): Informal Financial Institutions and Poverty Reduction in Informal Sector of Offa Town, Kwara State. A Case Study of Rotating Savings and Credit Association. *Journal of Social Science Vol.*20(1): 71-81

Zaman H 1999. Assessing the Impact of Micro-credit onPoverty and Vulnerability in Bangladesh. *WorldBank policy Research Working Paper No. 2145.*

The Global Financial Crisis (GFC) and Industrialization in Nigeria: The Implications of Reform Reversal

Osmund Osinachi Uzor[1]

Abstract

Nigerian government's microeconomic interventions are characterised by policy shifts and policy reversals. The industrial policy objectives and strategies in Nigeria are often subject to either modifications or neglect or even total abandonment. This paper employs a holistic approach in analysing Nigeria's industrial policy measures before the GFC dating from 1900 to 2007. The paper highlights possible implications of an industrial policy reversal as a result of the current global financial crisis impacting on Nigerian economy. The author argues that productive interventions aimed at stabilising market institutions and the mobilisation of domestic capital supported by Foreign Direct Investment in Nigeria's agro-industrial sector are necessary measures for a sustainable economic growth after the crisis.

1 Introduction

Nigeria is made up of about 350 ethnic groups or tribes with separate languages and over 140 million inhabitants. The country is diverse in culture and has abundant natural resources (UNDP, 2004, p. 1). The discovery of the mouth of the River Niger at the Bight of Biafra in 1830 made it possible for European traders to penetrate the hinterland. Lagos was annexed as a colony of Britain in 1861. The Royal Niger Company was entrusted to administer

---

[1] Holds a PhD degree in Economics from the University of Bremen, Researcher on African development in Bremen, Research Associate of the Institute for World Economics and International Management (IWIM), University of Bremen, and Coordinator of the Impacts of the GFC on the Economic Reforms in Africa Conference in Bremen, January 2010.

the territory by the British government in 1886 (Coleman, 1969, p. 75). In 1900, the Royal Niger Company handed over the administration of the area to the British government (Coleman, 1969, p. 41). Until recently, the country's economic and development policies have been subject to different ideological backgrounds and changes. In terms of industrial development, between 1900 and 1954 the colonial administration refrained from active participation in productive activities. This was as a result of the British tradition of *laissez-faire* and a rather negative attitude to a central economic planning system (Dauda, 1993, p. 75).

Between 1954 and 1986 subsequent regimes in Nigeria opted for a direct involvement in production, thereby circumscribing the autonomy of the private economic agents (Ohiorhenuan, 1989, pp. 141-151). The policy objectives were both inconsistent or ill-conceived ideas and subject to frequent reversals. The location of the so-called Core Industrial Projects (ICPs) and of other public industries was ethnically motivated - without any economic consideration. The pervasive nature of the policy objectives, coupled with a poor governance system, made the economy volatile to domestic and external shocks.

This paper presents the pattern of Nigeria's industrial development efforts and shows how policy shifts and policy reversals have contributed to the poor industrial policy outcomes. The paper also highlights the implications of the policy reversal as a result of the GFC. The paper is based on outcome of the research work conducted in Nigeria between 2003 and 2008 and is organised as follows. Section 2 highlights the problems with Nigeria's industrial policy strategies. Section 3 looks into the policy reforms and reform reversals. Section 4 discusses the recent reforms towards realising gains from a free market economy, and the consequences of the policy reversal as a result of the GFC. Section 5 highlights the challenges for sustainable development, while section 6 concludes with recommendations.

2 Pervasive Industrial Policies in Nigeria and Outcomes

Nigeria's industrialization efforts started actively between 1900 and 1954 through the provision of infrastructure for the easy movement of people and goods across regions. Furthermore, the creation of regional and provincial administrative authorities allowed not only a decentralization of administrative functions but also the establishment of an institutional framework for industrial development in the various regions. The Nigerian Local Development Board (NLDB) and the Department of Commerce and Industry (DCI) were also established. These institutions provided the framework for a grassroots industrial development as well as the promotion of trade and commerce. The activities of the NLDB were directed towards promoting grassroots industrial development, especially the development of rural agro-processing and of rural handicrafts. The DCI was assigned to promote the commerce across regions (Asiodu, 1967, p. 161; Ikpeze, 1991, p. 585).

Nigeria's industrial development strategy changed from 1954 onwards, when the regional governments and the legislative councils were established. Active government intervention was perpetuated through the legislative statutes, namely Industrial Development Acts (IDAs). The IDAs comprise the Import Duty Relief Act of 1957 which gave tax concessions to pioneer industries; the Income Tax Relief Act of 1958 aimed at offsetting investment costs against profits during the tax holiday period; and the Customs Duties Act of 1958 aimed at preventing dumping (Ikpeze, 1991, p. 587). Arguably, IDAs laid the foundation for protecting industries in Nigeria and for the framing of the import substitution program in Nigeria (Ohiorhenuan, 1989, p. 146).

Government's active involvement in industrial develop-ment became more visible from 1958 onwards. The justification of their actions was based on the assumption that the private sector was still very weak, hence industrial development requires proper planning and programming. This would encourage the private sector to channel their investment strategies towards areas of greater priority (Asiodu, 1967, p. 162). To strengthen their involvement in industrial development activities, industrial development initiatives were later integrated into the National Development Plan (NDP). Under the first NDP framework, a regulated open-door-policy was maintained (Dauda, 1993, p. 76). However, the call for a nationalisation of the Nigerian business became intensive in 1970, following massive criticisms on the government's poor implementation of the first NDP. Subsequent events led to the enactment of the Nigerian Enterprises Promotion Decree in 1971.

Nigerian Enterprises Promotion (NEP) Decree of 1972 (Indigenisation Decree) created two schedules of business ownership in Nigeria. Schedule 1 contained the list of enterprises which were exclusively reserved for Nigerians. Schedule 2 contained businesses which foreigners could engage in, but under certain conditions in terms of size and ownership. In other words, in relative terms foreigners lost the right to own a business in Nigeria. Soyode (1989, p. 195) argues that the policy of indigenisation was a complement to political sovereignty. The implication of the NEP Decree 1972 was – according to this argument - an implicit end of *imperialism* in Nigeria's political and economic discourse (Dauda, 1993, p. 75).

Gradually, Nigeria's industrial policy shifted from an open door policy to increasing government dominance in production activities (Ohiorhenuan, 1989, p. 148). Between 1973 and 1982, Nigeria witnessed a rapid industrial expansion, and the compound growth rate of the manufacturing sector rose by 9.5 per cent relative to a GDP growth rate of 2.3 per cent. In order to sustain the NEP policy, the government introduced different types of import restrictions with the aim to protect its new industries. The impacts of NEP and of the government's pervasive policies were such that about 600 public enterprises (PEs) at the federal level and about 900 smaller PEs at the state and local levels were established. The share of employment, value added and gross fixed capital formation of public enterprises generally exceeded those of other African countries. By 1997, an estimated 1,500 public enterprises accounted for about 57 per cent of aggregate fixed capital investment and for about 66 per cent of formal sector employment in Nigeria (Jerome, 2008, p. 4).

In 1982, the symptoms of economic downturn started to emerge as access to foreign exchange became persistently difficult. Firms could no longer import spare parts and the required raw materials, and hence industrial capacity utilisation began to contract. Contrary to expectations, the NEP policy and government's active involvement in economic production failed to meet their desired objectives in terms of reducing foreign dominance in the Nigerian economy. In spite of massive subsidies enjoyed by the PEs, the firms were operating at about 10-35 per cent of their capacity with poor returns and sub-standard outputs (Jerome, 2008, p. 4). The expected gains from nationalisation, such as employment generation, acquisition of skills and development of local technological capability, became a total flop (Ikpeze, 1991, p. 593). In general, government's active involvement in production processes and the NEP policy explicitly exposed Nigeria's weaknesses in terms of business environment. Such policy should not have been a priority policy option in a country that was in serious need of FDI (Aremu, 2003, p. 56).

3 Reforms and Reform Reversals in Nigeria

The Nigerian government introduced the Economic Stabilization Acts of 1982 and 1983 which, unfortunately, failed to rescue the ailing economy. After national debate in 1986, a Structural Adjustment Program (SAP) was launched in July 1986 in order to restore confidence in the economy. Deregulation and liberalization of the market were simultaneously introduced. An independent National Planning Commission (NPC) as part of the civil service reform was established in 1988 (Dauda, 1993, p. 80). The privatisation and commercialisation decree No. 25 of 1988 was promulgated. A Technical Committee on Privatization and Commercialization (TCPC) was subsequently established. The Committee succeeded in privatizing about 34 firms across several sectors through public floatation (Mahmoud, 2004, p. 1). The persistent economic downturn in Nigeria forced the government to make a further review of NEP in 1989. The three schedules were reduced to a single schedule in NEP Act No. 54 of 1989. Foreigners were no longer restricted in the proportion of shareholdings in their investment (Aremu, 2003, p. 59).

Unfortunately, the 1986 economic reform that tended to restructure the economy towards efficiency and prudent macroeconomic management was reversed in 1988/9 and abandoned in 1993. The general economic management processes became distorted as a result of the reform reversals. Consequently, the Nigerian economy collapsed and left behind huge foreign and domestic debt, soaring inflation, large-scale unemployment as well as widespread corruption (Bureau of Public Enterprise, 2006, p. 2). As a result of persistent pressure from the organised private sector, the Exchange Control Act of 1984 was repealed and was replaced by Foreign Exchange Decree No. 17 of 1995[2]. An Autonomous Foreign Exchange Market (AFEM) was subsequently created. The modalities for capital importation by foreign investors were deregulated and simplified. The Nigerian Investment Promotion Commission (NIPC) Act No. 16 was also established in 1995. The Act was designed to promote, coordinate and monitor all investment in Nigeria.

4 Reforms towards Free Market Economy

4.1 Policy Shift and Sectoral Changes in Nigeria

The impact of policy shift and policy reforms can be reflected on the change in gross domestic product (GDP) and sectors. Table 1 shows the changes in the production structure in terms of annual growth rates of the GDP and by sectors. The average annual growth rate of the GDP increased from 3.1 per cent between 1960 and 1970 to 4.6 per cent between 1970 and 1980. The GDP recorded the lowest annual growth rate of 1.6 per cent between 1980 and 1990 but rose to 6.0 between 2000 and 2006. The total farm output in Nigeria had recorded between 1960 and 1970 an annual average negative rate of –0.4 per cent and of -0.1 per cent per annum between 1970 and 1980.

---

[2] The Exchange Control Act of 1984 was the principal legislation regulating foreign currency transactions in Nigeria.

Table 1: Annual Average GDP, Sectoral and Population Growth Rates, in Percentage

	1960-1970	1970-1980	1980-1990	1990-2000	2000-2006
GDP	3.1	4.6	1.6	2.4	6.0
Agriculture	-0.4	-0.1	3.3	3.5	5.8
Industry	12.0	7.3	-1.1	1.0	5.5
Manufacturing	9.1	5.2	0.7	1.2	8.8
Services	4.9	9.6	3.7	2.9	6.5
Population	2.5	2.5	3.2	2.8	2.7*

Key: GDP=Gross Domestic Product; * = Population Growth 1990-2006
Source: The World Bank, World Development Report 1981, p. 136, p. 166; 1982, p. 142; 1992, p. 268; 1993, p. 240 ; 2002, p. 233; 2008, p. 199; The World Bank, World Development Indicators 2000, p. 183; 2002, p. 205

The negative growth in farm output between 1960 and 1980 is an evidence of the change in development policy as resource allocation shifted to other sectors. Between 1980 and 1990, the total farm output improved at an annual average rate of 3.3 per cent and rose slightly to 3.5 per cent between 1990 and 2000. As indicated in the Table 1, there was a remarkable improvement in the agricultural sector in Nigeria between 2000 and 2006 with a 5.8 per cent growth rate.

Industrial output expanded at an annual average rate of 12 per cent between 1960 and 1970 but grew rapidly at an annual average of 7.3 per cent also between 1970 and 1980. There was a drastic contraction in industrial output between 1980 and 1990 with a negative average annual growth rate of –1.1 per cent. Between 2000 and 2006, industrial output recovered and grew at an annual rate of 5.8 per cent. Relative to a lower annual growth rate of 4.9 per cent between 1960 and 1970, the annual growth rate in the service sector rose to 9.6 per cent between 1970 and 1980. However, the output fell to 3.7 per cent between 1980 and 1990 and to 2.9 per cent between 1990 and 2000 respectively. Between 2000 and 2006, the output growth in the services sector increased annually by 6.5 per cent. In general, the structural changes can be linked to policy shifts and policy reversals.

4.2 Policy Reforms and its Gains

Nigeria actively embraced the free market economy with private sector development as a core policy objective in 1999. As part of its globalisation strategy, the Federal Government of Nigeria (FGN) set up a privatization programme with the goal of divesting about 100 PEs through privatization or commercialization in July 1999. The privatization of utilities such as power and telecommunications made little progress in Nigeria (Jerome, 2008, p. 9). Arguably, the utilities are large and complex companies. Opposition from the parliament and from labour unions contributed to the slow pace in the second phase of the privatization programme (Mahmoud, 2004, p. 1). To facilitate the inflow of FDI in the economy, an Investment and Securities Act was signed into law in 1999. The aim was to deregulate the Nigerian capital market in order to harmonise the Capital Gains Tax Act, the Venture Capital (Incentives) Act, and the NIPC Act (Aremu, 2003, pp. 63-4).

In capital markets, there has been a steady improvement following the replacement of the call over trading system with an automatic trading system in 1999. In 2000, the settlement and clearing cycle was reduced from 5 days to 3 days. Subsequently, new financial instruments, such as long term government and corporate bonds as well as trading in options and futures, were created. As shown in Table 2, market capitalisation (or capital market value) in Nigeria grew from US$1,372 millions in 1990 to US$86,347 millions in 2007 and fell drastically to US$49,803 millions by 42.3 percent in 2008. The drastic decline was a result of the global financial crisis. The relative increase in the overall size in stock market values between 2005 and 2007 can be linked to the reform in Nigeria's financial institutions and capital markets. The market capitalisation (MC), expressed as a percentage of GDP, shows the rate at which securities are traded in the capital markets. It also projects the size of the market and shows the extent to which the liquidity position in the market has improved relative to the 1990s. A 52.2 per cent market capitalisation (expressed as a percentage of GDP) in 2007 suggests that securities can easily be bought in Nigeria's capital market in 2007 compared to 1990 with a market capitalisation value of only 4.2 per cent.

The turnover ratio, which is the value of traded shares expressed as a percentage of market capitalisation, has improved in Nigeria from 0.9% in 1990 to 29.3% in 2008. This also suggests that the transaction costs have been reduced in Nigeria's securities market relative to the 1990s, and that high liquidity exists in the market. It also suggests that the ability to mobilise foreign and domestic capital and to diversify risks in the market have increased in recent times. In general, the number of listed domestic stocks (LDSs) has increased from 131 in 1990 to 213 in 2008 by 62.6 per cent.

Table 2: Capital Market Position in Nigeria

	1990	2000	2005	2006	2007	2008
MC (mil. US$)	1,372	4,237	19,356	32,819	86,347	49,803
MC (% of GDP)	4.2	10.3	19.6	8.5	52.2	n.a
TR*	0.9	7.3	11.5	13.8	28.7	29.3
Number of LDSs	131	195	214	202	212	213

Key: n. a. = not available at present year; * turnover ratio is the value of shares traded in a year as % of market capitalisation, MC= Market Capitalisation, Size of LDSs = Size of listed domestic stocks; TR=Turnover Ratio
Source: World Bank, World Development Indicators, 1997, 2002 and 2006-2009

To support market development in Nigeria, the banking sector consolidation began in 2005. The basic argument for banking sector consolidation is centered on macroeconomic stabilization via monetary control in terms of exchange rate and interest rate control. Fundamentally, consolidating the banking sector was aimed at stabilising the foreign exchange market, strengthening the Dutch Auction System (DAS), and narrowing the premium between the DAS, Bureau De Change and Inter-Bank rates (Balogun, 2007, p. 11). The expected outcome was such that the reform would create a healthy and competition environment which is attractive for domestic and foreign investors. To achieve this, an investment-friendly interest rate regime, which would be in line with government's economic growth objective, was pursued (Balogun, 2007, p. 20). The post-consolidation evaluation as shown in Table 3 below indicates that the number of banks was reduced from 89 to 25, while the number of bank branches increased from 3382 to 4500 by 33,1%. Consequently, the total asset base of the banks rose from 3209 Billion Naira to 6555 Billion Naira by 104 per cent. The bank capital and reserves base increased from 327 Billion Naira to 957 Billion Naira by 192 per cent. The capital adequacy ratio increased from 15.18 per cent in 2004 to 21.6 per cent in 2006. As a result of the consolidation policy, the ratio of non-performing credit to total credit declined from 19.5 per cent to 9.5 per cent by 51.3 percentage points. In other words, the reform created a healthier financial sector, needed for the mobilization of domestic and foreign capital for the development in the economy.

In 2002, the Nigerian government introduced innovative financial incentive measures to promote small and medium scale enterprises (SMEs). The government launched the Small and Medium Enterprises Equity Investment Scheme (SMEEIS). Under the scheme, commercial banks were mandated to set aside 10 per cent of pre-tax profits for equity investments in SMEs[3]. Equity investment could be in the form of cash injections and/or the conversion of existing debts with additional funds as loans by the banks (World Bank, 2002. p.16; Oyekanmi, 2004, p. 66). By June 2009 a total sum of about N28.2 billion had been distributed to SMEs. Firms in Lagos State received about 41.25 per cent of the total sum, followed by Cross River State and Ogun State with 21.95 and 6.82 per cent respectively. 28.73 per cent of total disbursement went to the Manufacturing sector, 26.43 per cent to Tourism and Leisure, 16.91 to the Service sector, and 8.20 per cent went to Agro-allied Industries (CBN, 2009).

Table 3: Basic Indicators of Banking Sector Consolidation

	2004	2006	% of Growth
No. of Banks	89	25	-71.9
No. of Bank Branches	3382	4500	33.1
Total Assets Base of Banks in Billion Naira	3209	6555	104.3
Capital and Reserves in Billion Naira	327	957	192.7
Capital Adequacy Ratio (%)	15.2	21.6	42.6
Ratio of Non-performing Credit to Total Credit (%)	19.5	9.5	-51.3

Source: Balogun, 2007, p. 7

In 2004, Nigeria launched a new policy framework called the "National Economic Empowement and Development Strategy" (NEEDS)[4]. The NEEDS policy document explicitly recognised the role of economic growth, and the promotion of the private sector became the central objective of the NEEDS policy package. The policy targeted specific sectors, such as agriculture, agro-industries, agro-businesses, services, oil and gas, and solid minerals. The policy document also recognised the importance of small and medium scale enterprises (SMEs) in the economy in terms of employment

[3] NEEDS documents were created in March 2004, pp. 78-83

[4] A critical view of the policy framework shows that NEEDS is a revised SAP that aimed at reforming government institutions by encouraging effective budgetary implementation, fighting corruption, promoting accountability and transparency (NEEDS, 2004, p. 12). The basic difference between the NEEDS concept and the SAP concept is that NEEDS is a locally groomed concept with a neo-liberal background.

generation and wealth creation. Enterprises clusters were also regarded as a key strategy in Nigerian industrial development in the policy document (NEEDS, 2004, p. 7).

Furthermore, the telecommunications sector was actively deregulated. This gave room for entries of many telephone and internet service providers in the country. Hence, there was a rapidly increased access to mobile phone and internet in the country. The energy sector was partially deregulated in order to allow for public and private partnership investment. This was followed by the establishment of a Small and Medium Enterprises Development Agency of Nigeria (SMEDAN) through the parliamentary process. The agency was assigned to promote, facilitate and coordinate all government policies on SMEs (NEEDS, 2004, p. 80). A new national policy on Micro, Small and Medium scale Enterprises (MSMEs) was launched in 2008. The fundamental objectives of the policy according to the report are, to provide an overall framework of action as a guide for well focused, harmonious and coordinated programming by all actors. The implication is that policies on SMEs in Nigeria are now a macroeconomic issue which has to be centralised with unified policy measures and coordinated and supplemented with other policy measures.

4.3 The GFC and the Implications of Reform Reversals

A reform reversal is defined as a downgrading in the level of an average reform indicator (Merlevede, 2003, p. 1)[5]. Current reform may affect growth negatively for some time, while ongoing reform may affect growth positively and may eventually lead to consolidation (Merlevede, 2003, p. 14). This suggests that reform initially produces adjustment shocks, but as the reform continues it generates and supports a sustainable growth path on the long run. Economic reforms can arouse opposition if they are perceived to be redistributive and selfish. Incidentally, many economists in developed countries have come to the consensus that policy elements such as fiscal rectitude, competitive exchange rates, free trade, privatisation, undistorted market prices, and limited intervention, which tend to encourage export, and support educational development as well as infrastructure development, constitute an appropriate economic development strategy (Rodrik, 1996, p. 9).

---

[5] The reform indicators relate to the policy stance and include – the index of private entry in markets (large scale privatisation, financial market reform and enterprise reform); the index of trade and foreign exchange rate liberalization; and the index of price liberalization.

Two factors often mitigate reform processes and often lead to reversals. The first is the commitment problem while the second is the fear of changing the political equilibrium. The former suggests that an attempt to implement good policies, for example improving the business environment enhancing investment opportunities, may be resisted by political groups. The resistance could be coming as a result of fear of future expropriation of their returns. The later argument means that adopting good policies could lead to a change in future political equilibrium. Hence, the current administration/government may refrain from adopting the good policy for fear of losing their future political position (Robinson, 1998, pp. 31-33).

The impact of reform reversals is reflected on the existence of reversal costs. Such costs can be in the form of a general distortion of the economic system, the creation of uncertainty in the business environment, and the waste of scarce resources. In general, reversals often generate an immediate negative contribution to real output growth (Merlevede, 2003, p.15). Taking into account the level of reform a country has achieved, a reversal is found to be more costly at higher levels of the reform indicator. In this context, Nigeria should consolidate its gains in the banking sector reform and increase the pace of economic, social and political reforms in order to be more competitive after the GFC. As put forward by Merlevede (2003, p. 4), the closer to a market system the country is, the more beneficial will be the effects of reform on generating higher (allocation) efficiency and growth.

Nigeria should consolidate the gains from its banking sector reforms and should even increase the pace of its general economic, social and political reforms in order to be more competitive after the GFC. Reversing policies as a result of the GFC implies *resetting the clock back*. The danger is that such a behavior will lead to further distortions of the general economic management and as well will create uncertainty in the economy. This will invariably retard the progress made towards a free market economy in terms of learning how to act in an entrepreneurial environment and spirit. No economic system is perfect but a re-emergence of government dominance in economic production activities will reduce competition and will retard growth. It will also reduce the rate of innovative activities in the economy and will lead to a loss of scarce resources as experienced from 1970s to the 1990s in Nigeria. Government intervention should focus on short and medium term measures aimed at mitigating the impact of the GFC on the socio-economic environment. Important structural measures of a long-term nature are: creating the enabling environment for a competitive private sector; promoting SMEs and SME clusters and networks; and promoting agro-processing and agro-industries. These policy areas should remain the central focus of Nigeria government's long term industrial policy measures. This will help to promote sustainable economic growth and will help to counter future external shocks like the GFC.

5 The GFC and Sustainable Development in Nigeria

The major challenges facing policymakers in Nigeria are how to stabilise economic reforms in the face of the global financial crisis, how to translate the gains from globalisation (economic growth) towards improving living conditions, and how to reduce inequalities and inequities. As expressed in the UNDP 2007/2008 report, the problem of income distribution in Nigeria is clearly portrayed by the ratio of the richest to the poorest income groups. According to the report, for every 1 per cent of the national income allocated to the 10 per cent of the poorest population the 10 per cent of the richest population get 17.9 per cent of national income. For every 1 per cent of the national income allocated to the poorest 20 per cent of the population, the richest 20 per cent of the population get 9.7 per cent of the national income (UNDP, 2007/8 p. 337). Reducing the inequality gap is a major step towards the stability of the economic reform processes.

The first basic step towards sustainability of the reforms is to restructure Nigerian development policies. Emphasis should focus on human capital and skill development. This will have a positive impact in terms of distributing more evenly the gains from economic reforms. It will also contribute to per capita income growth, because increasing investments in skill enhancement will not only generate higher wages for workers, but also will increase the productivity level of the economy (Stockey, 1991, p. 588). Arguably, the inflow of FDI requires an effectively skilled labour force which can quickly adapt and apply relatively advanced foreign technologies in production (Caves, 1996, p. 6). Hence, differences in the efficiency of labour across time and countries can be explained by differences in the average years of schooling per worker (Benhabib and Spiegel, 1994, p. 144). Table 4 shows the trend in Nigeria's Human Development Index (HDI) performance between 1975 and 2005. The HDI values improved considerably from 0.321 in 1975 to 0.470 in 2005 by 46.4 per cent.

Table 4: Nigerian Human Development Index Trends

	1975	**1980**	**1985**	**1990**	**1995**	**2000**	**2005**
HDI	0.321	0.378	0.391	0.411	0.432	0.445	0.470

Source: UNDP Human Development Report 2007/8, p. 236

Despite the improvement, the country has not been able to reach so far the 0.5 minimum performance benchmark of the HDI. Investment in human capital development can be seen as the basic measure aimed at long term sustainability of the economy.

The second step is to improve the governance structure and the economic and political system. Sustainability of the reforms and Nigeria's further integration into the world economy depend on the nature of governance. If the governance structure and the governance system are infected with corruption, a successful development path cannot be achieved. Good governance is reflected on macroeconomic stability, equitable distribution of the resources, transparency, accountability, and government commitment to uphold the constitution (Gradstein, 2004, p. 516). Poor governance signifies poor management of the scarce resources and promoting ineffective and corrupt public institutions. For example, in manufacturing and services sectors, investors tend to choose countries with a low corruption index in order to avoid risks (Te Velde, 2002, p. 5).

Good governance is an essential factor for investment opportunities in the sense that unpredictability of reforms and reversal of policies discourage investment. Uncertainty in the political and economic environment and arbitrary behaviour of government officials in terms of interpretation of the laws discourage investors (World Bank, 1989, p. 189). In addition, ownership of reforms is imperative and should be an integral part of more comprehensive governance programmes, especially in public administration reforms (Wohlmuth, 1998, p. 75).

The third step is to diversify the economy and to promote economic growth after the GFC. Industrial development strategies should focus on areas where the country has comparative advantage for sustainable economic growth. Productive interventions aimed at stabilising market institutions and mobilising domestic capital supported by FDI in the Nigerian agro-industrial sector are necessary measures for a sustainable economic growth after the crisis. As a developing country, the problem with Nigeria's industrialisation efforts was the neglect of small-scale industries, especially in agro-industrial processing. The pattern of Nigeria's industrial development process laid more emphasis on unsustainable public large-scale enterprises. Such industrial development strategies failed to promote sectoral and industrial linkages (Osoba, 1991, p. 634).

Industrial policy objectives should focus on how to promote agro-industrial processing, sectoral linkages and SME linkages with large international firms in agro-processing. Agro-industry provides the crucial framework for the diversification of the economy, for strengthening farm-industry linkages, and ultimately contributes to the rapid development of the agricultural sector. The economic advantages of agro-processing include value addition to farmer's produce, creating opportunities for employment, and increasing the farmer's net income. The process opens up possibilities for agricultural development because the farmers will be motivated to increase production.

The fourth step is a continuous improvement of the capacity in corporate governance with focus on how to strengthen the economy through the gains from corporate sector and banking sector consolidation. This can be achieved by increasing the share of bank lending to productive sectors, such as agriculture, manufacturing, and mining sectors. Despite of increased lending in the Nigerian financial market, the costs of borrowing remain very high in Nigeria. Lowering the costs of borrowing would induce credit expansion and as well would act as a catalyst to investment activities (Balogun, 2007, p. 20). Furthermore, informal microfinance has been the major source of fundraising by micro-enterprises. Informal microfinance originated as a result of the inability of the formal financial institutions to provide financial services to the urban and rural poor. The small enterprises in the informal sector cannot provide the required collateral for loan security. Even government sponsored credit schemes failed to provide grassroots development financing. Hence, the informal microfinance institutions continue to flourish but at the expense of the poor due to the high interest rate. For sustainability of the reform, it is imperative to strengthen the Micro Finance Institutions (MFIs) in Nigeria. Despite high lending interest rates, there has been evidence of a high repayment rate and a low incidence of default in the loan grouping system due to sanction mechanisms within each group in the MFIs (Anyanwu, 2004, p. 6).

If the economy had been already more diversified away from overdependence on the petroleum sector and/or there had been a more effective mobilisation of domestic resources for income generation, the impact of the GFC on the economy of Nigeria would have been less severe. Economic development is measured not only by a rising national income but also by an increased capacity for self-sustained growth. Hence, development is a process that involves the ability to add value (Helmboldt et al., 1988, p. 343). The private sector therefore possesses the capacity to add value, and private investment remains the key factor for development (Söderbom and Teal, 2002, p. 27). To strengthen the economy against future external shocks like the GFC, the aforementioned steps are necessary and hence there is need to increase the pace of reforms that support private sector development. The major policy failure in Nigeria over the last three decades was giving only limited opportunities for the growth of the domestic private sector. The pervasive nature of policy objectives coupled with poor governance made the Nigerian economy to be volatile to external shocks.

6 Conclusions and Policy Recommendations

As Nigeria is currently undertaking economic reforms, there could be some initial setbacks as a result of the GFC. The challenge that the Nigeria policymakers face now is how to stabilize the reforms and how effectively to integrate the country in the global economy. The country can effectively overcome the crisis by containing the situation through short and medium policy measures. The experience gained will encourage the policymakers to speed up political and economic reform processes. The paper argues that the current crisis should not be used as an excuse to disengage from reforms, or even to reverse policies or to initiate measures that are contrary to long-term macroeconomic stability efforts.

The paper has advanced several steps for the sustainability of the economy after the crisis. Specifically, the paper recommends that an intensive accumulation of human capital is needed in order to support a sustainable development and a wide learning process. It is also imperative to create the environment that is conducive for the transfer of know-how and for building linkages of the local SMEs with large foreign firms in agro-processing. Furthermore, policy reforms should continue to focus on creating stable institutions that support and enhance access to global finance sources.

In a country like Nigeria with about 350 ethnic groups, there is the need to promote social cohesion. To promote social cohesion - needed to boost the confidence of the local and the foreign private economic actors - democratisation and stabilisation of political institutions are essential ingredients; more effective ethnic and social interactions will follow from such measures.

Furthermore, investment in infrastructure is a condition for the sustainability of the gains from reforms. Infrastructure represents a precondition that drives the acceleration of economic activities. It has potentially a high payoff in terms of economic growth. It increases productivity and reduces costs of production, and therefore remains a major factor in attracting foreign investors (Wheeler and Mody, 1992, p. 69). Infrastructure is the key factor for countries to compete internationally in trade (World Bank, 1994, p. 17). Hence, Nigeria's integration in the world economy depends on consolidating reforms, but also on adequate supplies of goods and services and a reliable infrastructure. Nigeria should redefine its industrial development strategy and focus on the sectors where the country has comparative advantage (agro-processing, mining, etc.), in order to diversify the economy and to increase the country's share of the global market and income.

The policy packages as proposed in this paper can prevent in future, if implemented deliberately and comprehensively, the occurrence of such high costs of global crises as Nigeria has experienced recently. Economic management - during and after crises - will then become more sustainable.

References

Anyanwu, C. M. (2004), Microfinance Institutions in Nigeria: Policy, Practice and Potentials, Paper presented at the G24 workshop on "Constraints to Growth in Sub Saharan Africa", Pretoria, South Africa, November 29-30, 2004.

Aremu, J. A. (2003), An Overview of Foreign Private Investment in Nigeria, in: O. J. Nnanna and C. M. Okafor, eds., Foreign Private Investment in Nigeria, Proceedings of the Twelfth Annual Conference of the Regional Research Units Research Department, CBN 01.09.03 -5.09-03, Kaduna, Nigeria.

Asiodu, P. C. (1967), Industrial Policy and Incentives in Nigeria, Nigerian Institute of Social and Economic Research, Ibadan, NISER Reprint Series No. 44.

Balogun, E. D. (2007), A Review of Soludo's Perspective of Banking reforms in Nigeria, MPRA Paper No. 3803, posted 07 November 2007/03:28, mpra.ub.uni-muenchen.de/3803.

Benhabib, J. and Spiegel, M. (1994), The role of human capital in economic development: evidence from aggregate cross-country data, in: Journal of Monetary Economics Vol. 34, pp. 134-173.

Bureau of Public Enterprises (2006), Nigeria: www.bpeng.org/10/0317731265632b.asp.

Caves, R. E. (1996), Multinational Enterprises and Economic Analysis, 2nd Edition, Cambridge: Cambridge University Press.

CBN (2009), The Central Bank of Nigeria, Small & Medium Enterprises Equity Investment Scheme (SMEEIS), SMEEIS 434 and 435. http://www.cenbank.org/documents/smeeis.asp.

Coleman, J. S. Nigeria (1965), Background to Nationalism, University of California Press, Berkeley and Los Angeles.

Dauda, B. (1993), Industrial Policy and The Nigeria Bureaucracy, 1900-1988, in: Elizabeth Eldredge, Toyin Falola, Paul Lovejoy, Donna Maier, and Ann O'Hear, Eds., African Economic History, Vol. 21, pp. 73-96.

Gradstein, M. (2004), Governance and Growth, in: Journal of Development Economics, Vol. 73, issue 2, pp 505-518.

Helmboldt, N. E., West, T. & Hardy, B. H. (1988). Private Investment and African Economic Policy, in: Robert J. Berg and Jennifer S. Whitaker (Eds.), Strategies for African Development, A Study for the Committee on African Development Strategies, Sponsored by the Council of Foreign Relations and the Overseas Development Council, pp. 331-357, University of California Press, Berkeley, Los Angeles, London.

Ikpeze, N. I. (1991), New Industrial Policies and Perspectives for Manufacturing in Nigeria, in: Karl Wohlmuth, Peter Oesterdiekhoff, Robert Kappel. Dirk Hansohm, Barbara Worch, Hans H. Bass, Elke Grawert, Gaby Zdunnek, Jutta Franz, Marlene Conrad and Klaudia, Kleine (Eds.): Industrialisation based on Agricultural Development, African Development Perspectives Yearbook, Vol. 2, Münster/Hamburg, Lit Publishers, pp. 585-608.

Jerome, A. (2008), Privatization and Enterprise Performance in Nigeria: Case Study of Some Privatized Enterprises, AERC Research Paper 175, African Economic Research Consortium, Nairobi.

Mahmoud, D. (2004), Privatization and Poverty Reduction in Nigeria, www.odi.org.uk/events/nigeria_2004/mahmoud web paper.pdf.

Merlevede, B. (2003), Reform Reversals and Output Growth in Transition Economies, Department of Economics, Ghent University, Belgium.

NEEDS (2004), Nigeria: National Economic Empowerment and Development Strategy, The NEEDS Secretariat, National Planning Commission, Federal Secretariat, Abuja.

Ohiorhenuan, F. E. (1989), The State and Economic Development in Nigeria Under Military Rule, 1966-79, in Tekena N. Tamuno and J. A. Atanda (eds.), Nigeria Since Independence: The First Twenty-Five Years, Vol. IV, Government and Public Policy, pp. 141-151.

Oyekanmi, R. (2003), Concepts of Equity Financing and its Implications for SMIEIS, in: Seminar on the Small and Medium scale Industries Equity Investments Scheme (SMIEIS), The Central Bank of Nigeria, Central Bank of Nigeria Training Centre, Lagos, Publication No. 4, pp. 66-84.

Osoba, A. M. (1991), The Missing Middle - New Chances and Programmes of developing the small-scale Industries in Nigeria, in: Karl Wohlmuth, Peter Oesterdiekhoff, Robert Kappel, Dirk Hansohm, Barbara Worch, Hans H. Bass, Elke Grawert, Gaby Zdunnek, Jutta Franz, Marlene Conrad and Klaudia Kleine (Eds.), Industrialisation based on Agricultural Development, African Development Perspectives Yearbook, Münster/ Hamburg, Lit Publishers, Vol. 2, pp. 529-546.

Robinson, J. (1998), Theories of Bad Policies, Journal of Policy Reform, Vol.2 (1), pp. 1-4.

Rodrik, D. (1996), Understanding Economic Policy Reform, in: Journal of Economic Literature, Vol. XXXIV, pp. 9-41.

Söderbom M. & Teal, F. (2002), The Performance of Nigerian Manufacturing Firms: Report on the Nigerian Manufacturing Enterprise Survey 2001, CSAE, University of Oxford, UK.

Soyode, A. (1989), Indigenization, in: Tekena N. Tamuno and J. A. Atanda, Eds.: Nigeria Since Independence: The First Twenty-Five Years Government and Public Policy, Vol. IV, pp. 191-208.

Stockey, N. (1991), Human capital, product quality and growth, in: Quarterly Journal of Economics, Vol. 106, pp. 587-616.

UNDP (2004), United Nations Development Programme, Human Development Report, Lagos, Nigeria.

UNDP (2007/8), United Nations Development Programme, Human Development Report, New York: The United Nations Development Programme.

Uzor, O. O. (2007): "Oil Palm Production in Nigeria and the Improved Export Chances: The Need for Upgrading", in: Karl Wohlmuth, Mareike Meyn, Tobias Knedlik, Achim Gutowski, Afeikhena Jerome, Chicot Eboue, Touna Mama, Alexandre Schouame (Eds.), Africa's Commodity Dependence, Resource Curse and Export Diversification, African Development Perspectives Yearbook, Vol. 12, 2007, pp. 273-294, Lit Verlag: Muenster, Hamburg, Germany.

Uzor, O. O. (2010), The ISMED Model and Public-Private Partnership in the Promotion of Agro-Industrial Clusters in Nigeria, Andreas Knorr, Alfons Lemper, Axel Sell and Karl Wohlmuth (Hrsg.), Berichte aus dem wirtschaftlichen Colloquium der Universität Bremen, Nummer 118, Bremen: IWIM, University of Bremen.

te Velde, D. W. (2002), Foreign Direct Investment for Development, Policy Challenges for Sub-Saharan African Countries, Overseas Development Institute.

Wheeler, D. /Mody, A (1992), International investment location decisions: The case of U.S. firms, in: Journal of International Economics, Vol. 33, pp 57-76.

Wohlmuth, K. (1998), Good Governance and Economic Development, New Foundations for Growth in Africa, in: Berichte aus dem Weltwirtschaftlichen Colloquium der Universität Bremen, No. 59, Hrsg. von Andreas Knorr, Alfons Lemper, Axel Sell, Karl Wohlmuth, Bremen: IWIM, University of Bremen.

World Bank (1989), Sub-Saharan Africa, From Crisis to Sustainable Growth, A Long-Term Perspective Study, Washington D. C.: The IBRD/The World Bank.

World Bank (1981, 1982, 1992, 1993, 2002, and 2008), World Development Report, The World Bank, Washington D.C. The IBRD/The World Bank.

World Bank (1994), Infrastructure for Development, World Development Report, The World Bank, Washington D.C.: The IBRD/The World Bank.

World Bank (1997, 2000, 2002 and 2006-2009), World Development Indicators, The World Bank, Washington D.C.: The IBRD/The World Bank.

The Impact of Emerging and Developed Stock Markets on the Nigerian Stock Exchange

Peter Njiforti[1] and Terfa Williams Abraham[2]

Abstract

Towards the end of the fourth quarter in 2007, the Nigerian Stock market witnessed a steady rise. Globally however, this period was the beginning of a recession. Available data showed that between 5th March 2008 and 3rd April 2009, the All Share index of the Nigerian Stock Exchange (NSE) dropped from 66,370.2 to 19,954.15 points: a decline of 69.94% in just one year. The decline (though at varying levels) was also witnessed among emerging stock markets in Africa and those of developed economies like the US, UK and Japan. The aim of this study is to examine two issues: 1) to measure the size and impact of emerging and developed stock markets on the Nigerian stock exchange and 2), to establish whether the Nigerian stock market is integrated with the emerging and developed stock markets. For this purpose, five day weekly data were collected from 10th December 2007 to 3rd July 2009. The data were stock market closing indices collected for three African Emerging markets (South Africa, Egypt and Tunisia) and three developed stock markets (US, UK and Japan). Autoregressive Distributed Lag (ADL) model, Granger Causality test and Augmented Engle Granger (AEG) cointegration test were the econometric frameworks employed for the study. For the emerging African stock markets, it was found that the JSE had a positive and significant impact on the NSE, while the granger causality test provided evidence that the JSE and the Egyptian stock market had unidirectional influence on the NSE in the short run. The AEG cointegration test however, showed no evi-

---

[1] Dr. Peter Njiforti (njifortica@yahoo.com) is a lecturer in the Department of Economics, faculty of Social Sciences, Ahmadu Bello University, Zaria (Nigeria).

[2] Terfa Williams Abraham (lorenzcurve@yahoo.com) is a graduate student of Economics in the Faculty of Social Sciences, Ahmadu Bello University, Zaria (Nigeria).
His contribution to the paper was supported by the Small Grant for Thesis Writing Funding by CODESRIA (Council for the Development of Social Science Research in Africa) during its 2009 17th Competition (Grant Award number: SGRT. 60/T09).

dence of integration connecting the NSE and the selected African emerging markets. On the other hand, all the developed stock markets were found to significantly impact on the performance on the Nigerian stock exchange at varying lag length. Asides the US (which had a negative relationship with the NSE) others had a positive relationship with the Nigerian stock exchange. When tested for cointegration, it was found that the Nigerian stock exchange was integrated with the developed stock markets. It was concluded that the short run and cointegrating relationship connecting the Nigerian stock exchange with the developed stock markets is a link for these markets to impact on the performance of the NSE in crisis times. However, the NSE could also benefit from these markets in times of market recovery and positive externalities. The study recommended that, increased stock market integration should be pursued in Africa; so as to reap the benefits of stock market integration within the continent as well.

1 Introduction

In the 1980s, many emerging markets' opened their stock market to foreign investors. By the 1990s, most of these countries in Asia, Latin America and Russia faced severe financial crises (Yang *et al*, 2002).

The global economic melt down which originated from *Developed Markets* towards the beginning of the fourth quarter in 2007, has continued to have wide spread impact on *Emerging markets* across the globe. Available data showed that between 5th March 2008 and 3rd April 2009, the All Share index of the Nigerian Stock Exchange (NSE) dropped from 66,370.2 to 19,954.15 points: a decline of 69.94% in just one year. The decline (at varying levels) was also witnessed among emerging stock markets in Africa and of developed economies over the same period. These events have helped in stimulating a debate about the response of emerging stock markets to developed stock markets and the benefits of stock market integration.

By focusing on Nigeria, the objectives of this study are: 1) to measure the impact of selected emerging and developed stock markets on the Nigerian stock exchange, and 2) to establish whether the Nigerian stock market is integrated with the selected emerging and developed stock markets.

The study is organized into five (5) sections. Section one presents the introduction of the study, while section two presents the conceptualization, theoretical and empirical literature review. In section three, the research methodology is presented and the analysis and interpretation of the result are presented in the fourth section. Finally, section five presents the summary and conclusion.

2 Review of Literature

2.1 Conceptualization

Collins and Biekpe (2004) in their study conceptualized Emerging Stock Markets using five indices: market capitalization ratio to GDP, market value traded as a ratio to GDP, market turnover, number of listed companies and the IFCI (International Finance Corporation Investibles) composite index. They noted that emerging stock markets are markets that are dynamic and have increasing possibilities of improving upon the five indices earlier mentioned closer to those of the Developed Stock Markets. The following African countries were listed as having stock markets that are emerging: Egypt, Ghana, Kenya, Nigeria, South Africa and Tunisia. Recent data from IFCI fact book confirms the position of these African Stock markets as Emerging.

According to Cerny (2004), a developed stock market for short, is any Stock Market that is known to drive (or influence to a great extent) the activities of other stock markets across the globe. Cerny identified these markets to include the US stock market, the UK stock market and Asian (i.e the Japanese) stock market. He provided evidence that the Asian stock markets opens first, followed by the European stock markets and then the US market. These markets are known to be highly capitalized and very volatile.

In looking at the cause of the global financial crisis of 2007 – 2009 (as it is often referred), Wikipedia.org offers the following explanation: "The **financial crisis of 2007–2009**, often referred to as "the credit crunch" or "credit crisis", began in July 2007 when a loss of confidence by investors in the value of securitized mortgages in the United States resulted in a liquidity crisis that prompted a substantial injection of capital into financial markets by the United States Federal Reserve, Bank of England and the European Central Bank. The TED spread, an indicator of perceived credit risk in the general economy, spiked up in July 2007, remained volatile for a year, then spiked even higher in September 2008, reaching a record 4.65% on October 10, 2008. In September 2008, the crisis deepened, as stock markets world-wide crashed and entered a period of high volatility, and a considerable number of banks, mortgage lenders and insurance companies failed in the following weeks".

2.2 Theoretical Literature

2.2.1 The Vector Autoregressive (VAR) Model

The VAR system rests on the general proposition that economic variables tend to move together over time and also to be autocorrelated (Johnston and DiNardo, 1997). The VAR is commonly used for forecasting systems of interrelated time series and analyzing the dynamic impact of random disturbances on the system of variables. The VAR approach side steps the need for structural modeling by modeling every endogenous variable in the system as a function of the lagged values of all the endogenous variables in the system.

The mathematical form of a VAR is:

$$y_t = A_1 y_{t-1} + \ldots + A_p y_{t-p} + Bx_t + \varepsilon_t \qquad 2.1$$

where y_t is a k vector of endogenous variables, x_t is a d vector of exogenous variables, $A_1,\ldots, A_p$ and B are matrices of coefficients to be estimated, and ε_t is a vector of innovations that may be contemporaneously correlated with their own lagged values and uncorrelated with all of the RHS variables. The VAR model however does not model the influence of current x_t on y_t. it only models the influence of past values of x (i.e lagged values of x) on y.

2.2.2 Autoregressive Distributed Lag (ADL) Model

The ADL model focuses on the relation of a dependent variable y_t on its lagged values and current and lagged values of one or more explanatory variables. The simplest example of an ADL scheme is:

$$y_t = m + \alpha_1 y_{t-1} + \beta_o X_t + \beta_1 X_{t-1} + \varepsilon_t \qquad 2.2$$

Here the current value of y depends on the current and all previous values of x and ε. Alternatively, this relation shows that the current value of x has an effect on the current and future values of y. The ADL (p,q) scheme gives a richer lag structure that still retains the specification of just one explanatory variable:

2.3 Empirical Literature

Kolari and Min (2002), examined the long- run relationship and short-run dynamic among the US, Japanese and 10 Asian stock markets with particular attention to the 1997- 1998 Asian financial crisis. The study employed Vector Auto regression (VAR) technique of the generalized impulse response analysis to estimate short-run dynamic causal linkages across stock markets. The data consist of daily stock index closing prices of two developed stock markets and ten Asian emerging markets (Hong Kong, India, Indonesia, Japan, Korea, Malaysia, Pakistan, Philippines, Singapore, Thailand, Taiwan and US). The sample period is from 2nd January 1995 to 15th May 2001 (i.e 1662 daily observation). The study found that in Asia both long-run cointegration relationships and short run causal linkages among these markets strengthened during the financial crisis than before the crisis. And that these markets have generally been more integrated after the crisis than before the crisis. The study also found that the U.S stock market exerted substantial influence on most Asian stock markets in all three sample periods. They conclude that the degree of integration among countries tends to change overtime, especially around periods marked by financial crises.

In another study, Click and Plummer (2003) examined stock market integration in Indonesia, Malaysia, the Philippines, Singapore and Thailand (these five countries are the original member of the Association of Southeast Asian Nations and now includes Brunei, Cambodia, Laos, Myanmar and Vietnam) in the aftermath of the Asian financial crises. The paper specifically considered whether these five ASEAN countries are cointegrated. Using daily stock index data in local currency from 1st July 1998 through 31st December 2002 (i.e. 1175 observations), the empirical results showed that ASEAN were cointegrated after the Asian financial crisis. And that, the results would be consistent whether daily data or weekly data are used or, analyzed in local currency, the US dollar or the Japanese Yen. This finding brings to focus that such studies could be done using index denominated in local currency or dollar denominated and the findings would still yield very close results.

Marashdeh (2005) examined the linkages among four emerging stock markets in the MENA region (namely Egypt, Turkey, Jordan and Morocco) with developed stock markets represented by the US, UK and Germany stock markets. The study employed monthly stock market data covering 115 months for the period Dec 1994 to June 2004. The stock prices were expressed in local currencies. The Augmented Distributed Lag (ADL) model was adopted to evaluate the impact of these stock markets on one another. Using Egypt as a dependent variable, the study found that U.S and U.K markets have significant influence on the MENA stock markets as well as having a significant long run relationship with the Egyptian stock market. When Turkey was used as a dependent variable, it was found that Egypt and Morocco had a significant influence on Turkey. For Jordan, only Egypt and Turkey had long-run impact on the Jordanian bourse. Lastly for Morocco, the results showed that both Egypt and Turkey have long-run impacts on Morocco. However it was found that the stock market in Turkey affected the stock market in Morocco negatively.

Abraham (2008) examined the fluctuation of prices on the Nigerian stock exchange from 31 December 2007 to 5 September 2008. The focus of the paper was to examine the influence of US stock market (DJIA), Japan (NIKKEI) and South Africa (JSE) on the Nigerian stock exchange (NSE). The study which employed Autoregressive Distributed lag model found that the JSE and the NIKKEI do not significantly explain the variation in the NSI and that the DJIA at lag four positively influenced 3.7 percent of the variation in the NSE. The granger causality test provided evidence of a short run two – way relationship between the NSI and the DJIA. The major strength of the study is that it provides an empirical evidence for the use of the autoregressive distributed lag model in modeling how other stock markets can influence the performance of the Nigerian stock exchange.

This paper therefore builds on the study of Marashdeh (2005) and Abraham (2008) by including Nigeria in the model and extending the sample size over the period of the recent global financial crisis. It further employs cointegration test to examine whether the Nigerian stock exchange is integrated with the selected stock markets.

3 Research Methodology

To conduct this study, secondary data was collected on a 5-day weekly basis for Nigeria's All Share Index along side three emerging stock markets (i.e. Case30-Egypt, Tunindex-Tunisia, and JSE -South Africa); and United States (Dow Jones Industrial Average-DJIA), United Kingdom (FTSE 100) and Japanese stock market (NIKKEI 225), from www.africanfinancialmarkets .com (for Nigeria, Tunisia and Egypt), www.reuters.com (for US,UK and Japan) and www.jse.co.za (for JSE). Other sources of data were from BBC website/news, www.nigerianstockexchange.com, *the Economist* magazine, CNN news and Nigerian dailies. The stock prices were closing prices and were local currency denominated. The five-day weekly data were collected from 10th December 2007 to 3rd April 2009 i.e. a sample size of 345days (or 68weeks). The choice of this sample period was to capture the performance of the Nigerian stock market within the crisis period. And because its index is available on a 5-day trading basis (i.e. Monday's to Friday's), the indices for other stock markets were also collected on a 5-day trading basis.

3.1 Model Specification and Analytical Framework

To carryout the first objective of the study, Autoregressive Distributed Lag (ADL) model adapted from Marashdeh (2005) and Abraham (2008) was employed. The model is specified as follows:

$$NSE_t = C + \alpha_1 NSE_{t-1} + \ldots + \alpha_n NSE_{t-k} + \beta_o JSE_t + \beta_1 JSE_{t-1} + \ldots + \beta_n JSE_{t-k} + \Phi_o TNSE_t + \Phi_1 TNSE_{t-1} + \ldots + \Phi_n TNSE_{t-k} + Þ_o CASE_t + Þ_1 CASE_{t-1} + \ldots + Þ_n CASE_{t-k} + \varepsilon_t \quad \textbf{(3.1)}$$

$$NSE_t = C + \alpha_1 NSE_{t-1} + \ldots + \alpha_n NSE_{t-k} + g_o FTSE_t + g_1 FTSE_{t-1} + \ldots + g_n FTSE_{t-k} + h_o DOW_t + h_1 DOW_{t-1} + \ldots + h_n FTSE_{t-k} + k_o NIKKEI_t + k_1 NIKKEI_{t-1} + \ldots + k_n NIKKEI_{t-k} + \upsilon_t \quad \textbf{(3.2)}$$

Emerging markets = JSE, TNSE and CASE (i.e. S/Africa, Tunisia and Egypt respectively). Developed markets = DOW, FTSE, and NIKKEI (i.e. United States, United Kingdom and Japan respectively). ε_t and υ_t are their residuals respectively. While α_n , $\beta_{n,}$, Φ_n, $Þ_n$, g_n ,h_n and k_n are parameters to be estimated, **m** and **f** represents the intercept (i.e the transformed mean of NSE) of the model. The lag length will be determined by using the Schwartz information criterion.

However, before the above model will be estimated, the series will be logged and tested for stationarity. Were the data are not stationary; they will be differenced to ensure stationarity and the models estimated by using the ordinary least square method.

Granger causality test will also be employed to examine the short run relationship between emerging/developed stock markets and the Nigerian stock exchange.

For the cointegrating relationship among the stock markets, the Augmented Engle Granger (AEG) Cointegration test was employed. The AEG framework begins with testing for stationarity of all the series. Where these series are nonstationary at levels *I*(0), a linear regression is then estimated and the residuals obtained from the regression and tested for stationarity using the Augmented Dickey Fuller (ADF) test. If the residuals are stationary, then cointegrating relationship holds. If otherwise, there will be said to be know cointegration among the variables. Thus the test of this cointegration technique is based on the Augmented Dickey Fuller (ADF) test.

4 Data Analysis and Interpretation

The stationarity test result for the stock market data collected is presented below:

Table 4: Stationarity Test: Augmented Dickey Fuller (ADF) Test				
Level test *I*(0)		Critical Values		
ADF Stat	Bourses	1%	5%	10%
-0.157	Nigeria (NSE)	-3.448	-2.868	-2.571
-1.506	South Africa (JSE)	-3.448	-2.868	-2.571
-0.297	Tunisia (TUNINDEX)	-3.448	-2.868	-2.571
-0.902	Egypt (CASE30)	-3.448	-2.868	-2.571
-1.2126	United States (DOW JONES)	-3.448	-2.868	-2.571
-1.5533	United Kingdom (FTSE 100)	-3.448	-2.868	-2.571
-1.5108	Japan (NIKKEI 225)	-3.448	-2.868	-2.571
First Difference Test *I*(1)				
-12.129	Nigeria (NSE)	-3.448	-2.868	-2.571
-22.633	South Africa (JSE)	-3.448	-2.868	-2.571
-18.626	Tunisia (TUNINDEX)	-3.448	-2.868	-2.571
-16.859	Egypt (CASE30)	-3.448	-2.868	-2.571
-21.0315	United States (DOW JONES)	-3.448	-2.868	-2.571
-21.904	United Kingdom (FTSE 100)	-3.448	-2.868	-2.571
-21.125	Japan (NIKKEI 225)	-3.448	-2.868	-2.571

Source: Eviews Output

The upper part of the table shows that the critical ADF values are greater than the ADF statistic. This implies that the variables are not stationary at levels. The lower part of the table shows the ADF result at first difference i.e. *I*(1). The result shows that all the variables become stationary after taken first difference.

4.1 Impact of Emerging Stock Markets on the NSE

To determine the extent to which emerging and developed stock markets influences the performance of the NSE, the ADL model is applied.

For the emerging markets, the estimation of the impact of Emerging Stock markets on the NSE showed that only the South African stock market (JSE) at lag 4 significantly explained the variation in the NSE (but significant only at 10% level). The R^2 Adjusted was found to be 23.01% and the DW statistics value of 1.99 showed no evidence of autocorrelation. The Eviews result is presented below:

Table 4.1(a): ADL Model of Emerging Stock markets on the NSE: Estimated (3.1)

Dependent Variable: NSE
Method: Least Squares
Date: 03/20/10 Time: 13:18
Sample(adjusted): 12/18/2007 7/03/2009
Included observations: 404 after adjusting endpoints

Variable	Coefficient	Std. Error	t-Statistic	Prob.
C	-0.000288	0.000307	-0.935506	0.3501
NSE(-1)	0.404429	0.051146	7.907418	0.0000
NSE(-2)	0.180834	0.054909	3.293357	0.0011
NSE(-3)	-0.092233	0.055453	-1.663275	0.0971
NSE(-4)	-0.044173	0.054812	-0.805906	0.4208
NSE(-5)	0.032778	0.050868	0.644375	0.5197
JSE	0.032542	0.030310	1.073640	0.2837
JSE(-1)	-0.005180	0.031675	-0.163532	0.8702
JSE(-2)	-0.009355	0.031498	-0.297020	0.7666
JSE(-3)	-0.023175	0.031511	-0.735471	0.4625
JSE(-4)	0.054474	0.031581	1.724923	0.0854
JSE(-5)	-0.028414	0.031395	-0.905031	0.3660
TUN	-0.007311	0.092742	-0.078830	0.9372
TUN(-1)	-0.023367	0.091811	-0.254511	0.7992
TUN(-2)	-0.060879	0.092949	-0.654973	0.5129
TUN(-3)	0.068900	0.093027	0.740639	0.4594
TUN(-4)	-0.085247	0.093340	-0.913293	0.3617
TUN(-5)	0.098871	0.091377	1.082022	0.2799
CASE	0.028367	0.029993	0.945808	0.3448
CASE(-1)	0.035054	0.030380	1.153833	0.2493
CASE(-2)	0.023985	0.030189	0.794485	0.4274
CASE(-3)	-0.011139	0.030189	-0.368973	0.7124
CASE(-4)	0.042861	0.030005	1.428463	0.1540
CASE(-5)	0.042664	0.029056	1.468305	0.1428

R-squared	0.279497	Mean dependent var	-0.000751
Adjusted R-squared	0.235887	S.D. dependent var	0.006613
S.E. of regression	0.005781	Akaike info criterion	-7.410919
Sum squared resid	0.012699	Schwarz criterion	-7.173212
Log likelihood	1521.006	F-statistic	6.409085
Durbin-Watson stat	1.999633	Prob(F-statistic)	0.000000

Source: Eviews Output

The model was then re-estimated (after excluding insignificant variables). The R^2 Adjusted improved to 24.03%. The JSE index then became significant at 5% level, while the DW value of 1.97 confirmed that there was no serial correlation among the residual of the independent variables. Generally, the F-stat was found to be 43.59 with a probability value of 0.000. This implied that information spilling out of the South African stock market significantly and positively explains current variation of NSE. The re-estimated model is shown below:

Table 4.1(b) Reduced ADL Model of Emerging Stock markets on the NSE

Dependent Variable: NSE
Method: Least Squares
Date: 03/20/10 Time: 12:23
Sample(adjusted): 12/17/2007 7/03/2009
Included observations: 405 after adjusting endpoints

Variable	Coefficient	Std. Error	t-Statistic	Prob.
C	-0.000322	0.000289	-1.116169	0.2650
NSE(-1)	0.402183	0.049103	8.190556	0.0000
NSE(-2)	0.143536	0.049125	2.921857	0.0037
JSE(-4)	0.064184	0.028262	2.271028	0.0237

R-squared	0.245945	Mean dependent var	-0.000749
Adjusted R-squared	0.240303	S.D. dependent var	0.006605
S.E. of regression	0.005757	Akaike info criterion	-7.466906
Sum squared resid	0.013291	Schwarz criterion	-7.427361
Log likelihood	1516.048	F-statistic	43.59704
Durbin-Watson stat	1.970361	Prob(F-statistic)	0.000000

Source: Eviews Output

4.1.1 Granger Causality Test

When Granger causality test was performed, it was confirmed that the JSE had unidirectional granger causality with the NSE in the short run. The Egyptian stock market was also found to have unidirectional granger causality with the NSE in the short run. The granger causality result is presented below:

Table 4.1(c): Granger Causality Test for NSE VS Emerging Markets

Pairwise Granger Causality Tests			
Date: 03/20/10 Time: 12:34			
Sample: 12/10/2007 7/03/2009			
Lags: 2			
Null Hypothesis:	Obs	F-Statistic	Probability
JSE does not Granger Cause NSE	408	5.92134	0.00292
NSE does not Granger Cause JSE		0.59667	0.55113
TUN does not Granger Cause NSE	408	0.06277	0.93917
NSE does not Granger Cause TUN		0.52485	0.59205
CASE does not Granger Cause NSE	408	10.8633	1.5E-05
NSE does not Granger Cause CASE		0.73594	0.17546

Source: Eviews Output

4.1.2 Cointegration Test

When tested for cointegration using the Augmented Engle Granger cointegration test, it was found that the NSE had no long run relationship with the selected African stock markets. This suggests that the NSE is not integrated with the selected emerging stock markets in Africa. This was because the ADF test statistic value of 1.943 (taking absolute value), was not significant at the 1% Mackinnon critical value. The Augmented Dickey Fuller test result used for this analysis is presented below:

Table 4. 1.(d): ADF Result to ascertain Cointegration between the NSE and the selected Emerging Stock Markets

ADF Test Statistic	-1.850726	1% Critical Value*	-3.4484
		5% Critical Value	-2.8688
		10% Critical Value	-2.5706
*MacKinnon critical values for rejection of hypothesis of a unit root.			

Source: Eviews Output

The AEG cointegration was also performed at country specific levels and was found that the NSE had no cointegrating relationship with the JSE, Tunisia and Egypt. Their respective ADF test statistic values were -2.409, -0.7193 and -1.2191 against the critical values -3.4484 (at 1%), -2.8688 (at 5%) and -2.5706 (at 10%). These results clearly indicate that African stock markets are not integrated. Thus going by the granger causality estimation, it can be said that the impact of the JSE on the NSE is short termed and might not be sustained in the long run. The trend showing the movement in stock market index for the NSE and the selected African Emerging stock markets is presented below:

Figure 1:

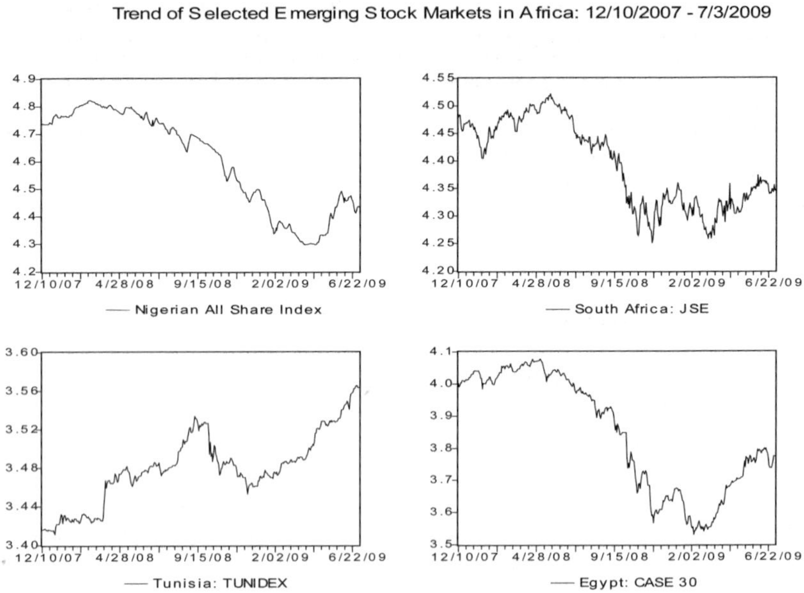

Source: Own Presentation

4.2 Impact of Developed Stock Markets on the NSE

The estimation for the impact of the developed markets (when lagged to 5) on the Nigerian Stock Market; showed that NSE_{t-1}, NSE_{t-2}, $FTSE_t$, DOW_{t-3}, $NIKKEI_{t-2}$ and $NIKKEI_{t-3}$ significantly explain part of the present variation of NSE going by their individual t-statistics. This result is presented in table 4.2 below:

Table (4.2): ADL Model for Developed Stock Markets on the NSE: Estimated (3.2)

Dependent Variable: NSE
Method: Least Squares
Date: 03/20/10 Time: 13:16
Sample(adjusted): 12/18/2007 7/03/2009
Included observations: 404 after adjusting endpoints

Variable	Coefficient	Std. Error	t-Statistic	Prob.
C	-0.000350	0.000296	-1.184759	0.2369
NSE(-1)	0.389690	0.051248	7.603976	0.0000
NSE(-2)	0.212275	0.054954	3.862769	0.0001
NSE(-3)	-0.083306	0.055821	-1.492362	0.1364
NSE(-4)	-0.050113	0.055269	-0.906713	0.3651
NSE(-5)	0.049027	0.051118	0.959085	0.3381
FTSE	0.112221	0.049956	2.246387	0.0253
FTSE(-1)	0.009234	0.054299	0.170052	0.8651
FTSE(-2)	-0.022001	0.054318	-0.405041	0.6857
FTSE(-3)	0.000935	0.054552	0.017140	0.9863
FTSE(-4)	0.024995	0.053936	0.463423	0.6433
FTSE(-5)	0.002164	0.051113	0.042332	0.9663
DOW	-0.036070	0.051212	-0.704324	0.4817
DOW(-1)	-0.021434	0.055099	-0.389008	0.6975
DOW(-2)	-0.072384	0.057039	-1.269041	0.2052
DOW(-3)	-0.127833	0.058354	-2.190625	0.0291
DOW(-4)	-0.104448	0.057427	-1.818784	0.0697
DOW(-5)	-0.035331	0.054715	-0.645724	0.5188
NIKKEI	-0.004619	0.038273	-0.120675	0.9040
NIKKEI(-1)	0.026801	0.041201	0.650495	0.5158
NIKKEI(-2)	0.118853	0.041776	2.844998	0.0047
NIKKEI(-3)	0.107149	0.041716	2.568544	0.0106
NIKKEI(-4)	0.044496	0.040424	1.100718	0.2717
NIKKEI(-5)	0.036578	0.032386	1.129428	0.2594

R-squared	0.286357	Mean dependent var	-0.000751
Adjusted R-squared	0.243163	S.D. dependent var	0.006613
S.E. of regression	0.005753	Akaike info criterion	-7.420487
Sum squared resid	0.012579	Schwarz criterion	-7.182779
Log likelihood	1522.938	F-statistic	6.629530
Durbin-Watson stat	2.004309	Prob(F-statistic)	0.000000

Source: Eviews Output

The model was then re-estimated after dropping the insignificant variables. The adjusted R-Squared then improved from 24.3% to 25.2%. The re-estimated model is presented below:

Table (4.2a) Reduced ADL Model of the Developed Stock markets on the NSE

Dependent Variable: NSE
Method: Least Squares
Date: 03/20/10 Time: 13:23
Sample(adjusted): 12/14/2007 7/03/2009
Included observations: 406 after adjusting endpoints

Variable	Coefficient	Std. Error	t-Statistic	Prob.
C	-0.000276	0.000287	-0.963161	0.3361
NSE(-1)	0.394865	0.048802	8.091140	0.0000
NSE(-2)	0.164082	0.048904	3.355171	0.0009
FTSE	0.080215	0.030871	2.598423	0.0097
DOW(-3)	-0.084127	0.041328	-2.035627	0.0424
NIKKEI(-2)	0.069592	0.030388	2.290150	0.0225
NIKKEI(-3)	0.064479	0.029183	2.209471	0.0277

R-squared	0.263086	Mean dependent var	-0.000747
Adjusted R-squared	0.252005	S.D. dependent var	0.006597
S.E. of regression	0.005706	Akaike info criterion	-7.477606
Sum squared resid	0.012990	Schwarz criterion	-7.408531
Log likelihood	1524.954	F-statistic	23.74125
Durbin-Watson stat	1.990492	Prob(F-statistic)	0.000000

Source: Eviews Output

The model showed that the Nigerian stock exchange responds positively to changes in the FTSE and NIKKEI stock market indices, while in responds negatively to the US stock market. The adjusted R-square of 25.2% implies that the present performance of the Nigerian stock market can is partly explained by it's on past values, the current value of the FTSE index, and the Nikkei index at lags 2 and 5. The US stock market index however (i.e. the Dow Jones) had a negative impact on the Nigerian stock exchange implying that both markets might be responding to different factors. The result was significant at 1, 5 and 10% critical values and the Durbin Watson statistic of 1.99, shows that there is no autocorrelation problem in the model.

4.2.1 Granger Causality

To see the direction of short run influence of the developed stock markets on the Nigerian stock exchange, the granger causality test was also employed. The Eviews output is presented below:

Table 4.2b: Pairwise Granger Causality Tests For NSE VS Developed Markets

Sample: 12/10/2007 7/03/2009

Lags: 2

Null Hypothesis:	Obs	F-Statistic	Prob.
FTSE does not Granger Cause NSE	408	9.24514	0.00012
NSE does not Granger Cause FTSE		0.68555	0.50440
DOW does not Granger Cause NSE	408	9.04478	0.00014
NSE does not Granger Cause DOW		0.95659	0.38507
NIKKEI does not Granger Cause NSE	408	10.0585	5.5E-05
NSE does not Granger Cause NIKKEI		0.03071	0.96976

Source: Eviews Output

For all the developed stock markets, it was found that they had a unidirectional influence on the NSE. That is, in the short run, it is the developed that markets that influences the performance of the NSE and not the other way round. These results were significant at 1, 5 and 10% critical values.

4.2.2 Cointegration Test

The ADF test for the long run relationship connecting the Nigerian stock exchange and the developed stock markets is presented below:

Table 4.2.c: ADF Test for Cointegration between NSE and Developed Markets

ADF Test Statistic	-4.965624	1% Critical Value*	-3.4484
		5% Critical Value	-2.8688
		10% Critical Value	-2.5706
*MacKinnon critical values for rejection of hypothesis of a unit root.			

Source: Eviews Output

Since the ADF test statistic value of 4.96 is greater than the 1% critical (Mackinnon) value of 3.44, it can be drawn that the Nigerian stock exchange and the selected developed stock markets are integrated. Thus, the developed stock markets are more likely to influence the performance of the Nigerian stock market than the emerging African stock market would.

The trend showing the movement in stock market index for the NSE and the selected developed stock markets is presented below:

Figure 2:

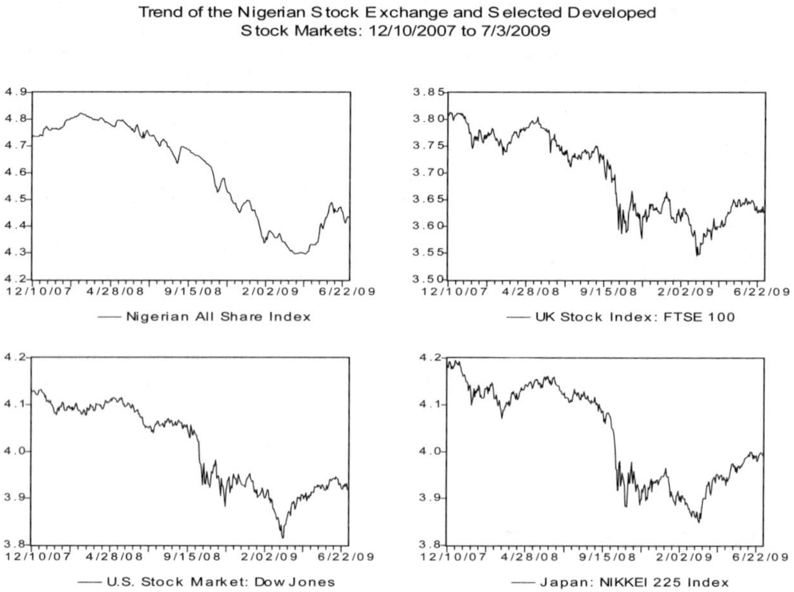

Source: Own Presentation

5 Summary and Conclusions

The recent global economic melt down has adverse effect on national economies brought about by the inter linkages of markets. The literature suggests that, as a subset of the financial market, the stock market can be a source of contagion. This study evaluated the impact of emerging and developed stock markets on the Nigerian stock market. The aim was to suggest the pattern of integration that would minimize shocks to the Nigerian economy through the stock market.

The Autoregressive Distributed Lag (ADL) model was applied to estimate the impact of the emerging and developed stock markets on the Nigerian stock market. For the emerging markets it was found that the South African stock market (JSE) positively influenced the Nigerian stock market significantly at lag 4. Though the model had a general goodness of fit, the Egyptian (CASE 30) and Tunisian (TUNINDEX) markets were not significant at their individual t-statistics level. The granger causality result also confirmed that the JSE influenced the NSE in the short run. Granger evidence running from the Egyptian stock market to the Nigerian stock exchange was also found. When tested for cointegration however, it was found that the Nigerian stock market was not cointegrated with the selected emerging stock markets from Africa.

For the developed stock markets, it was found that they significantly explained variation of the Nigerian stock market at varying lag length and signs. While the UK stock market (FTSE 100) was found to influence the performance of the Nigerian stock exchange at lag 0, the Japanese stock market index (Nikkei 225), was found to influence the performance of the Nigerian stock exchange at lags 2 and 3. Both the FTSE and the NIKKEI bourses however, had a positive impact on the performance of the Nigerian Stock exchange. The US stock market however, was negatively related to the Nigerian stock market at lag 3. The granger causality test then showed that, in the short run, all the selected developed stock markets used, had unidirectional causality with the Nigerian stock exchange. This means that the Nigerian stock exchange would in the short run respond to the FTSE, DOW and NIKKEI stock indices, but not the other way round. When tested for cointegration, it was found that the Nigerian stock exchange was cointegrated with the developed stock markets.

In conclusion, the short run and cointegrating relationship connecting the Nigerian stock exchange with the developed stock markets is a link for these markets to impact on the performance of the NSE in crisis times. However, the NSE could also benefit from these markets in times of market recovery and positive externalities. Thus, increased stock market integration should be pursued among African stock markets; so as to reap the benefits of stock market integration within the continent.

References

Abraham, Terfa Williams (2008) "An Econometric Investigation of the Fluctuation of Prices on the Nigerian Stock Exchange". *Journal of Marketing Management Ahmadu Bello University Zaria* Vol. 2 No. 1

Cerny, Alexandr (2004). "Stock Market Integration and the speed of information Transmission". *Charles University CERGE-EI, Czech Republic, Prague CERGE-EI, politickych veznu 7, III 12Working paper series , electronic version 242pages 1 – 27*

Click, Reid and Plummer, Micheal (2003). Stock market integration in ASEAN after the financial crisis. Working paper series Vol. 2003 – 2006.

Collins, Daryl and Biekpe, Nicholas (2004). Contagion: A fear for African Equity Markets? The African Capital Markets Forum Contemporary issues Vol. II pages 198 - 209

Johnston, Jack and DiNardo John (1997). "*Econometric Methods*". *4th* Edition McGraw Hill publications,NewYork, pages 244 - 280

Marashdeh, Hazem (2005). 'Stock Market Integration in the MENA Region: An Application of the ARDL Bounds testing Approach'. *Faculty of Commerce-Economics working paper, university of Wollongong.* http://ro.uow.edu.au/commwkpapers/133 pages 1 - 14

Stiglitz, Joseph (2002). "*Globalization and its discontents*". The penguin press, London

Yang, Jian; Kolari, James and Min, Insik (2002). Stock market integration and financial crisis: the case of Asia. Applied Financial Economics Journal (Google search).

Implications of the Global Financial Crisis on Health and Education Sectors in Nigeria

Abigail Ngozi Alio[1]

Abstract

The global financial crisis evolved from the bursting of the speculative bubble in the US housing market as well as the failure of regulation and lacking adherence to strict corporate governance principles in the United States of America. The world economy is greatly interdependent on each other, and is to a large extent - at the macro level - directed by the most advanced countries of the world which United States of America represents. The global financial crisis was transmitted to the economies of the developing countries (for example Nigeria) primarily through the financial capital market and especially through the real economy sectors. This paper presents the implications of the global financial crisis (GFC) on health and education in Nigeria. It discusses the impacts, the government's responses, the reforms, and the policy issues with regard to the education and health sectors in Nigeria. The paper highlighted the reasons for the meltdown. The analysis of the implications of global financial crisis on these key development sectors of Nigeria will help the government of Nigeria to be apprehensive of a re-occurrence of such a crisis. The findings of this paper will help Nigeria to guard itself better against future crises.

1 Introduction

Financial crisis can lead to recession or downturn in a nation's economic activities. The consequences of the downturn negatively impact on institutions, agencies and human elements. When the phenomenon occurs, the so-

[1] Dr. (MRS) Abigail Ngozi Alio, Department of Technology and Vocational Education, Enugu State University of Science ad Technology (ESUT), Enugu, Nigeria, Email: abygalio@yahoo.com

ciety suffers tremendously with all sorts of setbacks especially in human health and in education. It is worthy to note that health is a state of complete physical, mental and social well-being and not merely the absence of diseases and infirmity (Eneh, 2004). The meaning of health may be viewed in many contexts – historical, cultural, social, philosophical, and spiritual. These meanings are sometimes contradictory and sometimes overlapping. Health as a concept relates to all aspects of people's lives from physical well-being to social interactions, mental and emotional capacities, and even people's spiritual lives (Achalu, 2001).

Education is a process of teaching, training and learning, especially in schools or colleges, to improve knowledge and to develop skills (Hornby, 2004). It is a known fact that no nation can achieve meaningful development without human capital development (Nwajinka and Odogo, 2010). Education has been a driving force or tool for any type of development. That is why nations all over the world articulate policies and strategies for a strong and sustainable education system as the base for the much needed human capital and economic development.

The world economy is greatly interdependent and to a large extent at the macro level directed by the most advanced countries of the world which the United States of America represents. In other words, when there is any downturn/crisis in the United States of America, most developing counties, which Nigeria represents, are adversely hit by the uncontrolled spiral effects due to over-dependency of developing countries.

The current global financial crisis started in America's sub-prime mortgage market and later snowballed into a full scale global economic recession. The main cause of the financial disaster is believed to be the sub-prime' loans which were risky mortgage loans given to borrowers with unstable incomes or low credit worthiness who do not meet the usual criteria for lending. Such loans were given relying on the value of the collateral which in this case was the property under the mortgage.

This lending process was adequate at the time because there was a boom in the property market and it was regarded as a safe heaven by lenders since the realization of the collateral through a forced sale was easy. The said loans were given out as floating interest rate loans during the low interest rate regime. Both lenders (financial institutions) and the borrowers (households) did not see any problem in the business transaction since the monthly repayment was small enough for the borrowers to cope with. However, the Federal Reserve Bank (the US Central Bank) increased the lending rate in the country, in line with the country's monetary policy. With the US interest rate rising, the monthly installments to be paid to the banks also increased. Higher monthly installments had hit the sub-prime borrowers hard and they defaulted (Odikenmelu 2010).

Odikenmelu (2010) also noted that the housing market of the US started to feel the pain of high interest rates between 2004 and 2006, which had risen sharply resulting in an unprecedented rate of default on sub-prime loans. As more and more borrowers started defaulting, this created panic within the lending institutions and they quickly tried to get out of the bad loan situation by selling the property hitherto used as collateral for mortgage loans.

This drastically forced the prices of the property downward as the supplies far outweighed the demand. Returns from the mortgage loan repayment usually made to the institutional investors around the globe stopped, leading to huge losses. It is very important, and needing an immediate attention to note, that although the loans originated in the USA by a complex method of sophisticated securitization based on globalization strategies, the assets were held by institutions in Europe, Asia, and even at a minor scale in Africa who had also become investors in the US markets.

The financial crisis has continued to spread and to deepen in several countries, including Nigeria, this resulting into economic shocks, bank failures in the US and in Europe, declines in various stock indexes, a large reduction in the market value of equities and commodities, as well as large-scale job losses and unemployment.

This paper therefore adopts a research design which focuses on determining the impacts of the global financial crisis (GFC) on the economy, especially on the health and education sectors in Nigeria. Government responses to the GFC are also discussed. Reforms and initiatives that can mitigate the effects of the GFC on health and education are also highlighted. Conclusions and policy recommendations are also made. Section 2 is on the impacts of the GFC on the economy and the government responses in Nigeria. Section 3 is on the impacts of the GFC on the Nigerian health sector and the policy initiatives to mitigate the effects. Section 4 is on the impacts of the GFC on the education sector and the policy initiatives to mitigate the effects. Section 5 presents Conclusions and Policy Recommendations.

2 Impact of the GFC on the Economy of Nigeria and Government Responses to the Crisis

2.1 Impact of the GFC on the Economy of Nigeria

The world is becoming a global village due to the dynamics of technology and the enhanced communication system. When the US markets were over-saturated with a high debt burden the impact of the recession was drastically felt in Nigeria which has a mono-product source of revenue. Nigeria is to 90% dependent on oil revenue, and therefore was greatly exposed to external shocks resulting from the price crash/burst in the international oil market due to the financial meltdown. There was a sharp decline in export volumes. Demand for oil in the international market fell drastically from $7.3 billion in March 2008 to $ 3 billion in February 2009 for Nigeria. There was a steep fall in commodity prices, and a drastically reduced inflow of foreign capital and remittances also occurred (Ajakaiye, Fakiyesi and Oyinlola, 2009)

The first noticeable impacts of the recession in Nigeria were with regard of market capitalization, which fell by 45.8% in 2008, and the decline of the crude oil price from US $147 per barrel in July 2008 to $ 47 per barrel in January 2009, leading to a decline in external reserves and hence accruable revenue (Oyesola, 2010). Ajakaiye, Fakiyesi and Oyinlola (2009) reported that Nigeria's debt profile also deteriorated, and that foreign portfolio investors withdrew over $15 billion. The remittances and the official development assistance (ODA) fell greatly in 2009.

The exchange rate which was N 116/118 to a dollar went up to N160 per dollar (Odikenmelu, 2010). The exchange rate also affected the prices of goods and services since Nigeria is an import-dependent country. Consequently, there occurred a ripple effect on other sectors such as transport, health, education, etc.

The dwindling foreign exchange earnings led to reduced budgetary allocation to all tiers of government and sectors. The effect is such that cost of transportation, energy, and health care increased abruptly.

2.2 Government Responses to the GFC in Nigeria

The official response of the government to the crisis was slow (Ajakaiye et al. 2009). Oyesola (2010) noted that, although the global financial crisis has affected both poor and rich nations, the severity of the impact on individual countries will vary according to their economic, social, political settings.

Sensing the panic mood in Nigeria shortly after the financial crisis erupted in the United States of America, and having widespread social and economic effects around the globe, the then Governor of the Central Bank of Nigeria (CBN) Charles Soludo proclaimed that the Nigerian economy, because of its low integration into the global economy, would not suffer serious adverse impacts. He then started reassuring the public that all Nigerian banks were safe, and he promised that the CBN would do whatever that was necessary to keep the banks healthy. Soludo's early optimism was dictated by the view that economies without developed financial markets or only with rudimentary financial markets, which are connected or linked with the global economy, are less likely to suffer from impacts of the financial crisis. However, everyone in Nigeria knows that he (Soludo) wanted to be positive and optimistic just because of the fact that any indication of expressing doubts about the health of the banking sector would have triggered off a serious national panic. The leaders have however started to sing a different song as they have realized that the society would not escape unharmed by the global financial crisis because Nigeria is part of the global economy.

In order to survive the financial stress, the federal government of Nigeria (FGN) put in place some of the policy measures to reduce the problems of the global financial crisis in Nigeria, thus - reduction in the monetary policy rate (MPR) from 10.25% to 9.75%, reduction in the cash reserve requirement (CRR) for banks from 4% to 2%, and cutting the liquidity ratio from 40% to 30%. In addition, the CBN has given a directive to banks that they have the option to restructure the already crystallized margin of loans up to 2009, and that inter-bank lending facilities to banks are expanded and extended up to 360 days. The discount window facilities were expanded.

According to the CBN, all the above policy adjustments were designed to inject about N150 billion into the system and to improve the liquidity situation in the economy. All the above measures are part of government's initiatives to forestall any unforeseen development in view of the high degree of uncertainty believed to be emanating from the international financial markets. The rules and regulations above are an attempt to expand liquidity to counteract any contractionary implications of the global financial crisis on domestic economy, while at the same time introducing more regulation on financial markets and tightening the conditions for operations in the capital market (Ajakaiye and Fakiyesi, 2009).

In order to discourage corruption in financial institutions and in the capital market, CBN has reduced the interest rate of fixed deposits from 2.5% to 0.5% in order to discourage dumping huge amounts of money into the banks. The Federal Government of Nigeria (FGN) wants to encourage people to put their money into business instead of putting their money into the banks. So lowering the interest rate should stimulate business activities.

3. The Impact of the GFC on the Nigerian Health Sector and the Policy Initiatives in the Health Sector to Mitigate the Effects

3.1 The Impact of GFC on Nigerian Health Sector

The Human Development Index (HDI) is a composite measure of three dimensions of human development - living a long and healthy life (measured by expectancy), being educated (measured by adult literacy and enrolment at primary, secondary and tertiary level), and having a decent standard of living (measured by purchasing power income). It has not shown any remarkable improvement since 1970 for Nigeria (Ajakaiye, Fakiyesi and Oyinlola, 2009). The human development index for Nigeria stood at 0.499 in 2006 which gave the country a rank of 158 out of 177 countries. Ghana has a HDI of 0.553, ranked in position 135 and therefore classified as a medium HDI country (higher than 0.50). The paper also noted that Nigeria has a poverty profile as captured by the human poverty index for developing countries.

This suggests that the living conditions of Nigerians were deplorable even before the occurrence of the GFC. Hurley and Schlaadt (1992) argue that "wellness" is an approach to personal health that emphasizes individual responsibility for well-being through the practice of health-promoting life style behavior. According to the authors, wellness can be referred to as a process of moving towards optimal health.

The impact of the GFC on health can be analyzed based on the national health policy issues, thus:

Health Status

The definition of health denotes that the majority of Nigerians are not living in healthy conditions. The most vulnerable in society were the worst hit with respect to the global financial crisis. The financial crisis led to even lower levels of economic activity in the economy, especially in the informal sector where most of the vulnerable groups conduct their economic transactions. People find it difficult to eat three times in a day. A vast majority of the people are mere walking corpses. Obi (2009) argues that every year about 60,000 women die during pregnancy and child birth. 70% of these deaths are preventable; many Nigerian women are ignorant and cannot afford antenatal care and so develop complications that could have been prevented.

In Nigeria, people die of minor diseases that could have been prevented with simple medications and a healthy lifestyle (Acho, 2005). The ripple effect of the global financial crisis gives rise to the state of ill health, poor sanitation or poor sanitary conditions, a debilitating environment where bacteria in their millions co-habit with human beings as if that is the norm, illiteracy, and a poor economic status.

Pharmaceutical and Medical Supplies

Although remarkable progress has been made with regard to pharmaceutical and medical supplies, fake, substandard, adulterated and unregistered drugs are still prevalent in Nigerian markets. Due to the GFC, the Nigerian pharmaceutical drugs producing companies lack adequate foreign exchange to import quality chemicals to produce high quality drugs. Even those who import drugs from foreign pharmaceutical manufacturers do specify lower quality drugs for Nigeria to enable them to make more profit in their business in Nigeria.

Many people lost their job as a result of the GFC, and instead of staying idle they entered into the drug production market and started to produce fake drugs. The federal government has set up some agencies in a bid to fight against fake, substandard, adulterated, unregistered, and illicit drugs. The agencies are the National Agency for Food and Drug Administration and Control (NAFDAC), which was established in January 1994. This agency was established in order to control the quality of drug production, food production and their administration. The National Drug Law Enforcement Agency (NDLEA) was earlier established - in 1989. This agency is responsible to fight against drug trafficking and faking. These agencies are trying to fight these developments but the war is in the verge of collapsing due to funding and operational problems of the agencies. Some programmes or agencies rely on funds from offshore financers to fund mega projects such as the struggle to sustain the anti drugs war, but problems are the poor motivation of officers, out dated weapons to respond, a tax command and control structure, criminal conspiracy, and connivance with drug barons by top ranking officials. They have all combined to whittle down the performance of the anti drugs agencies. With the crisis, meeting up the challenges is an uphill task.

The Nigeria Health Care System (HCS) is known for the erratic supply and non-availability of essential drugs and related materials. The out of stock syndrome exposes the consumers of the HCS to the risk of fake and substandard drugs seen all over the country which have a negative impact in the treatment of the individual and also pose a great threat to the lives of the populace. The GFC gave rise to high prices of quality drugs as a result of the lack of adequate foreign exchange to procure them.

Primary Health Care

Primary Health Care (PHC) is in shamble, and this should not be the case in a nation so greatly endowed as Nigeria. Consequently the frightening statistics on the health status indicators show that Nigeria's people do not benefit from constitutional provisions. There is conflict of roles by the various tiers of government as to who should be responsible for the funding and running of the PHC system. Primary health care supposedly is the bedrock of the nation's healthcare system. The GFC brought a reduction in the allocation to the health sector. Consequently, funding and maintaining the PHC facilities and programmes became a big problem. Most of the laudable initiatives made by the government to address issues that border on the health status of the nation at the grass root level, like free maternal and child health services and the national programme on immunization to mention a few, have been discarded as they lack funds to run the programmes. Hence, the current state of the PHC, lacking adequate personnel in quality and quantity, essential drugs, facilities and infrastructures, is serious. This has resulted in a deterioration of the health status of the nation. According to the constitution, it is the responsibility of the local government to manage the PHC, though they may not have the capacity at this level of government to perform this role. However, if the available funds are utilized and prioritized in a better way the state of health can be improved to provide health care services that are needed at the grass root level.

Health Service Delivery and Quality

The crisis exposes Nigerians to poor health service delivery and quality. Health care services are activities geared towards the provision of a comprehensive package of integrated care to the beneficiaries at primary-local government level, secondary-state government level, and tertiary- national/federal government level. It is worthy to note that health care services in Nigeria are provided by a multiplicity of health care providers – public, private, for profit and not for profit, pharmacies, patent medicine vendors, and the traditional health care providers. Nigeria relies on several foreign grants and on funding from developed countries to complement public spending on education, health care delivery, and transportation amongst others. The crisis has resulted in a squeeze on grants to Nigeria as donor countries themselves are struggling to contain the crisis. Limited coverage of basic health services can contribute significantly to poor health outcomes.

Supplies of services in the health facilities are limited and vary across the zones - with 31% - 87% for women antenatal clinics (ANCs), 84% – 73% delivery for health facilities across the zones, and 0.5% - 90% for the PHC facilities providing immunization services in the North, West, South-West and South East zones (WHO, 2009). Capacity to provide basic emergency obstetric services remains very limited as only 20% have the capacity (WHO, 2009). Most services provided by private and public facilities are clinics that have a minimal outreach and are home based and community based services. The major sources of worry are the emergency health care situation, the dependency of the state of Nigeria on Medicare, and the rising incidence of wrong diagnoses. Many have lost their lives under circumstances occasioned by poor diagnostic management and by inadequate facilities (Obi, 2009). For effective treatment to take place, efficient laboratory tests are needed by doctors.

Health Finance

In 2001 at a special session of the OAU in Abuja, African leaders recommended the allocation of 15% of the total national budget to health. Nigeria committed to this percentage between 1999 and 2008. Ugwuoke (2008) argues that the quality of health care coverage depends on the national income and the total government budget allocation to health. Unfortunately, Nigeria with a rather high gross national income relative to other countries in West Africa has recorded the lowest health expenditures. The poverty level is a major factor responsible for individual and household decision making in the utilization of health services. Oyesola (2010) observed that the GFC has become a major concern for high, middle, and low income earners and even for the political leaders in Nigeria. The paper noted that Nigeria is not just an underdeveloped nation but it is classified as one of the poorest nations of the world. Poor utilization of modern health services resulting in poor health outcomes of the citizenry is not so much influenced by lack of knowledge and negative perceptions but by the high cost of health services and the high cost of drugs, factors further intensified by the GFC. Even travels to overseas for visiting health facilities are now affected by the GFC. Health care financing in Nigeria is based on a combination of different sources. The sources comprise federal government budgetary allocation, funding from state and local non-government organizations (NGOs), grants from donor countries, and most importantly private out of the pocket expenditure. The implication of the GFC is such that financing of health care in Nigeria was scaled down as resources were channeled to measures to rescue the economy.

3.2 Policy Initiatives aimed at Reducing the Negative Impact of the GFC on the Health Sector in Nigeria

Poverty is the central problem in Nigeria (Njoku, 2005). The challenge governments face include how to reduce the pervading poverty and the high and growing unemployment. Unemployment has worsened with the retrenchment of staff arising from the public sector reforms at different levels of government.

In an effort for Nigeria to achieve the Millennium Development Goals (MDGs), the National Economic Empowerment and Development Strategy (NEEDS), the State Economic Empowerment Development Strategy (SEEDS), and the Local Economic Empowerment Strategy (LEEDS) were launched. Development partners, like WB/World Bank, WHO, ILO etc., have been helping Nigeria to tackle the problem of poverty incidence. The objectives of the programmes of reform undertaken under NEEDS, SEEDS and LEEDS include:

- helping households and communities to sustain their livelihoods in the face of economic, political environmental, health or others shocks as well as reducing the likelihood of such shocks occurring;
- contribute to equality through (a) promoting levels of livelihood sufficiently to ensure enhanced equality of opportunity by allowing all households to achieve basic education for their children, as well as

standards of health and nutrient being necessary for human development, and (b) raising the level of consumption and livelihood of the poorest;

- promote growth through (a) ensuring a skilled productive workforce, (b) reinforcing values of social solidarity, thereby contributing to levels of social cohesion being necessary for long-term economic development, and (c) providing an environment where individuals and households are able to adapt and to change livelihood strategies without fear of calamity should such strategies fail.

Some specific programmes are discussed now in detail:

National Health Insurance Scheme

The National Health Insurance Scheme (NHIS) was launched in 2005 with the aim to improve access to healthcare for the majority of the Nigerians. The NHIS, as conceived, was meant to bridge an existing gap and to give wider opportunities for access to qualitative health care with strong private sector participation, and with government defining the policy and the framework. Abati (2010) argues that the NHIS was initiated with the aim to improve Nigeria's health indicators. Five years after the inception of the NHIS scheme, the program failed to deliver, and really nothing has improved. The poverty index has risen and the country's health indicators have not improved (Abati, 2010).

Currently, some of the providers under the NHIS have been suspended, except those integrated into the community health programmes for maternal and child health. This programme cannot be said to have served the purpose, mainly because of efficiency reasons. The states do not have to fold into the federal NHIS progamme. The states can have their own separate programmes which should not run contrary to the objectives of the federal NHIS. The states having their own/separate programmes can enhance variety and diversity rather than contribute to over-centralization. Over-centralization of any programme does not give opportunity for proper management and success. Decentralization helps to answer some of the integrity questions with respect to any federal government project in the country. Federal government should always allow the local and the state government to be involved in any programme initiated by the federal government.

Other important programmes on health policies are aimed at protecting infants:

Vitamin A Supplement Programme

The Vitamin A Supplement Programme (VASP) is designed to control or to reduce Vitamin A Deficiency (VAD) among infants. Average coverage of Vitamin A distribution in the country is 70% of the children aged 6-59 months. The programme is targeted at all children, but special provision is not made for the poor and the vulnerable. There is need to expand the coverage of distribution

National Programme on Immunization

The aim of the National Programme on Immunization (NPI) is to achieve universal child immunization in Nigeria. Currently, the NPI is being implemented in all of the 774 local government areas of the 36 states of the federation and in the federal capital territory. Implementation of the NPI is carried out during the National Immunization Days (NIDs). Distribution and administration of the vaccines are carried out under auspices of the NPI agency under the Ministry of Health.

The GFC brought reductions in the allocation of fiscal funds to the health sector. Consequently lack of funds hindered an effective distribution and administration of VASP and NPI programmes to reach the infants in Nigeria. No allowance is made for the poor and the vulnerable children. There is need to expand the coverage of the distribution.

Reforms on Human Resources for Health

This comprises, first of all, that the health personnel has to undergo professional training (this refers to formal health workers), but also for informal health workers, such as traditional health care providers, training is requested. Human resources for health play a major role in improving health system performance. It should reflect the right number, in the right place, where needed, and the appropriate skills to provide the needed services. Nigeria has one of the largest stocks of human resources for health in Africa though it is inadequate to meet the country's health needs. The management and the development of human resources for health pose a major challenge to the implementation of health sector reforms in the country, resulting in poor staffing ratios, poor utilization, and poor coordination at all levels.

Poor remuneration and discrepancies in salaries, allowances, incentives, and other conditions of service lead to high attrition of health workers. It is also noteworthy that people that go abroad for Medicare report that thousands of Nigerian doctors and health personnel work there and are experts in their field but cannot work in Nigeria due to lack of basic infrastructure. All the issues raised above should be harmonized for better results in the health situation of Nigeria.

Reforms on Mass Media and Consumer Rights

It is the right of the populace to be aware of relevant issues concerning their health. The citizens should be made to have the knowledge and behavioural skills to protect individuals against societal scourges, such as HIV/AIDS. Strong social skills that enable individuals to conduct themselves responsible in the society are requested. However, there has been an increase in activities and programmes aimed at improving the awareness and the knowledge of the population in recent years. The proportion of population exposed to health issues via the mass media has increased over time, and there is increased awareness about many health issues. This should be sustained for a better health situation to emerge.

Rebranding Reforms

Africa is the most corrupt region in the world, and this has been hindering the progress on improvement of living conditions in the region. He reported that corruption has killed 11 million children under five years of age who die from curable diseases or due to lack of water/sanitation. The situation in Nigeria is in this respect serious. Corruption has been fingered as being chiefly responsible for the country's stunted socio-economic and political development in spite of her enormous wealth in human and material resources. The management of health services is centralized and bureaucratic, allowing different actors in the health service sector to absolve themselves from various roles and responsibilities. In the 2007 rating of Transparency International (TI), Nigeria scored 2.2 out of 10.0 and ranked at 178th position out of 179 (TI Index, 2007). In the 2008 rating, Nigeria scored 2.7 out of 10.0 and ranked at the 121st position out of 179 (TI Index, 2008). According to the Transparency International Reports, government and corporations were accused of indulging in corruption, thereby pertaining poverty that the populace lives in (Oyesola, 2010).

The management of a health care system with better results requires leadership, a careful management, and capacity building. Rebranding is a process in Nigeria which advocates the necessity for changes of attitudes and realizing integrity and patriotism by Nigerians in Nigeria and outside of Nigeria. Nigeria's change from its corrupt practices will be made more difficult because of the effects of the global financial crisis.

4 Impact of the GFC on the Educational Sector in Nigeria and Policy Initiatives on Education to Mitigate the Effects

4.1 Impact of the GFC on the Educational Sector in Nigeria

Education helps in determining the level of development in any society. This explains why the education sector has been given preference in every country's annual budget (Obunadike, 2010).

Nigeria's economy depends on exports of crude oil. The major trading partners such as the United States of America, Europe, and some Asian countries were affected adversely by the impacts of the GFC. As these countries continue to face the credit crunch, Nigeria's commodity export is directly affected. This has a great impact on the revenue from oil with low demand and falling oil prices. The reduction of the government's revenue base was directly translated via reduced budget allocation to the education sector in 2009.

The GFC has induced high cost of schooling in Nigeria in the sense that importation of educational materials became difficult and expensive as a result of the exchange rate devaluation and an increase in school fees. Far-reaching impacts can be expected from such budget cuts for education. Nwajinka and Odogo (2010) noted that UNESCO had recommended an annual budget share of 26% for Education, but over the years the average allocation for education in the budget of Nigeria has been 10%.

There are severe consequences of the budgetary constraints:

Teachers are not well motivated

Obunadike (2010) observed that there is an argument that lack of proper motivation adversely affects the effectiveness of the Nigerian teachers in relation to their counterparts in other professions. Nzewi (1990) and Nwafor (2010) observed that in any organization, the goal of productivity is usually the major task of the leadership. Most of the teaching personnel in Nigeria is trained through institutions that are faced with major handicaps resulting from the quality of entrants, the staffing situation, the very low level of funding, and inadequate training facilities (Alio, 2008).

It is noteworthy that our educational system has already been witnessing inadequate facilities prior to the recession, but with the global financial crisis the situation became worse. Before the GFC the government of Nigeria used to organize seminars, workshops, and some retraining programmes for teachers where they could update their knowledge. Currently, such programmes have been abandoned because the government of Nigeria is still struggling to contain with the effect of the GFC.

It is worthy to note that in Nigeria the Information and Communication Technology (ICT) still seems to be a new technology. The government of Nigeria has so far no plan of how teachers will be trained in order to acquire the necessary ICT skills. The situation became worse with the GFC.

Inadequate Facilities for Teaching and Learning

It was observed that the use of facilities and resources for teaching has at least three advantages:

(a) They inspire children to ask questions;
(b) They serve as sources for finding answers to questions;
(c) They serve to make the science concept more real.

It appears that these advantages are not yet fully appreciated and exploited, hence the alleged poor performance in science education. Alio (2007) maintained that at schools where the laboratories are poor, the results are always poor even when there is no acute shortage of teachers for science education. Sharing the same view, Ezikiel (1998) studied the relationship between the use of laboratory equipment and the performance of students in the West African School Certificate (WASC) Agricultural Science Examination in secondary schools. The results are alarming and show that adequate laboratory equipment is mostly lacking. He found that schools with better laboratory equipment performed better in the WASC Agricultural Science Examination than those with less equipped laboratories. It is noteworthy that the need for adequate tools and equipment in teaching requires the teacher to have all the personal qualities expected of any good teacher. As a result of poor funding resulting from the reduction in the allocation to the educational sector due to the effect of the GFC, Nigeria's educational institutions lack modern and up to date teaching and learning materials. Foreign donor agencies and institutions were not in a position to bring modern equipment and materials to Nigeria due to the global economic downturn. The underfunding of tertiary education institutions made it impossible to purchase/to import modern materials for teaching and learning.

Libraries lack modern textbooks and information and communication technology equipment; even many laboratories have never used up-to-date chemicals for research and learning. Besides, the exchange rate of the Nigerian currency – N/Naira - is so high that importation of educational materials for teaching and learning became too difficult. Social problems, such as cultism, have escalated in the Nigerian educational institutions as a result of the economic downturn, induced by the global economic recession. Cultism is a system of religious beliefs and practices. It is a way of life, an idea that has become very popular but with negative effects among the youths. People who belong to this group act strangely against the norms of the society that exist.

People join cults mostly as a result of hard times and frustration. They join them in a search for temporary relief from their problems.

Limited resource allocation to education has two major negative effects on the education sector:

Firstly, the lecturers and teachers in tertiary and primary/secondary schools are owed arrears of salaries and subventions. This situation obviously makes the teachers to look for alternative means of survival to the detriment of academic activities. This led to a tremendous drop in the quality of teachers' output as teachers look for alternative sources of income.

Secondly, the students who had observed the decadence in the quality of the lecturers' output with regard of teaching competences turned to a high level of secret hooliganism and youthful misdemeanors, all in the projection of seeking relevance on campus and even outside. Clandestine intimidation and anti-social behaviour became the order of the day. The proliferation of small arms among the youths constitutes a great danger to government and to the society. The effects of cultism further worsened the already felt negative impacts of the global economic downturn even as the incidence of armed robbery and brazen gangsterism become a common feature.

The youths are the undisputed leaders of tomorrow. The quality of leadership correspondingly depends on a high level of teaching and learning; the higher the quality of learning, the greater the refined behaviour of youths and the leadership qualities. Social problems such as the cultism have escalated in the Nigerian education institutions as a result of the economic downturn induced by the global economic recession. Limited resource allocation to education has therefore major negative effects on the educational sector and on the whole society.

4.2 Policies to Protect Core Expenditures for Education and to Sustain the Educational Reforms in Nigeria

Okeke (2007) emphasized that the standards of education in Nigeria have declined, and hence there is a need for reform. Nwajinka and Odogo (2010) argue that reform is necessary in order to meet current development trends as the world is increasingly becoming interdependent. There have been ongoing reform initiatives in Nigeria's education sector before the GFC, and it is important to sustain them.

The then Minister of Education, Mrs. Oby Ezekwesili, initiated several reform measures which include, among others, the privatization of unity schools, the introduction of nine year compulsory basic education, and the introduction of a home grown school meal programme (FGN, 2007). Furthermore, polytechnics and colleges of education were to be merged, their programmes were scrapped and integrated into those of neighbouring universities. Nwajinka et al. (2010) argued that the reform initiatives were narrow by looking at a cost saving strategy with less emphasis on a performance enhancement strategy. They also noted that the objectives of the reform cannot be met as a result of poor funding (only 10% of the annual budget for education) of the educational sector in Nigeria. According to Nwajinka et al. (2010), for such reform initiatives to impact positively on the educational sector, 26% of the annual budget as recommended by UNESCO must be allocated and implemented.

Universal Basic Education

Universal basic education (UBE) was introduced to cater for children of ages 6 - 14 years. The proportion of the population of Nigeria in the age group 6-14 years is 25.3%, with 66.7% of them being poor, 30.1% of them being core poor, and 36.3% of them being moderate poor (Ajakaiye and Fakiyesi, 2009). The aim of UBE is to ensure that every Nigerian child has access to a qualitatively high basic education. The strategy is to make basic education compulsory and universal up to the junior secondary level (Alio, 2007). However, the nation has not been able to achieve this aim of universal basic education owing to a number of gaps in the operational modalities of the educational programmes, among which are infrastructure, equipment, and an inadequate ratio of teachers to pupils. The programme can only become a success if government devotes adequate funds to the education sector to secure the lacking facilities. Non-governmental bodies and philanthropists' help in funding can improve the standards of education in Nigeria, but cannot substitute for government action. GFC has impacted negatively on the chances to realize the aim of UBE.

Education Tax Fund

The Education Tax Fund (ETF) is meant for all levels of education and is designed to improve the financing of infrastructure and of resources that will lead to an improvement in the quality of education in the country. Currently the fund has no mechanism for targeting the poor or the schools they attend, which makes it regressive in nature. Irrespective of the effect of the GFC, the ETF mechanism should be designed in such a way that the fund allocation has an equitable distribution to schools irrespective of the location.

Curricula Reforms

The instructional practice should be reformed in all forms and levels of educational concepts, contents and methods in order to meet the challenges of the 21st century. The mode of training should be reformed. Special emphasis should be laid on the curriculum restructuring, strengthening of practical training, and developing of teachers who will be versatile in theory and practical skills.

For curriculum review and implementation to be possible, adequate facilities should be provided by government and voluntary agencies since the GFC has brought a reduced allocation of funds to the educational sector. Curriculum reform can help to sustain the economy, the environment, and the education system after the GFC by organizing workshops for teachers on environmental and resource scarcity issues.

Reforms Relating to Administration and Incentives

The head teacher should be appointed to be suitable to a particular type of school. The school should be divided to sub-departments with their heads being qualified in related fields. Qualified people in their respective duty post will achieve a lot even under monetary constraints.

Educators should be given incentives to encourage them to do better work. Such incentives include opportunities for further studies, prompt payment of salaries and allowances, etc. These incentives are necessary to reduce the exodus of teachers from the teaching field. The teachers can be retrained in the schools, by strengthening the skill base and by improving the service delivery in this education sub-sector.

Both administration and incentives are key areas for the future, and the GFC has constrained further such improvements.

Reforms on Student Enrolment

If the youths are left unguided, they are exposed to occupations that attract their fancy. With good occupational information such effects as later frustration and fast changes in the occupation are minimized (Oranu, 2001). For instance, there are courses that are preferred by the majority of the candidates. There are others where people don't always like to enter. Guidance and counseling services should be offered more than before to expose students on occupational choice and to correct their wrong impressions of some programmes of study. If there is a decline in students' enrolment in some programmes, for example in vocational subjects, the teaching of pre-vocational subjects in primary and junior secondary schools should be pursued more vigorously to raise the interest of students for vocational programmes. Various strategies should be taken to recruit new entrants into the system. These may include various measures, such as award of scholarships, free lunch at schools, etc. However, the impacts of the GFC have not made easier the support of such guidance systems.

Integrating ICT into Every School Programme

The development of information and communication technology and the acceleration of globalization trends give young people more life choices and opportunities than before (UNESCO, 2004). In order to help the youths to cope effectively with the challenges of the time, every programme needs to focus on developing them into productive, responsible persons, well equipped for life and work in today's technology based and globalized society. For people to compete favourably in this rapidly changing world, people should be equipped with skills that include, among others, analytical and problem solving skills, and creativity and entrepreneurship. Based on this, ICT and knowledge about global changes and interactions should be made important components of every programme's curriculum.

Teacher Education Reforms

The teacher occupies a very important position in the development of any system, be it the education system, or systems for technological, industrial and economic development. The outcome of any programme can never be better than the quality of teachers that are implementing the programme. For this reason, Alio (2008) pointed out that the teacher's utterances, actions, leadership style, knowledge of the subject he teaches, and skills in teaching are considered as important factors having implications for students' learning. So, no educational reform programme will succeed without the provision on a continuous basis of highly qualified and motivated teachers. In addition to the available teacher training programmes, creative ways of developing and mobilizing the capacity of teachers should form important parts of the reforms for a sustainable education system. It is desirable to promote collaboration between schools and industries in the teacher training, through work-study programmes in order to strengthen education in entrepreneurship and in professional ethics and to adopt a more functional mode of educational delivery.

Reforms on Education Funding

The running of educational programmes is very expensive because of the high cost of personnel training, machines, equipment, and materials. The high cost of these facilities is the ripple effect from the global financial crisis. As a result of reduced development funds, teachers have been forced to work under the conditions of limited resources, such as classrooms, laboratories, etc. There will be less funding available for much needed investment in infrastructure and other educational projects. This problem clouds the prospects for achieving the set targets on various areas of the Millennium Development Goals (MDGs), particularly on achieving universal basic education.

For education to be effective, it must be adequately funded by government, non-governmental organizations and other agencies. The impacts of the GFC have had severe consequences for the needed restructuring of the education system, and the government of Nigeria has to react vigorously to these new conditions.

5. Conclusions and Policy Recommendations

5.1 Conclusions

The GFC has led to a severe reduction in foreign exchange earnings of Nigeria, and also the government revenues were affected considerably. There have been policies adopted by the government to address the financial crisis in Nigeria. The Federal Government of Nigeria has released funds to cushion the impact of the global financial crisis. The Federal Government of Nigeria reduced the interest rate of fixed deposits from 2.5% to 0.5% to stimulate business.

Primary health care in Nigeria is in a deplorable state. There is a poor health service delivery and a low quality. The vicious cycle of poverty has a great impact in Nigeria. There is a high cost of schooling. Teachers are not motivated in their teaching job. There is an increase in the obnoxious activities of cultism in Nigerian educational institutions. Against all these, various reforms and initiatives have been put in place to ameliorate the ugly situation. The standard of education in Nigeria has declined. There is need for an effective implementation of the reforms in education in order to meet current development trends as the world is increasingly being interdependent.

The GFC has brought about a considerable reduction in the allocation to the health sector and education sectors. Sequel to that, funding of education systems and maintaining of primary health care felicities have become a big problem in Nigeria. Some government responses are announced, but the government reform programmes are as well affected by the GFC repercussions.

5.2 Recommendations

Ten important recommendations follow from this analysis:

1. Sectors like the agricultural sector, which contributed 39.8% out of 80.7% of the total contribution of the non-oil sector to the Nigerian GDP in the first half of 2008 (Nigerian Export Promotion Coun-

cil/NEPC: http://www.nepcng.com and National Bureau of Statistics/NBS: www.nigerianstat.gov.ng), should be given a chance.

2. In order to encourage the production in the agricultural sector, government should tighten controls on the illegal importation of agricultural products.
3. Government should abide by the declaration of the United Nations Summit of an allocation of 15% of the national budget to the health sector.
4. Government should implement the 26% target for the annual budget of education as recommended by UNESCO.
5. There should be a revitalization of all tiers of the health facilities, with great emphasis on preventive health care and on PHC as the foundation of the health care system.
6. Government should ensure the provision of basic amenities, such as water supply, power supply, and environmental sanitation which will greatly improve the health status of the nation.
7. Government should see that all the policy issues and the reform strategies considered as necessary in this paper to improve the performance of the health and education sectors are seriously pursued; this will help the country to achieve the MDGs and also to sustain her development.
8. It is the responsibility of the Department of Planning and of the Planning Commission at the federal and state levels to cooperate with international and national health development partners; there has been a lack of a harmonized framework for coordination between the Federal Ministry of Health and the health development partners from donor countries and agencies. Consequently, effective coordination has been poor with donors working separately through various departments. Currently, there is little or no intersectional collaboration with key relevant ministries like Finance, Agriculture, and Environment.
9. All these measures when implemented will also be helpful to overcome the depth and the severity of the impacts of the GFC on Nigeria's economy and its health and education sectors. In order to protect the health sector and the education sector with respect to the GFC, a holistic approach to health and education sectors must be mobilized - through good governance and storing political will and commitment to galvanize all stakeholders towards a common purpose to the benefit of all citizens.
10. The findings of the analysis on the impact of the global financial crisis on Nigeria's health and education sectors should help the Nigerian government to guard against the recurrence of such crisis phenomena.

References

Abati, R. (2010), Nigeria's Problematic health insurance scheme, *This Day 14* (600) 19

Achalu O. E. (2001), The current status and future of health education in the emerging Nigerian Nation, in: *Nigeria School Health Journal 2 (1), pp. 1-7*

Ajakaiye, O. and Fakiyesi, T. (2009), Global Financial Crisis, Discussion Paper Series, ODI/Overseas Development Institute, London, *Paper 8*

Ajakaiye, O., Fakiyesi, T. and Oyinlola M. (2009), Impact of the Global Financial Crisis on the Social Services Sectors in Ghana and Nigeria, ODI/Overseas Development Institute, London, *Papers 8*

Acho, O. (2005), Poor health care system: Nigeria's moral indifference, http://www.kwenu.com/publications/orabuchi/poor_healthcare.htm , Sourced on 13.12.2010, 15.40 pm

Alio A. N. (2007), Modern approaches for effective teaching of technology education subjects for self-reliance in technical colleges and comprehensive secondary schools, A paper presented at the national conference organized by the Nigerian Primary Teacher Education Association (NPTEA) on the Nigerian Education System: Which Way Forward, at the University of Jos from 30th July -2nd August

Alio, A. N. (2008), Utilization of tools and equipment for teaching of radio/television and electronics crafts/trades in technical colleges in Abia, Anambra, Enugu and Imo states, in: *Journal of Educational Management and Policy, 2 (1), pp. 61-67*

Asup (2007), Asup's position on the federal government plan to merge polytechnics and colleges of education with universities in Nigeria, *Asup new bulletin* (3), 2

Eneh, O. C. (2004), *Health, wellness and longevity,* Enugu: Chesten Books

Ezikiel A. A. (1998), A study of awareness and application of modern agricultural techniques by agricultural science teachers in Imo state, *Unpublished Master of Education Thesis,* Department of Vocational Teacher Education. University of Nigeria, Nsukka

FGN/Federal Government of Nigeria (2007), Strengthening the Education System to Meet National Economic Empowerment and Development Strategy Goals, Lagos: Federal Government Press

Hornby A. S. (2004), *Oxford advanced learner's dictionary of current English,* Oxford University Press

Hurley J. S. and Schlaadt R. R. (1992), *The wellness lifestyle,* C. T. Dushkin Publishing Group

Nwajinka C. O. and Odogo N. I. (2010), Educational reform in Nigeria, The challenges of technical/vocational education, in: Nworgu B. G. (Ed.), *Education in the Information Age: Global Challenges and Enhancement Strategies,* Proceedings of the First International Conference of the Faculty of Education, University of Nigeria, Nsukka

Nigerian Export Promotion Council (NEDC), http://www.nepcng.com

National Bureau of Statistics (NBS), www.nigerianstat.gov.ng

Njoku, W. N. (2005), *Financial Education for Financial Freedom,* Enugu: Wireni Financial Freedom Communications, Subsidiary of Wills Ventures International

Nwafor, F. (2010), Job performance and teachers motivation, *Unpublished M. Sc. Study Thesis,* Department of Psychology, Enugu State University of Science and Technology (ESUT), Enugu

Nzewi, E. (1990), Teachers motivation and effectiveness in the Nnewi local government area of Anambra state, *Unpublished M. Sc. Thesis,* Department of Education, Nnamdi Azikiwe University, Awka

Obi A. (2009, September 29), Diagnosis and Quality of Health Care, *Guardian Newspaper,* pp.18

Obunadike, J. C. (2010), Effective motivation of primary school teachers for attainment of the Millennium Development Goals, in: B. G Nworgu (Ed.), Education in *the Information Age: Global Challenges and Enhancement Strategies,* Proceedings of the First International Conference of the Faculty of Education, University of Nigeria, Nsukka

Odikenmelu, A. (2010), The global economic recession and the Nigerian economy, *The Mind Opener,* 101, pp. 14-17

Okeke, B. C. (2007), Preparation for Entrepreneurship and Entrepreneurial Opportunities in Industrial Technical Education in Contemporary Nigeria, Apapa, Presented at a Public Lecture Organized by the School of Industrial Technical Education Umunze: FCE (T)

Oranu, R. N. (2001), Vocational education and manpower development, Onitsha: Noble Graphics Press

Oyesola, B. (2010, January 11), Global Economic Meltdown and its Implications for Nigeria, *Daily Sun,* pp. 36

TI/Transparency International, 2007, Transparency International Corruption Perceptions Index, accessed: http://www.infoplease.com/world/statistics/2007-transparency-international corruption-perceptions.html

TI/Transparency International, 2008, Transparency International Corruption Perceptions Index, accessed: http://www.infoplease.com/world/statistics/2008-transparency-international corruption-perceptions.html

Ugwuoke, F. (2008, September 21), State of Health Care, Guardian, pp. 10

UNESCO (2004), Promoting skill development, *Report of an international seminar,* Paris: UNESCO Publishing

WHO, (2009), Details for the Report of the WHO Commission on Macroeconomics and Health (CMH): Country Cooperation Strategy, The World Health Organization, Regional Office for Africa

The Impact of the Global Financial Crisis on the Socio-economic and Political Landscape of Cameroon

Joy Alemazung and Christelle Wonkam[1]

Abstract

The Global Financial Crisis (GFC) has had far reaching effects in developing countries. Cameroon, a Central African nation with over 19.5 million inhabitants, has not been spared by the crisis. The country Cameroon is an example of a non-reforming state in Africa where the GFC had significant impacts. The effects of the crisis in Cameroon range from the agricultural to the industrial and to the social and political sectors. As a result of the GFC, some industries, especially in forestry and sugar sectors, had to scale down production what consequently led to job losses. Government resistance to reform the country's political and economic management system raised questions on how the external shocks of such a magnitude can be handled. This paper analyses the effects of the global financial crisis on Cameroon; some empirical data and case studies are presented. The paper also seeks to examine the severity of the GFC for the people of Cameroon in terms of unemployment and poverty. It analyses the immediate and the long term measures adopted by the government. As policy recommendations, the paper also presents alternative reform measures for a sustainable development, ranging from short-term to medium-term and long-term responses that are considered necessary to curb the effects of the crisis. In general, this paper argues that the immediate measures that were taken to reduce the negative impact of the crisis would have been effective if the government had effectively embraced

---

[1] Dr. Joy Alemazung is senior fellow of the African Good Governance Network and Lecturer and International Student Officer at the University of Applied Sciences, School of International Business in Bremen. Christelle Wonkam is currently rounding up her studies for M.A. in political sciences at the Center for Global Studies (CGS) of the University of Bonn.

reforms aimed at diversifying the economy and democratising the political institutions earlier.

1 Introduction

In 2006, the global housing bubble attained its peak in the United States and subsequently resulted in a plummeting of the collateral values tied to real estate prices. This development then led to an insolvency of parts of the banking system in the United States, setting the pace for a global financial crisis. Consequently, large financial institutions collapsed, associated with a downtown in stock markets around the world as national governments struggled to bail out their banks (Jain, 2010). In 2008, the global financial crisis (GFC) conspicuously broke out with its direct and immediate effects felt on industrial nations.

Initially, it was assumed that the impact of the crisis would be less severe in developing countries, including Africa. This assumption was based on the fact that African banks generally do not invest in subprime mortgages and/or are not related to toxic assets which tend to drain the foreign exchange assets in international trade transactions. The absence of an effective linkage of most African financial institutions to the international financial markets probably was an advantage to the continent in terms of contagion effects. However, the assumption that the impact of the crisis would not be felt much in African countries was ephemeral. The global recession which emerged as a result of the GFC subsequently generated direct and indirect impacts on the socio-economic environment of Cameroon and Africa at large. The global recession had serious impacts on the economy of Cameroon as well as of many other African countries due to the consequential shift in the demand (and the prices) for African products in the global markets. The decline in commodity prices in the international market and the reduction of the financial flows to African countries had adverse effects on the African economies (Export-Import Bank of the United States, 2009). Despite of weak direct linkages to the international financial markets, Cameroon was seriously affected by the GFC, largely as a result of over-dependence on primary commodities as the major export commodities. The central issue then was which policy instruments the government of Cameroon could use in order to mitigate the effects of the crisis on the country's socio-economic environment.

Cameroon is known for its reluctant and slow reform pace. According to the International Crisis Group Africa Report N°160 of 25 May 2010, the government has often failed to carry out meaningful reforms and when it did it was more to fortify the autocratic rule of the regime in power.[2] The aim of this paper therefore is to analyse the impact of the GFC on a non-reforming state in Africa, with Cameroon taken as an example. The paper provides policy suggestions on how the country would benefit from reforms. The analysis is focused on two political regimes in Cameroon after the independence in 1960. The first regime was between 1960 and 1982 under the leadership of Ahmadou Ahidjo. The second regime is at place between 1982 and the present date under the leadership of Paul Biya. This analysis is necessary in the sense that the governance system in both regimes was and still is based on "presidential decrees" in contrast to the background of democratic values and the rule of law.

This paper starts by presenting the political and the economic developments in Cameroon before the GFC. This is followed by an evaluation of the effects of the crisis on the country in the context of three major channels. The first channel is the shift in demand for African products; the second channel is global decline in commodity prices, while the third channel is the reallocation of financial flows to Africa. In analysing these channels, three sectors, namely oil, timber and agriculture, were used as case studies. The next step was to examine the social and the economic effects of the crisis in order to have insights on how the crisis has affected the MDGs in Cameroon. Another section of the paper focuses on the government's reactions to the crisis. In this context, the short and the long term measures to mitigate the effects of the crisis and to stimulate the economy towards sustainable growth were examined. The paper concludes and gives policy recommendations by firstly, examining the factors that led to the slow pace of reforms in Cameroon, and secondly, proposing alternative possible reform measures for sustainable growth.

The structure of sections is as follows. In section 2 of the paper the political and the economic development since independence is outlined in a short overview. In section 3 the effects of the GFC on Cameroon are presented. In section 4 there is a discussion of the GFC impacts on selected sectors of the Cameroonian economy. Section 5 discusses the government responses to the crisis and the policy measures pursued. Section 6 presents conclusions and some policy recommendations.

---

[2] See International Crisis Group Report titled: Cameroon: Fragile State. Africa Report N°160 – 25 May 2010. Available online at: http://www.crisisgroup.org/~/media/Files/africa/west-africa/cameroon/160Cameroon%20Fragile%20State.ashx (24.10.2010).

2 Political and Economic Development since Independence

2.1 Demography and Governance in Cameroon

Cameroon is a Central African country with an estimated population of about 19.5 million inhabitants (Hermes, 2009). Over the past five years, the population had recorded a steady growth rate of about 2.3 percent, and nearly 52 percent live in urban areas (Ministère du Dévelopement Urbain et de l'Habitat, 2010). The rural labour force has decreased rapidly and the annual rate of urbanisation has reached 3.5 percent (UNDP, 2007/8). Cameroon is among the poorer nations of the world. In 2001 the population living under the poverty line of one US dollar per day was about 17.1 percent (see World Health Statistics 2008 available online).[3] United Nations 2007[4] data indicate a slight improvement in the sense that only about 39.9 percent of the population are now living under the poverty line of one US dollar per day since 2004. The amelioration with regard of the poverty rate in Cameroon could be seen as a result of an economically favourable age structure as shown in Table 1 below.

Table 1: Cameroon's Population Structure

0 - 14 years	41.2 percent
15 - 64 years	55.3 percent
65 years and over	3.5 percent

Source: UNDP, 2007/8, p. 245

The demographic structure of Cameroon indicates that about 55.3 percent of the population falls within the population group of the economically active age. Thus, more than half of the population is supposed to participate actively in economic activities to take care of the 41.2 percent of youths and the 3.5 percent of adults. However, a large share of the economically active population is unemployed. According to the latest available data, the unem-

[3] World Health Statistics (UD Data) on population living under the poverty line of less than US $1 a day: http://data.un.org/Data.aspx?d=WHO&f=inID%3ASDEC15 (24.10.2010).

[4] United Nations Statistics Divisions, Millennium Development Goals Database, Found in: http://data.un.org/Data.aspx?d=MDG&f=seriesRowID%3A581 (accessed 08.10.2010).

ployment rate in Cameroon was about 30 percent in 2000 (Bolzen, Online Länder-Lexikon, 2010).

Cameroon gained its independence in 1960, and the principle of democratic governance and the rule of law were entrenched in the country's constitution. Like many African countries, the first national governments of Cameroon were democratically elected. However, a centralised unitary system of government was systematically introduced thereafter (NDI, 1993). A multiparty democracy was abandoned in favour of a centralised one party state. The country remained a centralised unitary autocracy until the resignation of the first president in 1982 (NDI, 1993). The one party-centralised state system, installed by the first president and fortified by the incumbent with a strong patrimonial political base, rendered the country to a reform-resistant and autocratic status with a persistent bad governance record until today (Konings, 1996; Ngoh 1987). Despite local and international pressure for effective economic and political reforms aimed at sustainable economic development in the country, the Cameroonian government has failed to embrace and to implement effectively reforms. In 1987, President Paul Biya launched the New Deal programme aimed at guiding Cameroon through towards a process of gradual democratic transition, liberalisation of the economy, and promotion of economic growth. Regrettably, the programme was ineffective because the government failed to embrace democracy. The situation deteriorated until in the late 1980s when the international institutions forced the government to embrace democracy as the norm of governance (NDI, 1993).

2.2 Governance and Reform Processes in Cameroon prior to the GFC

In transforming the multi-party independent Cameroon into a centralised unitary one party state President Ahidjo has created an authoritarian and patrimonial state. The consequence was that such a strategy helped in forming a hegemonic alliance out of the numerous ethnic groups in the country. It also implied loyalty to the ruler with severe consequences what means also access to state resources and other rent-seeking activities (Konings, 1996, p. 245). Cameroon's economy witnessed positive growth after independence until the early 1980s, not as result of good governance but rather due to the windfall earnings from the oil rent. Cameroon had positive growth between 1960 and 1985, with economic growth averaging 8 percent each year between 1970 and the early 1980s (NDI, 1993, p. 9). The economy surged ahead as oil became the country's most important source of foreign exchange earnings in the late 1970s, with the offshore exploration of oil fields being the base for this development. This positive trend was coming to an end as a result of the rapid decline in the price of the country's major export produce - oil.

As a result of the plummeting of oil and commodity prices at the world markets, coupled with an overburdened civil service as well as the non-diversification of the Cameroonian economy, the country was gradually plunged into recession and poverty (NDI, 1993). Between the period of 1985-1986 and 1990-1991, Cameroon witnessed an annual drop in its real per capita income of 7.4 percent (Tambi, 1998, p. 201). In addition, the decline in commodity export prices and the rise in import prices resulted in an aggravation of the terms of trade of the country from 172.1 in 1984/85 to 102.7 in 1987/88 with 1980 = 100 (Tambi, 1998, p. 201)[5]. Konings (1996, p. 252) further argues that the country's terms of trade deteriorated by 70 percent between 1986 and 1993 due to the decline in commodity prices in the world market and a slide in the USA dollar against the CFA Franc. The situation was further aggravated in the 1980s through a loss of billions of Franc CFA due to capital flight and the departure of many foreign investors following the deteriorating economic and political environment (Konings, 1996, p. 252). Foreign exchange earnings declined sharply, leading to a decrease in GDP by 6 percent between 1989 and 1990 (NDI, 1993, p. 9). The fall of the oil and commodity prices in the mid-1980s led to a drop in custom and export tax revenues (NDI, 1993). Consequently, there was a drastic drop of government revenues by 51 percent between 1985 and 1991 (Gauthier, Soloaga and Tybout, 2002, p. 451). Konings (1996, p. 252) mentioned that state oil revenues decreased from US $350 million in 1985 to US $207 million in 1988. The government's attempt to finance the revenue shortfall through accumulation of salary arrears of civil servants and arrears with domestic suppliers resulted in a banking sector crisis and a strong recession of the economy (Gauthier et al. 2002, p. 451).

As the economic situation worsened the government of Cameroon needed external assistance and appealed to the World Bank and the International Monetary Fund (IMF) for financial assistance. Cameroon received loans from these institutions on conditions to liberalise the economy and to introduce reforms in the political processes. The government accepted it to cut state spending by reducing the size of the civil service. In the late 1980s, the government embarked upon a series of economic reform programs supported by the World Bank and the IMF (US Department of State, 2010). However, a partial implementation of the Structural Adjustment Programme

[5] Import/domestic price ratio rose from 1.00 in 1983/84 to 1.17 in 1989/90

(SAP) in 1989 failed to rescue the plunging economy. By 1993, the per capita income in Cameroon fell to half of its 1986 value (Gauthier et al, 2002, p. 451).

The measures and conditions for reforms were painful to the masses in Cameroon, especially the slashing of civil service salaries by 50 percent in 1993. In addition, the devaluation of the Franc CFA by 50 percent resulted in a decline of approximately 63 percent of the purchasing power of the citizens (Gauthier et al, 2002, p. 451). By early 1990s, it became clear that implementation of President Biya's political and economic reforms were symbolic rather than real. The government failed to liberalise the political process and to introduce democratic reforms in the political institutions (Takougang, 1997, p. 166). The centralised unitary patrimonial state, already introduced by the previous regime and encouraging rent-seeking activities and corruption, was rather fortified (Konings, 1996, p. 245).

In general, government failed to meet the conditions of the past IMF programs. For example, after the Board of Directors of both the IMF and the World Bank had approved Cameroon's Poverty Reduction Strategy Paper (PRSP) with high marks in 2003, the country still failed to reach the completion point of the Highly Indebted Poor Countries Initiative (HIPC) programs in late 2004, due to a lacklustre reform performance of the government (US Department of State, 2010). The interventionist approach to industrialisation and development adopted by the government after independence in 1960 was continued under the subsequent regime. For example, the present government tax code selectively protected the firms owned by political clients of the ruling party. The firms owned by the sympathizers of the opposition were marginalised and even have to pay higher tax rates (Gauthier et al, 2002, p. 449). The implication is that the tax discrimination often limits competition and hurts the economy in general.

As a result of domestic and international pressures for reforms, the present government of Cameroon is engaged in ad-hoc liberalisation by focusing on selective privatisation of few state enterprises. The opposition blamed the government for moving too slow in the implementation of the economic and political reform processes. Hence, by 1990 the economic crisis deepened and the opposition to the government escalated. Consequently, the government was forced to introduce a multi-party system and to recognise the importance of good governance and the liberalisation of the economy. In May 1989 the World Bank approved an initial structural adjustment loan to help strengthening the economy of Cameroon. The loans were approved under the following conditions: first, reforms of the banking sector; reducing the bureaucratic bottlenecks in the public administration and privatisation of government-owned enterprises; deregulation of trade and marketing organizations for raw agricultural materials; as well as firm control and reduction of government expenditures (BTI, 2010). Despite government promises to reform the economy and the political system, evidence shows that by the mid-1990s there were no meaningful results due to the sagging pace of the reforms. In 1994, the regional currency, the Franc CFA, was devaluated in order to boost exports in member states, including Cameroon (Gauthier et al, 2002). The measure was also intended to spur the economies of the whole Economic Community of Central African States (ECCAS). The objective of this measure was however not attained, and this failure pushed the economy of Cameroon into a deeper crisis.

3 The Global Financial Crisis and its Effects on Cameroon

3.1 The Cameroonian Economy and the GFC

When the GFC broke out, experts thought that Africa was relatively sheltered from the negative impact of the crisis (BBC News, 10.10.2008). However, in November 2008 the World Bank Chief Economist for Africa, Shanta Devarajan, expressed concerns about the threefold impact arising from the global recession as a result of the GFC (World Bank Group, 2008). The threefold impact as argued by Devarjan is: first, there would be a slowdown in private capital flows to Africa. The implication is that countries that had been relying on these flows for investment in infrastructure will be adversely affected; secondly, the falling commodity prices will hurt exporters in Africa while the importers in industrialised nations will gain as a result of lower prices; thirdly, there will be a drop in remittances which could be at a loss of about \$15 billion a year, and foreign aid to Africa will be scaled down as well (World Bank Group, 2008).

The global recession induced by the GFC dampened also the growth prospects of the Cameroon economy and of the rest of the African countries. This was seen as a result of diminished "trade opportunities, reduced access to global finance, reduced international migrant remittances and foreign direct investment" (World Bank Group, 2008). The recession affected different economic sectors of Cameroon differently. However, the Cameroonian economy has been experiencing large structural changes prior to the GFC. Table 2 shows the recent changes in the shares of economic sectors of Cameroon prior to the GFC. As shown in Table 2, the contribution of agriculture to the GDP in Cameroon declined drastically from 41 percent in 2005 to 19 percent in 2008; this is a decline by 53.7 percent. This suggests that the agricultural sector has been experiencing severe government neglect in terms of budgetary allocation and in terms of investment in rural infrastructure. It also reveals that Cameroon has moved from an agricultural surplus economy to a food import-dependent economy. Hence, there was a rapid increase in food prices as a result of the external shock. Table 2 also shows that between 2005 and 2008 the contribution of industry and oil subsectors as well as of manufacturing to the GDP has increased by 121.4 percent and 142.9 percent respectively. This also suggests that government resources have moved from agricultural development to industry, oil, and manufacturing sectors. Arguably, this resulted in a drastic reduction of the rural labour force as farmers and youths abandoned the rural areas and migrated to urban areas in search for jobs in other sectors. Table 2 also shows that 50 percent of the sector contribution to the GDP came from the services sector.

Table 2: Cameroon's Major Economic Sectors (in percent of the GDP)

	2005	**2006**	**2007**	**2008**
Agriculture	41.0	20.0	19.0	19.0
Industry & Oil	14.0	33.0	31.0	31.0
Manufacturing	7.0	18.0	17.0	17.0
Services	45.0	47.0	50.0	50.0

Source: The World Bank, World Development Indicators 2007, p.194; 2008, p. 202; 2009, p. 208; 2010, p. 230

As argued by Fonjong (2004, p. 14), the agricultural sector provides about two-third of the overall employment but has been severely neglected over the last three decades. After independence, the government recognised the importance of agriculture to the Cameroonian economy and introduced several measures to promote agricultural development. The measures include the creation of agro-pastoral institutions, like the *National Centre for Studies and Experimentation in Agricultural Mechanisation* (CENEEMA), the *Mission de Development des Cultures Vivrières, Marachaires et Fruitières* (MIDEVIV), and the agricultural extension service of the Ministry of Agriculture (Fonjong, 2004). The objective of the CENEEMA was to study the adaptability of agricultural tools to local environment and fixing prices for these tools. MIDEVIV was assigned to produce high quality seedlings for small farmers involved in food production (Fonjong 2004). In addition, agricultural research centres were created in different regions of the country as well as rural development agencies. According to Fonjong (2004), systematic neglect of the agricultural sector and of the rural infrastructure led to a scaling down of the activities in the rural development agencies and of the agriculture-supporting institutions, all this resulting in a severe deterioration of rural infrastructure. The degree of government neglect of agricultural development is reflected on budgetary allocation. For example, in 2009 the Cameroonian government budgeted $309 million for the military expenditures, $105 million for the office of the president, and only about $106 million for agriculture which accounts for about 70 percent employment in the country (Business Mirror, 2009).[6]

Prior to the GFC Cameroon was the economically strongest country in the CEMAC region and was experiencing steady growth in GDP since the beginning of the 2000s (Bundesagentur für Außenwirtschaft, 2005). The GFC hamstrung the positive trend of economic growth experienced in the last years. The negative impacts on Cameroon and on other African countries come from the resulting global recession. The most serious indirect impact of the recession is the increase in the poverty level of the population. Table 3 reveals the impact of the GFC on the macroeconomic environment of Cameroon. As shown in Table 3, the nominal GDP which increased from US$16,588 million in 2005 to US$24,030 million in 2008 then fell to US$23,760 million in 2009 (and so by 1.12 percent). This is reflected on the GDP per capita which fell in 2009 to US$1,220 as against US$1,260 in 2008. The real GDP growth fell sharply from 3.9 percent in 2008 to 1.0 percent in 2009. This shows how severely the GFC had affected Cameroon's economic performance.

The fiscal balance of -0.4 percent recorded in 2009 shows the extent to which the government has borrowed in order to reduce the impact of the GFC. The implication is that a relatively high budget deficit, financed through the Central Bank and government external borrowing, will contribute to the increase in domestic and external debt and as well is crowding out private sector investment. It will also impact on the foreign exchange reserves as well as inducing adverse effects on relative prices. The current account balance, expressed as a percentage of the GDP, explains the contribution of the country's external sectors to the general performance of the economy. As shown in Table 3, the contribution of the external sector to the GDP has declined from 0.2 percent in 2008 to -2.1 percent in 2009. Following the debt-relief initiative of 2005, more than half of the country's debts were erased. As shown in Table 3, the government efforts recorded successes

---

[6] Business Mirror (2009): Government bribes in Cameroon divert funds from food amid riots, Lexusplus.com, 6. January 2009. Found in: http://www.lexpressplus.com/Government-bribes-in-Cameroon-divert-funds-from-food-amid-riots_a673.html (23.08.2010).

until 2008, when its external debt went down to about 13 percent of the country's GDP. The sharp fall of external debt registered between 2005 and 2006 was due to the 2005 debt-relief initiative. The debt relief initiative resulted in a writing off of the country's external debt by over 40 percent in 2005 and by about 18 percent of the GDP in 2006 (Ioannou and Singh, 2007). In the subsequent years, Cameroon's government managed to reduce its debts. The slight reverse in the trend as observed in 2009 was seen as a result of the GFC. The challenge for the government to face is to keep the debt level to its previous lowest record. This could be possible by embracing political and economic reform measures.

Table 3: GFC impact on Selected Economic Indicators in Cameroon (2005 -2009)

Selected economic indicators	2005	2006	2007	2008	2009
Nominal GDP (USD mn)	16,588	17,920	20,475	24,030	23,760
Population (mn)	17.82	18.24	18.66	19.09	19.53
GDP per capita (in USD)	931	982	1,097	1,260	1,220
Real GDP growth (in %)	2.2	3.0	3.3	3.9	1.0
Inflation (percent, average)	2.0	5.1	1.0	5.3	3.0
Fiscal balance (in % of GDP)	1.9	16.7	2.2	2.1	-0.4
Current account balance (% of GDP)	-4.7	-0.8	-2.7	0.2	-2.1
Foreign exchange reserves (USD mn)	946	171	290	308	250
External debt/GDP (percent)	44.4	18.8	15.4	13.3	14.3

Source: Euler Hermes (2009): Country Review Cameroon

3.2 The Effects of the GFC on Cameroon's External Transactions

The global recession has interrupted the positive economic trends observed in the country from 2005 until 2008 prior to the GFC. It has reduced the progress made in real GDP growth and has affected fiscal and current account balances negatively as shown in Table 3. In general, the economic progress made in the external transactions was coming to a halt in 2009 and has been estimated to deteriorate to -2.8 of the GDP in 2011 as seen in Table 4 (African Development Outlook 2010).[7] The rise of imports relative to exports as shown in Table 4 below suggests that the economy will continue to be dependent on food imports as agricultural output continues to decline. It also suggests that the export volume in the oil sector has declined and that the non-oil sector has not been exploited sufficiently. Hence, there is the need for a diversification of the country's export base.

According to data from the African Economic Outlook (2010), tax revenue accounted for 18.4% of the GDP in 2009. This implied a drop of a 0.1 percentage point from 2008 (Table 4). Projections, however, indicate a return to the slow and steady increase in tax revenue as experienced during the years prior to the GFC (African Economic Outlook 2010)[8]. Despite the expected drop, loans for investment projects and grants (external budget resources), however, exceeded the 2009 projections by 22.6%, as a result of a XAF 68 billion loan allocated to Cameroon by the International Monetary Fund (IMF) under the Exogenous Shocks Facility (African Economic Outlook 2010). Grants to Cameroon also experienced a downward trend from 2008, and according to projections for the years to 2011 this trend may go on for some time.

Net bilateral aid flows from the Development Assistance Committee (DAC) donors, that is, net disbursements of official development assistance (ODA) from the DAC donor member countries to Cameroon, dropped following the outbreak of the GFC. According to Trading Economics (2010), except for Luxembourg, most of the other DAC members saw a drop in their net flows of aid to Cameroon (see Figures 1a and 1b).

---

[7] See Data from BEAC and the Cameroon Ministry of Finance and Economy found in the online version of the African Economic Outlook, available at: http://www.africaneconomicoutlook.org/en/countries/central-africa/cameroon/ (24.10.10).

[8] African Economic Outlook (2010) of OECD and African Development Bank: Country Report on Cameroon. Found in: http://www.africaneconomicoutlook.org/en/countries/central-africa/cameroon/ (15.08.2010).

Table 4: GFC Impact on Tax Revenue, Grants, Exports and Imports of Goods (% of GDP, with estimates for 2009 and projections for 2010 and 2011)

Selected economic indicators	**2005**	**2006**	**2007**	**2008**	**2009**
Nominal GDP (USD mn)	16,588	17,920	20,475	24,030	23,760
Population (mn)	17.82	18.24	18.66	19.09	19.53
GDP per capita (in USD)	931	982	1,097	1,260	1,220
Real GDP growth (in %)	2.2	3.0	3.3	3.9	1.0
Inflation (percent, average)	2.0	5.1	1.0	5.3	3.0
Fiscal balance (in % of GDP)	1.9	16.7	2.2	2.1	-0.4
Current account balance (% of GDP)	-4.7	-0.8	-2.7	0.2	-2.1
Foreign exchange reserves (USD mn)	946	171	290	308	250
External debt/GDP (percent)	44.4	18.8	15.4	13.3	14.3

Source: African Development Outlook 2010

Figure 1a. World Bank Indicators - Cameroon – ODA from France

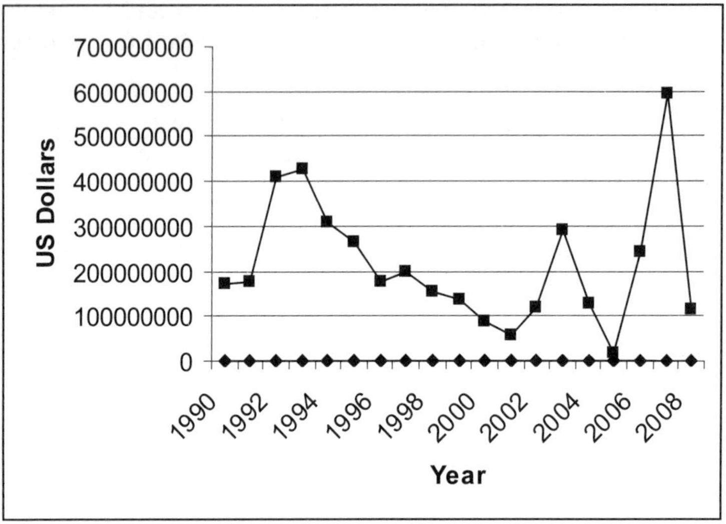

Source: Trading Economics 2010

Figure 1b. World Bank Indicators - Cameroon – ODA from Luxembourg

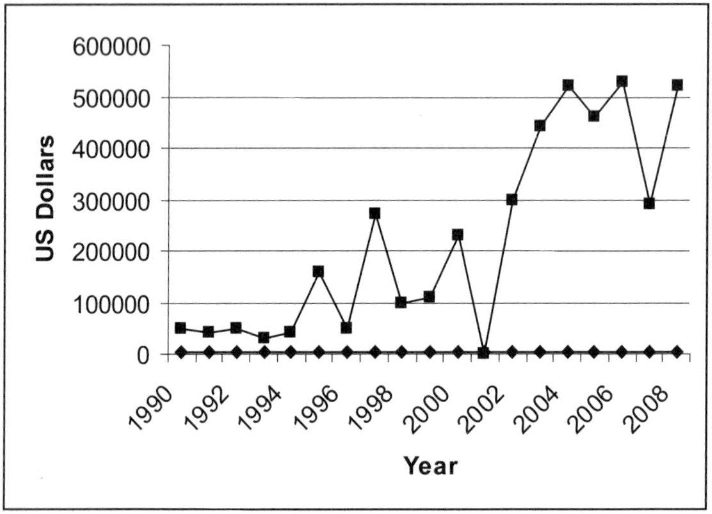

Source: Trading Economics 2010

As indicated in Table 4, the rise in exports in the past years had supported an increase in the GDP of the country for the same period. The global recession, however, brought a plunging effect to this trend. Table 5 below shows the impact of the global recession resulting from the GFC on the export volume in terms of millions of US $ for Cameroon. The implication of the GFC was such that the contraction of the economies of the developed countries had an immediate effect on the economy of Cameroon. For example, imports by the US and the Asian countries from Cameroon declined due to the crisis. Exports from Cameroon to the countries of the European Union, constituting the country's largest trading area, declined by a total of 5 percent (US Foreign Trade Division, 2010). The most affected sectors in Cameroon are timber and oil, which constitute together almost three-quarter of the country's exports.

Developing countries in general and in Africa in particular have observed an important rise in their exports during the last decade. Due to preferential export agreements, such as the African Growth and Opportunity Act (AGOA) with the USA, and an increased demand for African natural resources, African countries have seen their rate of exports growing at an average of 5 percent during the past years; this is also the case of Cameroon (World66, 2010). Like many countries in Africa, Cameroon experienced a rise in its exports from the early 2000s through to 2008 as indicated in Table 4. This is also reflected in export revenue as shown in Table 5 below: Between 2005 and 2008 the export revenue increased from USD 3,265.2 million to USD 5,890.0 million by 80.4 percent. It subsequently declined to USD 4078.6 million in 2009, by 30.8 percent, as a result of the GFC (also see IMF Statistical Yearbook 2010, p. 288).

Table 5: GFC and Cameroon's export in Millions of US Dollars

	2005	**2006**	**2007**	**2008**	**2009**
Export of Goods (in million US Dollar)	3.265,2	3.848,6	4.956,0	5.890,0	4.078,6

Source: IMF Statistical Yearbook, July 2010, p. 288

Apart from the economic boom of the 1990's, the entry of new global players, such as China, Brazil, India and South Africa, has opened new windows of opportunities for African products. The industrialisation of these countries and their consequent need for raw materials and other products supported the growth rate of the GDP in many African countries, including Cameroon. However, the GFC did not spare this category of countries either;

on the contrary, the effects of the crisis were felt almost as hard as in the Western world. The reduction of their consumption also affected demand for Cameroon commodity products in their respective markets. The low demand for products in turn led to a sharp decline in their prices. For example, the price for oil declined between July 2008 and March 2009 by 70 percent to US $ 50 (Legicam, May 2009). The price for other export goods, such as cotton, timber, coffee, or cocoa, plunged severely. This brought sizable reductions in Cameroon's revenues, considering the fact that the country's economy is strongly export-oriented. Consequently, the fiscal balance that was on a positive course turned towards the negative side.

4 GFC Impact on Selected Sectors and the Socio-economic Base of Cameroon's Economy

4.1 The Oil, Forestry and Agriculture Sectors

Oil is the largest export commodity for Cameroon and is the most important source of export revenues for Cameroon. In 2002, the International Court of Justice ruled the Bakassi peninsula in favour of Cameroon and so the estimates on oil reserves are expected to rise, since the peninsula, which is located in the Gulf of Guinea, is suspected to contain significant oil reserves. Cameroon is the sixth biggest oil-producer in Sub-Saharan Africa; with oil reserves estimated at about 400 Million barrels in 2004 (Mbendi Information Services, 22.02.2010). Recent estimates suggest that the quantity is about 200 Million barrels (CIA World Factbook, 2010). Cameroon produces around 74,000 barrels of oil a day, and the national consumption lies around 30 percent of the production (CIA World Factbook, 2010).[9]

The immediate impact of the GFC on the Cameroonian economy was the rapid drop in the demand for natural resources products, particularly oil. The decline of the oil price in the international market has had a severely negative effect on the government revenues. Oil exports contributed to about 8 percent of the GDP in 2008. Oil production output declined from 30.70 million barrels in 2008 to 26.68 million barrels in 2009 by 13.08 percent (Dongmo, 2010). The implication is that government projects and programs have to be suspended or cancelled as revenues contracted (Dongmo, 2010). For example, between March 2008 and March 2009, the revenues from oil dropped

[9] CIA World Factbook (2008/2010): Found in:
https://www.cia.gov/library/publications/the-world-factbook/geos/cm.html (12.04.2010)

drastically from FCFA 131 billion to 43.2 billion by 67 percent (Chendjou, 2009). Transfers to the state treasury dropped from FCFA 651.75 billion in 2008 to FCFA 331.716 billion in 2009 by almost 50 percent (Chendjou, 2009). The sharp drop led to a decline in the fiscal revenues of the country and to a significant deterioration of the fiscal balance what resulted in a reduction of public investments. Furthermore, the decrease in the oil price did not only affect the national treasury but also slowed down overall investment.

The forests in Cameroon are part of the Congo Basin Forests, which is the second largest tract of rainforest in the world after the Amazon (Congo Basin Forest Fund, 2010). The forest area of Cameroon covers about 22.5 million hectares of land mass (Eba'a Atyi, 1998). This made Cameroon to become a major exporter of timber to European countries. In recent times, Asia has emerged as new competitor to Europe for Cameroon's timber products. The proportion of revenues that came from the logging industry has risen since the 1990s. The revenues from the logging industry, expressed as a percentage of the Gross National Product (GNP), increased from 3,5 percent in 1990/1991 to 6,7 percent in 1995/96 (Eba'a Atyi, 1998). In 2007, government revenues from timber exports of Cameroon were about 500 billion FCFA. Currently, timber constitutes the second major source of Cameroon's export revenues with a share of 13.3 percent after oil with a share of 50.5 percent (Les Afriques, 2008).

The forestry sector employs about 45,000 people and has a share of up to 6 percent of the GDP. It is one of the sectors of the Cameroonian industry most affected by the global recession (Chendjou, 2008). According to Cameroon's Prime Minister's office, the forestry industry saw a dramatic fall in the demand in international markets. The industry was adversely affected by the credit rationing in the banks. According to the President of the association of forestry exploiters in Cameroon, about 170,000 metric tons of orders made by European and American clients in late 2008 were cancelled. Timber export in Cameroon dropped by more than 200,000 metric tons by the end of 2008. Consequently, about 10,000 workers were temporarily sent on "technical leave" (Nyuylime 2008).

Various agricultural sectors, especially the rubber industry, were adversely affected as a result of the global recession. The price of rubber products dropped in the international market by a half. The scenario was becoming drastic in the sense that despite of a sharp drop in the price of rubber in the international market the export activity was also limited for Cameroon due to the non-availability of buyers (Mbom, 2009). By mid-2009, the price for a kilogram of rubber had fallen by more than 50 percent (Njoka, 2009). This had affected the Cameroon Development Cooperation (CDC) severely, as its most important export crop, rubber, got accumulated in its warehouses with no buyer coming forth despite of drastically falling rubber prices following the GFC (Mbom, 2009). The impact of the GFC was such that not only the large corporations and companies were adversely affected, but also the small peasants in rural areas. A small farmer from south west Cameroon revealed that the rubber he had supplied months ago had not been paid for. The local buyers have reduced the price from 500 to 200 FCFA and are threatening to reduce the price even further (Njoka, 2009).

Furthermore, the cotton producers in Cameroon have witnessed a sharp drop in income. The aggregate income of cotton growers has declined from 68.9 billion FCFA in 2007 to 38.46 billion FCFA in 2008 by almost 50 percent (Njoka, 2009). By May 2009, about 370,000 jobs were at risk, hence there has been an enormous pressure on government to take action (Njoka, 2009).

4.2 Unemployment, increasing Poverty and Risk of Political Destabilization

The impacts of the GFC are observable on every sector in Cameroon, including the social sectors. The expected drop in international aid was a concern to policymakers in Cameroon. The drop in foreign aid would invariably limit investment in infrastructures and would reduce spending on social sectors such as health, education, and environmental protection. It would also have adverse effects on the efforts to contain malaria, to reduce infant mortality, and to manage and reduce the HIV/AIDS pandemic. The reduction in the fiscal revenues could lead also to a reduction in the public efforts towards development. The consequence of this tendency would be to bring to a halt the positive growth observed in the country during the last years (BTI, 2010). The decline of fiscal revenues could also bring to a halt the government efforts to engage into meaningful reform processes to improve the situation of the country and to enforce diversification and development (African Economic Outlook, 2010).

One of the most severe consequences of the global recession in Cameroon is the increasing unemployment rate. The recent survey conducted by the Employers Union of Cameroon indicates that about 100 companies in Cameroon are close to bankruptcy. Among them, about 40 companies have lost more than $600 million as a result of the GFC. The loss was due to the inability to maintain production levels because of the low demand for their products (The Herald, April 2009). The decrease in exportation contributed to a loss of revenues which made companies to scale down or to stop production and to lay-off workers. In 2009, a study conducted by Cameroonian Chamber of Commerce also projected that the country would lose more than 370,000 jobs if immediate measures were not taken to attenuate the impact of the crisis (Njoka, 2009).

The direct impact of unemployment on poverty threatens the state's ability to fight poverty and reduces the ability of the state to realize the MDGs (World Bank Group, 2010). Furthermore, the GFC had also a negative impact on the flow of remittances into Cameroon. According to the Integrated Regional Information Networks (IRIN) News (2010) remittances to Sub-Saharan Africa, including Cameroon, were set to fall considerable in 2009. This is very bad news as private remittances have gained a significant role as it provided income for families in Africa through their relatives in the Diaspora (Schmelz, 2007; Ngome and Mpako, 2009). In other words, remittances have become a principal source of income for many households and contributed to raising the living standard of many households in the region. Ngome and Mpako (2009) argue that significant parts of the private remittances are used not only for household consumption but also for investment in human capital development.

Apart from private remittances, public remittances are also an important instrument for development and for fighting poverty in Africa. For example, the International Fund for Agricultural Development (IFAD), through the Finance Facility for Remittances (FFR), provides support for rural development projects from financial inflows into Cameroon through remittances (FUNDSFORNGOs, 2010). The implication is that a fall in remittances, coupled with the rising rate of unemployment rate as a result of the GFC, would adversely affect the efforts to reduce poverty in Cameroon. A further implication of the GFC is that measures to curb the increasing rate of HIV/AIDS infection and efforts to attain the MDGs may be rendered futile in Cameroon. According to BTI's (2010) projection, only goal number 2 in the context of the 8 MDGs could be achieved in Cameroon. In other words, achieving universal primary education seems to be possible in Cameroon. Achieving other MDGs set by the UN, especially fighting poverty, remains uncertain in Cameroon (World Bank Group, 2010).

Cameroon received support from the international community which helped to reduce the negative impacts of the GFC. For example, in May 2009, the United Nations through its International Fund for Agricultural Development (IFAD) signed up a \$13.5 million loan and a \$200.000 grant for poverty reduction projects in the rural areas of Cameroon (UN News Center, 2009). The IFAD Microfinance Scheme was aimed to support the growing number of youths who abandoned the urban areas due to increasing unemployment and returned to rural areas to engage in agricultural production. The IFAD Microfinance Scheme was designed to reduce the difficulties associated with access to credit for the new young rural farmers (UN News Centre, 2009).

Apart from the increasing unemployment rate through loss of jobs, the global recession is worsening the living conditions and could lead to risks of political and social instability in the Cameroon. There has been a noticeable rise in the price for consumer goods. The price increases, coupled with the rising unemployment rate and the high poverty level, consequently exposed the country to severe social turbulences. The direct consequence of the scenario was mass protest and increased pressure on the government to ameliorate the situation (BTI, 2010). As a result of poor management of the economic system and the undemocratic nature of governance, the government could no longer manage the turbulences surrounding the impact of the GFC. Consequently, about 100 people lost their lives in the February 2009 protests in Cameroon (BBC online, 2009). The increasing dissatisfaction with the system of governance and the rising costs of living coupled with a high unemployment rate as a result of the current GFC made the country to become politically affected and volatile. This could result in another round of political instability if there are no meaningful reform initiatives undertaken by the government.

5. Government Responses and Policy Measures to React to the Crisis

Following the outbreak of public protest, social unrest and violence due to public frustration over rising prices of consumer goods in February 2008, the government announced a reduction in food import tariffs. The government introduced other measures aimed at reducing the cost of basic commodities (Travel Document Systems, 1996-2009). The government policy document released in November 2009 (The Prime Minister details Government's Economic, Financial, Social and Cultural Programme for fiscal year 2010, Crtv Nouvelles 20.11.2009)[10] also revealed several steps aimed at responding to the external shock.

The first measure was to scrap bank deposits usually demanded from tax payers in the timber sector and the factory-entry tax for the second and third stage of timber processing (Crtv Nouvelles, 20.11.2009). The measure helped to reduce the constraints that limit business activities in the timber sector.

[10] The Prime Minister's complete policy presentation can be found in: http://www.crtv.cm/cont/nouvelles/nouvelles_sola_fr.php?idField=5467&table=nouvelles&sub=special (04.02.2009).

Hence, there was a net improvement of cash-flow in the sector to the effect of about CFAF 13 billion. The second measure was the suspension of custom duties and dues on certain consumer goods, but the Common External Tariff (CET) on cement remained in force (Crtv Nouvelles, 20.11.2009). The government tightened price controls and intensified the promotional campaigns to increase the production of staple food as well as beefing up consumer protection policy with a new institution known as the Quality and Standard Agency (Crtv Nouvelles, 20.11.2009). In general, trade policy measures which include a reduction or a waiving of import taxes on equipment, tools and goods required for the research on oil exploration were put in place.

One would argue that the GFC has exposed Cameroon's woes and has forced the government to reconsider the need of reforming the country's political and economic system. Besides the aforementioned measures, the government quickly assembled a group of scientists, researchers, experts and analysts in economic and political circles for policy advice. The group was assigned to forward long term policy proposals reflecting the situation in the country[11]. After months of intensive deliberations, the group outlined measures that covered economic, political and social areas of the country (Rapport du Groupe de Reflexion sur la Crise Financiere et Economique Internationale)[12]. The measures reflected different channels through which the GFC has affected Cameroon. The group's proposal was divided into two major sections:

The first section focused on policy implementation and promotion of growth. The measures comprise; first, execution of investment in terms of restructuring and securing the infrastructure cycle[13]; second, effective implementation of sectoral policies which cover agriculture, industry, forestry, housing and public works[14]; and third, development of human resources, research and technology. The second section of the policy document focused on the instruments to realise the proposed growth measures. The instruments comprise; first, implementation of the public financing policy[15]; second,

---

[11] The group known as "Groupe de Reflexion sur la Crise Financiere et Economique Internationale" headed by Emmanuel N. Djoumessi deputy secretary general at the Prime Minister's office finished the task and submitted their report dated January 2009 to the government.

[12] Report available online: http://www.camticdevelop.net/article-31589111.html (23.10.2010)

[13] L'exécution des investissements structurants et l'arrimage au cycle des infrastructures

[14] La Mise en oeuvre effective des politiques sectorielles

[15] La mise en oeuvre de la politique de financement

implementation of Public Finances and Budget Policy[16]; third, strengthening the institutions and promoting good governance[17]; and fourth, intensifying measures aimed at attracting Foreign Direct Investment (FDI)[18].

Arguably, these measures are similar to the World Bank and the IMF conditions necessary to promote growth. However, past experience indicates that government has never been committed to political and economic reforms for fear of losing control of the political power and the state resources. This invariably cast doubts on the seriousness of the Cameroonian government to implement the group's recommendations. Particularly, the present regime has been reluctant to implement the reform measures aimed at liberalising the economy and the polity in the past. The trade-off between written policies and the implementation of policies continues to cast doubt on the government commitment to embrace political and economic reforms.

In November 2009, the Prime Minister of Cameroon presented to the National Assembly the government policy document (The Prime Minister details Government's Economic, Financial, Social and Cultural Programme for fiscal year 2010, Crtv Nouvelles 20.11.2009)[19] on measures to improve the economic situation in the country. The policy document suggests that the government has acknowledged the need for long term reform measures being necessary for sustainable growth. The presentation of the government's policy at the National Assembly implies that the government has indicated the desire to improve the living conditions in the country. According to the policy document, the long term measures were classified into two, namely: i) the Cameroon vision 2035 Paper aimed at transforming the country into a democratic and unified nation; and ii) the Growth and Employment Strategy Paper which marks the start in the concretisation of the government's growth vision for the country. It documents the stipulated government strategy to improve infrastructure, rural development, industries and services, health, education, social development, and governance (Crtv Nouvelles, 20.11.2009).

Some government action already has started. Government investment in infrastructural projects covers repairs and the construction of new access roads for an easy flow of traffics, transportation of goods and persons. Amongst the road projects indicated by the Prime Minister is the 35 multi-

---

[16] Les Finances Publiques et la Politique Budgétaire
[17] Les Institutions et la Gouvernance
[18] L'attractivité des investissements directs étrangers
[19] The Prime Minister's complete policy presentation can be found in: http://www.crtv.cm/cont/nouvelles/nouvelles_sola_fr.php?idField=5467&table=nouvelles&sub=special (04.02.2009).

year project aimed at reducing communication problems in Cameroon. Education and health sectors will receive more government attention in terms of budgetary allocation for improvement of existing facilities and the construction of new schools and health institutions; investment in modern facilities will take place. Government also undertook several measures aimed at improving the energy sector. In 2009, some of the energy development projects were launched, and other measures have also been planned for the later years (Crtv Nouvelles, 04.02.2010). For example, two important projects were already started: the construction process of the Kribi gas plant, and the signing of a CFAF 365 billion service contract to finance the construction of the Memve'le storage dam, effected between the Cameroonian government and SinoHydro. The government has signed a memorandum of understanding with a South African Consortium, BUILT AFRICA, on June 16, 2009, laying out a framework agreement on pre-feasibility studies on the economic, technical, environmental and social viability in view of developing a 1.200 Megawatt Noun-Wouri hydro-power dam (Crtv Nouvelles 20.11.2009).[20] The memorandum is for a feasibility study on. Furthermore, the rural electrification programme has been intensified with additional 161 projects connecting different localities in rural areas.

Furthermore, the government took some steps towards increasing the production of profitable foodstuffs like roots and tubers, rice, plantain, manioc, potatoes, and palm oil (African Economic Outlook, 2010).[21] In addition, the government provided multi-faceted support in the production of key cash crops like cocoa and coffee. As estimated by the African Economic Outlook (2010), the production of cocoa will to reach 306,381 tonnes in 2009. This is an increase of about 28 percent over the 2008 production level. The increase can be seen as a result of the commencement of production from new cocoa plantations. Development of the plantations was supported by the national cocoa development firm (Société de Développement du Cacao) which provided cocoa growers selected high-quality seedlings.

The sum of CFAF 430 million was granted by the government to various common initiative groups and cooperatives for milk production projects (Crtv Nouvelles, 20.11.2010). Assistance was also given to "non-conventional"

---

[20] See more of this in the Prime Minister's 20.11.2009 policy programme for Cameroon, Tribune (09.09.2009), available online on Muslim TV: http://www.237online.com/200909091683/Actualites/Politique/cameroon-south-africa-implementation-of-bilateral-agreements-under-review.html (23.10.2010).

[21] African Economic Outlook Online version: http://www.africaneconomicoutlook.org/en/countries/central-africa/cameroon/ (15.08.2010).

livestock initiatives for the training of about 1,500 farmers. The sum of CFAF 1 billion was allocated to about 29,665 piggery owners in the Porcine Sector Development Programme (PSDP) (Crtv Nouvelles, 20.11.2010). Over CFAF 9 billion development assistance funds came from the Spanish government for the construction works on the National Nautical Arts and Fishing Trade Institute at the coastal town of Limbe (Crtv Nouvelles, 20.11.2010). Regarding basic food shortages, the government sharply reduced VAT and customs duties on basic food staples as well as on imports of agricultural inputs and at the same time raised civil service wages (Wodon and Zaman 2008).

The educational sector also profited from the programmes to counter the effects of the GFC so as to gain additional recognition and attention from the government. Thus, amongst the government measures taken to counter the effects of the GFC is an increase in the budget allocation to educational institutions for the improvement of the quality of education. In April 2009, the President opened an earmarked account for the modernization of Research in the State Universities. This was intended to illustrate the government's determination to support Research and Development (Crtv Nouvelles, 04.02.2010).

In the area of governance, the decentralisation process which was launched through Presidential Decree No. 96/06 of 18 January 1996 has also taken a priority stage following the GFC. Cheka (2007, p. 182) has argued that decentralisation has long been entrenched in Cameroon's constitution[22]. Regrettably, more than 15 years after the launch of the decentralisation process the government of Cameroon came up to initiate the implementation process. One cannot overemphasize the importance of a decentralised system in promoting democracy and participation in Cameroon. Decentralisation would facilitate active participation of citizens at local level in decision-making processes, especially on economic, political, and cultural development issues.

6 Conclusions and Policy Recommendations

From the economic and social point of view, Africa and Cameroon in particular were adversely affected by the GFC. However, the GFC has apparently forced the government of Cameroon to acknowledge the need to reform

---

[22] Article 55 of the Cameroon constitution stipulates that "decentralised local entities of the Republic shall be regions and councils ... decentralised local authorities shall be legal entities recognised by public law."

the economy and also the political process in the country. Regrettably, for more than two decades the Government of Cameroon has now been receiving conditional aid geared towards reforms but has failed so far to implement the necessary reforms. The continuous flow of aid helped the government to strengthen its "authoritarian" control of the country and its resources with reforms as good as futile. The continual flow of aid to a non-reforming state like Cameroon helps governments in Africa to consolidate the grip on power and the control of resources. This in turn hinders development and political and economic prosperity in the region and exposes these countries to the ills of global crises like the GFC.

The recent reform package announced by the government of Cameroon may appear promising. Past experiences still leave reasons for doubt regarding the implementation of all these policies. The negative impacts of the GFC, as indicated by the major macroeconomic variables and the sector indicators in this paper, could be tackled through short and long term measures. However, the success of the reforms depends on government's commitment to and the willingness to implement good governance practices, especially with regard of the rule of law[23]. The sever impacts of the GFC have offered another chance for the Cameroonian government to rethink on its political and economic development strategies in order to improve the living conditions its citizens and to create a healthy business environment for domestic investors and foreign direct investment (FDI). Any substantive reform which can bring sustainable growth and development in the country greatly depends on how far the government can adopt consistent economic policies, democratic principles, and the rule of law.

Pro-active change, especially on the issues relating to effective rule of law, transparency and accountability on the part of governmental and non-governmental actors, is necessary at this stage of development and is requested for confidence-building after the crisis. The recovering global economy provides reasons for hope, but recent IMF reports revealed a disappointing outlook for the Cameroonian economy and concern about the government's willingness to embrace reforms. Disappointedly, a recent report (IMF, as quoted in Ngalame, 2010) from the head of the IMF evaluation team suggests that Cameroon has not recovered from the impact of the GFC. On the other hand, government programmes, especially the priority infrastructure

[23] The absence of the rule of law (see the World Bank Worldwide Governance Indicators 1996 – 2008 for Cameroon) and the persistence of corruption in the institutions not only scare foreign investors but also neutralise national or local industrial and socio-economic activities in the country that could account for development (see Corruption in Cameroon, published by the FES in 1999).

projects initiated, have not been abounded (Ngalame, 2010). According to the IMF (IMF, as quoted in Ngalame, 2010)[24] the government had concentrated on micro reforms which did not have a strong impact on the growth of the economy and failed to prioritise major projects that would boast the economy. For example, the Cameroon - Nigeria highway project, funded mainly by the African Development Bank (AfDB), has not taken off. Despite the AfDB having provided its own share of the funding, the construction of this highway is still not underway. Recently, Cameroon's Minister of Economy, Planning and Regional Development attested that the country lost most of its markets within and outside the country due to bad roads (Ngalame, 2010). The implication of the delay on the Cameroon-Nigeria highway project is that regional integration and trade across borders within the region will continue to be limited. This has negative effects on Cameroon's economy because infrastructure is definitely a determining factor for economic growth.

Lessons drawn from the impacts of the GFC and its effects on government reform policies are in three dimensions; first, the impact of the GFC has sent a direct and strong signal to the Cameroonian government to redirect its policies and its leadership style; second, the government should consider setting an agenda towards long term reform measures that is credible and also implemented; third, the government should not see reforms as a dangerous undertaking with risks of losing the political equilibrium and the control of state resources, rather as necessary measures aimed at improving the living conditions in Cameroon and securing future prosperity on the basis of good governance.

References

African Economic Outlook (2010) of OECD and African Development Bank: Country Report on Cameroon. Found in: http://www.africaneconomicoutlook.org/en/countries/central-africa/cameroon/ (15.08.2010).

BBC News (10.10.2008): Financial Crisis „worries Africa". Found in: http://news.bbc.co.uk/go/pr/fr/-/2/hi/africa/7662893.stm (23.03.2009).

[24] Ngalame, Ntungwe Elias (2010): Cameroon's Economic Growth: IMF disappointed with Cameroon's stagnated economy. Found in: http://www.edennewspaper.com/index.php?option=com_content&view=article&id=11482:449&catid=14:economy&Itemid=163 (02.08.2010).

BBC online (28.05.2009): Global Crisis hits "human rights". Found in: http://news.bbc.co.uk/2/hi/africa/8071347.stm (25.01.2010).

Biya, Paul (1987): Communal liberalism, Macmillan: London.

Bolzen, Thomas: Länder-Lexikon (2010): Kamerun, 26. January 2010. Found in: http://www.laender-lexikon.de/Kamerun (26.01.2010).

BTI (Bertelsmann Transformation Index) (2010): Cameroon country report 2009. Bertelsmann Stiftung. Found in: http://www.bertelsmann-transformation-index.de/fileadmin/pdf/Gutachten_BTI2010/WCA/Cameroon.pdf (13.08.2009).

Bundesagentur für Außenwirtschaft Bfai: Kamerun, Wirtschaftentwicklung 2004. Found in: http://www.gtai.de/ext/anlagen/PubAnlage_776.pdf?show=true (10.06.2010).

Business Mirror (2009): Government bribes in Cameroon divert funds from food amid riots, Lexusplus.com, 6. January 2009. Found in: http://www.lexpressplus.com/Government-bribes-in-Cameroon-divert-funds-from-food-amid-riots_a673.html (23.08.2010).

Cameroon Tribune (09.09.2009): Cameroon-South Africa: Implementation of Bilateral Agreements Under Review, available online on Muslim TV: http://www.237online.com/200909091683/Actualites/Politique/cameroon-south-africa-implementation-of-bilateral-agreements-under-review.html (23.10.2010).

Cheka, Cosmas (2007): The State of the Process of Decentralisation in Cameroon, in: *Africa Development,* Vol. XXXII, No. 2, Council for the Development of Social Science Research in Africa: 181–196.

Chendjou, Leopold (2008): Le Cameroun dans la Crise: le secteur forrestier camerounais dans la tourmente, 20. October 2008. Found in: http://www.cameroon-info.net/stories/0,23787,@,le-cameroun-dans-la-crise-le-secteur-forestier-camerounais-dans-la-tourmente.html (25.01.2010).

Chendjou, Leopold (2009): Finances Publiques. Le Cameroun perd 71 milliards FCFA en trois mois, Le Messager 10. June 2009. Found in: http://www.cameroun-online.com/actualite,actu-10615.html (24.02.2010).

CIA World Factbook (2008/2010): Found in: https://www.cia.gov/library/publications/the-world-factbook/geos/cm.html (12.04.2010).

Congo Basin Forest Fund/CBF Fund (2008-2010): The forests of the Congo Basin, the second largest rainforest in the world, are an essential resource providing food, shelter and livelihoods for over 50 million people. Found in: http://www.cbf-fund.org/cn/why/index.php (23.02.2010).

Cramer, Christopher, Deborah Johnston and Carlos Oya (July 2009): Briefing, Africa and the credit crunch: From crisis to opportunity?, in: African Affairs, 108/433, P. 643-654. Found in: http://afraf.oxfordjournals.org/cgi/content/short/108/433/643?rss=1 (27.02.2010).

Crtv Nouvelle (03.02.2010): Compte à rebours : 2010 est année de la décentralisation. Found in: http://www.crtv.cm/cont/nouvelles/nouvelles_print_fr.php?idField=6055&table=nouvelles (04.02.2010).

Crtv Nouvelles (20.11.2009). The Prime Minister details Government's Economic, Financial, Social and Cultural Programme for fiscal year 2010. Found in: http://www.crtv.cm/cont/nouvelles/nouvelles_print_fr.php?idField=5467&table=nouvelles (04.02.2009).

Crtv Nouvelles (01.12.2009) : Message du Chef de l'Etat à la Nation 31 décembre 2009. Found in: http://www.crtv.cm/cont/nouvelles/nouvelles_print_fr.php?idField=5775&table=nouvelles (04.02.2010).

Dongmo, Stéphanie (2010): Pétrole : Les recettes de Cameroun baissent de 320 milliards FCFA en 2009: Le Jour Quotidien, 23. February 2010. Found in: http://www.africatime.com/cameroun/popup.asp?no_nouvelle=511116 (24.02.2010).

E/ECA/COE/28/6 AU/CAMEF/EXP/6(IV) (13.05.2009): The global financial crisis: impact, responses and way forward. Found in: http://www.uneca.org/cfm/2009/docs/FinancialCrisis_RegComm.pdf (30.01.2010).

Eba'a Atyi, Richard (1998): Cameroons's Logging Industry, Structure, Economic Importance and Effects of Devaluation. Found in: http://www.cifor.cgiar.org/publications/pdf_files/OccPapers/OP-14.pdf.

Erlassjahr.de-Briefing (2009): Kamerun in der entschuldungsinitiative. March 2009.

Export-Import Bank of the United States (2009): Impact of the Global Financial Crisis on Sub-Saharan Africa, March 2009.

Fonjong, Lotsmart (2004): Changing fortunes of government policies and its implications on the application of agricultural innovations in Cameroon, in: Nordic Journal of African Studies 13(1): 13–29.

Friedrich Ebert Stiftung/FES (1999): Corruption in Cameroon. Yaounde: Saagraph.

FUNDSFORNGOS (2010): IFAD's Rural Remittances and Development Projects under Finance Facility Remittances, 25. March 2010. Found in: http://www.fundsforngos.org/free-resources-for-ngos/ifads-rural-remittances-and-development-projects-under-finance-facility-for-remittances-ffr-1 (16.08.2010).

Gauthier, Bernard, Isidro Soloaga, and James Tybout (2002): A Firm's-Eye view of the commercial policy and fiscal reforms in Cameroon, in: The World Bank Economic Review, Vol. 16, No. 3: 449-475.

Hermes, Euler (2009): Cameroon country review, 31. July 2009. Found in: http://www.eulerhermes-aktuell.de/de/dokumente/country-review-cameroon-20090731.pdf/country-review-cameroon-20090731.pdf (15.02.2010).

IMF (04.03.2010): Relief?, IMF African Department. Found in: http://www.imf.org/external/pubs/ft/survey/so/2007/CAR0628A.htm (04.03.2010).

Crisis Group Africa Report N°160 (25 May 2010): Cameroon: Fragile State? Found in: http://www.crisisgroup.org/~/media/Files/africa/west-africa/cameroon/160Cameroon%20Fragile%20State.ashx (04.10.2010).

Ioannou, Iacovos and Raju Singh (2007): Cameroon: What Next After Debt Relief, IMF African Department. Found in:

http://www.imf.org/external/pubs/ft/survey/so/2007/CAR0628A.htm (10.02.2010)

IMF (2010 July): International Financial Statistics Yearbook, International Monetary Fund, Washington D.C.

IRIN News (2010): West Africa: Remittances set to fall in 2009, 11. November 2008. Found in: http://www.irinnews.org/Report.aspx?ReportId=81410 (16.08.2010).

Jain, Sachin (2010): Rural Marketing in India: A strategy to fight global Recession, Research Papers/Rural Marketing: Faculty, PCTE Group of Institutes. Found in: http://conf.pcte.edu.in/IMCTWGB2010/ResearchPapers/Rural%20Marketing.pdf (26.08.2010).

Konings, P.J.J. (1996): The post-colonial State and economic and political reforms in Cameroon Liberalization in the developing world: institutional and economic changes in Latin America, Africa and Asia. London/New York: Routledge.

Legicam.org (May 2009): Impact de la crise financiere et economique sur le Cameroun. Les propositions du GICAM. Found in : http://www.legicam.org/index2.php?option=com_docman&task=doc_view&gid=168&Itemid=92, (24.02.2010).

Les Afriques (03.11.2008): La crise financière mondiale casse le bois camerounais. Found in: http://www.lesafriques.com/cameroun/la-crise-financiere-mondiale-casse-le-bois-camerounais.html?Itemid=44 (21.01.2010).

MBendi Information Services (22.02.2010): Oil and Gas in Cameroon. Found in: http://www.mbendi .com/indy/oilg/af/ca/p0005.htm (22.02.2010).

Mbom, Francis Tim (2009): Cameroon: CDC hit by World Economic Crisis – GM, 09. September 2009, found in: http://allafrica.com/stories/200902091240.html (26.01.2010).

Ngalame, Ntungwe Elias (2010): Cameroon's Economic Growth: IMF disappointed with Cameroon's stagnated economy. Found in: http://www.edennewspaper.com/index.php?option=com_content&view=article&id=11482:449&catid=14:economy&Itemid=163 (02.08.2010).

Ministère du Développement Urbain et de l'Habitat (2010): Cadre de Politique de Recasement (Phase 3 – Financement Additional), June 2010. Found in: http://search.worldbank.org/all?qterm=cameroonpercent20urbanisation http://www.edennewspaper.com/index.php?option=com_content&view=article&id=11482:449&catid=14:economy&Itemid=163 (02.08.2010).

National Democratic Institute (ed.) (1993): An Assessment of the October 11, 1992 Election in Cameroon, Washington D.C./Yaounde.

Ngoh, Victor Julius (1987): Cameroon 1884 – 1984. A Hundred Years of History, Navi-Publication Group, Cameroon.

Ngome, Ivo & Judges Mpako (2009): Cameroon: In-flow of remittances: Use, trend, and factors affecting inflow of remittances. First African Remittance Conference (AREC-2009) in Yaoundé, Cameroon, 23-25 November 2009. Found in: http://www.africafiles.org/printableversion.asp?id=21792 (17.08.2010).

Njoka, Kingsley F. (2009): World Financial crisis: Cameroon's agricultural sector suffers major setback, L'Effort Camerounais 06. may 2009. Found in: www.leffortcamerounais.com/2009/05/world-financial-crisis-cameroons-agricultural-sector-suffers-major-set-back.html (25.01.2010)

Nyuylime, Lukong Pius (2008): Cameroon**:** Global Financial Crisis - Cameroon Feels the Pinch, l'Effort Camerounais, 21. October 2008. Found in: http://allafrica.com/stories/200810210847.html (23.02.2010)

Schmelz, Andrea (2007): The Cameroonian Diaspora in Germany: Its Contribution to Development in Cameroon. Eschborn: Deutsche Gesellschaft für Technische Zusammenarbeit (GTZ) GmbH.

Tambi, N. Emmanuel (1998): Trade liberalization effects on commodity imports in

Cameroon, in: Journal of Economic Studies, MCB University Press, Vol. 25 No. 3, 1998, pp. 193-202.

The Herald, April (2009): Global financial crisis: GICAM hatches coalition to cushion impacts, Issue 2208, Wednesday 22 -Thursday 23 April 2009. Found in: http://www.theheraldcameroon.com/business.htm (25.08.2010).

Trading Economics (2010): World Bank Indicators - Cameroon - Official Development Assistance. Found in: http://www.tradingeconomics.com/cameroon/net-bilateral-aid-flows-from-dac-donors-luxembourg-us-dollar-wb-data.html (20.09.2009).

Travel Document Systems (1996-2009): Travel document systems 2005-2009. Cameroon, Economy. Found in: http://www.traveldocs.com/cm/economy.htm (05.02.2010).

UNDP (2007/08): Fighting climate change: Human solidarity in a divided world. The United Nations Development Programme, New York, USA

UN News Centre (2009): Cameroon: UN funds multi-million dollar scheme to boost rural employment, 11 May 2009. Found in: http://www.un.org/apps/news/story.asp?NewsID=30758&Cr=rural&Cr1=development (18.02.2010)

US Department of State (2010): Background Note: Cameroon, Bureau of African Affairs (February 2010). Found in: http://www.state.gov/r/pa/ei/bgn/26431.htm (accessed 12.02.2010).

US Foreign Trade Division (2010): Cameroon's trade-balance statistics, 10. February 2010. Found in: http://www.census.gov/foreign-trade/balance/c7420.htm (04.03.2010).

Velde, Dirk Willem de (October 2008): The global financial crisis and developing countries, in: Background Note: Overseas Development Institute.

Wodon, Quentin and Hassan Zaman Rising Food Prices in Sub-Saharan Africa: Poverty Impact and Policy Responses. The World Bank Human Development Network & Poverty Reduction and Economic Management Network: Policy Research Working Paper 4738. Found in: http://papers.ssrn.com/sol3/papers.cfm?abstract_id=1277057 (24.10.2010).

World Bank (2007): World Development Indicators, The World Bank /IBRD;Washington D.C.

World Bank (2008): World Development Indicators, The World Bank /IBRD;Washington D.C.

World Bank (2009): World Development Indicators, The World Bank /IBRD;Washington D.C.

World Bank (2010): World Development Indicators, The World Bank /IBRD;Washington D.C.

World Bank Governance Indicators (1996 – 2008): Found in: http://info.worldbank.org/governance/wgi/sc_country.asp (02.08.2010)

World Bank Group (2009): World Bank to Help Mitigate Impact of Global Financial Crisis on Africa's Development. Found in:

http://web.worldbank.org/WBSITE/EXTERNAL/COUNTRIES/AFRICAEXT/0,,contentMDK:21984811~pagePK:146736~piPK:146830~theSitePK:258644,00.html (23.03.2009)

World Bank Group (2010): Millennium Development Goals. Found in: http://ddp-ext.worldbank.org/ext/ddpreports/ViewSharedReport?&CF=&REPORT_ID=1305&REQUEST_TYPE=VIEWADVANCED (14.08.2010).

World66 (2010): Economy in Cameroon. Found in: http://www.world66.com/africa/cameroon/economy (22.02.2010)

WTO Report. Press/TPRB/170 (20.07.2001): Trade Policy Reviews: First Press Release, Secretariat and Government Summaries: Trade Policy Review Body: Review of Cameroon.

Unit 3: Book Reviews and Book Notes

Global Financial Crisis and Developing Countries

OECD, *The Financial Crisis. Reform and Exit Strategies,* 2009, Paris: OECD, ISBN: 978-92-64-07301-2, pages: 99

Although the financial crises still persist, the OECD has delivered a short booklet which is intended to focus on two questions which are outlined in the introduction: "How and when can governments safely wind don their emergency measures? And how can we sensibly reform financial markets?" (p. 3). Since it is assumed that economic recovery is beginning, there is a debate on the future role of government after the "extraordinary measures to support financial markets and institutions" (p. 3). Thereof questions about actions to be implemented are to be discussed, which is a common subject among national policy makers, the financial industry and the central banks as ell as international financial institutions.

The structure of the study approaches the questions being raised by a very well documented and easily understandable survey of the origins, the schedule and of the overall impact of the financial crisis in the OECD member countries. Additionally, there authors deliver a clear survey of government interventions which have been implemented. Furthermore, the booklet summarises the actions which are proposed in the negotiations of the international serving as the floor of the debate on the economic policies being geared to overcome the financial crises. The study outlines the elements of the policy packages of the G 20, the European Union and related institutions which have been installed either by the financial industry or by the multilateral financial institutions. The first part of the publication is devoted the actual situation and the exit strategies. Two further chapters deal with the priorities which are recommended when reforming the financial markets and the timeline to phase out emergency measures. The first of these chapters discusses in detail the well-known and widely applied structure of actions by referring to the regulatory framework, the integrity and the transparency in financial markets and the capital adequacy rules. This chapter includes the tax policies' adjustment as it is necessary to remove distortions in the financial markets, the accountability of the financial industry, the corporate structures for complex financial firms and strengthening financial education programmes and consumer protection.

The user of the book is enabled to get insight into the various measures by a well founded and complete presentation as of early autumn 2009. It is noted that a strategy is only partly the outcome of the discussion and that relevant actions are not yet been underway. The study also underlines at various occasions that the policy approach implies to be effective adequate response from the financial industry. This argument is stressed also when considering the schedule of actions. The report calls on rollback measures as well as strengthening the corporate structures and competition. Privatisation of recapitalised banks (among others pools of long-term capital for equity), privatisation and the instalment of bad banks as well as a reinforcement of pension agreements should be put on the schedule.

The OECD has provided by this publication a very well organised presentation which refers to the state of art as of mid 2009. The book offers a very impressive insight into the intellectual analysis and offers a toolbox to be applied by policy-makers. There is a clear distinction between the gains from financial market liberalisation and the cost of any regulation efforts. The study confines itself to economic considerations and leaves out economic policy mechanisms, which among others are needed to understand why the actual policy design lagged in relation to the many G20 and G8 announced intentions. It is line with the state of art that the report does not hint at recent deliberations as in the IMF on crisis adjustment policies which should imply actions by the governments to return to sound budgeting practices. The paper refers mainly to the OECD member countries. However, African policy makers should look into the proposed tool box when designing reforms the financial industry and when pursuing policies to have a better access to the international capital markets.

Karl Wolfgang Menck, Hamburg

OECD, *From Crisis to Recovery. The Causes, Course and Consequences of the Great Recession*, 2010, OECD Insights series, Paris: OECD, ISBN: 978-92-64-06911-4, pages: 147.

OECD Insights is a series of primers commissioned by the OECD Public Affairs and Communications Directorate. They draw on the Organisation's research and expertise to introduce and explain some of today's most pressing social and economic issues to non-specialist readers.

The book consists of seven chapters. After chapter 1 including the introduction, chapter 2 looks at the roots of the financial crisis, including how techniques like securitisation greatly increased the vulnerability of banks to fail. Chapter 3 examines the routes of the recession – how a financial crisis developed into a crisis for the global economy. Chapter 4 looks at the impact on jobs, including the risk that the recession will be followed by a jobless recovery that contributes to a "lost generation" of young people in the workforce. Chapter 5 looks at the impact on pensions: the crisis highlighted issues in both funding and benefits that population ageing and changing career patterns could aggravate. Chapter 6 considers the push for new rules and standards in three key areas: financial markets, tax evasion and business and economic ethics. Finally, chapter 7 examines some long-term issues arising from the recession, including rising national debts, the prospects for turning the recovery into an opportunity for "green growth" and the challenges facing economics as a profession.

At the end of each chapter, there is a section offering pointers to further information and reading from the OECD and links to other intergovernmental bodies and information sources.

Achim Gutowski, Bremen

IMF, *Post-Crisis Growth in Developing Countries – a special report of the Commission on Growth and Development on the Implications of the 2008 Financial Crisis*, 2010, Washington D.C.: IMF, ISBN: 978-0-8213-8165-6, pages: iv+96.

The 2008 financial crisis has raised a number of questions about the best strategy for achieving sustained growth and poverty reduction in developing countries; foremost among them whether the failure of the financial system also signifies the broader failure of market-oriented capitalist systems. The Growth Commission of the IMF looks at this issue in this report. It assesses the 2008 financial crisis′ long term impact on developing countries, explains how developing countries can make themselves more resilient and examines what international institutions and forums can do to help.

IMF, *Global Financial Stability Report: Responding to the Financial Crisis and Measuring Systemic Risks,* 2009, Series: World Economic and Financial Surveys, Washington D.C.: IMF, ISBN: 978-1-58906-809-4, pages: xv+146.

The Global Financial Stability Report assesses key risks facing the global financial system with a view to identify those that represent systemic vulnerabilities. In normal times, the report seeks to play a role in preventing crises by highlighting policies that may mitigate systemic risks, thereby contributing to global financial stability and the sustained economic growth of the IMF′s member countries. In the current crisis, the report traces the sources and channels of financial distress and provides policy advice on mitigating its effects on economic activity, stemming contagion and mending the global financial system.

The report consists of the chapters. Chapter I called Stabilizing the Global Financial System and Mitigating Spillover Risks provides a global financial stability map. It shows that the crisis even has engulfed emerging markets; it also gives a deteriorating outlook for households and corporate defaults in mature markets and implications for the financial system. The stability risks and the effectiveness of policy responses are discussed. The costs of official support, potential spillovers and policy risks are analyzed.

Chapter II named Assessing the Systemic Implications of Financial Linkages provides four methods of assessing systemic linkages and explains how regulators assess systemic linkages and states policy reflections.

Chapter III called Detecting Systemic Risk questions what constitutes systemic risk and states fundamental characteristics of intervened and non-intervened financial institutions. Severe market perceptions of risk and financial institutions are mentioned and systemic risks through regime shifts are identified. The role of global market conditions during episodes of stress and policy implications are outlined. Finally, a conclusion follows.

all by Achim Gutowski, Bremen

IMF, Occasional Paper series, 2009, Washington D.C.: IMF:

***Fiscal Implications of the Global Economic and Financial Crisis*, no. 269, ISBN: 978-1-58906-850-6, pages: x+85.**

The financial and economic crisis is affecting the fiscal accounts of virtually all IMF members through several channels. It is now critical to reassess the state of public finances in light of the crisis and pursue strategies to ensure fiscal solvency. Major doubts about fiscal solvency would lead to destabilize expectations and might shake market confidence. A clear strategy to ensure fiscal solvency is, therefore, an important element for the resolution of the current crisis.

The paper prepared by a staff team from the IMFs Fiscal Affairs Department quantifies the fiscal implications of the crisis, assesses the status of fiscal balances after the shock and discusses the strategy to ensure fiscal solvency. The focus is primarily on advances and emerging market economies. While, for practical purposes, some of the empirical evidence presented refers only to the G-20 countries, information is provided also for other countries, and the analysis also applies to them. Section I provides an overview, section II estimates the fiscal costs and contingent liabilities arising from direct support extended to financial institutions and markets, looking both at the gross costs and the likely recovery from asset sales. Section III assesses the budget impact of the recession related to other non-discretionary effects (eg revenue losses from asset price declines) and the discretionary stimulus. Section IV looks at fiscal risks arising from the losses suffered by funded pension schemes. Section V presents the overall fiscal outlook for advanced and emerging economies, adding together the effects discussed in the other sections, and discusses risks to the baseline. Section VI assesses the outlook for fiscal solvency, calls for the early identification of a fiscal strategy to ensure solvency, and outlines the key components of such a strategy.

***Structural Reforms and Economic Performance in Advanced and Developing Countries*, no. 268, ISBN: 978-1-58906-818-6, pages: v+51.**

This paper examines the impact on economic performance of structural policies that increase the role of market forces and competition in the economy, while maintaining appropriate regulatory frameworks. It examines the effects of structural reforms on two aspects of economic performance: medium-run growth and macroeconomic stability and resilience. It improves the analytical basis of IMF policy advice by drawing on the lessons from broad-cross country experience. Therefore, major data collections were implemented, involving the compilation of indicators of structural reforms for a large sample of 91 developing and developed countries over the past three decades.

It includes indicators of liberalization in domestic product markets, international trade, several indicators of liberalization of the domestic financial sector and measures of external capital account liberalization.

The papers consists of VIII sections dealing mainly with the empirical survey; section V describes structural reforms and economic growth; section VI is about the sequencing of real and financial sector reforms; section VII deals with financial sector reforms and resilience; section VIII concludes.

***Developing Essential Financial Markets in smaller Economies – Stylized Facts and Policy Options*, no. 265, ISBN: 978-1-58906-775-2, pages: x+73.**

This paper was written due to the fact that there is a lack of guidance for the development of key financial markets for one important group of countries: smaller economies. They face a qualitatively different set of policy challenges than do their medium-sized and large counterparts, but there has been much less policy work done for them. The paper is meant to inform regular financial market surveillance and technical assistance, and be helpful to central banks and government agencies. It draws on Financial Sector Assessment Programm (FSAP) documents, technical assistance reports, IMF country reports, and central bank websites and documents in order to provide the appropriate cross-country data on smaller economy markets. 107 countries were chosen based on size and level of development; some of them have successfully developed their essential financial markets and thus offer positive policy lessons.

Section II is about the impediments to financial market development in smaller economies; section III describes foreign exchange markets; section IV deals with money and secondary government securities markets; section V informs about secondary equity markets; section VI is about regional integration.

all by Achim Gutowski, Bremen

World Bank, *Protecting Progress: The Challenge Facing Low-Income Countries in the Global Recession*, 2010, Working Paper Series, Background paper prepared by World Bank Group staff for the G-20 Leaders' Meeting, Pittsburgh, USA, September 24-25, 2009, no ISBN/ISSN, pages: iii+23.

This paper looks at the extraordinary range of challenges faced by low-income countries (LICs) as a result of the global financial crisis. It points out that, while not caused by LICs, LICs nonetheless suffer particularly. LICs don't have the financial means at their disposal that more advanced economies do, to overcome or even mitigate the crisis. As a result more people are estimated to slip back into poverty.

The crisis has led to a shortfall in funds of about 11,6 bn USD in the poorest countries, that is needed to protect the most vulnerable elements of society. Without the money to bridge shortfalls achievements fighting poverty will be lost, people will slip back into poverty and long-term prospects for development will erode. The World Bank concludes that more money is needed if poverty is to be reduced. LICs have made progress in recent years improving their macroeconomic policies, public sector governance and their private sector environment, which could enable governments to put money to better use, when the money is there. But the money is not there.

Beyond the current crisis the World Bank feels that there is need for a Crisis Response Facility (CRF) under the International Development Association's (IDA) umbrella to promote quick and effective assistance to LICs following severe shocks, according to performance based allocation rules.

While the paper highlights the present and long-term challenges and illustrates the urgent need for action, it fails to address some finer points in greater depth. The idea of a Crisis Response Facility is problematic. Few people doubt that there is a need to improve aid coordination and that crisis response measures are of vital importance to LICs. But what shape is this CRF to take? How and at what level will it be implemented? Who will fund it? Without an adequate and functioning information system a CRF may result in poorly timed, dirigisté responses. Waste of funds may be avoided in some cases, but performance based criteria may put some countries at a disadvantage over other countries, with better, more efficient institutions. The money may be sent elsewhere as a result. For a CRF to be successful at the global macro level, local micro and macro level coordination of stakeholders and governments may need to be improved first. Micromanaging this from a single location is bound to cause problems. Therefore a decentralized system of multiple regional CRF working together with local authorities, stakeholder and aid groups may serve a greater common good than one CRF can and is likely to be met with a warmer reception by the countries involved.

First and foremost institutional coordination at various levels needs to be strengthened and the flow of information needs to be improved. A CRF can oversee this process during its early stages of formation and propose improvements before being phased into action. But ultimately the question with a CRF is "Quis custodiet ipsos custodes?" (i. e. who watches the watchmen), where does the ultimate power reside? Any CRF must be subjected to rigorous external evaluation. Until these questions are sufficiently addressed and a more detailed proposal is put forth many doubts to the feasibility of this idea remain. The idea itself is laudable, but institutional design and implementation will be vital.

In the short-run more pressing matters such as bridging the funding shortfalls in LICs, preventing more people from slipping back into poverty and restoring long-term growth prospects need to be addressed.

Christopher Langelage, Himmelpforten

World Bank, *The World Bank Group's Response to the Global Crisis: Update on an ongoing 'Independent Evaluation Group' Evaluation*, 2009, World Bank Brief, Washington DC: World Bank, no ISBN/ISSN, pages: 32.

The Independent Evaluation Group (IEG) has undertaken an evaluation of the World Bank Group's response to the current economic crisis, focusing on developments since mid-2008. The purpose of the evaluation is to provide inputs for enhancing the impact of World Bank actions. The approach paper for the evaluation stated that IEG should deliver two main reports to the Committee on Development Effectiveness (CODE) by the end of fiscal 2010 and 2011, as well as interim notes for management and CODE. This first interim note presents a status report on the first year of the World Bank's response to the crisis.

This evaluation reviews the World Bank's attention to outcomes. A rigorous framework to track results is vital, as the volume of lending is at an all-time high much of it in the form of development policy loans. Whereas the approach to conditionality relies mainly on a small number of prior actions. An early sign of greater results focus today is the Bank´s mainstreaming of a requirement for results frameworks to underpin any type of financial support. In International Financial Corporation´s (IFC) case, the results framework embedded in recent initiatives includes implementation targets and expected development benefits. But in both IFC and the Bank, resources for implementation are tightly constrained, creating tensions between speed and quality. The World Bank´s crisis response will need to ensure oversight and careful attention to quality and impact.

World Bank, *Global Financial Crisis and Implications for Developing Countries*, 2008, Working Paper Series, Washington DC: World Bank, no ISBN/ISSN, pages: 9.

According to this working paper, the current financial crisis has evolved differently from other major crises that have hit the developing world in recent decades. Not only is it occurring in a world of unprecedented financial globalization, where the financial sector plays a historically large role in economic activity, but it is also an ´imported` crisis, with origins outside the developing world. The crisis also comes on the heels of a major global shock from high food and fuel prices that has imposed a heavy economic burden on many countries and significantly increased the incidence of poverty and vulnerability. The uniqueness of the current configuration of economic challenges has important implications for the nature and effectiveness of the policy options available to developing country governments.

It implies that the policy responses of individual developing countries are unlikely to measurably affect the depth and length of the global crisis. However, their actions can affect the impact of the crisis on their own economies. The authors mention that policy-makers need to be ready to react forcibly and quickly at the first signs of domestic weakness, including the rapid involvement of external assistance as necessary. More generally, countries need to maintain sound macroeconomic and financial-sector policies, while focusing on mitigating the potential negative impacts of the crisis on those living at the margin. The unprecedented scope of the crisis calls for innovative solutions to complement those more traditional policies. Further, the importance of multilateral and coordinated actions is highlighted.

all by Achim Gutowski, Bremen

World Institute for Development Economies Research (WIDER); The United Nations University (UNU), Helsinki: UNU/WIDER, Working Paper Series:

***Development Progress in sub-Saharan Africa – Lessons from Botswana, Ghana, Mauritius and South Africa*, Naudé, W., 2010/7, ISBN: 978-92-9230-242-9, pages: 10.**

The paper states that Botswana, Ghana, Mauritius and South-Africa are sub-Saharan African countries that have, in comparison, better development progress than other countries. Each of these countries has succeeded against forecasts and expectations. The paper synthesizes the common ingredients of these countries′ success and derives lessons. It concludes that smallness, landlockedness, tropical location, distance from world markets, racism, colonialism and other challenges can be overcome through appropriate institutions, governance and good economic policies.

***The Triple Crisis and the Global Architecture*, Addison, T. et al, 2010/1, ISBN: 978-92-9230-236-8, pages: 25.**

This paper deals with the global economy which is passing through a period of profound changes. The immediate concern is with the financial crisis, originating in the North. The South is affected via reduced demand and lower prices for their exports, reduced private financial flows and falling remittances. This is considered to be the first crisis. Simultaneously, climate change remains unchecked, with the growth in greenhouse gas emissions exceeding previous estimates, which is the second crisis. Finally, malnutrition and hunger are increasing and getting worse through recent inflation and global food prices. This constitutes the third crisis. These three crises interact to undermine the prosperity of present and future generations. Each has implications for international aid and underlines the need for concerted action.

World Institute for Development Economies Research (WIDER); The United Nations University (UNU), Helsinki: UNU/WIDER, *The Global Ecnomic Crisis after one Year: is a new Paradigm for Recovery in Developing Countries Emerging?*, Policy Brief, 2009, no. 2, ISSN: 1814-8026, pages: 7.

This policy brief is about the fact that is has become clear that after the global financial crisis the paradigm for international development has changed irrevocably. With leadership, moral authority and the capacity of the West diminishing, developing countries′ recovery and future growth will critically depend on their own initiatives and solutions.

The paper asks how the paradigm of international development has changed, what developing countries can do, on their own, to recover from the crisis and suggests how to avoid the long-term consequences of short-term policy choices. Mainly, rising food and energy prices coupled with poor growth in rich countries will pose a deadly combination for poor countries′ development prospects. The way forward for most developing countries may hinge on whether or not exports can continue to be relied on to fuel growth.

all by Achim Gutowski, Bremen

Oxfam International, *The Impact of the Global Financial Crisis on the Budgets of Low-Income Countries*, 2010, A research report for Oxfam by Development Finance International, Oxford: Oxfam, ISBN: 978-1-84814-112-4, pages: 42.

This report examines the impact of the global financial crisis on the budgets of low-income countries (LIC) to reach the Millennium Development Goals. Oxfam International commissioned this study to quantify the fiscal hole created for LICs by the crisis, and to examine their governments' policy responses. The key value-added of this study, compared with others, is that it is based on direct and detailed analysis of 43 LIC budget documents produced in June–December 2009, rather than just using global IMF datasets. Section 1 provides an introduction. Section 2 presents the fiscal hole in budget revenue created by the crisis. Section 3 analyses fiscal policy responses in terms of budget deficits and expenditures, looking in detail at expenditures needed to reach the MDGs. Section 4 looks at how the expenditures were paid for. Section 5 shows that countries have the fiscal space to spend more on making progress towards the MDGs.

The report urges the international community to make strong new aid commitments:

- The IMF to encourage LICs to spend more on MDG goals and on combating climate change and to report regularly on such spending;
- LIC governments to increase spending on social protection and education; taxation of income; property and foreign investors; and efforts to fight tax avoidance.

Achim Gutowski, Bremen

Oxfam International, *The Global Economic Crisis and Developing Countries*, 2010, Oxfam International Research Report, Oxfam: no place, no ISBN, pages: 72.

Oxfam's research on the global economic crisis in twelve countries, involving 2.500 individuals, is combined in this report with the findings of studies by a range of universities, think tanks and international organizations. The report reveals the depth and complexity of the impacts of the global economic crisis, and the vulnerabilities and resilience of poor people and countries worldwide.

The report consists of two main sections. Section 1 is about the impact, the resilience and vulnerability of poor countries and includes an overview of sub-Saharan Africa. Section 2 states responses to the crisis. For SSA, fiscal and monetary responses, economic policy and job creations as well as social responses are mentioned.

The crisis has highlighted social protection as a development issue, and the importance of managing risk and volatility at all levels. According to the authors, it is not enough to pursue economic growth now and social welfare later – the two must come together in pursuit of improved well-being. Poverty is not just about income or the lack of it; it is about fear and anxiety over what tomorrow may bring. This crisis will not be the last, but if one of its lessons is that reducing vulnerability and building resilience are the central tasks of development, then future crises may bring less suffering in their wake.

Achim Gutowski, Bremen

Oxford Policy Management, OPM briefing notes, 2009, Oxford: Hunts, no ISBN/ISSN:

***The 2009 Crisis and the developing countries*, 2009/03, pages: 4.**

This briefing note describes the impact of the global financial crisis on developing countries. According to the note, it is premature to assess in great detail the depth and the duration of these impacts or to identify which among the world´s poorest countries will face the biggest hits. The note is designed with the more modest intentions of first reviewing the current state of play, second summarising the channels of negative influence and third commenting on how these influences might best be mitigated. Four ways to mitigate the effects on developing countries are stated: the solution must be a collective one involving coherent policy response from a wide range of rich, emerging market and transition country governments. Also, the global system needs to nurture continued positive growth. Additionally, the financial sector spillovers of the crisis need to be understood and addressed explicitly as a part of the collective mitigation effort. Finally, the enhanced aid programs of the main multilaterals such as the World Bank and key bilaterals should address particular problems in some developing countries and those eligible for concessional flows.

***Effective targeting of poverty-focussed programmes – how to reach the poorest households*, 2009/01, pages: 4.**

Many poverty-focused programs, e.g. cash transfer programs, explicitly aim to target assistance or services at the poorest households. It is important, in terms of both poverty-reduction and financial efficiency, that such programs manage to target these households effectively. This briefing note outlines the key technical challenges to effective targeting. First, in establishing the target population; and second in designing an operationally feasible mechanism to reliably identify this target population.

Achim Gutowski, Bremen

Global Financial Crisis and Africa

Allen, Emma; Sam Maghimbi, *African Cooperatives and the Financial Crisis*, 2009, CoopAfrica Working Paper No. 3, CoopAfrica, Cooperative Facility for Africa, Cooperative Programme (EMP/COOP) of the Job Creation and Enterprise Development Department (EMP/ENT) of ILO, Geneva, Dar es Salaam: ILO Office for Kenya, Somalia, Tanzania and Uganda, Dar es Salaam, United Republic of Tanzania, International Labour Organization, ISBN: 9789221227434; 9789221227441 (pdf), pages: 31.

Because of the severe impacts of the global financial crisis (GFC) on the incomes of the producers and on the household budgets of consumers in Africa, also the cooperatives in these countries are affected considerably. Cooperatives are suffering from the GFC because declining incomes and restrictive household budgets impede the repayment capacity of debtors to financial cooperatives; therefore the potential for new credit granted from these financial institutions is further reduced.

The working paper brings out the impacts of the GFC on African economies and on individual producers and households, and then analyses the role of financial and agricultural cooperatives. Cooperatives have a huge potential for development, also in times of crisis as they are more resilient to external shocks than other ventures. Cooperatives are also motivated by long term gains and do not work on the basis of short term yields. Their investment strategies are more conventional and less risky. However, the working paper shows that the cooperatives are not immune against such shocks as the GFC.

The study analyses in detail the management problems of financial and agricultural cooperatives in the crisis. The effects of the crisis (shrinking global demand for African products and increasing volatility in commodity markets) reduced the incomes of the members of African cooperatives. Because of these direct impacts, the growth of the financial cooperatives is impeded – they become more cautious in extending credit to members. A sharp decrease in the growth of loan portfolios since 2007 is observed. It is also becoming quite clear from the working paper that state support is needed to keep cooperatives intact during and after such crises. Financial and agricultural cooperatives work in areas and sectors where commercial banks are not active, and therefore they can have beneficial effects on the welfare and on the productivity of producers, of workers and the self-employed in the agricultural sector. However, the cooperatives are not strong enough to insulate themselves from shocks and crises so that the state has a role to play. There is interesting material in the study on the role of such cooperatives in Kenya and Tanzania, as well as data coverage on the characteristics of such cooperatives in other African countries.

The Cooperation Facility for Africa/CoopAfrica was launched in October 2007 by ILO. ILO is working in this project for nine countries in Eastern and Southern Africa to assist cooperatives to improve their governance, efficiency and performance. Their capacity should be strengthened by the project – to create jobs, access markets, generate income, reduce poverty, provide social protection, and give people a voice in society. ILO is since more than 80 years active in cooperative development and has in this area a unique position among the institutions of the UN family. ILO sees in recent years a "renaissance" of cooperatives in Africa, what has various reasons (poverty reduction, growth enhancement, agricultural and rural development, deepening of the financial sector in rural and low income urban areas, etc.). However, a more favourable legal and institutional environment is needed for this to happen on a much broader scale (see: http://www.ilo.org/global/What_we_do/ Projects/..). The project is providing support services, is promoting effective coordinating structures, and is establishing and maintaining a challenge fund mechanism (which can provide support services). Three types of challenge funds are there: for subcontracting, for innovative cooperative ventures, and for training. A demand-driven and competitive selection of projects is envisaged. The project has also published widely assessments on cooperatives in other African countries.

Karl Wohlmuth, Bremen

José Brambila Macias; Isabella Massa, *The Global Financial Crisis and Sub-Saharan Africa – The Effects of Slowing Private Capital Inflows on Growth*, 2009, London: Overseas Development Institute, Working Paper 304, ISBN: 978-0-85003-906-1, pages: v+18.

The authors of the paper investigate the impacts of capital flows on the economies in Sub-Saharan Africa (SSA). They seek to identify what effects different types of capital flows have on economic growth, and examine the impact of a possible reversal in the inflow of private capital on the region due to the global financial crisis. To do so, Macias and Massa research what types of private capital inflows enhance economic growth and their importance for the economies in SSA, and also to which extent a decrease or a reversal in these private capital inflows might affect the economies in SSA countries.

The paper is divided into five sections. The first is the introductory part. The second section deals with the trends and composition of private capital flows to SSA, while the third section gives an overview of the literature dealing with the relation between private capital flows and economic growth. Section four and five investigate the types of private capital flows that enhance economies in SSA and conclude the paper respectively.

When the global financial crisis broke out, experts expected it to spare Africa as the continent was not profoundly integrated in the international banking system. It emerged later on that the continent will not escape the swirl of the crisis. Due to the contraction in the world economy, capital flows into SSA knew a sharp drop, and the economies of the region are experiencing a slowdown. The authors of this paper are trying to shed light on the importance of certain forms of capital flows for the economies of SSA countries.

In the introductory section, Macias and Massa sum up the situation of capital inflows in SSA before and right after the outbreak of the global financial crisis. The authors go on with identifying the types of capital flowing into SSA, putting a focus on cross-border bank-lending, FDI, bond flows and portfolio equity flows. Massa and Macias assert that "private capital flows into SSA have experienced a remarkable increase since the early 2000s". However, the financial crisis has affected the attractiveness of the SSA markets to foreign investors leading to a slowdown of the economies and a decline in real GDP growth. The next section presents literature available on the effects of certain categories of capital flows on the economies, simultaneously deplores the low number of studies of the effects on certain types of capital flows on developing countries. Finally, they deal with the fostering effects of four types of private capital inflows into SSA, coming to the conclusion that FDI and cross-border bank lending have significant effects of growth in SSA whereas Portfolio equity and bond flows have insignificant effects on growth.

In the light of these results, the authors in their conclusion assert that "the global financial crisis is likely to have an important effect on growth through the private capital inflows channel".

Macias and Massa created a paper which may help experts in advancing their researches but whose understanding might be difficult for the novice, who make first steps in the field of political economics. To reach the aim presented in the introduction, the authors use a panel cointegration regression analysis to study the private capital flows in a sample of selected countries. The authors have made their point and the aim of their paper clear, and the results they obtain are quite convincing as far as they seem to having considered most of the factors influencing growth. I'll agree with the authors concerning that the impact of FDI on economic growth is of great importance for the economic growth in the SSA region. Another positive side of the paper is the variety of the selected countries. The regional location of the selected countries allows a generalization of the study and enforces the results obtained by the authors. The reproach that can be made to the authors is that they did not explain the tables they used. The availability of the data and the lack of explanations leave the readers in a kind of fog and do not foster understanding. Summing up, the paper gives, in a convincing manner, a good outlook on capital flow in SSA and may be useful for policymakers while defining the focuses of their politics.

Christelle Sidoine Wonkam, Bonn

African Development Bank, *Policy Briefs on the Financial Crisis*, 2009, Dakar: ADB, no ISBN/ISSN.

The policy briefs on the financial crisis are produced by a complex of the chief economist with contribution from other departments of the African Development Bank (ADB). The policy briefs are intended to present analyses of experiences and lessons emerging from the financial crisis, so as to encourage policy debates that guide the search for sustainable solutions to the crisis. Examples are as follows:

***The financial crisis and access to financing*, no. 12, 2009, pages: 9.**

Africa´s access to international capital has been substantially reduced as a result to the financial crisis. Foreign lines of credit have virtually closed. Local African banks that have depend on credit lines from international capital markets have had to scale back operations or have turned to alternative sources of financing from regional development banks, such as the ADB. Private capital flows are now severely at risk of drying up as a result of the crisis. The situation calls for increased efforts to improve domestic resource mobilization. The paper deals with the increasing scarcity of financial resources, strategies for domestic resource mobilization, the role of the ADB and provides some suggestions to solve those problems.

***Africa and the financial crisis: an agenda for action*, no. 13, 2009, pages: 9.**

The economic and financial crisis affects all drivers of African growth: prices and demand for primary commodities, capital flows and foreign direct investment and regional integration, especially in low-income countries and fragile states. Many countries face the risk of twin deficits (current account and fiscal deficits) and the crisis threatens the positive results achieved in the last decade in the fight against poverty. The ADB engaged in several projects to provide additional funding and mobilizing existing programmatic instruments to support all countries, especially fragile states. The papers discusses those projects; the ADB is actively trying to initiate an early general capital increase to boost its risk-bearing capacity and to better position it to support member countries to face the adverse effects of the crisis.

Achim Gutowski, Bremen

African Development Bank, *Impact of the Global Financial and Economic Crisis on Africa*, March 2009, Working Paper, Dakar: ADB, no ISBN/ISSN, pages: 35.

The paper was successful in pointing out, as well as addressing, a number of essential areas in Africa's economy that were affected by the global financial crisis (GFC)[1].

By emphasising key statistics on financial integration, stock market capitalisation and financial globalisation indicators, the paper provides valuable perspective on why the global banking crisis has not affected Africa as much as other developed and emerging economies. It is, however, pointed out in the paper that some African countries have been more exposed to the contagion effects due to their larger foreign bank presence. The comparison of the impact of the GFC on African financial markets, sovereign debt spreads, the volatility of foreign exchange markets and commodity markets highlights key areas of vulnerability that need urgent addressing to enhance Africa's ability to withstand crises. This also applies to prioritising the streamlining of long

[1] Note that the paper still needs some minor editing such as, for instance, in the second-last paragraph of the executive summary.

and medium term transmission channels to address possible obstacles to trade and capital flows in a way that improve Africa's global competitiveness, as stressed in the paper. Africa's dependence on primary exports and its limited investment attractiveness is of particular concern in this regard. The papers' focus on specific sectors in the economic outlook after the financial crisis is also particularly significant for identifying areas of largest concern for specifically job loss and creation. Africa's economic development is especially prone to structural weaknesses as regards job creation as unemployment remains the main problem of the continent's poverty conditions.

Finally, with Africa having been somewhat insulated from the worst of the GFC, the paper draws attention to the fact that its anticipated growth-recovery will be essential in getting it back on track (or closer) to achieving the Millennium Development Goals. Although a recovery in global demand is necessary for Africa's growth drivers to start performing, it can create a head start by ensuring increased resource mobilisation.

Arno J. van Niekerk, Bloemfontein

IMF, Ltaifa, N. et al, *Impact of the Global Financial Crisis on Exchange Rates and Policies in Sub-Saharan Africa*, 2009, Washington D.C.: IMF, ISBN: 978-1-58906-796-7, pages: iv+19.

The paper deals with the large depreciations in some African countries ongoing with the global financial crisis. Collapsing trade and financial flows led to substantial balance of payments gaps, triggering fast depreciations and higher exchange rate volatility, beginning in mid-2008.

The paper studies the evolution of the exchange rates of sub-Saharan African countries in the context of the global financial crisis. In particular, it analyzes the reasons behind the differences in the magnitude and volatility of the exchange rates among countries. To explain the severe problems, it takes a sample of seven countries, e.g. Kenya, Rwanda, Tanzania, Uganda and three others, which experienced large exchange rate losses at the onset of the crisis: Ghana, Nigeria and Zambia. Chapter 1 provides an introduction to the topic. Chapter 2 analyzes the movements of the exchange rates with respect to the US-Dollar and two major currencies. Chapter 3 tries to link the magnitude of their movements to key factors, relating to the external environment and the countries′ internal policies. Chapter 4 provides a conclusion, mentioning that additional measures could be explored to mitigate the impact of external volatility in the short run.

Achim Gutowski, Bremen

IMF, Iossifov, P.; Khamis, Pl; Credit Growth in Sub-Saharan Africa – Sources, Risks and Policy Responses, 2009, Working Paper, Washington D.C.: IMF, no ISBN/ISSN, pages: 29.

In this paper, the authors analyze credit growth in Sub-Saharan Africa over the past decade focusing on the post-2002 rapid credit growth in selected countries. They analyze the main drivers of credit growth over the past decade and examine opportunities, challenges and policy implications associated with it. They first document the financial deepening that occurred during 1997-2007 and highlight the post-2002 rapid credit growth in a selected group of countries (Section II).

The authors next examine the contribution of demand and supply factors and catching-up effects to the observed growth and level of bank credit to the private sector in Sub-Saharan Africa. They use the developed regression models to check whether they can fully explain developments in rapid credit growth countries (Section III). They then argue that rapid credit expansion, whether a manifestation of an unsustainable credit boom or driven by fundamentals, can give rise to prudential and macroeconomic risks. In Section IV, they elaborate on these risks and discuss the choice of policies to mitigate them.

They conclude by evaluating the likely impact of the ongoing global recession and financial crisis on credit growth in Sub-Saharan Africa (Section V). Section VI provides a summary on the main findings.

Achim Gutowski, Bremen

World Institute for Development Economies Research (WIDER); The United Nations University (UNU), Helsinki: UNU/WIDER, Discussion Paper series:

***The Global Economic Crisis – towards syndrome-free Recovery for Africa*, Fosu, A.; Naudé, W., 2009/3, ISBN: 978-92-9230-214-6, pages: 22.**

Many had hoped that Africa would be spared the fallout from the global financial crisis due to mainly three reasons: firstly, crisis originated in the financial sector of the US to which Africa has limited exposure; secondly, expansionary fiscal and monetary policies implemented by the US and European governments seemed promising and thirdly, given the expansion of trade between Africa and Asia, there might have been some de-coupling of Africa's growth dependency on US and European growth.

However, Africa's financial sector did not escape unharmed, bailout programmes for the financial sector and stimulus packages adopted by US and EU economies never realised. And the increased trade between Asia and

Africa could not protect Africa from lower US and European demand for exports. The Asian economies were also adversely affected by the crisis.

Resultantly, the global economic crisis has induced two negative external shocks for African countries namely, a financial shock and a trade shock. However, Africa's resilience to recover from a crisis has improved over the past four decades specifically in terms of macroeconomic management and good governance (that progress with the incidence of multiparty democracy).

The authors belief that Africa "can-and will-recover" and calls for policy responses that leads to a syndrome-free policy environment in Africa. Specifically, African governments should avoid anti-growth policy syndromes such as state controls, adverse redistribution, suboptimal intertemporal allocation, and state breakdowns. Not only should Africa avoid such policies that contain "seeds of destruction", but it should also sidestep unintentional consequences of the way in which the advanced economies address their own recession.

Guidelines to sidestep such consequences, firstly, entail that trade channels to Africa are open, aid is distributed at an accelerated pace and irresponsible lending is avoided. Secondly, from the advanced economies' side, the authors appeal for the avoidance of financial protectionism to banks and to restructure the global financial architecture in such a way that responses for resolving the growing number of global challenges are better coordinated.

Lizelle Janse van Rensburg, Bloemfontein

***The Financial Crisis of 2008 and the Developing Countries*, Naudé, W., 2009/1, ISBN: 978-92-9230-171-2, pages: 22.**

Following the beginning of the financial crisis in 2008, there is now serious concern about its impact on the developing countries. A deep global recession is predicted through some media. This paper critically discusses that and concludes that, as far as the developing countries are concerned, a bit more optimism should be implemented. Although there are particular countries that will be adversely affected, there will also be countries that may be less affected, may avoid recession and may recover sooner than expected.

According to the author, there are six major reasons for this conclusion which are discussed. Without this resilience in the developing world, prospects for the world´s richer countries would be worse. Finally, some options available to the developing countries for minimizing the impact of the crisis are discussed. The crisis accentuates the urgent need for accelerating financial development in development countries. Both through domestic financial deepening, domestic resource mobilization and reform of the international financial system.

Achim Gutowski, Bremen

World Institute for Development Economies Research (WIDER); The United Nations University (UNU), Helsinki: UNU/WIDER, WIDERAngle Newsletter, no ISBN/ISSN:

***Africa's Recovery from the Global Financial Crisis*, June 2009, pages: 7.**

African economies have been shaken by the global economic downturn which followed the financial crisis of 2008. Africa's growth rate for 2009 and 2010 has been revised substantially downward by international financial institutions. The consequences of a reduction in growth, even if African economies may avoid shrinking, are likely to be higher unemployment and poverty, increases in infant mortality, and adverse coping with long-lasting impacts such as higher school drop-outs, reductions in healthcare, environmental degradation as well as political instability.

The papers discusses some of the steps which can be taken to minimize the impact of the crisis on Africa and speed up recovery. Given that Africa should have learnt from the lessons from past external crises, it is argued that countries should avoid to implement programmes which introduce so-called anti-growth syndromes. The international organizations should also play its role in ensuring that trade channels to Africa are kept open. Also, that promised development aid is distributed; that irresponsible lending is avoided; and finally that fiscal stimuli and bank bailouts in the Western countries do not negatively affect the status quo of the current unsatisfactory global financial architecture.

***How will the Financial Crisis impact on the Developing World and what can be done about it?*, February 2009, pages: 3.**

According to the newsletter, there are three main channels through which the financial crisis can affect the economies of developing countries. Firstly, banking failures and reductions in domestic lending; secondly, reduction in export earnings; thirdly reduction in financial flows. Many developing countries are currently quite resilient as a result of good growth, better policies and having learnt hard lessons during the 1998 Asian crisis. Finally, due to the huge fiscal and monetary expansion programmes being undertaken in the advanced economies and the efforts at the G20, including a global financial architecture, developing countries should be able to achieve sustainable economic growth and face a better future.

all by Achim Gutowski, Bremen

Stuart, E.; *A Crisis Multiplied*, 2010, Oxfam Discussion Paper, June, Oxfam International, no place, no ISBN/ISSN, pages: 22.

The paper "A Crisis Multiplied – how the global economic crisis, coming on top of other shocks, is worsening poverty in Burkina Faso" documents the impacts of the global economic crisis on Burkina Faso, which exacerbated the effects of the previous food and fuel price crises and was then made worse by serious flooding.

The paper consists of six parts: introduction; the impact of the economic crisis at the macro level; the impacts of the crisis at the micro level; government responses; donor responses and what the future prospects for recovery.

Based on interviews with a number of international donors, government officials, economists, civil society organizations and local people in Burkina Faso, the paper reflects how the multiple crises have affected the country´s ability to achieve the MDGs and considers the response of the government. The papers states that the main transmission mechanism for the economic crisis has been the cotton sector, where a 40% drop in prices paid on the global market has reduced government revenue and further impoverished cotton producers. However, in the medium term, the crisis is likely to affect the Burkinabe economy more significantly – and poor people´s spending power had already been hit by the increase in the cost of food prices.

The government has responded to these crises by producing an ambitious plan , including social safety nets and measures to boost the cotton sector.

Achim Gutowski, Bremen

Global and African Economic Reports

- Global Economic Reports

OECD/Development Centre, *Perspectives on Global Development 2010, Shifting Wealth*, Paris: OECD, ISBN: 978-92-64-08465-0 (print) and ISBN: 978-92-64-08472-8 (pdf), pages: 174.

The book documents the new geography of growth in the world economy that has been built up in the last twenty years (1990 to 2010). The per capita growth rate in China and in India, but also in many other emerging and developing countries, is now more than twice the per capita income growth in the OECD world (in the "affluent world" as named in the book). Although in Brazil and in other developing countries growth is also accelerating, the per capita income growth rates are less than twice the growth rates of the OECD countries. The growth of the emerging countries is interpreted in the book as a sign of a global shift in wealth, and also as a shift towards a greater role of emerging economies in deciding on the course of the world economy.

The theoretical foundation of the book is a statistical classification of countries into four groups of economies based on per capita income growth rates and income levels achieved over the two periods of the 1990s and the 2000s – the four groups of countries are the affluent economies, the converging economies, the struggling economies, and the poor economies. The "four speed world economy" considers the speed of convergence and the level of income reached in the process of catching up towards the OECD countries. The methodology is referring to two indicators, based on income levels and on per capita income growth rates achieved. Countries are classified according to the average per capita growth rate for the periods 1990 – 2000 and 2000 - 2007 and the level of income reached at the end of the respective period. The study looks especially at the "converging economies", as these are the "catching up" economies in the sense of "strong convergence". A country being able to reach an average per capita income growth rate more than double the rate of the high-income OECD countries is considered as a potential candidate to converge to the "affluent world" (although it may be still a low income country and not a middle income country). The period of the 2000s saw a large number of countries converge in this sense towards the OECD world, while the number of poor countries was halved in this period. The "four speed world economy" has important policy implications. The "struggling countries" and the "poor countries" have achieved less than twice the growth of the OECD countries at their respective level of development (the middle income level for the struggling economies and the low income level for the poor countries).

The book analyses the global macroeconomics of this change. The converging economies, but also some struggling economies like Brazil and Mexico, have built up huge foreign exchange reserves, and an important trade and foreign investment position; however these countries have also contributed to growing macroeconomic imbalances at the global level, especially so China with its current account surpluses, huge foreign exchange reserves, and an alleged undervalued currency. The financial crisis is related to these developments that have occurred since the 1990s and the 2000s, although the converging and emerging countries came out of the world economic crisis economically more powerful than before, even setting the pace in the world economy. The addition of 1.5 billon workers to the labour market had resulted in a supply shock to the global labour market, with overall decisive impacts and consequences. Interactions among the Southern economies have increased considerably, and the converging economies have increasingly built up their position in the struggling economies, many Latin American middle income countries and some African middle income countries, and in the poor economies, low income countries mainly in Africa, but also Pakistan. The geography of trade and investment has completely changed, as the converging and struggling economies began to dominate the commodity markets in low and middle income countries.

There has emerged also a huge technological divide in the "four speed world". The converging economies and also some struggling economies became important technology providers for other developing countries, especially for the poor countries, but they also became technological competitors to the OECD countries. Multinationals of these countries, from China and India, but also from Brazil and Mexico, more and more penetrated the markets of other developing countries and even became technology generators and R&D partners of OECD multinationals as the cost advantage of skilled personnel from these countries is used.

All the developing countries have now to adapt to these changes, implied by the "four speed world", by reorganising economic policies, especially trade and investment policies, so as to maximise national benefits. Trade liberalisation among developing countries is now seen as a huge benefit for all developing countries. A new division of labour is emerging among developing countries (including converging, struggling, and poor countries), which has been overlooked for long by policymakers in OECD countries, but also in developing countries, and also by international organisations being active in developing countries. Complementary factors, endowments, and resources can be used more fully among the developing countries in the "four speed world economy". At the global level, new forms of collective decision-making and new global governance mechanisms will give the developing countries new roles and new responsibilities, and some of the large converging and struggling economies are spearheading this process. Also the poor countries could benefit from this new role of the spearheading countries.

Altogether, the book is describing quite well the win-win situation being inherent in this global shift. Therefore, the book will contribute to a more positive view of these global changes and will also encourage an informed discussion about a pro-active support, continuation and acceleration of this positive trend. It should be made clear in further studies how strong the win-win situation is that emerges as an outcome of this process in various economic sectors, policy areas, countries and regions. The book is just an introduction to give a better understanding of this complex process, and deeper reviews will have to follow.

Karl Wohlmuth, Bremen

International Monetary Fund, *World Economic Outlook, Sustaining the Recovery*, 2009, World Economic and Financial Surveys, Washington D. C.: IMF, ISBN: 978-1-58906-807-0, pages: xviii+208.

The regular issues of the World Economic Outlook (WEO) are of great relevance for the multilateral surveillance of the functioning of the world economy by the International Monetary Fund (IMF). The IMF has in earlier reports of the WEO discussed some issues of global economic policy: the cycles and spill-overs in the world economy, the causes and the emergence of the crisis, the characteristics of the crisis, and the recovery after the crisis. This report analyses how to sustain the recovery, and this is a most important issue now as countries need advice how to avoid wrong policy actions that would threaten the recovery. The complex balance between maintaining supportive measures while preparing for reducing extraordinarily high levels of public interventions has to be realized at the global level. The IMF as an institution is well placed to give advice to countries and regions how to go along with this task.

Although there are signs of recovery according to the IMF Report, the overall pace of recovery is considered as slow. The IMF discusses the risk of a reversal, and the danger arising from the fact that uncertainty in the world economy that was reduced by public intervention and by central bank intervention at global level is still in the market. However, the IMF can only raise warnings that a premature exit from accommodative monetary and fiscal policy will be a danger for some time to come; the IMF can only propose concerted action at the global level to avoid such an outcome. The balance between public and private activity has to be sought by all countries individually and found at a multilateral decision-level. Important is it therefore how strong the rebound of private demand in the world economy is. And important is it also which shocks could disturb the more positive picture that has arisen on horizon. From advanced country to advanced country there may be different patterns of expectations, and a different pace in rebuilding confidence. The IMF Report discusses the type of recovery that has to be reckoned with.

The IMF Report also gives a frame for a medium-term strategy to rebuild the global economy at sustainable growth levels. Such a strategy has two major pillars – adjusting to the lower potential output and rebalancing the demand side. Financial crises in the past have had impacts on the output in the aftermath of crises, and a permanent loss of potential output can therefore be expected. Capital stocks may be reduced and unemployment may remain at high levels. Rebalancing of demand between current account surplus and deficit countries may be needed to avoid the re-emergence of global imbalances in the world economy. The IMF Report gives a long list of measures how to rebalance demand and how to generate adjustments on the supply side which are concomitant with demand side action. From all this it becomes clear that a sustained recovery depends on a global economic policy (along the lines of a G 20 approach and intensified IMF surveillance).

The IMF Report is also rich in the area of policy challenges discussed. In fact there is a middle course proposed between unwinding pubic interventions too early and leaving these measures in place too long. Therefore, four crucial elements are discussed: first, timing the tightening of accommodative monetary policy; second, maintaining fiscal support while safeguarding fiscal sustainability; third, healing financial sectors while reforming prudential frameworks; and fourth, responding to structural and social policy challenges. All this has to be considered globally – in advanced countries, in emerging countries, in developing countries, and in least developed countries, as interdependence in the global economy has dramatically increased.

The IMF WEO Report covers these issues in chapters on global prospects (chapter 1), country and regional perspectives (chapter 2), lessons for monetary policy from asset price fluctuations (chapter 3), assessing the overall loss by analysing the output dynamics after financial crises (chapter 4), and then it contains an evaluation of the report by the IMF Executive Board and a Statistical Appendix. The Statistical Appendix is useful as containing full information on data sources, methodologies, and a rich collection of important tables.

As a base for world economic policy, these reports are becoming more and more influential. In times of the G 20 governing the world economy such a multilateral surveillance framework is more and more needed to prepare decision-making of the world economic leaders. The particular IMF Report also signifies a new thinking in the IMF – conventional wisdom and simple macroeconomic decision rules are no longer the base of evaluations, projections, and policy descriptions. Keynesian elements of policy design are seen as relevant to reach sustainable global growth; unconventional reforms of financial sectors and proactive measures to deal with poverty, inequality, and unemployment are increasingly the order of the day. The old image of the IMF as a rigid creditor institution pursuing their conventional conditionality agenda in relation to poor countries is these days replaced by a new image of the IMF as an institution in the forefront of formulating frameworks for coherent world economic policies. The long-term trend of globalization, the rapid integration of developing countries into the world economy, the issue of high poverty and inequality in and between countries, the pervasive nature of global imbalances, and the high degree of cyclicality of the world economy are taken as the key elements that have to be considered in a future-oriented policy-making mechanism for the global economy.

However, it appears from the Report that the IMF is not only aiming at a new image, but that a real commitment for global sustainable recovery and long-term equitable growth is driving now this important institution.

Karl Wohlmuth, Bremen

World Bank, *World Development Report 2010, Development and Climate Change*, Washington D.C.: The IBRD/The World Bank, 2010, ISBN: 978-0-8213-7987-5 (softcover), ISBN: 978-0-8213-7989-5 (hardcover), pages: 417.

The World Development Report 2010 is highlighting the important theme of Development and Climate Change because of estimates that developing countries will have to bear 75 to 80 per cent of the costs of the damage caused by the changing climate. The developing countries and especially the least developed countries for sure cannot afford to bear these costs of climate change, because the loss would affect seriously their development prospects. It is even not possible for these countries to adapt to the climate change, because of the high costs involved. Some more fundamental action is therefore needed at the global level to safe development in these countries. The World Development Report 2010 with such a theme is therefore overdue. It is in the particular interest of the developing world to switch to a low-carbon growth path at the global level so that vulnerability to climate risks can be reduced in the developing countries.

The World Development Report 2010 has to be understood as an urgent call for change. Developed countries (and to some extent also developing countries) have to mitigate the climate change with ambitious programs so as to limit the warming of the planet caused by man-made greenhouse gas emissions. Developed countries have to support developing countries in their mitigation and adaptation processes, and this is not a too great burden for them. Developing countries on their side have to face the realities of climate change, and especially they have to redirect their policies towards adaptation.

The World Development Report 2010 comes to the conclusion that a "climate-smart" world is possible if three imperatives are accepted: first, it is necessary to "act now" to overcome inertia, as there are very high costs of inertia, and of not acting now in front of these dangers to the whole planet. The second imperative is to "act together" by reaching collective agreements to mitigate the climate change and by supporting collectively adaptation programmes in favour of developing countries. Although developed and developing countries have to bear the costs of mitigation and adaptation to climate change, it is necessary to help the developing countries to adapt to the consequences of climate change. Otherwise poverty will increase and growth will be reduced in these countries. Growth and sustainable development can be reached in this context of collective agreements on mitigating climate change and financing adaptation and development. The third imperative is to "act differently" than it was possible in the past; all has changed with the increasing vulnerability caused by the climate change ("stationarity is dead"). Acting differently means that huge investments are needed into an energy revolution to mitigate climate change and to finance adaptations to a different environment in front of climate change. Especially in areas such as agriculture development, agro-industry development, and water and land development new approaches (for mitigation and adaptation purposes) are needed.

It is timely to devote the 32nd World Development Report for 2010 to this call for change and policy reversal. It is an interdisciplinary work, as many disciplines have contributed, such as development economics, science, energy, ecology, technology, finance, and theoretical thinking about effective international regimes and governance.

As first information on main results, the Main Messages of the World Development Report 2010 are presented. The Messages make it quite clear that under certain conditions a "climate-smart world" can be reached. It must not be an illusion, or a utopia. Evidence is presented in the Report that even targeting a maximum of 2 degrees warming above preindustrial temperatures can only be achieved on the basis of a massive mitigation effort with very high cost; at the same time the 2 degrees target is probably the minimum increase of temperature that the world is likely to experience and it is evident that even this degree of warming is full of dangers to the planet. Such a warming – if it really can be limited to 2 degrees – will result in permanent reductions of GDP of 4 to 5 per cent for Africa and South Asia, the most vulnerable developing regions in the world and affected with the highest levels of poverty.

Climate change policy is not assuming that there is a simple choice between a high growth high carbon world and a low growth low carbon world, and so optimism comes in. Mitigation actions – to prevent climate change by reducing the emission of greenhouse gases – have substantial co-benefits in public health, energy security, environmental sustainability, and financial savings. Climate policy therefore ensures to build a world with high growth and low carbon. The Case for Action is presented in the Report quite well. As large uncertainties about mitigation and adaptation costs play a large role in the economics of climate change, estimates about costs are differing widely. This has implications for strategies what is outlined in various chapters. A climate-smart world with high growth and low carbon is of importance for the planet, for the developed and for the developing world. The report shows that such a world can be realised. The economics of climate change reveals that reducing the climate risk is affordable, especially when estimating the total mitigation and adaptation costs under various time horizons and various targets for maximum warming. Spending less on mitigation today will mean that higher adaptation costs will come forth in the future. Mitigation and adaptation costs have therefore to be looked at together (using appropriate scenarios and simulations).

The Report outlines after the "Case for Action" a full programme for "acting now", of "acting together" and "acting differently". Acting now is necessary to keep open as many options as possible for a sustainable living on the planet in the future. Acting now helps to overcome the dangers of inertia today and to avoid the otherwise higher mitigation and adaptation costs in the future. Acting together is necessary so as to balance globally equity, effectiveness and efficiency considerations of climate policy; collective actions can definitely save resources, increase effectiveness of agreements, and avoid policy reversals. Acting together is necessary so as to provide energy and natural resources for future development, and adequate food and water for all. Especially the continual provision of food and water is endangered because of climate change and increasing population pressure. Acting differently implies nothing less than accepting the need for revolutionary changes, such as an energy revolution, which is basically a technology revolution with regard of energy efficiency and energy production. A technology revolution is required in all sectors being important for mitigation (especially in transport and housing) and adaptation (especially for providing social protection and disaster management, and for improving natural resources management). Acting differently requires also a revolutionary transformation of land and water management as the competing demands for land and water have to be balanced at the global level. So it is also an agriculture revolution, a transport, industry and housing revolution that is ahead of us.

Something like a revolution is also needed in decision-making as decisions have to be managed in a riskier and more complex environment. More robust strategies are needed that cut across a range of possible future outcomes. Robust strategies cope with increasing uncertainty – they build on flexibility, diversification and adaptability. Technologies that better cope with uncertainties – by inherent flexibility and adaptability and by allowing for diversification – are increasingly important for mitigation of climatic risks and for adaptation to climate change. The need for new technologies relates therefore to mitigation (in sectors such as transportation, construction, public services, local advocacy) and to adaptation (in areas such as social protection, disaster risk reduction, natural resources management).

Another issue in the Report after "Case for Action" and "Acting for a climate-smart world" is "Making it happen", by relying on new pressures, new instruments, and new resources. This section of the Report may be the weakest part, as the other two issues are dealt with in various chapters by drawing on wide interdisciplinary analysis and on broad-based evidence. But

"Making it happen" is different. There may be new pressures for mitigation and adaptation in our societies, as preferences for clean technologies and for a sustainable world globally increase, and there may be new instruments like better global deals, new types of global technology transfer agreements, innovative cost-sharing agreements for large-scale and high-risk technologies, and agreements on global technical standards so as to save costs for disseminating new technologies. There may also be new resources for mitigation and adaptation when agreements on funding schemes for clean technologies are improved.

But the call for an equitable, effective, and efficient climate deal is presented in a quite technocratic design, and the reader is left with so many questions how in this world such a deal might come forth with such properties (and after so much bad experience with internationally negotiated climate deals). It is proposed in the report to learn from the experience of aid transfers, and to do it better now with transfers for financing a low carbon agenda, but the next page in the Report reveals the same fragmentation of funds, approaches, operations in climate finance as with aid programmes. Climate finance also shows – with regard of quantity of resources available – how great the difference is between what is needed according to estimates of mitigation and adaptation finance for developing countries and what is currently available to finance such programmes in developing countries; this is sadly enough – according to the figures in the Report – not more than 3% - 5% of the annually needed mitigation and adaptation finance for developing countries. The Pricing carbon model (by a tax or a cap and a trading scheme) is presented in the Report as highly superior to the prevailing CDM (Clean Development Mechanism) model, but the Report makes it clear that we have to live for some time with CDM type models (which only reduce the cost of mitigation).

So what about "Making it happen"? So many additional finance sources are discussed, and the role of private and public sectors is assessed in mitigation and adaptation. Public-private partnerships are also referred to in this context, especially in case of new large infrastructure projects. Also the view is correctly expressed that the climate issue is incorrectly perceived as a long-term threat, as we see already severe consequences of climate change. Stimulation packages after the world financial crisis are considered as valuable actions to green the economy while restoring growth – they can be at least partly accredited with triple dividends of greater energy savings, fewer emissions, and more jobs. But now at global macroeconomics it is a time of getting back to fiscal restraint, and the danger is great that climate policy is again overlooked for many years.

As usual, the World Development Report 2010 is equipped with tables for climate and world development indicators and references attached to each chapter. It is a fine analytic report full of evidence but only two issues are treated in a convincing way – the "Case for Action" and "Acting for a climate-smart world", but the treatment of the issue "Making it happen" does not show any new pressures, nor any new instruments and resources that would really give a global push and lead to immediate action.

Karl Wohlmuth, Bremen

World Bank, *Global Monitoring Report 2010: The MDGs after the Crisis*, 2010, Washington DC: World Bank, ISBN: 0-8213-8316-7, pages: 172.

This report examines the impact of the worst recession since the Great Depression on poverty and human development outcomes in developing countries. Although the recovery is under way, the impact of the crisis will be lasting and immeasurable. According to the authors, the impressive pre-crisis progress in poverty reduction will slow, particularly in low-income countries in Africa. No household in developing countries is immune. Gaps will persist to 2020. In 2015, 20 million more people in Sub-Saharan Africa will be in extreme poverty and 53 million more people globally. Even households above the 1.25 USD-a-day poverty line in higher-income developing countries are coping by buying cheaper food, delaying other purchases, reducing visits to doctors, working longer hours, or taking multiple jobs.

The crisis will also have serious costs on human development indicators:

- 1.2 million more children under age five and 265.000 more infants will die between 2009 and 2015.
- 350.000 more students will not complete primary education in 2015.
- 100 million fewer people will have access to safe drinking water in 2015 because of the crisis.

The international financial institutions and international community responded strongly and quickly to the crisis, but more is needed to sustain the recovery and regain the momentum in achieving the MDGs. Developing countries will also need to implement significant policy reforms and strengthen institutions to improve the efficiency of service delivery in the face of fiscal constraints. Unlike previous crises, however, this one was not caused by domestic policy failure in developing countries. So better development outcomes will also hinge on a rapid global economic recovery that improves export conditions, terms-of-trade, and affordable capital flows— as well as meeting aid commitments to low-income countries.

The Global Monitoring Report 2010 is prepared jointly by the World Bank and the International Monetary Fund. It provides a development perspective on the global economic crisis and assesses the impact on developing countries – their growth, poverty reduction, and other MDGs. Finally, it sets out priorities for policy responses, both by developing countries and by the international community.

World Bank, *Global Monitoring Report 2010: Concept Note – Achieving the MDGs in the Aftermath of the Global Economic Crisis: Prospects, Policies and Actions*, 2009, Board Report, Washington DC: World Bank, no ISBN/ISSN, pages: 14.

The global economic crisis has reversed some of the gains in living standards that the developing world has made over the last decade. Concerns are mounting about lasting impacts in poor countries, especially in Africa, on extreme poverty and hunger, primary education, child mortality, gender equality, and the incidence of major diseases. The World Bank estimates that by the end of 2010, 89 million more people will be living on less than 1.25 USD a day than would have been the case without the crisis. The crisis may have caused even more disastrous and longer lasting impacts on health indicators. As a result, the MDGs, already difficult to achieve for most poor countries before the crisis, may be moving out of reach.

This board report first analyzes lessons from the past crises and examines the extents regarding growth in poor or fragile countries. Building on complementary and ongoing research at the World Bank, the IMF and other sources, the report then analyzes the implications for the likely long term trajectory of growth and development indicators. Finally, the report discusses priorities for policies in developing countries, developed countries and international financial institutions.

World Bank, *Global Monitoring Report 2009: A Development Emergency*, 2009, Washington DC: World Bank, ISBN: 0-8213-7859-7, pages: 227.

This Global Monitoring Report 2009, prepared jointly by the World Bank and the International Monetary Fund, provides a development perspective on the global economic crisis. It assesses the impact on developing countries, their growth, poverty reduction, and other MDGs. It sets out priorities for policy response, both by developing countries themselves and by the international community. The report also focuses on the ways in which the private sector can be better mobilized in support of development goals, especially in the aftermath of the crisis.

According to the report, the global economic crisis is rapidly turning into a human and development crisis. No region is immune. The poor countries are especially vulnerable, as they have the least cushion to withstand events. The crisis, coming on the heels of the food and fuel crises, poses serious threats to their hard-won gains in boosting economic growth and reducing poverty. It is pushing millions back into poverty and putting at risk the very survival of many. The prospect of reaching the MDGs by 2015, already a cause for serious concern, now looks even more distant.

Chapter I is about the Global Financial Crisis and its impact on developing Countries. Chapter II deals with the improvement of the private investment climate for recovery and growth. Chapter III provides information about leveraging the private sector role in human development. Chapter IV is about the increase of aid to poor countries. Chapter V is called pressing ahead with trade openness and promotes a liberal and free trade. Finally, Chapter VI deals with international financial institutions, crisis response and support for the private sector.

all byAchim Gutowski, Bremen

World Bank, *Global Economic Prospects 2010: Crisis, Finance and Growth in Developing Countries,* 2009, Board Report, Washington DC: World Bank, no ISBN/ISSN, pages: 157.

According to the authors of this report, the world economy is emerging from the outcomes of a deep and synchronized recession provoked by the bursting of a global financial bubble. The consequences of the initial bubble and the crisis have been felt in virtually every economy, whether or not it participated directly in the risky behaviors that precipitated the boom and bust cycle. This report examines the consequences of the crisis for both the short and medium-term growth prospects of developing countries.

Chapter I deals with the prospects for the developing economies regarding global growth. Regional outlooks also include Sub-Saharan Africa. The commodity markets are described and their grade of being affected by the crisis. The impact of the crisis on the very poor is mentioned and conclusions are drawn regarding the policy implications for developing countries.

Chapter II analyzes the impact of the boom in global finance on developing countries including the shadow banking system and developing-country finance. Chapter III discusses the impacts of the crisis for finance and growth in developing-countries over the medium-term. Tighter financial-sector regulations on developing countries and the consequences for the role of foreign banks in the developing world are stated. The impacts of higher borrowing costs and developing countries' strategies for dealing with a weaker international finance system are outlined.

The report concludes that the crisis and the regulatory reaction to the financial excesses of the preceding several years may have lasting impacts on financial markets, raising borrowing costs, lowering levels of credit, and international capital flows. As a result, as compared with its pre-crisis path, potential output in developing countries could be reduced by between 3.4 and 8 percent over the long run and trend growth in developing countries may be reduced by between 0.2 and 0.7 percent over the next 5 to 7 years as economies adjust to tighter financial conditions. The report further finds that the very liquid conditions of the first half of the decade contributed to the expansion in credit available in developing countries and that this was responsible for more than 50 percent of the approximately 1.5 percentage point acceleration of the pace at which many developing country economies could grow without generating significant inflation.

Achim Gutowski, Bremen

- African Economic Reports

OECD/African Development Bank, *African Economic Outlook 2010*, Paris: OECD Publishing, 2010, ISBN: 978-92-64-08652-4 (United Nations Economic Commission for Africa/UNECA being a third partner to the project beside of OECD and AfDB), pages: 281.

This is a valuable and very informative annual publication of OECD, AfDB and UNECA to present an economic outlook for the countries on the African continent. Four parts cover the economic developments in Africa, and they are of equal importance for the whole publication project. In the Part One there is an Overview of the Macroeconomic Situation and Prospects in Africa, of the External Financial flows to Africa, of the Trade Policies and Regional Integration Developments in Africa, of the Progress towards the Millennium Development Goals in Africa, and of the Political and Economic Governance Developments in Africa. In the Part Two of this Yearbook 2010 the special focus is on Public Resource Mobilisation and Aid to Africa. Covered are in this section important definitions and concepts, analyses of the state of Public Resource Mobilisation, challenges for African policy makers, and Policy Options. In the Part Three Country Notes are presented for almost all African states, with further information in full-length Country Notes being available online at: www.africaneconomicoutlook.org, to give additional information on the economic and political situation of the countries. The Part Four covers the Statistical Annex with key tables on the economic, human, and political situation. The four parts are integrated, so that the reader is not only informed about general themes but also gest information what follows from all this for the specific country. Country Notes and Statistical Annex allow it to compare the situation of countries (and this on the basis of mostly up to date information).

The main objective in the chapters of Part One is it that it is necessary to review the economic situation of Africa after the food price increases in 2008 and after the Global Economic and Financial Crisis in 2009 and to look at the crisis management. The main questions are: how were the countries and regions affected, how have the countries responded, which countries have shown resilience in times of crisis, and what can be done to increase resilience in future crises. The various regions of Africa had been differently affected by the global economic and financial crisis, the South African region the most, and the East African region the least. It is also important to learn more about the prospects of recovery in African countries and about the policies that are used or should be used so as to reach more sustainable development.

The Yearbook 2010 shows that African countries with sustained fiscal policy reforms in the past could use successfully countercyclical fiscal policy measures to combat the consequences of the global crisis. Obviously because of this fact the editors of the Yearbook found it as important to study in a special survey the role of public resource mobilisation. Public resource mobilisation can reduce the high dependence on external funds, and so also the negative impacts of global crises can be reduced. This survey is presented in the Part Two. Africa had been affected during the global crisis by the decline of foreign capital and of remittances, and it is therefore important to see how public resource mobilisation can make the country more resilient in times of crises, but also more stable in pre- and post-crises periods.

The other two parts of the Yearbook give valuable information on the country characteristics. The Part Three gives – in the form of Country Notes – a short but very concise view on the actual situation of the country and also on the most pressing needs for further economic and political reforms. The Part Four contains very important tables on key economic indicators, but also on human development indicators and on governance indicators. These tables add to the information in the Part Three, and so allow a comparative assessment of the situation of African countries.

The prior issues of the African Economic Outlook were all reviewed in other issues of the African Development Perspectives Yearbook, and in this volume of the African Development Perspectives Yearbook there is to be found a review of the three volumes of the African Economic Outlook for

2009. In the review of the African Economic Outlook 2009 (as well as in the prior ones) the approach used is analysed in detail and the model and the methodology of short-term forecasts is evaluated. The African Economic Outlook 2010 is an integrated report, containing all four parts in one book, while the African Economic Outlook 2009 was organised into an Overview volume and tow Country Notes volumes. It may that this 2010 volume can be more easily used as all four parts are included in one book. It also seems that the coverage of countries in Country Notes and the presentation of the focus issue of Public Resource Mobilisation are even better integrated with the forecasting exercise.

The volume for 2010 of the African Economic Outlook also highlights some new developments for Africa, like the increasing importance of donors outside of OECD's Development Assistance committee (DAC), but the new powers like China are increasingly active not only in aid and debt relief, but also in South –South trade, transfers of experts, knowhow and technology, and in direct investment. A serious data gap increases as not enough data are available on the activities of the new powers (from outside of the OECD world) in Africa, especially with regard of South-South aid, debt relief, trade, technology and manpower flows, and direct investment flows.

With the Part One (the Overview Part) the report is increasingly becoming a source on new developments in macroeconomic policy formation, external flows to Africa, trade policy and regional integration, progress towards reaching the Millennium Development Goals (MDGs), and on new developments in terms of economic and political governance. The current report emphasizes the increasing role of the eight Regional Economic Communities (RECs) in Africa, in view of the global crisis and in times of still so many outstanding issues in WTO Doha Round negotiations and negotiations with the EU on the Economic Partnership Agreements (EPAs). The role of the RECs is increasing, and the African Economic Outlook 2010 reports on new initiatives and new developments in various important spheres of activity, especially in infrastructure development. The reporting on the MDGs shows the impact of the global crisis on Goal 1 – Eradicating Extreme Poverty and Hunger, but also the need for public resource mobilisation and for more regional integration to act more forcefully in Africa on poverty and hunger. Some countries, like Niger, Burkina Faso, Madagascar, and Eritrea, should be given a closer look as they are not successful yet in eradicating extreme hunger and poverty in their countries. Uneven progress marks also the development with regard of others MDG Goals. The main message is that public resource mobilisation and accelerating regional integration can also be helpful for the realisation of the MDGs in Africa.

The Special Issue Focus on Public Resource Mobilisation in the Part Two of the African Economic Outlook 2010 is therefore quite timely. Reflecting on the sources of tax income, on the small tax base, and on the weak tax administration in Africa, the Report favours in this Part some new ways to broaden the tax base, to use the taxes in a more developmental way, and to reach the richer segments of the society. Pursuing a more redistributive tax policy instead of focussing mainly on a highly progressive income taxation policy is outlined as a new strategy, but the issues are not further elaborated. The view that urban property taxes, taxes and fees on luxury goods, and excise taxes should play a greater role in taxation policy is not new, but it is definitely an important point although political realities have prevented such a route in most of the countries. Combined with proposals for a more redistributive public expenditure policy, some new aspects for reforms and immediate actions in public resource mobilisation are presented. Too many African countries have concentrated fiscal effort on raising natural resource rents, what has shifted incentives in revenue collection away form more politically demanding forms of taxation, like income taxation. Resource-rich countries have increasingly shifted revenue effort away from taxation towards resource rents. These countries have also shown little interest in redistributive revenue and expenditure policies. The Special Issue Focus is in this volume is therefore of great relevance, but so far action towards these objectives is minimal in Africa. The idea presented in the Report to devote more aid towards improving the systems of public resource mobilisation is of great relevance.

This volume of the Yearbook is of great use to all those working in and for Africa.

Karl Wohlmuth, Bremen

OECD, African Development Bank, *African Economic Outlook 2009, Overview*, Paris: OECD, Development Centre Of The Organisation For Economic Co-operation And Development/African Development Bank, 2009, ISBN: 978-92-64-06170-5/41 2009 02 1P, pages: 196.

OECD, African Development Bank, *African Economic Outlook 2009, Country Notes, Volume 1*, Paris: OECD, Development Centre Of The Organisation For Economic Co-operation And Development/African Development Bank, 2009, ISBN: 978-92-64-07614-3/41 2009 07 1P, pages: 317.

OECD, African Development Bank, *African Economic Outlook 2009, Country Notes, Volume 2*, Paris: OECD, Development Centre Of The Organisation For Economic Co-operation And Development/African Development Bank, 2009, ISBN: 978-92-64-07615-0/41 2009 08 1P, pages: 381.

The collaborative work of the OECD Development Centre and the African Development Bank (AfDB), and since the *African Economic Outlook 2007/2008* with the United Nations Economic Commission for Africa (UNECA), resulted now in the eighth edition of the *African Economic Outlook.*

These publications – supported by the European Commission – aim to provide to policy makers, private sector operators, experts in donor organisations, and to researchers on an annual basis an objective analysis of economic and social developments and prospects of countries on the African continent. Major conclusions of the past reports were that Africa's economic performance, while showing considerable variation among countries, continued on the positive trend path that was observed in the recent years. In this report for 2009 one can see that the global financial crisis (GFC) has turned the international environment for Africa quite negative. GDP of Africa is expected to contract sharply in 2009 and to stagnate in 2010. This overshadows the fact that growth in Africa was in 2008 with 5.7 per cent for the fifth consecutive year in the range above 5 per cent. This positive trend had to do with favourable growth conditions, the settlement of some civil conflicts, with the continuation of reforms, and with some external improvements, such as favourable commodity prices, increased debt flows, and debt forgiveness. However, human security in Africa was still severely affected by weak governance, ongoing conflicts, and by vulnerability in the context of extreme poverty. With regard to the realisation of the Millennium Development Goals (MDGs) the results were also mixed. The new edition for 2009 looks carefully at the impacts of the GFC on African economies, examines the consequences of the crisis for the progress that has been made in the past with reforms, identifies the problems hindering a more rapid development and a realisation of the Millennium Development Goals (MDGs), and gives a short-term forecasting exercise for the current and the two following years. Also specific topics are covered in the Reports: while drinking water and sanitation was the theme in the *African Economic Outlook 2006/2007,* and technical and vocational skills development in the *African Economic Outlook 2007/2008,* the major theme in the *African Economic Outlook 2009* is Innovation and ICT in Africa. The theme is of great importance for policies to overcome the impacts of the GFC and to sustain long-term growth in Africa.

The "African Economic Outlook 2009, Overview" provides a general overview regarding the international environment, the macroeconomic performance in Africa, a progress report on the MDGs, and information on governance and political issues. The special theme of "Innovation and ICT in Africa" is taken up in the Overview Report and again in the two Reports with Country Notes. It is made very clear throughout the three volumes for 2009 that STI (Science, Technology and Innovation) are of crucial importance for

Africa's development. ICT (Information and Communication Technology) is presented as an instrument to make the economic systems in Africa respond dynamically to the need for upgrading STI. Many examples show that ICT and STI infrastructures create new possibilities to connect markets, to integrate landlocked countries, to make value chains more effective from producers to markets and consumers, and to allow for an application of STI to private and public sectors. Many continent-wide and region-wide initiatives in Africa aim at speeding up the establishment of ICT infrastructure. It is also good news that the private sector is active in responding dynamically to the demands for information and telecommunication technologies, even running ahead of donor funded initiatives. Despite of the financial crisis, Africa telecommunication companies attract investors. Africa is still the fastest growing cellular market in the world, and so the interest of the investors is unabated, although there are trends of restructuring and consolidation in the industry. Still rather weak is the power and the effectiveness of the African regulators of ICT sectors. Because of complicated taxation issues, reforms in regulation and taxation are needed to make telecommunication infrastructure really available to all sectors of the economy – formal and informal ones – and to use taxes on the ICT sector for the further improvement of connectivity. The chapter is of interest also because new ICT business models for low income households are presented. Micropayment systems, microfinance and microcredit systems play a role as well as connecting the small producer to market information, weather information, and technical advice on inputs and repair by mobile phones. Solar panels are increasingly used for maintaining rural radio stations and the excess energy for recharging mobile phones. The Report gives numerous new applications of ICT so as to use it for E-Banking, E-Agriculture, E-Education and E-Government. E-Government Reforms, E-Taxation and E-Trade are of great relevance for Africa so as to avoid the high transaction costs of traditional administration, customs, trading, and taxation procedures. Also in incubating African business ICT is increasingly important, and various initiatives are of importance for entrepreneurship development. The report concludes with a plea for E-Waste reduction strategies as also Africa is increasingly affected by the greenhouse emissions from ICT technologies and related waste from ICT installations.

The special themes of the various succeeding reports are of great importance for the policymakers. While technical and vocational skills development was the major theme in the *African Economic Outlook 2007/2008*, drinking water and sanitation was the special subject area in the *African Economic Outlook 2006/2007.* In the *African Economic Outlook 2005/2006* the crucial issues of transport infrastructure development in Africa were discussed. In the *African Economic Outlook 2004/2005* the key issue introduced was the financing of small and medium-sized enterprises. In the *African Eco-*

nomic Outlook 2003/2004 a discussion of another important key policy issue for Africa was presented – energy sector policies, and the interaction of energy and poverty issues. The first two *African Economic Outlook* reports for *2001/2002* and *2002/2003* did not contain specific themes, but were already discussing some structural issues. A gradual improvement of the project can be observed.

In the "African Economic Outlook 2009, Country Notes Volume 1" and in the "African Economic Outlook 2009, Country Notes Volume 2" we find analyses for now 47 African countries, what is up from 35 countries in the *African Economic Outlook 2007/2008*. In the Report for 2009 countries with 97 per cent of Africa's population and 99 per cent of Africa's GDP are now covered. While in the *African Economic Outlook 2003/2004* only reports for 22 countries were included, the *African Economic Outlook 2009* contains reports for 47 African countries what is really an impressive extension. This comprehensiveness allows for a deeper understanding of the challenges and the opportunities facing countries and regions in Africa.

This gradual enlargement of the number of countries that are reviewed in the *African Economic Outlook* is an important improvement to the overall Yearbook project. However, Zimbabwe is again excluded from the coverage, and this has obviously to do with the further aggravating political and economic situation in the country, but also with the lack of any reliable data coming from national sources. Otherwise the exclusion of African countries from such reviews is not a good idea as comparisons with other countries and evaluations of the situation in Zimbabwe over the years are no longer possible. Even under the current political and economic situation of Zimbabwe, and taking into account the serious prospects for the country, such an analysis would be important, not only for the international community, but also for the Africa region, and especially so for the future of the country Zimbabwe. However, the country cases covered are more or less representative for the five African sub-regions, and it is good that the number of countries evaluated increases gradually up to the high level of today, although it would be better to stay with the chosen selection and inclusion of countries from the first three issues also in subsequent reports, and not to delete any country like Zimbabwe that was already considered in a previous *African Economic Outlook.*

In the two Reports for 2009 containing the Country Notes the special theme "Innovation and ICT in Africa" is again taken up country by country under the heading of Structural Issues, giving more detailed inputs and experiences to the general discussion as presented in the Overview Report. In the two volumes with the country reports for 2009 we find reviews of the recent economic developments, macroeconomic policies, various structural issues, and also political and social context considerations. The analysis of country developments with regard to these four areas is useful, allowing for comparisons with regard of policies, projects, programmes, and adaptations to the changing international environment. It is also possible to use the experiences of countries that are presented in the two volumes for learning from good performance cases.

The "African Economic Outlook 2009, Overview" contains in Part Three: Statistical Annex" tables that cover not only basic indicators, but also demographic and poverty indicators, social indicators, and also political indicators. The political indicators are especially important for assessing the real foundation of governance and the support for reforms that are prevailing in the respective country (as, for example, the Corruption Perception Index, the Civil Tensions Index replacing the Political Troubles Index of former editions, the Softening of the Regime Index, and the State Pressure over Civil Liberties Index, replacing the Hardening of the Regime Index of former editions). The Methodology for all these tables is carefully explained. The Statistical Annex is valuable as including a selection of very important and so then also largely comparable data for African countries. An additional advantage is it that also the left out countries like Zimbabwe are represented in the Statistical Annex tables with some data, especially also on governance.

The editors consider their publication as a joint project by the African Development Bank (AfDB) and the OECD Development Centre, and now joined also by the United Nations Economic Commission for Africa (UNECA). The idea behind is it to combine the expertise and the experience of the OECD– when working on the OECD Economic Outlook and in the OECD Development Assistance Committee (DAC)– with the expertise and insight of the African Development Bank– when working on policies, pr ojects and programmes in and for African countries. The inclusion of UNECA makes sense as it coordinates – having a mandate for this – continent-wide the economic policies and programmes for Africa, and as it cooperates now intensively with the African Union on the annual Economic Report on Africa. An explicit aim for the *African Economic Outlook* is the analysis of the trends and of the short-term evolution of selected African countries by using a unique analytical model design for all country case studies. The common framework includes a forecasting exercise for the current and the following two years by using a simple macroeconomic model, together with an analysis of the social and political situation in Africa. Mainly policymakers, donor agencies, academic experts, and business people should benefit from these analyses.

A problem with the *African Economic Outlook* is the fact that the background to the modelling work is not explained more deeply. Reference is made to a standard macroeconomic model called Africalook (see the short description of the prediction models in the African Economic Outlook

2001/2002, p. 19). It is argued that the specific structural peculiarities of the countries are considered also in this framework. The modelling for the OECD Economic Outlook is used to forecast world demand as well as the prices of the non-traditional imports and exports being of relevance for the particular African countries that are included in the form of case studies, while predictions of the (traditional) raw materials prices come from World Bank sources.

A much greater problem is it that there are two important competing reports coming from Africa, the *African Development Report* from the African Development Bank (AfDB) and the *Economic Report on Africa* from the UN Economic Commission for Africa (UNECA) and in cooperation now with the African Union. Therefore it is not yet clear to what extent the joint project of the OECD, the AfDB and the UNECA really can contribute to a better understanding of Africa's development, and what the comparative advantage of the three (or four with the African Union) institutions and of the various reports really is, as the other reports also present analyses, forecasts, regional economic profiles, and country case studies. Both the *African Development Report* of the AfDB and the *Economic Report on Africa* of the UNECA (and African Union) are very rich in analyses, in forecasts, in policy recommendations, and in informative regional economic profiles and country cases. It may be that a new division of labour emerges over time with regard to the three reports. It could be that the *African Economic Outlook* focuses on country reports and on specific policy themes, the *African Development Report* on policy reforms and financing issues, and the *Economic Report on Africa* on sector and regional integration issues.

However, compared with earlier reports of the *African Economic Outlook*, the messages from the more recent ones are much clearer and stronger – the focus on international assistance strategies for Africa is stronger, structural impediments and solutions to Africa's development problems are highlighted more deeply, more and more country reviews are included, the comparability of country cases is strengthened, and the relevance of the presented data and of the forecasts has improved. The specific policy field that is covered – in this report the issues of innovation processes and the role of ICT for development – is always important a nd the analysis to the point, and the information presented in all the three Volumes for 2009 is useful for further analyses and for projections. It may however be quite important to work further on a clear division of labour between these three (to four) institutions that are producing such reports, in order to strengthen them as instruments for policy assessment and reform at the international, regional and national levels.

The *African Economic Outlook* can play a great role if the new trends in global development cooperation with Africa are reflected even more in the context of the annual focus theme of the *African Economic Outlook*, and as well in the frame of the policies of the specific African country cases that are considered and reviewed. The *African Economic Outlook* is highlighting the development cooperation issues in general and also with regard to specific structural, policy, and infrastructure development issues. So the country cases highlight now more than in the past the role of national priorities and policies and the development assistance implications of macroeconomic policies and sector development policies; also the issues of aid dependency and the debt problems of the countries are reflected, as well as the objectives, means and strategies for improving aid assistance to these countries. This is where the basic competences of the OECD policy departments, of the OECD/DAC forums, and of the OECD Development Centre really lie, and this vast knowledge should be utilised properly. It should also be made quite clear that the *African Economic Outlook* is a joint OECD-Africa project with considerable and fast increasing African inputs. This is not so clear and obvious from the image and the logo of the presented volumes of the *African Economic Outlook*. The inputs coming from Africa towards making possible these informative volumes are becoming greater, and this can be made better visible in the format and layout of the Reports. So it would be better to show that these are really joint OECD/Africa reports and not OECD reports on Africa assisted by some African institutions. Encouraging is the fact that the primary responsibility for the project had been taken over by the African Development Bank.

Karl Wohlmuth, Bremen

International Monetary Fund (IMF), *Regional Economic Outlook Sub-Saharan Africa – Weathering the Storm,* World Economic and Financial Surveys, 2009, no. 0258-7440, Washington D.C.: IMF, ISBN: 978-1-58906-857-5, pages: vi+92.

This Regional Economic Outlook (REO) for Sub-Saharan Africa (SSA) is part of the research work of the IMF African Department, and since 2008/2009 the Global Financial Crisis (GFC) and the "Great Recession" (as defined so by the IMF) are analysed in their impacts and effects on Sub-Saharan Africa and on the growth and development perspectives as well. In the first chapter of the REO one can find analyses of the impacts of the crisis on country groups, by the degree of affectedness, the policy reactions of governments by using countercyclical policies and by mixing financing and adjustment policies, the lessons to be derived from prior cyclical recoveries in Africa, the outlook for growth in the medium-term, and the policy shifts that are becoming necessary when recovery emerges what will require adequate action by governments to support the medium- and long-term growth agenda while preserving macroeconomic stability. In chapter two important issues of fiscal policy and economic performance in Sub-Saharan Africa are analysed, with emphasis on three core roles of fiscal policy (fiscal policy as a stabilization tool; fiscal policy as an instrument to preserve debt sustainability; and fiscal policy as an instrument for capital accumulation and growth). These three roles of fiscal policy have to be considered in the context of the current crisis, having in mind the immediate policy actions that are needed, but having in view also the future requirements and perspectives.

With this Report and with various other studies done by the IMF on the Global Financial Crisis and the Great Recession, a new role of the IMF becomes visible. The IMF is no longer propagating fiscal and monetary stability at any price and irrespective of the economic situation, but is recommending countercyclical policies where they are feasible so as to avoid negative effects on output and employment in Africa. Thereby, the gains from the growth and development process over nearly a decade should be preserved. At the same time, the IMF looks in the Report at the right point of time to switch from output stabilizing measures and countercyclical policies to medium- and long-term policies for growth so that the recovery is followed by more capital spending and better provision of public services in the context of improved public sector efficiency while preserving debt sustainability. Serious infrastructure gaps, the neglect of investment in productive sectors of the economy, such as agriculture and industry, education and health, low productivity and efficiency in sectors and enterprises, and weaknesses of social security and poverty alleviation systems require more capital spending and productive consumption.

The limitation of the Report is the confinement to the countries of Sub-Saharan Africa. Important are the models giving the base for the projection of the speed of recovery and the expected medium-term developments. It is also part of the policy of the IMF to give more general lessons to policy-makers, as it is the case in this Report with the advice on governance reforms and measures for the improvement of public financial management (PFM). The IMF refers to unique conditions of individual countries, but does not like to give cases of successful achievers or cases of countries with deteriorating governance systems (rather vaguely a group of fragile countries is mentioned). The Statistical Appendix is quite rich and methodologically sound, and the country groupings and methods of aggregation referred to in the tables are convincing and well explained.

Karl Wohlmuth, Bremen

Hamburgisches WeltWirtschaftsInstitut (HWWI)/Berenberg Bank, Axel Borrmann et al, *Afrika, Strategie 2030*, 2010, Hamburg: Berenberg Bank, no. 11, Vermögen und Leben in der nächsten Generation – Eine Initiati-

ve des Hamburgischen WeltwirtschaftsInstituts und der Berenberg Bank, no ISBN/ISSN, Access via presse@berenberg. de, pages: 112.

Economists of the Hamburgisches WeltWirtschaftsInstitut and experts of the Berenberg Bank, both based in Hamburg, have produced a report which provides a more than a short term review of the development potential of the whole continent Africa. The subjects being dealt with cover a long list of topics being relevant to assess the risks and chances for investors who plan for a period up to 2030.

The strategy to be pursued for the next 20 years in Africa proposes that the resources of the continent should be spent for diversification of the economic structure and of the markets being supplied especially delivering to emerging economies in Asia and Latin America. Sectors which inhibit the exploitation of the potential of the African countries should be strengthened by further investment. Local and foreign capital has to be mobilised by an economic environment which creates "good governance". Such a policy enables African countries to integrate into the world economy, to benefit from specialisation and to resist to global economic shocks. Official development assistance – as it is often requested by many African speakers – is not needed in the medium term. The proposal is elaborated from a comprehensive description of the economic situation, of the integration of the continent into the world economy. Sectors which are relevant to the future growth opportunities are additionally elaborated. Special consideration is given to the banking industry and the financial sector. It is not only the perspective which is worthwhile to mention.

The study identifies also the different economic exposure in various African countries. However, representatives from African countries may claim that the long-term focus should not put aside policy recommendations which match the short run challenges to the African policy makers as for instance the impact of the commodity markets trends and of the global financial crisis.

It has to be taken into account that the editors of the study focussed on economic issues. Social and political items and the links to economic policies are not dealt with extensively. The Hamburgisches WeltWirtschaftsInstitut and Berenberg Bank are recommended to provide an English version. Otherwise the results of the publication (written in German) which should be studied by representatives in Africa and international financial institutions cannot be communicated to those who should read it carefully when designing short and long-term strategies.

Karl Wolfgang Menck, Hamburg

Post-Conflict Reconstruction in Africa

Jean A. P. Clement; Shanaka J. Peiris (eds.), *Post-Stabilization Economics in Sub-Saharan Africa – Lessons From Mozambique*, 2008, Washington D. C.: International Monetary Fund, ISBN: 978-1-58906-677-9, pages: viii+397.

This is an interesting study about a country that has so far successfully managed its post-stabilization economics, although still great tasks and huge efforts are ahead to consolidate the achievements. The book is organised around important themes.

Three essays discuss the complex issues of growth takeoffs and of sustaining growth in the long term, with corresponding analyses of repercussions on the Millennium Development Targets (MDGs) of halving the poverty rate by the year 2015 in Mozambique. It is argued that the growth takeoff in Mozambique since the end of the civil war has some similarities to the growth takeoff in several fast-growing Asian countries, such as some ASEAN countries and China, India and Vietnam, but that now much more is needed in Mozambique to consolidate reforms and to reach sustainable long-term growth. Especially the governance-related and growth-supporting institutions have to be strengthened, and more participation by civil society is needed so that growth can become more broadly shared. The relatively high costs of doing business in Mozambique are an expression of institutional weaknesses and impede export diversification, structural change, and employment creation. Also the spending and the absorption of aid require much better institutions in the country.

Lessons are drawn in all chapters of the book from the case of Mozambique for other African countries, especially being of relevance for countries that had suffered from civil war and from the mismanagement of windfall profits from natural resources. The experience of Mozambique shows that much more than macroeconomic stability is needed for growth and equity. As important are a prudent external borrowing strategy, a strategic orientation for spending (by government) and absorbing (by central bank) aid, continuous improvements along the key human development sectors, and capacity building measures at all government levels. Although in this book it comes out clearly that a very specific growth strategy is needed to consolidate inclusive growth and to spend and absorb aid productively, the productive sectors of the economy (agriculture, industry, agro-industries, infrastructure, education and health, and the promotion of backward regions and of small and medium enterprises) are not adequately covered.

This is a severe neglect as all the studies on post-stabilization economics show how important these sectors really are for sustainable growth and poverty reduction. It comes however out that the MDG targets can only be met if the strategy over the next years is balanced between agriculture and non-agricultural sectors, if direct attempts are made to improve the income-earning opportunities of the poor households, if priority is given for expanding access to education, and if determined action is undertaken to increase agricultural productivity. Sustaining growth is much more dependent in the coming phase of development on technological catching-up strategies associated with institutional reforms and capacity building measures at all government and private sector levels. By doing all this in the three introductory chapters, the book is definitely a valuable addition to analyses on reform policies and reform packages in countries after conflict.

In a further essay the basic issues and problems of monetary and financial policies are discussed, again by deriving conclusions for future reform policy requirements for Mozambique and lessons for Africa and especially so for the post-stabilization countries in Africa. Monetary policy handling and macroeconomic strategy formation are very complex in countries with weak institutions, with a high degree of aid dependence, with a high dependence on minerals and oil and gas export revenues and related price and demand volatilities, and with a significant debt overhang. All this is the case in Mozambique as a monetary-based stabilization programme will only be effective if it is supported by fiscal consolidation. However, also strengthening central bank independence, reducing the debt overhang, and deepening the money, finance, and foreign exchange markets are needed as policy actions, especially if a full-fledged inflation targeting regime is followed as in Mozambique. The outreach of the financial system to rural areas, to backward regions, and to poor producers and consumers has to be extended, what also means that rural households and small venture in the country have to be reached by new institutions being able to deal with microenterprises and poor segments of the population. Lessons to be learned from Mozambique are that financial sector reforms are an important element of macroeconomic policy reforms and of improving the business environment so that this sector has to be given high priority in the new phase of post-stabilization economics.

In three further essays the broad, complex and important issues of spending and absorbing aid in Mozambique are covered. This is done by working with a DSGE (Dynamic Stochastic General Equilibrium) model in order to understand the conduct of monetary policy under alternative policy scenarios, by analysing the macroeconomic management problems and monetary policy rules in case of scaled-up foreign aid, and by discussing the government-donor relations and the new partnership models for government-donor coordination. There is a great emphasis on the issues of spending and absorbing optimally the aid flows to Mozambique. The main question is how monetary, fiscal and exchange rate policies can be conducted in a situation where aid flows are important for the fiscal budget and for the whole balancing of resources of the country, while they are highly volatile; however, also the natural resource exploitation revenues are volatile so that exogenous shocks have to be modelled. As aid flows and resource revenues may affect the real effective exchange rate (REER) an therefore also export competitiveness, the spending decisions of government and the absorption decisions of the central bank of its aid and other resource inflows have to be considered in various forms and scenarios and optimal monetary policy rules are to be derived. This modelling is useful not only for the case of Mozambique, although data limitations, structural conditions, and other operational issues have to be considered in application to other country cases. The complexity of formulating monetary policy rules and of pursuing fiscal consolidation in such an environment of volatile inflows is high; difficult choices have to be made of spending such flows by the government and of absorbing such flows by the central bank what leads to demands for appropriate models that can help in decision-making by outlining potential outcomes of alternative policy decisions. This is important for Mozambique but as well for an increasing number of other African countries as they are already or are becoming oil and gas exporters and minerals exporters. The DSGE model as developed for Mozambique is therefore applicable to an ever increasing number of countries in Africa. Although Mozambique has fully spent and mostly absorbed its aid inflows (of 10 to 20 per cent of GDP) so far, scaled-up foreign aid in the future may bring problems if not institutional reforms and capacity building efforts are speeded up in the coming years.

Careful management of further aid flows is therefore needed, but has to be accompanied by institutional reforms, by capacity building efforts, and by speeding up structural changes in the economy to overcome the megaprojects bias of the country. In order to avoid a pressure on the real exchange rate to appreciate which would hurt the export sector it is necessary to look at the supply response in the productive (and priority) sectors, such as agriculture, small and rural industries, education, health care, and infrastructure. Again initiatives for the development of productive sectors come in, as aid spending (as government expenditures) and aid absorption (as foreign exchange made available to the real economy by the central bank) have to be seen in the context of highly needed productivity increases and a requested much better public service delivery. To optimize the spending and the absorption of aid in the Mozambican policy environment is therefore an important management task, and all this depends on the path of development of the productive efficiency of the productive sectors and on the speed of improving the quality of infrastructural services and of public service delivery. At the same time, an exit strategy has to be developed so as to reduce aid dependency and dependency on megaprojects exports and minerals and oil and gas exports in the long run; fiscal consolidation, broadening of the tax base, financial deepening, and export diversification are the requested strategies. Only then will monetary policy and fiscal policy recapture their important role for development and policy autonomy. A further contribution in this group of essays relates to Mozambique as a model of donor coordination and cooperation with donors, as the country is indeed improving on various criteria of measured aid effectiveness. Much of the successes of the model are due to the increasing use of government systems and government institutions, so that parallel systems for aid delivery are avoided. From all this lessons for other African countries can be derived, although the unique case of post-stabilization economics in Mozambique has to be acknowledged.

In a further study the management problems of mineral and other natural resources in Mozambique are considered. Also in this area of policy new programmes and new avenues for action are recorded. The main policy problem is how to move from a system with large, ad hoc and arbitrarily negotiated fiscal benefits for exploitation companies to a system that is more neutral with regard of the type of resources and the size of the resource exploitation companies and more beneficial for the economy of Mozambique in terms of government revenues and spill-over effects to sectors and regions. Such a system is needed in order to attract investment on a more sustainable basis by strengthening control over using land and natural resources and by creating sufficient fiscal revenues so that the fiscal benefits can be more widely spread. The fact that old and new fiscal regimes/investment regimes will coexist side by side for a long time also creates management problems. Capacity building is thus important to handle these management problems. Creating linkages with other sectors, supporting neighbouring regions and providing benefits for the inclusion of affected communities are important objectives and elements of the new investment regime. New and encouraging moves to increase good governance and transparency in these sectors are visible at all levels; they are part of the new regime, but capacity building efforts are desperately needed to provide for the required human resources. In order to realize the new programmes for sustainable natural resources management Mozambique has accepted to become a member of all important regional and international good governance and transparency initiatives for the sector. Many lessons can be learned from the Mozambican case, and especially so the necessity to use fiscal and financial models for devising an optimal mineral and oil and gas exploration and taxation strategy and policy. Also the need to continuously review the mineral policy of the country is a lesson for other countries. However, it is not made clear in this and in other chapters how the human resource constraints can be overcome. Especially in the field of minerals and natural resources exploitation the new operational actions and the policy moves of the government in Mozambique have to be followed carefully.

In two final chapters important issues for private sector development are covered: improvements of the business environment and improvements of the export performance. Mozambique undertakes serious assessments of the overall business environment, and then after these assessments proceeds to change the regulations and the policies accordingly. In doing such assessments Mozambique uses comparator countries to analysis the business environment in detail and by looking at important policy areas. The evidence for comparator countries in Africa and in Asia shows that governance, institutional, financial, and regulatory issues are important, but also infrastructure provision and building up a credibility for macroeconomic stability. The respective action plans in Mozambique to transform assessments into new policies and regulations are important and convincing. A whole system of action plans and policy changes is in place. The action plans and programmes are related to potential growth impacts, and continuously there is a process of taking stock of reform effects. Lessons for Africa can be derived from the way how Mozambique is handling the issue. It is – as was done in Mozambique – always necessary to use windows of opportunity, to exploit quick win situations, to coordinate in the process all concerned agencies, and to look always at new demands for reforms. Again, also this area of policy shows that there is still a strong donor influence and donor impact, but it is emphasized again and again in the book that ownership of reforms is increasing in Mozambique. More evidence for supporting this statement is however not presented.

In the last chapter on Mozambique's export performance it is convincingly shown that it is necessary to go beyond promoting exports resulting from the megaprojects towards a much broader export sector activity with a diversified export portfolio. Limiting exports to minerals, oil and gas, coal, and hydropower from megaprojects will just continue the severe neglect of small and medium producers. Employment generation and poverty reduction depend on an expansion of exports from non-megaproject sectors. However, there are other areas of importance for redressing polices. Especially the fact that the Real Effective Exchange Rate (REER) is to some extent overvalued leads to corrective policy requirements in order to increase the overall export competitiveness. It is however not clear how to overcome the unfavourable situation with: a slightly overvalued REER, the concentration on megaprojects in exports, and the declining world market conditions for traditional export products. It is argued that manufactured exports should be promoted, but it is not said how this can be achieved at the prevailing level of development, and especially what type of agricultural and agro-industrial development strategy and/or natural resources related production of manufactured goods may be feasible. Improving the business climate and moving further towards broad-based MFN trade liberalization are mentioned as strategies to be followed, as well as making trade at sub-regional African levels less discriminatory. But again, the book is rather weak on concrete recommendations and especially so on sector issues. It is not at all clear which sectors, which sizes of firms, and which regions in the country may benefit from all this, and how the positive effects could be broadened. A move away from the capital-intensive resource sectors requires a new agro-industrial development strategy. But the issue is not covered at all in the book. While strategies to correct the overvaluation of the REER – by appropriate corrective monetary and fiscal policies and by avoiding Dutch disease effects resulting from aid and mineral resource inflows – are mentioned in a more general way, an overall strategy to support non-megaproject exports is not becoming visible.

The book is an impressive volume to highlight the post-stabilization economics of Mozambique, and many lessons can be learned from this country case for other African countries. However, the focus is narrowly on policy areas such as promoting growth by preserving macroeconomic stability, improving monetary and financial policies, reregulating investment and fiscal regimes for the exploitation of minerals, and assessing and promoting business climate and export competitiveness. But there is a gap with regard of all aspects of the development of productive sectors in Mozambique. A problem for the reader is the fact that there is no summary and synthesizing chapter at the end in the book. An Overview chapter is there, but it consists of short versions of the Chapter conclusions and the respective lessons derived for Africa. Nevertheless the book is of relevance for a number of post-stabilization countries in Africa (like Sierra Leone, Liberia, DR of Congo, Rwanda, Sudan/South Sudan, and still others). It is obvious that less developed and least developed countries after conflict and especially when endowed with rich natural resources should take the macroeconomic, governance, and institutional risks of aid and resource inflows seriously. However, the construction of a sustainable post-conflict economy depends also on choices with regard of developing productive sectors. The book is therefore of relevance for oil- and resource-rich countries after conflict which have to solve severe macroeconomic and economic policy problems but which have also to build up agriculture, small processing and manufacturing industries, and governance institutions by setting development priorities. The book is part of a series of IMF studies on post-stabilization economies in Africa, like the study on the DR of Congo (which was reviewed in another issue of the African Development Perspectives Yearbook). This study of IMF and World Bank experts is well presented and documented, but the composition and the methodology of the book reveal what matters most for the international experts of these organizations. This is the macroeconomics of stabilization. Most important is the respective collection of lessons that are derived from the case of Mozambique for other African countries. However, also the analysis of the role of aid in Mozambique and of the changing attitudes of government and private sector institutions toward the donors gives valuable insights.

Karl Wohlmuth, Bremen

Tony Addison; Tilman Brück (eds.), *Making Peace Work – The Challenges of Social and Economic Reconstruction*, 2009, Studies In Development Economics And Policy, UNU-WIDER, Houndmills, Basingstoke, Hampshire: Palgrave Macmillan; New York: United Nations University, Helsinki: UNU-WIDER, ISBN-13: 978-0-230-22245-8 and ISBN-10: 0-230-22245-5, pages: xx+346.

This collection of essays is important reading for all those working on the post-conflict reconstruction of countries after civil war. Social and economic issues of reconstruction are covered in the book in a multi-faceted way. It is an inter-disciplinary research work building on the experiences from many post-conflict countries and it is drawing from researches on reconstruction efforts, covering all important fields, actors, and sectors. External and internal actors are investigated as well as international and domestic policy approaches; sectors such as infrastructure and health, and economic sectors such as agriculture and industry are analyzed; fiscal institutions and a great variety of development institutions are examined. Based is the study on a Peace, Participation and Prosperity (PPP) perspective as it is argued that peace agreements will only lead to sustainable peace and to lasting reconstruction efforts if participation of people is ensured from the start and if prosperity creates a peace dividend great enough so as to avoid new violence.

Addison and Brück undertake it in their overview to highlight the interaction between peace, prosperity and participation. The PPP triad is of great importance throughout the whole book. The interrelations in the PPP triad are highlighted throughout all the essays of the volume. Fact is that the interaction between peace and prosperity is well documented in researches on countries in reconstruction, and it can be assumed that increases of per capita income will reduce the probability of conflict. Reconstruction has therefore to achieve quickly such increases, by generating fast responses of agricultural production and small industries and by increasing exports so as to exploit this important interrelation. The relation between peace and participation is less clear for countries under reconstruction after civil war, as country-specific and region-specific analyses matter. The reviewer is doing research on reconstruction of Sudan and South Sudan after the Comprehensive Peace Agreement (CPA) of 2005, and the review is therefore a good opportunity to confront the general messages of the book with the research results of our Governance Sudan Project (see the website on this project: http://www.iwim.uni-bremen.de/africa/Sudan.Drittmittel/Governance.html). The book review so becomes more of a type of review article. The case of Sudan shows the complex relationship between peace and participation. The CPA gives potential for participation, but there are so many unresolved questions surrounding the implementation of the CPA at all state levels, especially concerning the mandated Elections and the Referendum of 2011 for the independence of south Sudan. So the authors are right in asserting that participation will not lead in a linear way to peace. So many structural issues have to be solved to make peace and participation to become mutually supporting each other. Most uncertain is the relationship between participation and prosperity, as dictatorship and democracy can be associated with economic success, at least for some time. The "economic miracle" of Sudan after the discovery of oil for export is associated very much with civil wars and increases of poverty and inequality.

The book is an attempt to highlight all these interactions, but it becomes quite clear that only country-specific analyses will be of help to design appropriate reconstruction strategies after civil wars. It is necessary to look carefully at the causes of conflict, at the economic agenda of the groups that are competing for power, at the length of the conflict and the spread of the civil war. In Sudan, the last civil war has lasted from 1983 to 2005, and the Sudan has experiences conflicts and civil wars most of the time after independence. It is therefore necessary to look at the periods of peace, how stable they were in the past, and to see to what extent and if at all unresolved conflict causes have been tried to overcome. It is also necessary to look at the economic development problems in peace periods, as structural problems and inequalities have increased the fragility of peace. It is also necessary to study the extent of destruction of institutions and infrastructure in conflict periods. So it is important to see how agriculture, trade and transport sectors were affected by civil wars as well as the human resources base of the country. It is also necessary to look at the participation of people in decision-making processes at all state levels, prior, during and after conflict. If there was no participation in pre-conflict periods, a completely new political and economic approach is needed after conflict. The example of Sudan shows clearly that a formally agreed CPA cannot guarantee that a new approach is inaugurated. Participation in reconstruction of Sudan and South Sudan is not taken up and organized from the local levels to the higher levels of the state, but is organized exclusively by the representatives of the ruling forces in the Central Government of Sudan and the South Sudan Government. The authors and editors share in the book the hypothesis that PPP are mutually reinforcing each other, that the PPP triad is important for reconstruction work, but there is no clear understanding yet how all this fits together. So the volume is an attempt to bring some advance in the understanding of the PPP triad, so as to exploit the knowledge gained for a better reconstruction strategy in post-conflict countries.

The contributions to this volume give attention to all the factors that may support this hypothesis about the PPP triad. It is a great advance to highlight the "cautious" hypothesis in chapters 1 and 2 (Tony Addison and Tilman Brück). Instead of presenting wish lists for reconstruction of countries after civil war, the authors emphasize the necessity to use the interaction of the PPP triad for prioritization. Although the PPP triad is a theoretical construct, it can be exploited for prioritization. This is intended to be done step by step by the various authors to the volume under the guidance of the editors.

A first important element in exploiting the PPP triad for reconstruction is the analysis of the dynamics of civil war economies (chapter 3 by David Malone and Heiko Nitzschke). It is obvious that the complex dynamics of civil war economies – such as it is the case of oil resource-rich Sudan after the CPA – has to be understood in order to come to enhanced conflict prevention and conflict resolution, and to build up institutions and an economy for sustainable peace. Conflict transformation can only work if the economic dimensions of the conflict are really understood. The "greed versus grievance" debate was – according to the authors – too simple and then misleading in reconstruction efforts, so that the authors demand a real dynamic analysis of civil war economies. For the case of Sudan, although the CPA has taken up the issues of oil wealth and the long-term neglect of the South Sudan, the provisions for wealth-sharing and power-sharing in the CPA were inadequate. They were outlined in a rather simple and mechanistic way, and may be understood as a compromise between greed and grievance theorists, but not based on a dynamic analysis. In order to make progress, it would have been necessary to go beyond the incomplete peace agreement by devising long-term strategies and short- and medium-term actions to implement them. Regrettably, this was not done since 2005 in Sudan. Conflict transformation did not take place at a level needed for the sustainability of peace.

The next step in making the PPP triad relevant for reconstruction work towards peace is to look at democratization efforts (chapter 4 is written by Peter Burnell). The problem is to make synergies between peace-making efforts and activities towards building democracies. A look at the Sudan case again shows that such synergies were not aimed at and were not sought in the CPA. There was an agenda for peace-building and for fiscal transfers, but not an agenda to increase participation and to support democratization. The power-sharing agreement in the CPA did not advance democratization. To get a virtual circle from democracy and peace much more is needed. Trust between the partners – getting power and resources after the peace agreement – has to be created, what requests a permanent dialogue at all state, economy and society levels on long-term strategies and short- and medium-term actions. In the CPA some high level commissions were installed for this purpose, but not more. It was not made clear how trust and readiness for a dialogue could be promoted. The author sees some hope in some African countries; if multi-ethnic parties and broadly-based parties emerge, they can organize better for trust and dialogue. The case of Sudan again shows that nothing like this happened after the CPA in Sudan. There was no progress in inclusiveness of parties and movements – neither in the North nor in the South. The situation is worst for countries if all the three elements of the PPP triad are at a low level. In such cases the political awareness about PPP has to be created, and a clear prioritization of actions and a specific sequencing of reforms are needed to get forward with democratization based on PPP interactions which are mutually supporting each other.

Much more is needed. In order to get the PPP triad of such countries restored/created, the ethical dimension of post-conflict reconstruction has to be understood. In Chapter 5 (written by Sirkku K. Hellsten) the role of the social contract in post-conflict reconstruction is discussed. It is argued that the PPP triad can only be restored if a wider frame for justice is sought and implemented, going much beyond law and order (justice) towards justice in the sense of respecting local values, impartiality, and social cohesion. As civil wars lead to a breakdown/a transformation of moral values and of institutions, reconstruction of justice in a broader sense is requested. While peace agreements (like the CPA in Sudan) may have some value as incomplete social contracts, they have to be filled in the following periods by dimensions of justice which have to consider local values, reconciliation, and local rights, The tradeoffs in reconstruction policies are obvious, also in Sudan, as land rights in Southern Sudan are of a customary nature and have to be respected, although new investment may demand a balance between formal frameworks of justice and local values and rights. Formal justice frameworks and traditional ethical frameworks have to be balanced, what is difficult to realize; the case of Sudan shows that such a balance is even not existent in South Sudan. So the concept of justice has to be broadened from rule of law and order and security considerations to political justice, social and distributive justice, and reconciliation as a dimension of justice. It may be that so far all the reconstruction efforts in Africa and elsewhere have disregarded the broad concept of justice, by emphasizing property rights in a narrow sense mainly. These four dimensions of justice may be considered as basic requirements and as of strategic importance in post-conflict reconstruction so as to lay the foundations for peace, prosperity and participation. Reconstruction of justice in post-conflict countries is then becoming more concrete with regard of tasks than simply appealing for more democracy.

Another issue of great importance for policy reform during post-conflict reconstruction is the gender dimensions. In chapter 6 Marcia E. Greenberg and Elaine Zuckerman highlight these complex issues. The PPP triad can only be brought to work if three connected gender dimensions (women-focused activities, gender-aware programming, and gender role transformation) are considered adequately. It is argued that by such a new focus the returns to post-conflict aid can be enhanced and the stability of the peace settlement can be better preserved. The critical role of these three dimensions for the PPP triad is made quite clear in this essay. Otherwise new and additional gender imbalances can be the result. Again taking up the example of reconstruction in Sudan, the danger is great that post-conflict donor assistance creates further imbalances between men and women, or within these groups. The gender dimension has therefore an important and critical role for implementing the CPA. The authors give many examples from projects in post-conflict reconstruction showing how deficient so far the consideration of gender issues is. Demobilization programs and productive employment projects still ignore important issues of the gender dimension. Civil wars create new gender imbalances, and after the peace agreement misconceived reconstruction activity can lead to further imbalances. According to the authors of this chapter, the gender effects of war are the strongest indirect effects of civil war.

Good post-conflict reconstruction policies with regard of gender dimensions are in the interpretation by the authors always good development policies. The editors consider this as a basic message of the whole volume. However, because of the knowledge gaps as to the working of the PPP triad, it is extremely difficult to find out what good post-conflict reconstruction really is. It is interesting to see how difficult it is to use properly the vast experiences with gender projects and programs that international donors have recorded over decades. The experiences accumulated do often not fit the specific requirements of post-conflict countries. The dynamics of civil war and the dynamics of post-conflict reconstruction have to be considered as important elements of policy design and implementation of projects and programs. Gender dimensions also highlight the case that inequalities will cause conflicts but that conflicts may even be continued and accelerated in post-conflict reconstruction times – if not properly targeted programs for women, for wives of demobilized soldiers, and for women producers and traders are planned and implemented. Obviously most of such programs and projects in post-conflict countries do not fit in the context of the PPP triad.

Chapter 7 with a contribution by Frances Stewart on horizontal inequalities as an issue in post-conflict reconstruction is also important as the focus is on the (economic, social and political) discrimination of whole groups (ethnic groups, producer groups, religious and linguistic groups) or even of whole regions of a country (like South Sudan). The PPP triad implies that action is done to redress these inequalities as they cause conflicts but may also lead to new problems in case of ignorance during post-conflict reconstruction efforts. The case of autonomous South Sudan shows that a Dinka tribe-led rebel movement ultimately coming to power may provoke new problems in terms of horizontal inequalities, when the rights and opportunities of the other tribes are not considered. As ethnic groupings (Dinka and Nuer tribes) and economic groupings (activities as pastoralists or as sedentary agriculturalists) overlap, the responsibility of the government is great to respect the rights of all groups. Although the CPA has laid down a new relation between the North Sudanese and the South Sudanese, and also a federal structure in the North and in the South, the post-conflict reconstruction period since 2005 has not seen decisive action to overcome horizontal inequalities. Imbalances in social and economic opportunities even have increased since. Pastoral producer groups and sedentary producer groups may come into conflict if post-conflict reconstruction does not effectively care for their respective land use rights and for access to production inputs. If a government like those for the autonomous Southern Sudan is caring mainly for establishing central power in the capital city of Juba, and is not changing policies towards horizontal inequalities in the ten states of South Sudan, the post-conflict reconstruction may fail from the outset.

The issue is not only to have a constitution for balancing out the interests of the various state levels, but also of pursuing policies that aim at horizontal equalization of incomes and opportunities. Access of all relevant groups to assets and income, to social services and infrastructure, and to means for effective political participation is of importance. It seems now – one year prior to the referendum on the independence of South Sudan – that such policies are not becoming visible. Planning for post-conflict reconstruction all over Sudan means that all national and donor activities have to be in conformity with the principles of horizontal equalization. The handling of the Darfur conflict, of the issue of the displaced South Sudanese in the North, and of the wealth and power-sharing and border conflicts with South Sudan are not enlightened by active policies to reach horizontal equalization in Sudan. Distributive justice is neglected, and also other dimensions of justice (rule of law and security, and social, political, and social cohesion dimensions of justice) are not considered in the post-conflict reconstruction of Sudan.

The chapter by Frances Stewart is of great relevance for post-conflict reconstruction as it becomes clear how the situation even can become aggravated if not decisive action is taken. Post-conflict reconstruction should not only highlight classical instruments for horizontal equalization – like quota fixing or other administrative measures to strengthen the position of groups – but should address economic processes so as to reach the centre of economic power. For Sudan after the CPA, some quota fixing at the state level political and administrative representation plays a role, but at the level of access to resources and economic processes whole ethnic groups and even regions are still marginalized. The reconstruction process in Sudan since 2005 shows deficiencies also because the international donors have so far not considered the key issue of horizontal inequalities in their projects and programs. Entrenched rights and privileges would have to be changed, what would imply fiscal reforms, a new fiscal federalism, new forms of dealing with the oil wealth, new priorities in taxation and public spending, and modifying economic processes and the access to resources. It becomes clear from chapter 7 that advances in the PPP triad depend on successful initiatives with regard of horizontal inequalities.

The chapter 8 on rebuilding fiscal institutions (by reforms of public spending and taxation after civil war) is also of great importance. The authors (Sanjeev Gupta, Shamsuddin Tareq, Benedict Clements, Alex Segura-Ubiergo and Rina Bhattacharya) consider a most important aspect of the PPP triad. Fiscal policy during post-conflict reconstruction is the most important instrument to consolidate peace, to advance prosperity, and to secure participation. From the case of Sudan/South Sudan we know that rebuilding fiscal institutions is an extremely complex and time-consuming task, despite of the fact that so much expertise is made available to Sudan from IMF, World Bank, regional development banks, etc. Although the case of Sudan is a special one with South Sudan having already an autonomy status and heading for a referendum on its independence by 2011 and because of the wealth- sharing agreement on oil revenues, a lot can be learned from this case for reconstruction of fiscal institutions in other post-conflict countries. While in South Sudan the basis for such institutions has to be laid, in the North it is necessary to reconstruct a system that is effective, equitable and efficient.

It is obvious that at early stages of reconstruction the fiscal systems and the fiscal institutions will have to be simple and manageable, and so less than optimal policies and institutions are needed to go ahead in the transitional period towards sustainable growth. The authors also consider the unique windows of opportunity to introduce new taxes, a new tax administration, and to increase the tax base by changing the balance of interest groups in post-conflict countries. It is also highlighted that various complementary reforms (in finance and banking, in local administration and in statistical services) are needed to move ahead. Fiscal institutions have to be built up on the basis of a limited state capacity, and a low fiscal capacity will not allow it to distribute the peace dividend to the people. This also leads to the fact that donor funds are not spent timely for development purposes despite of being part of the budget. The case of South Sudan shows that large amounts of donor funds for reconstruction are not spent what has its reason in the fact that budgets are accepted by legislative and executive powers, but not readily executed. However, taxation systems must not only be simple and efficient as stressed by the authors of chapter 8, but also have to be integral to development policies and enforceable vis a vis all the interest groups. It is obvious and well demonstrated in the chapter that the reconstruction of fiscal institutions is of central importance for the PPP triad.

Health as a crucial sector for post-conflict reconstruction is considered in chapter 9 (written by the authors Hugh Waters, Brinnon Garrett and Gilbert Burnham). This sector is to be considered in the PPP triad as a quick-win area. Huge direct and indirect costs of conflict occur in the area of health, and in this sector there are the greatest chances to move up quickly with the PPP triad. It is made clear by the authors that the conventional three stages concept or framework may be useful but will not always be appropriate: to start with immediate measures to reconstruct the health sector after the peace agreement, then to come up in the medium-term with a whole package of essential health services, and ultimately to rehabilitate the health system as a long-term venture. The case of Sudan/South Sudan shows that such a concept may be disrupted because of ongoing conflict, because of the uncertainty about a new round of conflicts, and because of donors' reluctance to go ahead along these stages in an environment of political instability. So it can be that immediate steps and measures will go on for long periods of time without coming to the stages with packages and long-term strategies. The idea of the stages concept/framework is criticized also by the authors. It may not be realistic to realize these three stages synergistically and as part of a continuum as such an expectation may become frustrated by reality. The authors are therefore questioning the use of wish lists and of optimal frameworks for the reconstruction of health sectors in post-conflict countries. Prioritization and sequencing of measures may demand another framework for action – ongoing immediate measures for long, packages only for some areas, and health sector reforms on certain aspects only. Such a framework may be implemented along the improving supply of state services in general. It is obvious that the reconstruction of fiscal institutions, of health institutions and of infrastructure services institutions may demand quite different and adapted approaches for supporting the PPP triad. Immediate steps and adapted packages may help to further participation, prosperity and peace at local levels. Systemic reforms of the health sector have to wait for improved macro-governance conditions.

Infrastructure rehabilitation is the theme of chapter 10 (authored by P. B. Anand). The author makes it clear that the quality of infrastructure determines the level of transaction costs of the economy, and so the speed of post-war recovery is directly related to the building up of infrastructure. Maintaining infrastructure for use in the future is a key aspect, and this relates to the capacity of public and private sector institutions to sustain the infrastructure for services delivery. Maintaining infrastructure is therefore linked to the functioning of institutions to keep up the services of infrastructure. Rebuilding such institutions is a key task in post-conflict economies. Infrastructure is – according to the author – not only a physical asset, but mainly an important governance task. Three interrelated questions are to be answered: first, whether infrastructure should be reconstructed (as it was before, or in a different way); second, when it should be reconstructed; and third, how it should be reconstructed. It is also correctly emphasized in the study that donors too often and too long look at the hard investments of infrastructure but not at the soft institutions which are needed so that the services can be supplied. Participation is for such supplies a key, and so the PPP triad comes in again. Related to the infrastructure issue is the setting of clear priorities on the development strategy. If agriculture, fisheries, livestock, and forestry sub-sectors (with abundant resources to be found in South Sudan) are taken as the basis for rebuilding infrastructure, then infrastructure rehabilitation should concentrate primarily on this sector and on human resources development. Actually, there are not too many signs of conforming to this prioritization in South Sudan.

The last chapter 11 (written by Wim Naude) is on entrepreneurship development in post-conflict countries. It is emphasized that entrepreneurship in post-conflict countries will not automatically improve on the PPP triad. It is important to eliminate unproductive and destructive forms of entrepreneurship what is a difficult task because of the still weak state after civil war, and because of limited capacities of the private sector and of the donors in such an environment. As entrepreneurs react always to particular sets of incentives, the structure of incentives becomes important, and even a post-conflict society may transmit incentives to continue conflict and to concentrate benefits to a small group of winners from civil war. In the case of Sudan/South Sudan one can easily see how distorted the economic incentives still are – productive sector development, like agriculture and small manufacturing, is given much less attention than specific types of trade (arms, food, consumer goods, etc.) and construction (building infrastructure and hotels in the capital cities). Incentives for agriculture, fisheries, forestry and livestock are not only distorted, but are also conditioned by unresolved land rights issues. So it may be quite right what the author says – that increasing the supply of entrepreneurship might be less important than giving incentives for the reallocation of entrepreneurial effort to productive sectors and productive entrepreneurship. Removing barriers to business development, supporting the inputs side of the entrepreneurial process and decentralizing the provision of support services and of decision-making would be useful strategies. However, the case of Sudan/South Sudan again shows that all this is not enough. Decentralization of competencies to states and counties in South Sudan needs to be supported by human resource development and capacity-building, while removing barriers to business development is a highly complex issue because of overlapping and conflicting institutions that are affecting company and investment actors. It is correctly argued by the author that a good development policy is the basis for a good entrepreneurial development policy in post-conflict countries. Although these are very general lessons, they are valid. However, the case of Sudan/South Sudan shows that implementing good development policies is extremely difficult in post-conflict societies. It is also of importance that ethnic, immigrant, and minority entrepreneurs and their networks are considered in reconstruction policy. Again, in South Sudan one can see that ethnic, minority, and immigrant entrepreneurs play a great role, and for realizing sustainable development a discrimination of these entrepreneurial groups might be harmful. On the other hand, some measures to promote local entrepreneurs, by giving them special assistance and incentives, may be important. Some government and donor concepts on private sector development may be too vague and too general to be suitable for reconstructing the private economy in post-conflict economies.

The book is delivering key messages. First, the tensions between the goals of development and of peace-building have to be overcome by the day to day decisions – de-activating the spoilers of peaceful development and encouraging the poor people about the course of development. Second, it is necessary to understand the motives for conflict so as to be able to act, may they be horizontal inequality, grievance, greed, gender inequality, income and/or non-income inequality, governance problems, historical and religious factors, or external impacts on conflict. Third, implementation of reconstruction and delivery of services are important after peace agreements, so that capacity-building, human resources development and building up institutions are key priorities; however, the strategy and all measures have to be adapted to the level of the state institutions. Fourth, prioritization is necessary in order to avoid that too many programs, objectives, and projects are swamping the overall goal of the PPP triad; it has to be avoided that donors and local policy-makers can set conflicting priorities and pursue inappropriate actions. Fifth, global dimensions are increasingly important for a successful reconstruction in particular countries and regions; only at the global level measures can be taken to prevent that climate change, proliferation of arms, trade in illegal and dangerous goods, and flows of mercenaries and finance perpetuate conflicts or lead to new conflicts. The book brings out these messages in a clear frame for action.

The book is concluded with a short essay by the editors on the Way Forward. The particular situation of economies after peace agreements leads to patterns of growth that favor particular sectors (like trade and construction) while other sectors (like agriculture and small manufacturing, being of great relevance for a broad-based development and for poverty reduction) are not supported. Because of weak state capacity the danger is also great that post-conflict development leads to over-exploitation of natural capital what is especially dangerous for the development course of low income countries after conflict. The role of the state further increases in post-conflict development so as to prioritize the allocation of investment funds in times of scarce savings. However, the policy space of governments in post-conflict countries is limited because of institutional weaknesses and because of international trade regulations that restrict largely the use of subsidies and of protectionist support measures. A limited role of the state in enhancing the private sector activities is there in post-conflict countries, but the basis for a state-led development like in East Asia is not any more given. The state capacity in some areas nonetheless has to be restored forcefully, especially in providing for a sound domestic financial system, for rational fiscal policies and a good public sector administration, and for an effective foreign investment support management. It is necessary to concentrate on these key areas of state capacity building and on human resources development, irrespective of the general problem to find a viable balance between state-led and market-led development in post-conflict countries.

The Way Forward has also other important implications. Reconnecting the post-conflict countries to the global economy has to be combined with a reconfiguration of the interactions with the global economy so that the PPP triad can be considered. This means that all the interactions with the global economy have to be scrutinized to see if they are supporting the PPP triad rather than just increasing the volume of transactions in a particular field. This means that trade in goods and services, investment, migrant, technology and finance flows have to be scrutinized carefully, what requires the building up of appropriate capacity for such actions. Simplistic definitions of peace and war can also be impediments to development in post-conflict countries The case of Sudan/South Sudan shows that reconnecting these economies effectively to the global economy requires new development priorities beyond the limitations of the oil-based economy. The case of Sudan/South Sudan also shows how inappropriate simplistic definitions of war and peace can be; the conflicts in the north and in the South of Sudan are part of a complex continuum between war and peace showing that these two boxes are not amenable to reconstruction policies. The PPP triad has to be restored and developed every day anew. The successful negotiation of the CPA for Sudan does not mean that a distinct separation between war and peace was assumed by the concerned partners, and that post-conflict reconstruction can be based on this distinction. Reconstruction has to be based on the continuum between war and peace from Darfur to East and South Sudan. Shocks from the world economy can do a lot of harm to post-conflict reconstruction (so the sharp oil price decline affects the fiscal budget for reconstruction in South Sudan quite heavily), and therefore reforms at the global level (to mitigate the effects of climate change, to speed up trade reforms and governance reforms for international organizations) matter a lot for a success of post-conflict reconstruction.

The book is a valuable source for all those people and institutions working on post-conflict reconstruction in the widest sense. Many of the ideas can be translated to particular country cases, as it was done by the reviewer in general terms for Sudan/South Sudan. The editors did a good job by providing a clear summary work on the themes and by integrating the messages from so many authors (coming from quite different backgrounds and institutions). This study is also finalizing the important research work done over many years by WIDER-UNU on post-conflict countries. Making Peace Work is therefore important reading.

Karl Wohlmuth, Bremen

Development Finance and Development Aid

Spratt, Stephen, *Development Finance. Debates, dogmas and new directions*, 2009, Routledge Advanced Texts in Economics and Finance, London: Routledge, ISBN10: 0-415-42318-X, pages: xiii + 418.

A short look at a survey of recent publications on development finance reveals that there only very few textbooks and extensive studies available. One of those publications which attract attention is the book by Stephen Spratt, director of the new economics foundation, UK based think tank.

Spratt deals with the subject development finance in a very comprehensive and extensive manner which may be explained by his activities as a lecturer in development finance at the University of Reading, in the City of London's financial markets at the Institute of Development Studies at the University of Sussex.

The title "development finance" is perceived a very extensive manner which implies two different modes of interpretation of the term "development finance". The publication focuses on the analysis and assessment of policies being directed to the financial sector's role in developing countries and the transmission to the real sector or the mobilising of resources to generate development.

The financial sector is defined as capital markets (bond and equity markets) and other financial markets as money markets, derivates markets and FX markets which trade currencies internationally. The respective institutions are commercial financial institutions (which include investment/ merchant, universal banks as well as mortgage banks, building societies, contractual savings institutions, asset management companies, venture capitalists/ private equity companies and finance companies) and besides that quasi-commercial financial institutions as state development banks, mutual/ cooperative banks, post office savings banks, credit unions/friendly societies and microfinance institutions. The role of government in the financial sector is defined by the intervention of the central bank and the regulation of the financial sector and by borrowing or investing in the financial sector (pp. 2). The financial sector should mainly mobilise internal savings, transfer risks of local capital owners and borrowers through time and allocate capital efficiently (p. 125). Also, the financial sector is a "channel" to distribute the inflow of external resources which arise either from commercial sources as for instance trade and foreign direct investment (FDI) as well as from of official development assistance (ODA) by bilateral and multilateral institutions. Having this in mind the publication elaborates mechanism of the financial sector – as defined above – and other instruments to generate financial internal and external resources to foster growth and to eradicate poverty in developing countries.

The textbook is introduced by a survey on growth and development theory, starting with the Solow and Harrod-Domar analysis and a very conducive presentation of development theories which were elaborated in the sixties up to recent stage of art. Thereafter the interrelationship between the financial sector development, growth and poverty reduction strategies are presented and assessed. Pros and cons of financial liberalisation are discussed by referring to the theoretical research as well as of the findings of empirical studies. Strategies of sequencing are deducted as well as requirements of financial liberalisation which is conducive to economic growth. The specifics of domestic financial markets in developing countries are described in the next step. The very informative overview directs the reader's attention to key factors influencing the structure, and detailed reports are devoted to macroeconomic stability, geography and climate, regulation and the institutional set-up and the property rights. In line with the definition of the financial sector the role of government is defined by the finance policy (among others provision of public goods, other government expenditure and taxation) and the banking regulation. The further analysis refers to firstly to the reforms of the domestic financial system and secondly to external resources mobilization. In the first part, monetary and fiscal policy proposals are presented in a very extensive analysis which refers to the recent theory and empirical studies findings. Proposals to reform the banking system take into account the deliberations on banking reforms after the financial crisis in 2008 and following years. The recommendations on the mobilisation of external financial resources are introduced by a description of the mechanism (ODA, IMF, WTO, and FDI) and the impact with special consideration of the Millennium Development Go and the Monterrey decisions. The actual financial crisis is focused in the subchapter 7.4 which refers to former financial crises and their respective management and the ongoing activities (pp. 223 and pp. 345). Further considerations are devoted to the lending mechanisms to the private industry and especially to small and medium enterprises. Spratt's summary proposes that governments in developing countries are recommended to mobilise savings through fiscal policy, pension reform, financial liberalisation and enlarging foreign borrowing and assistance. Also internal reforms as the World Bank proposes are required – as Spratt concludes – to generate an economic environment being conducive to saving and investment in developing countries. To foster financial and economic development and to fight against poverty the investment climate has to be improved, labour markets are to be liberalised, excessive risk taking has to be controlled, barriers which remove competition should be abolished and prudent macroeconomic regulation has to be implemented.

Teachers and students of development economics as well as of development finance are well advised to make use of the textbook as a study book as well as a reader in the course of preparation of reports and studies. All items are described and analysed by a well-founded theoretical and empirical approach and easily understandable. Teachers and students find in-between summaries and conclusions which enable an easy access to the issues being dealt with. The state of art is made available, and all relevant publications have been considered. Guiding principles as for instance the Meltzer report on the reform of multilateral institutions or the structural adjustment programmes of the IMF are outlined and assessed.

The user of the book receives all the relevant data and facts on the indebtedness of the developing countries since 1970. The role of the private sector is described and analysed, and the results convince. Spratt deliberations pertain to an approach which combines external support, trade liberalization and internal reforms to remove poverty and to foster economic growth. Education and health are focussed in line with the overall subject of the book in short subparts. A minor critical point is the short analysis of microfinance and its contribution to poverty-averting policies. Having in view alternative modes of the financial markets in developing countries Islamic banking may be added in a second edition. The chapter on small and medium-sized enterprises biases the positive impact of these industries and does not take fully into account its limitations. The textbook is dealing with development finance in all developing countries and partly in transforming economies in Eastern Europe. References are also made in case studies referring to developed countries.

The context to Africa (mainly south of the Sahara) and to Latin America, however, is not at all neglected, some users may complain that the examples and analysis regarding Asia is far shorter than for Africa and Latin America. Summarizing it is fair to conclude that Spratt has succeeded to fill the gap in the list of recent development finance publications which deserves – applying ratings denominations – an AAA assessment.

Karl Wolfgang Menck, Hamburg

Mold, Andrew, *Policy ownership and Aid Conditionality in the Light of the Financial Crisis – A critical Review*, 2009, Development Centre Studies, Paris: OECD, ISBN: 978-92-64-07551-1, pages: 93.

Andrew Mold's work marks a timely addition carefully hand-picked from collection of research and specifically crafted to drive a coherent discussion on the debate of Aid conditionality in the midst of the recent financial crisis.

The book publication addresses conditionality measures imposed by international financial lending institutions, mainly the World Bank (WB) and the International Monetary Fund (IMF) and donor agencies. The author begins by introducing the concept of conditionality and gives a brief historical background of Aid conditionality policy. His general conclusion is that conditionality has been ineffective in achieving the intended objectives.

This publication can stake its claim among other recent works on the changing landscape of Aid conditionality. It provides an analysis from the Aid suppliers and reflections of the Aid receivers.

The author has been meticulous in touching key subject areas related to Aid conditionality.

From giving a quick insight on the genesis of the recent economic recession and financial crisis since June 2007 to new paradigm shifts, new realism and China's approach to Aid. The publication summarily highlights and provides the justification and benefits of conditionality, including risk mitigation strategies, moral reasoning, and reform efficiency on lending.

Coupled with concrete illustrations, the author articulates classification of the Aid conditionality, pro and contra views of Aid conditionality, Aid incentives, defences to Aid and the implications.

The publication gets into the nitty gritty of types of conditionality policies ex *post* and *ex ante* scenarios in which they either flourished or dwindled. It encompasses comparative aspects of the conditionality strategies whether performance based, poverty reduction, e.g., those imposed for attainment of the Millennium Development Goals (MDGs), and outcome based vs. policy based approaches and many others. The author observes that some Aid agencies have shifted from *ex ante* to *ex post* policy.

Flanked with input, the reader is well prepared by having first being exposed to a detailed chronology of the Aid modalities from the 1940s to date. The eras discussed include: The post war period 1947-1960 a period when individual countries were major clients of Aid modalities. The author describes it as a phase when conditionality was *less obtrusive.* This was Marshal Plan era when the WB in 1947 exercised conditionality on France. The 1960s -1970 s characterised an era when developing countries received large scale loans from private banks. The terms of the loans were less stringent consequently occasioning repayment complications. In the 1980s era, there was a rise of conditionality manifested in Structural Adjustment Programmes (SAPs). The WB and IMF placed conditions to budget deficits, monetary expansion, and privatization and trade liberalization. This was followed by the 1990s era where there was a sudden increase in conditionality. It was also the phase when academics and NGOs intervened and wooed the International Financial Institutions (IFIs) and donors to widen their remits accusing them of adopting excessively narrow simplified view of the development process. The donor community become low spirited due to lack of concrete results from the SAPs and the after effects and some countries suffered economic stagnation. Around 2000 the WB declared conditionality as an instrument to promote reform has been a failure revealing 'policy fatalism'. This brought a new Aid era, a shift towards *ex ante* rather than *ex post*. Only countries that adopted 'good policies' were considered. The concept of 'ownership' became the central semantic that accorded the Aid receivers an opportunity to take control of their destiny. Assistance became channelled through Sector-Wide Approaches (SWAps) which entailed a combination of economic and political aspects with strong focus on governance and institutional issues arising out of negotiations between donors, recipient governments and other stake holders.

The author has by no means attempted to respond to the frequently raised question, that is; 'whether conditionality increasing or diminishing?' The response is evidenced in statistical analysis precisely illustrated (for example the WB in the 1980's imposed 5 conditions, in 1993 about 45 in 2000 about

25). The publication goes beyond to include other factors that have impacted on conditionality for instance the trade policy conditionality policy has been usurped by the developments in the world trade system like adoption of World Trade Organisation (WTO) and membership of the developing countries to the WTO.

Throughout the work, the author has provided mix of real country illustrations and incorporated empirical studies. The publication does not spare the reader from wealth information on the implications of conditionality and lessons learned overall by the Aid suppliers and receivers. The search for the ultimate strategies to help the poor nations carried debate about the right set of approach and between 'good' and 'bad' policies.

WB recognised lessons learnt in the 1990s that there is no single model of development. The author notes that economics still tended to take the reductionist and prescriptive approaches to economic problems. Backed by ideologies of Stiglitz who states that "…no consensus as to what strategies that are likely to help poorest countries," the author contends there is a difficulty in searching for universal rules that govern economic ideals of good governance and good policies. The shifting Aid policies and conditionality policies presented a challenge for economist in determining and delivering advice between 'good' and 'bad' policies. The author opines that the problem is compounded by lack of justification on the part of the donor community on the adoption of polices. The decision to adopt conditionality policies was marred by secrecy.

He summarises that "policy conditionality has become largely obsolete and the donors need to explore other ways to maximise the efficiency of the money." Inclusion of information on political conditionality aspects welcomes a discussion on why the donors continue providing Aid despite their dissatisfaction with the outcomes. The publication lays down the various reasons tied to political, economic, moral, historical repercussions such as career dependency and what he terms as the 'Samaritan Dilemma' where donors support becomes too crucial to let a country fail.

He then ponders into the motives of political conditionality stating the collapse of the Soviet Union gave most Western countries the impetus and confidence to impose on their recipients their ideologies manifested in democratized principles such as governance and anti-corruption precepts. According to the author, there was no evidence to show that donors funding was in line with the high-minded principles they espouse. They have sometimes supported countries despite their breach of conditions imposed. The author consistently introduces and distinguishes the donor motivations being either 'altruistic' or 'egoistical'. He arrives to a deduction is that "conditionality has had little or no impact on actual outcomes."

In looking ahead to the new Aid modalities, the author questions how donors can limit the difficulties associated with conditionality? He reveals the changes embraced by donors in working with actors such as private sector and civil society to develop innovative solutions. He cautions that the new Aid modalities show signs of being weak pointing out various opinions some of which suggest retreat or return to project financing having past mistakes in mind. Discussed are other alternatives such as SWAps where Aid is given to particular sector and their implication. The author briefly describes why China's approach to Aid was gaining popularity in Africa. He attributes it to low conditionality and project based approach geared towards long-term maturing projects, less bureaucratic process, with low transaction costs, efficient and allowance for policy space. This was quite a challenge to the traditional Western Aid. The chapter entitled 'Policy-Based Conditionality and the Economic Crisis – A Final Nail in the Coffin?' captures the gist of the publication. Although concise, the chapter provides food for thought for those who may be interested in furthering this discourse. This would include actual discussion on the actual implication of the financial crisis on donor funding. The author explains the shifting position of the IFIs prior and post the 2008 financial crisis. The fact that the Western countries had to massively turn to salvage their banking sector and provided financial support to the affected industries. The developing countries view Western countries as employing double standards as they were implementing the very measures that were prohibited to former. The author perceives the crisis provides a platform to rethink how conditionality is applied.

The authors ensures a comprehensive input in the final chapter by providing conclusions, recommendations and some thoughts as to the future of policy ownership and Aid conditionality vis-à-vis of the financial crisis including the efforts of some developing countries like Rwanda to find solutions to end Aid dependency.

The publication makes for enjoyable reading. It is a standard reference work for those consulting and interacting with Aid. Its title is reflected by its content. It only remains to be seen whether those to whom it is dedicated will take up what the author has recommended. It is also a publication which can be progressed into further research and contribution to Aid conditionality.

The book publication is an added value for readers already familiar with the subject and may inspire those who have not yet encountered the field to become involved. It is a must for the academia and practitioners involved with Aid, be it staff of the financial lending institutions, donor Aid agencies, personnel in government departments responsible or funding institutions, University institutions providing related studies, Non-Governmental Organizations, just to mention but a few.

Angeline Asangire Oprong, Bremen

World Bank, *Annual review of development effectiveness 2009: Achieving Sustainable Development – Management Comments*, 2009, Board Report, Washington DC: World Bank, no ISBN/ISSN, pages: 11.

The World Bank subjects itself to independent evaluation and uses the findings to enhance its development effectiveness by learning from experience. The Independent Evaluation Group (IEG) consistently ranks as the benchmark for independent evaluation in the development field. The risk, of course, is that the Bank´s effectiveness as measured by IEG in its evaluations may be taken out of the context of the challenges inherent in development assistance or compared across agencies with less strong evaluation functions.

The Annual Review of Development Effectiveness differs from most IEG outputs in that it draws on a wide range of evaluative findings and provides a summary overview. Because of the nature of the review, it does not make specific recommendations for management and does not name specific management responses to issues raised in the document. However, the management finds it important to provide its views on the report´s findings and to give an overview of a set of key management actions that are directly relevant to those findings.

Achim Gutowski, Bremen

Oxford Policy Management/Ministry of Foreign Affairs of Denmark (DANIDA), *Evaluation of Danish support for financial services in Tanzania*, 2009, Copenhagen: Ministry of Foreign Affairs of Denmark, ISBN: 978-87-7087-225-6, pages: 152.

This evaluation covers Danish support to the financial sector in Tanzania from 2003 to 2008. The overall objectives of the evaluation are to assess the outcomes achieved from the support during that period and to get key lessons from the support with regard to strategies and approaches to support financial services.

The papers consists of five chapters (introduction, context, Danish support for the financial sector in Tanzania, findings and finally conclusions/lessons learnt/recommendations).

A key focus for the evaluation is the channels for DANIDA support to financial services and their beneficiaries. Despite Tanzania´s achievements in terms of economic growth, income poverty statistics show a high proportion of the population in Tanzania living on less than the amount needed to cover basic needs, and a significant proportion of these are experiencing food insecurity. The DANIDA programme is designed, along with those of other donor agencies, to help the Government of Tanzania to tackle the problem in the context of an extensive framework of strategies and policies to reduce poverty and financial exclusion. This being most important with regard to the global financial crisis and its challenges.

Achim Gutowski, Bremen

Oxford Policy Management, OPM working papers, 2009, Oxford: Hunts, no ISBN/ISSN:

***An integrated approach to policy analysis: practical exercises for political economy*, 2009/02, pages: 8.**

The paper states that political economy analysis is increasingly recognized as central to the formulation of sound policy strategies. In recent years different toolkits have been created to facilitate this analysis. However, a tool that may address the totality of the multiple dimensions involved in complex reform scenarios is still much needed. The integrated framework for policy analysis aims to fill this gap by providing a comprehensive approach to policy change and reform processes.

The result is a flexible, handy tool that explores the diverse points, and the links between them, within the policy-change process from the perspective of the agents involved in it. By analyzing the incentive and motivation structures of actors taking part in policy and decision-making, the framework may provide important inputs to understand better how and why policy choices are made and implemented.

Achim Gutowski, Bremen

Oxford Policy Management/UNICEF, OPM/UNICEF briefing papers, 2009, Oxford/Dakar, no publisher, no ISBN/ISSN:

***Fiscal Space and public expenditure on the social sectors*, 2009/02, pages: 6.**

Until the onset of the global economic crisis, higher growth, tax revenues and aid flows improved public finances across much of West and Central Africa. Rising commodity prices, along with more prudent fiscal policies and debt relief, helped to boost revenues and reduce previously large deficits. Paradoxically, this did not bring about a large increase in public spending on the social sectors to accelerate progress towards the Millennium Development Goals; despite the commitments to do so in most poverty reduction strategies.

Since 2008, there have been serious setbacks, due to the rise in food and fuel prices and the adverse shocks from the global financial crisis.

***Increasing aid and its effectiveness in West and Central Africa*, 2009/02, pages: 6.**

This briefing paper firstly presents the trends in official development assistance (ODA) to West and Central Africa, focusing in particular on ODA to the social sectors. Secondly, it discusses the challenges of improving the quality of aid. West and Central Africa has seen significant increases in aid in the past few years, but this has not benefited all countries. Much of the increase has come from debt relief, which has so far been concentrated on about half the countries. Aid has to be scaled up significantly in order to meet the MDGs.

Achim Gutowski, Bremen

Oxford Policy Management/Bank of Zambia, *Measuring Financial Access to Zambia. The supply side*, 2007, Lusaka: Bank of Zambia, no ISBN/ISSN, pages: 8.

This study looks at the financial sectors′ policies and regulations, the players operating in the system, and the structures that enable the market to operate. The overall objectives of the supply-side study are to contribute to a better understanding of the constraints to financial sector expansion in Zambia. Further, to enable policymakers and financial service providers to develop strategies to expand the landscape of financial access and build a more inclusive financial system in Zambia.

The study provides new insights into the reasons for the low level of access to financial services in the country, and what might be done to tackle the problem. With a better picture of the financial market, the study suggests key focus areas for change that would contribute to building a more inclusive financial sector in Zambia over time.

Achim Gutowski, Bremen

Contents Volume 14
African Development Perspectives Yearbook, 2009
NEW GROWTH AND POVERTY ALLEVIATION STRATEGIES FOR AFRICA: INSTITUTIONAL AND LOCAL PERSPECTIVES

Call for Papers

African Development Perspectives Yearbook, Vol. 16

Macroeconomic Policy Formation in Africa

We are soliciting papers for Vol. 16 of the African Development Perspectives Yearbook on the Topic of Macroeconomic Policy Formation in Africa. Potential topics include but are not restricted to:

- Macroeconomic policy formation at national level
- Macroeconomic policy coordination in regional economic communities
- African Union initiatives for policy coordination and economic policy formation
- Exchange rate policy and currency unions in Africa
- Globalization and national economic policy formation in Africa
- Policies of IMF and World Bank towards Africa
- Interest groups in macroeconomic policy formation
- Institutions in macroeconomic policy formation

Manuscripts might be sent electronically to the Managing Editor (Tobias.Knedlik@iwh-halle.de) by the **Deadline July 1st 2012**.

African Development Perspectives Yearbook

Research Group on African Development Perspectives University of Bremen

Karl Wohlmuth; Philippe Burger; Achim Gutowski; Mohammed N. Hussain (†), Tobias Knedlik; Mareike Meyn (Eds.)

Africa – Escaping the Primary Commodities Dilemma

This volume XI of the African Development Perspectives Yearbook on *AFRICA – ESCAPING THE PRIMARY COMMODITIES DILEMMA* presents and analyses policy-oriented papers, development projections, and proposals of how to overcome African countries' dependence on few primary commodities. The relevance of the issue to escape the primary commodity trap and to diversify into new products and markets is without doubt one of the major challenges for African countries. In the era of globalisation and increasing international competition it has however become much more difficult for African countries to diversify into new products and processes and to enter new niche markets successfully. This Volume XI of the Yearbook discusses the state of primary commodity dependence of African countries by analytical surveys based on examples of countries, sectors and products. Options for horizontal and vertical diversification are analysed by detailed case studies, and supply- and demand-side constraints for successful diversification efforts are elaborated. Successful cases of diversification and upgrading activities are presented, possibilities to improve the position of countries and firms in the global value chain are outlined, and options for primary commodity producers to use their resources for successful diversification are discussed for the countries of the Southern African Development Community (SADC). Book Reviews and Book Notes are included, and News and Information follow with up-to-date entries.

This volume builds the foundation for a comprehensive strategy of policy reforms in Africa of how to escape the primary commodities dilemma. Complementary to this volume XI is volume XII on *AFRICA – COMMODITY DEPENDENCE, RESOURCE CURSE AND EXPORT DIVERSIFICATION.* Both volumes are of use for all who work in African countries as officials, executives, managers, researchers, and policy-makers, but also for all those in the world-wide donor community who actively support Africa's development concerns at the international, regional, country, local and project levels. Development practitioners, government officials, business executives, and development researchers as well as media people will experience this volume XI and also the complementary volume XII as indispensable sources of insight, reference and inspiration.

Bd. 11, 2006, 576 S., 69,90 €, br., ISBN 3-8258-7842-2

LIT Verlag Berlin – Münster – Wien – Zürich – London

Auslieferung Deutschland / Österreich / Schweiz: siehe Impressumsseite

Karl Wohlmuth; Reuben Adeolu Alabi; Philippe Burger; Achim Gutowski; Afeikhena Jerome; Tobias Knedlik; Mareike Meyn; Tino Urban (Eds.)

New Growth and Poverty Alleviation Strategies for Africa – International and Regional Perspectives

Volume XIII analyses the „NEW GROWTH AND POVERTY ALLEVIATION STRATEGIES FOR AFRICA“. Country cases in Africa for the integration of new growth and poverty alleviation policies are presented. New international strategies in the context of the Millennium Development Goals (MDGs), the New Partnership for Africa's Development (NEPAD) and the EU Strategy for Africa that aim at promoting pro-poor policies are discussed. Regional aspects of new growth and poverty alleviation strategies are analysed with regard to the case of South Africa. The South Africa of 2007 is a much different country from the South Africa of 1994, the year in which the country held its first democratic election. The country returned to positive per capita growth in the period since 1994. However, large challenges remain – the most glaring being the high levels of poverty and unemployment. Innovative strategies to address these challenges are discussed – incentives for sub-regional economic growth; improving the relationship between growth and employment; enhancing the role of education in the labour market; promoting Broad-Based Black Economic Empowerment; and moving step by step towards a South African welfare state. New researches, initiatives and publications related to the theme are reviewed carefully in this Volume. This Volume builds the foundation for a comprehensive strategy of policy reforms in Africa so as to integrate new growth and poverty alleviation strategies. Complementary to Volume XIII is Volume XIV on „NEW GROWTH AND POVERTY ALLEVIATION STRATEGIES FOR AFRICA – INSTITUTIONAL AND LOCAL PERSPECTIVES“. Both Volumes are of importance for all those who work in African countries as officials, executives, managers, researchers, and policy-makers, but also for all those who actively support Africa's development concerns at the international, regional, country, local and project levels. They will experience this Volume XIII and also the complementary Volume XIV as indispensable sources of insight, reference and inspiration.

Bd. 13, 2008, 648 S., 69,90 €, br., ISBN 978-3-8258-1542-4

LIT Verlag Berlin – Münster – Wien – Zürich – London

Auslieferung Deutschland / Österreich / Schweiz: siehe Impressumsseite

Myungkyu Park, Bernhard Seliger, Sung-Jo Park (Eds.)

Europe – North Korea

Between Humanitarism and Business?

Global Cultural and Economic Research LIT

Myungkyu Park; Bernhard Seliger; Sung-Jo Park (Eds.)
Europe – North Korea
Between Humanitarism and Business?

Given the imbalance of relatively dense relations (by North Korean standards for relations with the Western world) and relative underexposure of these relations in the media and in academic discussions the aim of this book is to review the many facets of European – North Korean relations. And indeed, the relations between Europe and North Korea have many facets, including exchanges based on humanitarian, political and business grounds and relations focusing on human rights, capacity-building and education as well as trust-building and cultural exchanges. The two nuclear tests of 2006 and 2009 as well as the hardened North Korean stance throughout 2008 to 2010 were not foreboding well for improved relations with Europe. However, the history of North Korea has been one where the invariable and the unpredictable always have been in a curious relationship. We hope, this volume can stimulate academic discussion but also exchange activities between Europe and North Korea and help to make relations, cumbersome as they are under the strains of North Korea's political and economic system and nuclear ambitions, a success story.

Bd. 6, 2010, 328 S., 29,90 €, br., ISBN 978-3-643-10351-2

LIT Verlag Berlin – Münster – Wien – Zürich – London

Auslieferung Deutschland / Österreich / Schweiz: siehe Impressumsseite